The BIG BOOK *of*
DIABETIC
RECIPES

The BIG BOOK of DIABETIC RECIPES

From Chipotle Chicken Wraps to Key Lime Pie, 500 Diabetes-Friendly Recipes

Marie Feldman, RD, CDE

Aadamsmedia

Avon, Massachusetts

Published by
Adams Media, a division of F+W Media, Inc.
57 Littlefield Street, Avon, MA 02322. U.S.A.
www.adamsmedia.com

Contains material adapted and abridged from *The Everything® Diabetes Cookbook, 2nd Edition* by Gretchen Scalpi, RD, CDN, CDE, copyright © 2009, 2002 by F+W Media, Inc., ISBN 10: 1-4405-0154-8, ISBN 13: 978-1-4405-0154-8; *The Everything® Low-Glycemic Cookbook* by Carrie S. Forbes, copyright © 2014 by F+W Media, Inc., ISBN 10: 1-4405-7086-8, ISBN 13: 978-1-4405-7086-5; and *The Everything® Glycemic Index Cookbook, 2nd Edition* by LeeAnn Smith Weintraub, MPH, RD, copyright © 2010, 2006 by F+W Media, Inc., ISBN 10: 1-4405-0584-5, ISBN 13: 978-1-4405-0584-3.

ISBN 10: 1-4405-9365-5
ISBN 13: 978-1-4405-9365-9
eISBN 10: 1-4405-9366-3
eISBN 13: 978-1-4405-9366-6

Printed in the United States of America.

10   9   8   7   6   5   4   3   2   1

Cover design by Alexandra Artiano.
Cover images © iStockphoto.com/t_kimura, iStockphoto.com/CharlesKnox.

This book is available at quantity discounts for bulk purchases.
For information, please call 1-800-289-0963.

ACKNOWLEDGMENTS

A sincere thanks to Adams Media for providing me with the opportunity to become a first-time cookbook author and allowing me to share my recipes with a wider audience through publishing this book. Professionally, I am also grateful to work under Dr. David Kayne, a wonderful mentor who has taught me so much about successfully diagnosing and treating diabetes through the patient care and clinical research we have conducted daily over the last decade together. I feel extremely fortunate to be a registered dietitian, clinical diabetes educator, and research manager at the Medical Group of Encino, where I work as part of an amazing team of physicians and staff and I interact with wonderful patients who challenge and inspire me constantly. In addition, a big thank you goes out to my good friend and colleague, fellow dietitian and seasoned chef/author Cheryl Forberg, who has been very helpful and informative during this entire project.

Many thanks to my husband, Ken—you are my best friend and I treasure our relationship, in which we motivate and elevate each other every day. You help ensure our household runs smoothly (has a clean kitchen!) and is filled with smiles and laughter, even in the most hectic of times. I also want to express my heartfelt gratitude to my parents, who have given me ultimate unconditional love and support throughout my life in countless ways. I lovingly acknowledge my daughter, Gabrielle, who inspires me every day to work hard to create a balanced, healthy, happy, and nourished life for us to share together. I appreciate my extended family, my friends, and the wonderful community of Playa Vista, where I live, along with the readers and supporters of my blog, *www.nourishyoudelicious.blogspot.com*, since its creation six years ago.

And last but not least, I thank you, the reader, for buying this book and taking the opportunity to cook and eat healthy as part of managing your diabetes and overall health. I hope you enjoy the recipes and find this book very useful!

CONTENTS

INTRODUCTION

WHEN IT COMES TO MANAGING DIABETES, KNOWLEDGE is power. The more you know about diabetes, the better you can control it and minimize your risk of complications. By reading this book and putting some ideas into practice, you will have taken the first steps toward learning all you can about diabetes.

DIABETES MELLITUS

Every time you eat, your body converts the foods you consume into glucose. Insulin is a hormone the body makes that enables the glucose to get into cells for use as energy. People with diabetes either lack sufficient amounts of insulin or are unable to use the insulin they make. When insulin is absent or ineffective, the body is unable to get energy into cells and the level of glucose in the blood increases. Genetics, obesity, and lack of exercise appear to be causal factors in most cases of diabetes.

TYPE 1 DIABETES

Approximately 5–10 percent of known cases of diabetes are classified as type 1 diabetes. Type 1 diabetes was formerly referred to as juvenile-onset diabetes because the onset typically occurs before the age of thirty. Type 1 diabetes is an autoimmune disorder that is thought to develop when stress factors (such as a viral infection) damage or destroy the beta cells of the pancreas. People with type 1 diabetes are always dependent upon insulin because their pancreases no longer produce insulin. Type 1 diabetes is usually not associated with obesity or lack of exercise.

TYPE 2 DIABETES

The vast majority of individuals with diabetes have type 2 diabetes. For most type 2 diabetics, the pancreas still produces insulin, but it is being produced in insufficient amounts or the body is unable to use the insulin in an efficient way.

Type 2 diabetes is generally diagnosed in mid- to late adulthood. Unfortunately, with the increase and prevalence of obesity among children, practitioners are now seeing children with type 2 diabetes as well.

Type 2 diabetes is usually related to a sedentary lifestyle and an overweight or obese status. If diagnosed early enough, this form of diabetes can often be controlled with weight loss, proper eating habits, and exercise. It is important to understand that diabetes is a disease that progresses, and while it can be controlled, it cannot be cured. Over time, many type 2 diabetics may require oral medications and/or insulin to effectively treat and manage the disease.

GESTATIONAL DIABETES

Gestational diabetes is similar to type 2 diabetes because the body still makes insulin; however, a hormone secreted by the placenta interferes with the action of insulin. The result is elevated blood glucose levels, usually starting around the twenty-fourth to twenty-eighth week of the pregnancy. In most cases, the pregnant woman's blood glucose returns to normal after the delivery of the baby and the diabetes is gone. A woman who has had gestational diabetes in the past has an increased risk of developing type 2 diabetes later in her life.

Gestational diabetes is usually treated in a similar way to type 2 diabetes: through proper eating habits, weight control, and exercise. If blood glucose does not normalize with these measures, it may become necessary to use insulin to control the diabetes for the duration of the pregnancy. Oral diabetic medications cannot be used during pregnancy.

The major health concerns with gestational diabetes are macrosomia (a fetus that has grown too large for normal delivery) and hypoglycemia (low blood sugar) in the infant after delivery.

SUMMARY

Careful and routine monitoring of blood glucose is extremely important for all diabetics. Activity and timing of insulin, medications, and meals must be taken into consideration to prevent highs and lows.

When blood glucose is very low (hypoglycemia), the individual may exhibit symptoms of disorientation, sweating, hunger, shakiness, pale skin color, or dizziness. If hypoglycemia occurs, the blood glucose should be tested immediately to verify a low. Hypoglycemia needs to be treated by consuming a form of carbohydrate that can get into the bloodstream quickly. All diabetics, and particularly type 1 diabetics, should understand and know how to treat hypoglycemia. One procedure for treating hypoglycemia is known as the "Rule of 15":

1. Take **15 grams** of carbohydrate (4 ounces of juice or soda, 4 glucose tablets, or 5 or 6 Life Savers).
2. Test blood glucose in **15 minutes**.
3. Treat with another **15 grams** of carbohydrate if blood glucose is still low.

As you read this book, you will see the common theme of having a plan mentioned throughout. It is through planning and know-how that you will achieve optimal management of your diabetes.

CHAPTER 1

MANAGING YOUR DIABETES

WHETHER YOU HAVE JUST BEEN DIAGNOSED WITH diabetes or you have dealt with it for many years, there are steps you can take to manage it effectively. A daily plan for diabetes includes a healthy eating plan, exercise, and possibly medication. Learning more about healthy eating habits and ways to prepare tasty, enjoyable foods can help you start making those changes. As you make small changes to your eating habits, you'll soon realize that you can have more control over your diabetes. Work closely with your doctor and dietitian to learn how healthy eating and lifestyle changes can make a big difference in achieving better health and better diabetes control.

WHERE TO START

Contrary to what you may have heard in the past, there is no strict diet you must follow. You will likely need to make some changes in your lifestyle, and sometimes changes can seem very difficult. It is usually not necessary to totally change everything about the way that you eat. Managing diabetes is more about adopting a healthier lifestyle by making small changes one at a time.

The American Association of Diabetes Educators believes that the following seven self-care behaviors are effective ways to make positive changes:

1. **Eat healthy:** Make healthy food choices, understand portion sizes, and learn the best times to eat.
2. **Be active:** Include regular activity for overall fitness, weight management, and blood glucose control.

3. **Monitor:** Self-monitor your blood glucose daily to assess how food, physical activity, and medications are working.
4. **Take medication:** Understand how medications work, and when to take them.
5. **Problem-solve:** Know how to problem-solve. For example, a high or low blood-glucose episode requires the ability to make a quick decision about food, activity, or medication.
6. **Reduce risks:** Effective risk-reduction behaviors such as smoking cessation and regular eye exams are examples of self-care that reduce risk of complications.
7. **Healthy coping:** Good coping skills that deal with the challenges of diabetes help you stay motivated to keep your diabetes in control.

There Is No Diabetic Diet

You may think that being diabetic means giving up everything you like to eat, especially carbohydrates. Nothing could be further from the truth! With the help and advice of a registered dietitian, you can adapt healthy eating habits that fit into your lifestyle. Here are several suggestions to get you started on your plan:

- Eat meals at regular intervals.
- Include nutritious snacks in your daily eating plan.
- Try new foods and experiment with whole grains, vegetables, or fruits you have never tried before.
- Work on maintaining good portion control.
- Drink plenty of water every day.

Food portion size is critical for controlling how many calories you eat every day, and of course, for controlling your weight. If you tend to overeat at certain meals, you can start controlling portions by eating 1/3 less than you usually do. Use a smaller plate and put 1/3 less food on your plate.

It's very important to avoid skipping meals. Regular meal times help prevent high or low blood sugar readings. When you skip meals, you run the risk of having unexpected low blood sugar. Skipping meals can also lead to overeating at the next meal, causing a blood sugar high. Snacking is a great way to prevent excessive hunger and keep your blood sugar at a healthy level. When chosen wisely, snacks can help you work in the recommended amounts of healthful foods such as fruit or vegetables.

Trying new foods can expand the options of foods in your eating plan. Today there are many more choices of whole or minimally processed foods available to the consumer. Shopping in the produce section of the grocery store or visiting your local farmers' market can give you plenty of ideas for including some foods that you may not have used before. Large grocery stores and health-food stores carry an array of different whole-grain products that, while not new, may be unfamiliar to you. Using some of the recipes in this book will introduce you to some of the lesser known but healthful whole grains.

Small Steps Every Day = Gradual Lifestyle Changes

Accept that you won't be able to change your eating habits overnight, and adopt the approach of taking small steps every day. Over time, you can make significant changes toward improving your health and reaching consistent near-normal blood glucose levels. Think of changes in your eating habits as goals rather than inflexible rules and regulations. Start by making a (honest) review of your current eating habits, then list what you'd like to change or improve. Decide exactly how you will work on each change, then select one or two changes to work on at a time. Your dietitian can help you with creative ideas for making changes. Here's an example: If you eat a candy bar as a pick-me-up late in the afternoon, try substituting a small piece of fruit and an ounce of low-fat cheese instead.

Once you've mastered a change, you can move on to something new. Some changes will be easy; others will be difficult or take more time. Start off by making easier changes first, then tackle something that would be very difficult for you.

WHAT CAN I EAT?

You may be surprised to learn that your eating plan will have the same foods that everyone else eats, and buying all sorts of specialty or diet foods is usually unnecessary. You may wish to use an artificial sweetener of your choice or certain sugar-free food items; however, this is not essential. You will not have to prepare one meal for yourself and something different for the rest of your household. As you look over the recipes in this cookbook, you will find a few specialty items, but in general the recipes use foods that everyone can eat.

Eating a balanced diet that includes foods from all of the essential food groups generally meets the nutritional needs of most adults. Some individuals have other health issues in addition to diabetes, and this may affect specific nutritional requirements. Discuss all of your health issues with your doctor and registered dietitian to determine whether you should take vitamin and mineral supplements or make special modifications to your diet to meet specific nutritional needs.

Carbohydrates and Diabetes: Facts You Should Know

Carbohydrates serve as the body's primary energy source. Simple carbohydrates include all kinds of sugars, sweets, juices, and fruits. Complex carbohydrates include all types of grain products and starchy vegetables such as potatoes or corn. General recommendations for a healthy diet with diabetes suggest that you get most of your carbohydrates in the form of complex carbohydrates rather than simple sugars. Complex carbohydrates provide an important source of vitamins, minerals, and fiber. Although fruits contain simple sugar, they are also good sources of vitamins, minerals, and fiber and therefore should be included. To get more fiber, make most of the fruit choices in your eating plan fresh fruit rather than juice.

You may be under the impression that because you have diabetes you must cut out all carbohydrates. This is definitely not the case, and you will be happy to learn there are many carbohydrate food options that you can include in your plan, as long as you choose carbohydrates that have good nutritional value—such as whole grains—and maintain an appropriate portion size.

Avoid Empty Calories

When simple sugars (found in sweets, soft drinks, etc.) comprise too much of your total carbohydrate intake, you'll be missing many important nutrients. These foods are often referred to as "empty-calorie" foods because there are plenty of calories but little nutritional value.

The FDA has defined whole grains as "the intact, ground, cracked or flaked fruit of the grains whose principal components—the starchy endosperm, germ and bran—are present in the same relative proportions as they exist in the intact grain." In other words, no part of the grain has been removed during the processing of the grain; you are getting all the parts of a grain.

Protein: Your Building Blocks to Good Health

Proteins are the building blocks of the body and are used for growth, building, and repair. Animal proteins such as meat, fish, eggs, and milk contain all nine essential amino acids. When all essential amino acids are present in food, it is called a complete protein.

Vegetable proteins are found in nuts, seeds, vegetables, whole grains, and legumes. All vegetable proteins, with the exception of soy, are considered incomplete proteins because one or more of the essential amino acids are missing. Even though a vegetable protein is considered incomplete, it is not considered less nutritious than a complete protein. Incomplete proteins simply need to be combined with other foods to provide the full complement of the nine essential amino acids. For example, combining rice (a grain) with beans (a legume) provides all of the essential amino acids. Combining grains, beans, nuts, vegetables, and seeds in various ways can provide a complete protein.

Fats: Polyunsaturated, Monounsaturated, Saturated, and Trans

All fats, regardless of the type, have a significant amount of calories; therefore, moderation of any fat is your best guide. Every gram of fat contains 9 calories.

Monounsaturated fats should make up most of the fats you consume. This type of fat is found in certain plant foods such as macadamia nuts, canola oil, peanut oil, and olive oil. Monounsaturated fats do not raise blood cholesterol and may actually help reduce blood cholesterol levels if they replace saturated fat in the diet.

Polyunsaturated fats should be used in moderation, and less often than monounsaturated fats. These fats come mostly from vegetable sources such as corn oil, sunflower oil, and some types of margarine.

Saturated fats should be used the least. This type of fat is typically found in foods made from animal sources such as meat, butter, cheese, and cream. Baked goods such as cakes and pastries may be high in saturated fat if lard, palm oil, or coconut oil is used. Excessive intake of saturated fat can increase blood cholesterol levels.

Trans fats are the result of a food manufacturing process called hydrogenation. This process converts a liquid vegetable oil to a solid fat to make shortenings and solid (stick) types of margarine.

Avoid Trans Fats Too

Check food labels and ingredients to avoid trans fats as much as possible. This form of fat can raise LDL (bad) cholesterol and increase your risk for heart disease. Trans fats can be found in vegetable shortenings, solid margarines, certain crackers, cookies, and other foods made with partially hydrogenated oils.

Foods containing omega-3 fatty acids are encouraged. Omega-3 plays an important role in the maintenance of immune function, brain development, and reproduction. There is considerable evidence to suggest that omega-3 fatty acid can have a positive effect on certain conditions due to its anti-inflammatory properties. Omega-3 fatty acids are found in soy oil, green leafy vegetables, walnuts, flaxseed, and most notably, oily fish such as salmon, sardines, and mackerel.

Cholesterol

Cholesterol is a waxy substance found in all body cells. It is part of some hormones, and essential for fat digestion. The liver manufactures much of the cholesterol your body needs, but cholesterol is also obtained from the foods you eat. Cholesterol is found in animal foods such as meat, eggs, butter, and whole dairy products. Too much cholesterol in the blood can increase your risk for heart disease. Diabetics have more risk for heart disease and should have their blood cholesterol checked routinely. Diabetics are advised to limit consumption of fatty meats and other high-cholesterol foods to 300 milligrams or less daily. Your doctor or registered dietitian may provide you with more specific recommendations for cholesterol control.

Sodium

Sodium is a mineral that does not affect blood sugar, but it can alter your blood pressure. Controlling blood pressure is yet another important aspect of managing your diabetes. The recommended sodium intake for healthy adults is 2,400–

3,000 milligrams per day. If you have high blood pressure, you may need to keep your sodium intake under 2,400 milligrams daily.

Follow these tips to reduce your sodium intake:

- Leave out or reduce the amount of salt in standard recipes by 25–50 percent
- Use commercial herb blends (or make your own) to season food instead of using salt
- Limit intake of highly processed foods such as boxed mixes, instant foods, or processed meats
- Make more soups, stews, casseroles, or side dishes from scratch
- Watch your use of salt when cooking or at the table

ABOUT FIBER AND WHOLE GRAINS

There are two types of fiber found in foods: soluble and insoluble. It's important to include foods containing both types of fiber in your daily eating plan.

Soluble fiber dissolves or swells when it's put into water. Soluble fiber helps keep blood sugar levels stable by slowing down the rate of glucose absorption into the bloodstream. When consumed in adequate amounts, soluble fiber can help lower blood cholesterol levels as well. Beans, fruit, barley, and oats are especially good sources of soluble fiber.

Insoluble fiber does not dissolve in water. It is not readily broken down by bacteria in the intestinal tract, so it passes through the body. Insoluble fiber is essential for preventing constipation and diverticulosis by helping to maintain regularity. Vegetables, whole-grain foods, and fruit are all good sources of insoluble fiber.

Label Know-How

Terms like "multigrain," "seven grain," or "stone ground" do not necessarily mean a product is whole grain. If a whole-grain ingredient is not listed as the first ingredient, the item may contain only a small portion of whole grains. One way to find a whole-grain product is to look for the Whole Grains Council stamp of approval, which has two different logos used to label foods containing whole grains. The logo with "100 percent Whole Grain" on it indicates the food has only whole grains and at least 16 grams per serving.

Getting More Fiber Every Day

Although all types of grains are sources of complex carbohydrates, those that have not been refined are better for you. Whole grains generally have more fiber and minerals. Because whole grains have not had the bran layer and germ removed during the milling process, fiber, vitamins, and minerals are preserved. Refined grains such as white flour and white rice have the bran and germ removed—this makes the refined grain much lower in fiber. Vitamins and minerals are also removed during this process, so they must be added back into the product after processing. Adding nutrients back into a processed food is called enrichment. When you see predominant ingredients such as enriched flour in a food, odds are it has been refined and is not very high in fiber. Eating refined grains instead of whole grains makes it difficult to achieve adequate amounts of fiber each day. Whenever you can, choose whole grains over refined grains. The recommendation for daily fiber intake is 25–30 grams per day, which is about twice the amount found in the typical American diet.

Great Ways to Get More Whole Grains

The best way to get more whole grains in your meals is to substitute whole-grain foods for refined products.

- When a recipe calls for white flour (all-purpose), experiment by replacing some of the flour with a whole-grain variety.
- Every week try one new grain. Quinoa, brown rice, bulgur, or kasha may be unfamiliar to you but are as easy to prepare as white rice.
- Use whole grains as a side dish or mixed with vegetables, lentils, or beans.
- Add whole grains to soups, salads, or casseroles instead of white rice or pasta.
- Try a cooked whole grain as a hot breakfast cereal.
- If you are not used to bran or other high-fiber cereals, try mixing them with equal amounts of your regular cereal.
- Switch to whole-grain crackers instead of saltines or snack-type crackers.
- Use oatmeal in place of bread crumbs in items such as meatloaf or meatballs.
- Gradually start replacing the refined grains in your kitchen cabinets with whole-grain foods.

READING AND UNDERSTANDING FOOD LABELS

The nutrition facts found on food labels contain plenty of information, but unless you understand how to read the label, you may be presented with information that doesn't mean very much to you.

UNDERSTANDING TERMS ON LABELS

- **Serving size:** Each label must identify the size of a serving. The nutritional information listed on a label is based on one serving of the food. Note that the serving listed on a package may not be the same as the size of your serving.
- **Amount per serving:** Each package identifies the quantities of nutrients and food constituents from one serving. From this information, you can find the calorie

value of the food in addition to how much fat (saturated or trans), cholesterol, sodium, carbohydrates, and protein per serving.

- **Percent daily value:** This indicates how much of a specific nutrient a serving of food contains in comparison to an average 2,000-calorie diet.
- **Ingredient list:** A list of the ingredients in a food in descending order of predominance and weight.

By comparing the calories from fat to the total calories in a food, you can identify foods that have lots of hidden fat. A typical hot dog has 110 total calories and 90 calories from fat. This means that 82 percent of the calories in the hot dog come from fat! Making this determination before buying a food can help you make healthier choices. Look for foods with 30 percent or less of its calories from fat.

Compare Carbohydrate Grams to Grams of Sugar

There are several parts to the carbohydrate section of the nutrition label. Total carbohydrates represent the amount of carbohydrate grams found in a food. Beneath the total carbohydrates line are other listings: fiber, sugars, and sometimes, sugar alcohols. These values are part of the total carbohydrates.

When you look at the grams of sugars in a product, be sure to compare it to the grams of total carbohydrates. For example, if a cup of cereal has 32 grams total carbohydrates and 16 grams of sugars, that means 50 percent of the carbohydrates in the cereal comes from sugars. Try to choose foods with 30 percent or less grams of sugars.

Fiber grams are also part of the total carbohydrates. Remember that fiber helps to slow down the absorption of glucose in the bloodstream. Choose foods that contain 4 or more grams of fiber per serving.

THE GLYCEMIC INDEX

The glycemic index (GI) measures how a food with carbohydrates raises blood glucose. Foods are ranked on a scale from 0 to 100, based on a comparison to a reference food. White table sugar is generally used as the benchmark for this comparison. A food with a high GI has more impact on blood sugar than a food with a medium or low GI.

Using the GI for meal planning involves choosing foods with a low or medium GI and limiting foods known to have a high GI. Eating foods with a lower GI can help control blood sugar and insulin levels in the body. Examples of carbohydrate foods with a low GI include dried beans and legumes, nonstarchy vegetables, most whole fruits, and many whole-grain breads and cereals. Foods that don't contain carbohydrates (such as meats or fats) do not have a GI.

Foods that are good sources of fiber tend to have a lower GI. In general, the less processed a food is, the lower the GI. The GI of a food can be affected by its degree of ripeness, the amount and type of processing it has sustained, or the method in which it has been cooked. For example, a very ripe piece of fruit will have a higher GI than one that is not as ripe. Pasta that is cooked al dente has a lower GI than soft-cooked pasta. Fruit juices, because of more processing, usually have a higher GI than fresh fruit.

When it comes to meal planning for diabetes, there is no right way that works well for everyone. The GI is one of several tools you can use in conjunction with maintaining portion control. If you choose to use the GI as a meal-planning tool, keep in mind that the total amount of carbohydrates you eat is still the most important factor. For more information about the glycemic index, go to *www.joslin.org* or *www.mendosa.com/gilists.htm*.

YOUR GROCERY SHOPPING LIST

Having a plan and the right foods on hand is the best way to keep you eating healthier. If you don't have a good plan and leave things up to chance, you could make poor food choices. Grabbing a fast-food or takeout meal at the last minute usually means you will be eating fewer vegetables, fresh fruits, or whole-grain foods. At the same time, you will be consuming plenty of calories, fat, refined grains, and possibly sugar.

Set aside some time each week to plan your meals. If you work or have a very busy schedule, a good time to plan or shop may be your day off or a quiet time of the day. A little bit of time invested in meal planning saves time and money.

Keep a weekly shopping list visible and handy; when you think of food items you need, you can write them on your list. Each time you plan, consider what meals and snacks you will need for the coming week. As you develop a shopping list, take stock of the types of foods you have in your kitchen cabinets, refrigerator, and freezer, then decide what you need to add.

Having plenty of healthy food choices available all of the time helps you avoid the pitfalls of eating too many empty-calorie foods that get in the way of weight loss or managing your diabetes.

TWENTY FOODS TO ALWAYS HAVE ON HAND

1. Vegetables: any fresh, frozen, or reduced-sodium canned
2. Fruits: any fresh, frozen (unsweetened), or canned (juice or water packed)
3. Whole-grain bread
4. High-fiber (low sugar) cereals with 4 grams or more fiber per serving
5. Canned beans, dry beans, or lentils—any variety
6. Boneless, skinless chicken or turkey breast
7. Egg substitutes or egg whites
8. Tuna or salmon canned in water
9. Low-fat cheese or cheese sticks—choose 1–1½ percent fat varieties

10. Nonstick cooking spray
11. Dried herbs and spices—any single varieties or mixes made without the addition of salt
12. Unsalted dry-roasted or raw nuts (walnuts and almonds are good choices)
13. Noncaloric sweetener
14. Reduced-fat mayonnaise or salad dressing
15. Low-sodium chicken, vegetable, or beef broth
16. Leafy lettuce varieties or bagged salad mixes using leafy varieties
17. One or more whole grains: quinoa, amaranth, barley, bulgur, kasha, brown rice, whole-grain pasta
18. Canned tomatoes or stewed canned tomatoes
19. Fat-free yogurt—plain, vanilla, or fruit flavored, artificially sweetened
20. Whole-grain crackers

Make Over Your Food Supply

Making over your food supply does not have to be extreme, costly, or stressful. You can gradually make over your cupboards by phasing out foods of lesser nutritional quality with newer ones that have more health benefits and fewer calories. As you run out of items that you already have, replace each item with something new.

SUGGESTIONS FOR SWITCHING TO HEALTHIER FOODS	
Instead of	**Replace it with**
Garlic or onion salt	Fresh garlic or onion
Fruit juices	Fresh fruit
All-purpose flour	Whole-wheat or rye flour
Vegetable oil	Olive or canola oil
Sour cream	Plain low-fat yogurt
Buttery snack crackers	Whole-grain crackers
Cookies	Graham crackers
Potato chips	Popcorn (make your own)
Half gallon of ice cream	Single-serving reduced-calorie ice cream
Bacon	Thin-sliced low-fat ham

There are many ways to prepare foods that preserve nutrients and good taste and minimize the use of sugar, salt, and fat. Some nutrients are lost if foods are cooked at very high temperatures or with too much water. For vegetables, the cooking process should have minimal contact with water and the least amount of cooking time required to retain the nutritional value. This makes steaming, microwaving, and stir-frying great options for cooking vegetables. All three save time and preserve the nutritional value of foods.

MAKING RECIPE ADJUSTMENTS

Your favorite recipes can be adjusted to reduce the fat, salt, or sugar content, yet still maintain good taste. Recipes that are cooked rather than baked can often turn out quite well with a simple reduction in sugar, salt, or fat. It is possible to substitute low-fat or low-sodium ingredients in certain recipes. As an example, using 1% milk instead of whole milk in a pudding recipe lowers fat and calories without significantly altering the taste.

Substitution Options

Milk is an easy ingredient to substitute in baking. Fruit juice, rice milk, almond milk, or soymilk can be used one for one, although it will alter the Nutritional Analysis of the recipe. Keep in mind you can substitute water, but that may produce a blander-tasting baked product.

Some of the recipes found in this cookbook may contain ingredients such as butter or salt in small amounts. These ingredients are usually part of a recipe because they improve the flavor of a food or aid in the baking process. When baking bread, cookies, or cakes, salt is usually required in the leavening process and should not be eliminated. If you must eliminate all butter from your diet, most recipes can use margarine or vegetable oil as a substitute. You and your dietitian can decide whether it is appropriate to include these ingredients in small quantities or make a substitution.

Completely eliminating sugar from baked desserts can be tricky. Although sugar is an empty-calorie food, it does serve as an important ingredient in certain baked foods by enhancing the flavor, texture, or appearance. When sugar is reduced or replaced with an artificial sweetener in a cake or cookie recipe, the result can be very different. The end product can be denser, lack a golden-brown color, or have a flavor unlike the original recipe.

The recipes for baked desserts found in this cookbook have different methods for addressing sugar in the recipe. Some recipes will simply have a reduction in the total amount of sugar used; others use a different type of sugar that has caloric value, such as honey or maple syrup. When these are used in the place of sugar, a lesser quantity is used; it is lower in sugar, but not sugar-free. Lastly, some recipes have a combination of an artificial sweetener with a very small amount of regular sugar. As you work with these, or with your own recipes, you will learn how to adjust ingredients to get good results.

Tips for Replacing or Reducing Sugar and Fat

- Try reducing a standard recipe's sugar content by 25–50 percent. It's usually best to start with a smaller reduction (25 percent) and gradually decrease the amount of sugar each time you make it. Be sure to note any significant or undesirable changes in the properties of the food, then adjust as needed.

- Use puréed, unsweetened fruit or fruit juices to replace some or all of the sugar in a recipe.
- Honey and maple syrup will affect blood sugar; however, either can add sweetness to a food. Carbohydrates and calories can be reduced in a recipe if you use a smaller amount of these sugars.
- Many recipes can withstand up to a 50 percent reduction in fat. To replace fat but not volume, try using plain yogurt, applesauce, mashed ripe banana, or other puréed fruit for half of the oil or shortening called for in a recipe. If the product requires sweetness in addition to volume, applesauce or mashed ripe banana make good options.

Using Sugar Substitutes

Sugar substitutes are never mandatory for diabetes management, but they can offer options to those who may wish to use them. Using a sugar substitute in recipes can slash sugar and a significant amount of calories. When using sugar substitutes in baking, keep in mind that sweetness is being added to the food, but other traits unique to a baked product (volume, texture, golden-brown color) may be altered.

The following sweeteners are all approved by the FDA. They vary in taste, uses, and suitability for cooking or baking. You will need to do a taste test on your own to decide which ones are best for you.

SUGAR SUBSTITUTES		
Sweetener	**Brand Name**	**Notes**
Saccharin	Sweet'N Low or Sugar Twin	Saccharin can leave a bitter aftertaste, and may need to be combined with other sweeteners to improve taste when used in cooking. Twenty-four packets replace 1 cup of sugar.
Aspartame	Equal, NutraSweet	High temperatures diminish sweetness, making this product less suitable for baking. Aspartame contains phenylalanine, which can be harmful to people with the rare disease phenylketonuria (PKU).
Sucralose	Splenda	There are several baking products using sucralose, including a granular version that measures cup for cup with sugar. There are also half sugar/brown sugar blends that contain sugar, so adjust accordingly.
Stevia	Truvía, Pure Via	Look for brands of stevia that use a purified portion of the stevia leaf known as rebaudioside A. Sugar-to-stevia ratios vary with each brand, so follow recommendations by the manufacturer if using in cooking or baking.

WHAT ABOUT ALCOHOL?

When it comes to alcohol and diabetes management, it's all about moderation. Consider the facts about alcohol, then decide whether including alcohol on a moderate basis fits into your diabetes plan. Alcohol does not provide any essential nutrients, but it is a source of calories. At 7 calories per gram, too much alcohol can promote weight gain. If you drink and are having difficulty losing weight, do not overlook the calories that alcohol adds to your overall intake. Alcohol can significantly impact blood lipid levels and elevate triglycerides; both of these health issues may already be a source of concern if you have diabetes.

The Definition of Moderate Alcohol Consumption

If your diabetes is well controlled, you may be able to drink a moderate amount of alcohol. Moderation is considered two drinks a day for men and one drink a day for women. One drink is a 12-ounce beer, a 5-ounce glass of wine, or 1½ ounces of 80-proof distilled spirits. Beverages with mixers (sodas, juices, etc.) have more carbohydrates. If you use mixers, decrease the calories and carbohydrates by using club soda, mineral water, diet soda, or diet tonic water in the drink.

Alcohol prevents the liver from producing glucose. While this sounds like it could be helpful, the results can actually be quite harmful. The diabetic who takes insulin or any diabetic medication designed to lower blood glucose may experience hypoglycemia (low blood sugar) shortly after drinking. The hypoglycemia can continue for many hours beyond that. In short, if you choose to drink alcohol, you should always limit the amount and take the alcohol with a meal to keep your blood glucose stable.

CHAPTER 2

BREAKFAST AND BRUNCH

EGG WHITE PANCAKES

SERVES 2; SERVING SIZE: ½ BATTER

4 egg whites

½ cup rolled oats

4 teaspoons reduced-calorie or low-sugar strawberry jam

1 teaspoon powdered sugar (optional)

Creative Toppings

Experiment with toast and pancake toppings. Try a tablespoon of raisins, almonds, apples, bananas, berries, nut butters (limit these to 1 teaspoon per serving), peanuts, pears, walnuts, or wheat germ.

1. Put all ingredients in blender; process until smooth.

2. Preheat nonstick pan treated with cooking spray over medium heat. Pour half of mixture into pan; cook for 4–5 minutes.

3. Flip pancake and cook until inside is cooked. Repeat using remaining batter for second pancake. Dust each pancake with powdered sugar, if using.

Nutritional Analysis (per serving): Calories: 197 | Protein: 13g | Carbohydrates: 31g | Fat: 3g | Saturated Fat: 1g | Cholesterol: 0mg | Sodium: 120mg | Fiber: 4g | PCF Ratio: 27-61-12 | Exchange Approx.: 1 Free Sweet, 1 Lean Meat, 1½ Breads

BUCKWHEAT PANCAKES

SERVES 2; SERVING SIZE: ½ BATTER

1 cup whole-wheat flour

½ cup buckwheat flour

1½ teaspoons baking powder

2 egg whites

¼ cup apple juice concentrate

1¼–1½ cups skim milk

1. Sift flours and baking powder together. Combine egg whites, apple juice concentrate, and 1¼ cups milk. Add milk mixture to dry ingredients; mix well, but do not overmix. Add remaining milk if necessary to reach desired consistency.

2. Cook pancakes in nonstick skillet or on griddle treated with nonstick spray over medium heat.

Nutritional Analysis (per serving): Calories: 220 | Protein: 11g | Carbohydrates: 44g | Fat: 1g | Saturated Fat: 0g | Cholesterol: 1mg | Sodium: 200mg | Fiber: 5g | PCF Ratio: 76-19-5 | Exchange Approx.: 2 Starches, ½ Skim Milk, ½ Fruit

BERRY PUFF PANCAKES

SERVES 6; SERVING SIZE: 1 WEDGE (⅙ PANCAKE)

2 large whole eggs

1 large egg white

½ cup skim milk

½ cup all-purpose flour

1 tablespoon granulated sugar

⅛ teaspoon sea salt

Powdered sugar for garnish

2 cups fresh berries such as raspberries, blackberries, boysenberries, blueberries, strawberries, or a combination

1 tablespoon powdered sugar

Syrup Substitutes

Spreading 2 teaspoons of your favorite Smucker's Low Sugar jam or jelly on a waffle or pancake not only gives you a sweet topping, but it can be one of your Free exchange list choices for the day.

1. Preheat oven to 450°F. Treat 10" ovenproof skillet or deep pie pan with nonstick spray. Once oven is heated, place pan in oven for a few minutes to get hot.

2. Add eggs and egg white to medium bowl; beat until mixed. Whisk in milk. Slowly whisk in flour, sugar, and salt.

3. Remove preheated pan from oven; pour batter into it. Bake for 15 minutes; reduce heat to 350°F and bake for an additional 10 minutes or until batter is puffed and brown. Remove from oven and slide onto serving plate. Cover with fruit and sift powdered sugar over top. Cut into six equal wedges and serve.

Nutritional Analysis (per serving): Calories: 110 | Protein: 5g | Carbohydrates: 37g | Fat: 2g | Saturated Fat: 1g | Cholesterol: 71mg | Sodium: 89mg | Fiber: 3g | PCF Ratio: 65-18-17 | Exchange Approx.: 1 Starch, ½ Fruit

BUTTERMILK PANCAKES

SERVES 2; SERVING SIZE: 2 PANCAKES

1 cup all-purpose flour

2 tablespoons nonfat buttermilk powder

¼ teaspoon baking soda

½ teaspoon low-salt baking powder

1 cup water

Nut Butter Batter

For a change of pace, try adding 1 exchange amount per serving of nut butter to pancake batter and use jelly or jam instead of syrup.

1. Blend together all ingredients, adding more water if necessary to get batter consistency desired.

2. Pour ¼ of batter into nonstick skillet or skillet treated with nonstick cooking spray. Cook over medium heat until bubbles appear on top half of pancake. Flip and continue cooking until center of pancake is done. Repeat process with remaining batter.

Nutritional Analysis (per serving): Calories: 143 | Protein: 6g | Carbohydrates: 26g | Fat: 2g | Saturated Fat: 1g | Cholesterol: 49mg | Sodium: 111mg | Fiber: 1g | PCF Ratio: 16-74-10 | Exchange Approx.: 1½ Starches

SWEET POTATO PANCAKES

SERVES 4; SERVING SIZE: ¼ BATTER

2 medium sweet potatoes (1½ cups cooked)

¼ cup grated onions

1 egg

3 tablespoons whole-wheat pastry flour

½ teaspoon ground cinnamon

½ teaspoon baking powder

½ cup egg whites

2 tablespoons canola oil

Whole-Wheat Pastry Flour

Whole-wheat pastry flour is a finer grind of soft white wheat. When used in quick bread and muffin recipes, it delivers more nutrition and fiber than white flour and yields a lighter texture than whole-wheat flour.

1. Scrub sweet potatoes; pierce skins with fork and microwave on high for 4–5 minutes. When sweet potatoes have cooled enough to handle, scoop sweet potato flesh out of skins; lightly mash with fork.

2. In medium bowl, mix together sweet potatoes, grated onion, and egg. Add in flour, cinnamon, and baking powder.

3. In separate small bowl, beat egg whites until rounded peaks are formed. Gently fold egg whites into potato mixture.

4. Heat oil in skillet (nonstick preferably) until hot. Spoon batter onto skillet to form pancakes approximately 4" in diameter. Brown on both sides.

Nutritional Analysis (per serving): Calories: 168 | Protein: 6g | Carbohydrates: 25.87g | Fat: 7g | Saturated Fat: 1g | Cholesterol: 0mg | Sodium: 139mg | Fiber: 3g | PCF Ratio: 13-49-37 | Exchange Approx.: 1 Starch, 1½ Fats

COUNTRY-STYLE OMELET

SERVES 2; SERVING SIZE: ½ OMELET

2 teaspoons olive oil

1 cup diced zucchini

¼ cup diced red pepper

1 cup skinned and cubed plum tomatoes

⅛ teaspoon pepper

4 eggs

1 tablespoon grated Parmesan cheese

1 teaspoon minced fresh basil

1. Heat oil in nonstick skillet. Add zucchini and red pepper; sauté for 5 minutes.

2. Add tomatoes and pepper; cook uncovered for another 10 minutes, allowing fluid from tomatoes to cook down.

3. In small bowl, whisk together eggs, Parmesan cheese, and fresh basil; pour over vegetables in skillet.

4. Cook over low heat until browned, approximately 10 minutes on each side.

Nutritional Analysis (per serving): Calories: 253 | Protein: 17g | Carbohydrates: 7g | Fat: 17g | Saturated Fat: 5g | Cholesterol: 493mg | Sodium: 221mg | Fiber: 2g | PCF Ratio: 27-12-61 | Exchange Approx.: 1 Vegetable, 2 Medium-Fat Meats, 3 Fats

FRUIT SMOOTHIE

SERVES 1

1 cup skim milk

2 exchange servings of any diced fruit

1 tablespoon honey

4 teaspoons toasted wheat germ

6 large ice cubes

Batch 'Em

Make large batches of smoothies so you can keep single servings in the freezer. Get out a serving as you begin to get ready for your day. This should give the smoothie time to thaw enough for you to stir it when you're ready to have breakfast.

Put all ingredients into blender or food processor; process until thick and smooth.

Nutritional Analysis (per serving): The nutritional analysis and exchange approximation for this recipe will depend on your choice of fruit. Otherwise, allow ½ Skim Milk exchange and ½ Misc. Food exchange. The wheat germ adds fiber, but at less than 20 calories a serving, it can count as 1 Free exchange.

YOGURT FRUIT SMOOTHIE

SERVES 2; SERVING SIZE: ½ SMOOTHIE

1 cup plain low-fat yogurt

½ cup sliced strawberries

½ cup orange juice

½ cup peeled and sliced nectarines

2 tablespoons ground flaxseed

Variations and Combos

You can vary this smoothie by substituting other fruits of your choice. Good combinations are strawberry and banana, strawberry and kiwi, or banana and peach. Keep portions of each fruit to no more than ½ cup.

Put all ingredients in blender; process until smooth.

Nutritional Analysis (per serving): Calories: 149 | Protein: 10g | Carbohydrates: 26g | Fat: 1g | Saturated Fat: 0g | Cholesterol: 2mg | Sodium: 96mg | Fiber: 2g | PCF Ratio: 25-67-8 | Exchange Approx.: 1 Milk, 1 Fruit

TOFU SMOOTHIE

SERVES 1

1⅓ cups frozen unsweetened strawberries

½ banana, peeled

½ cup (4 ounces) silken tofu

In food processor or blender, process all ingredients until smooth. Add a little chilled water for thinner smoothies if desired.

Nutritional Analysis (per serving): Calories: 289 | Protein: 20g | Carbohydrates: 35g | Fat: 11g | Saturated Fat: 2g | Cholesterol: 0mg | Sodium: 19mg | Fiber: 8g | PCF Ratio: 25-44-31 | Exchange Approx.: 1 Meat Substitute, 2 Fruits

OVERNIGHT OATMEAL

SERVES 4; SERVING SIZE: ¼ RECIPE

1 cup steel-cut oats

14 dried apricot halves

1 dried fig

2 tablespoons golden raisins

4 cups water

½ cup Mock Cream (see recipe in
   Chapter 6)

Another Overnight Method

For another way to cook steel-cut oats,
place 1 cup steel-cut oats, 4 cups water,
and dried fruit in medium saucepan; bring
to a quick boil. Turn off the heat and cover
saucepan. When cooled, place in covered
container and refrigerate overnight. In the
morning, the oatmeal will have absorbed
all of the water. Scoop one portion of the
oatmeal into a bowl; microwave on high
for 1½–2 minutes. Add milk and serve.
Heat up refrigerated leftover portions as
needed; use within 3 days.

Add all ingredients to slow cooker with a ceramic interior;
set to low heat. Cover and cook overnight (8–9 hours).

Nutritional Analysis (per serving): Calories: 221 | Protein:
9g | Carbohydrates: 42g | Fat: 3g | Saturated Fat:
1g | Cholesterol: 1mg | Sodium: 25mg | Fiber: 6g | PCF Ratio:
15-73-11 | Exchange Approx.: 1 Fruit, 1 Starch, ½ Skim Milk

EGG CLOUDS ON TOAST

SERVES 1

2 egg whites

½ teaspoon sugar

1 cup water

1 tablespoon frozen apple juice concentrate

1 slice reduced-calorie oat-bran bread, lightly toasted

Additional Serving Suggestions

Spread 1 teaspoon of low-sugar or all-fruit spread on toast (½ Fruit exchange) before ladling on the "clouds." For cinnamon French-style toast, sprinkle ¼ teaspoon ground cinnamon and ½ teaspoon powdered sugar (less than 10 calories) over top of the clouds.

1. In copper bowl, beat egg whites until thickened. Add sugar; continue to beat until stiff peaks form.

2. In small saucepan, heat water and apple juice over medium heat until it just begins to boil; reduce heat and allow mixture to simmer. Drop egg whites by teaspoonful into simmering water. Simmer for 3 minutes; turn over and simmer for an additional 3 minutes.

3. Ladle "clouds" over toast and serve immediately.

Nutritional Analysis (per serving): Calories: 57 | Protein: 4g | Carbohydrates: 9g | Fat: 1g | Saturated Fat: 0g | Cholesterol: 0mg | Sodium: 101mg | Fiber: 0g | PCF Ratio: 30-63-7 | Exchange Approx.: ½ Very Lean Fat Meat, ½ Starch

QUINOA BERRY BREAKFAST

SERVES 4; SERVING SIZE: ¼ RECIPE

1 cup quinoa

2 cups water

¼ cup chopped walnuts

1 teaspoon ground cinnamon

2 cups fresh berries

Single-Serving Quick Tip

Use this basic recipe to make four servings at once. Refrigerate any leftover portions; microwave 1–1½ minutes on high for single portions as needed. Use cooked quinoa within 3 days. Try other berries, nuts, or spices such as ginger or nutmeg to vary this nutritious breakfast cereal.

1. Rinse quinoa in fine-mesh sieve before cooking. Place quinoa, water, walnuts, and cinnamon in 1½-quart saucepan; bring to a boil. Reduce heat to low; cover and cook for 15 minutes or until all water has been absorbed.

2. Add berries and serve with milk, soymilk, or sweetener if desired.

Nutritional Analysis (per serving): Calories: 228 | Protein: 7g | Carbohydrates: 41g | Fat: 5g | Saturated Fat: 0g | Cholesterol: 0mg | Sodium: 2mg | Fiber: 5g | PCF Ratio: 12-69-19 | Exchange Approx.: 2 Starches, 1 Fruit, 1 Very Lean Meat, 4 Fats

OAT CREPES

½ cup oat flour

¼ cup liquid egg whites

½ cup low-fat milk

Cooking spray

Tips for a Perfect Crepe

Place paper towels in between each cooked crepe while stacking to keep them from sticking together. Always spray a new coat of cooking spray before making the next crepe so it can be easily removed from the pan. These crepes keep well in the refrigerator in a sealed container.

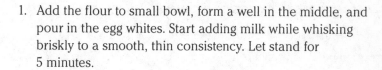

1. Add the flour to small bowl, form a well in the middle, and pour in the egg whites. Start adding milk while whisking briskly to a smooth, thin consistency. Let stand for 5 minutes.

2. Coat a medium-sized pan generously with cooking spray and warm on high heat for 2–3 minutes to get the pan very hot to start. Pour ¼ cup of the batter in a small circle in center of the pan. Rock and swirl the pan in a circular motion while holding a few inches above the heat to get the batter to thinly coat the pan. Then put the pan directly on the burner.

3. Heat for 1–2 minutes until the edges start to curl up. Use a large spatula to flip the crepe over and heat for 30–60 seconds on the second side until very lightly browned. Place each cooked crepe on a plate and cover with paper towel. Repeat this step to make three more crepes. Note: the crepes will begin to cook quicker as the pan gets hotter and may take as little as 30–60 seconds on each side.

Nutritional Analysis (per serving): Calories: 60 | Protein: 3g | Carbohydrates: 8g | Fat: 1g | Saturated Fat: 0g | Cholesterol: 0mg | Sodium: 30mg | Fiber: 1g | PCF Ratio: 21-60-19 | Exchange Approx.: ½ Starch, ¼ Skim Milk

GINGER APPLE WALNUT BARS

YIELDS 16 BARS; SERVING SIZE: 1 BAR

1 cup creamy or crunchy almond butter

½ cup pure maple syrup

1 tablespoon blackstrap molasses

¾ teaspoon ground ginger

1 tablespoon vanilla extract

¾ cup old-fashioned rolled oats

½ cup chopped dried apples

¼ cup chopped walnuts

Wax or parchment paper

1. In a medium-sized bowl, combine all of the ingredients and mix well.

2. Line an 8" × 8" pan with a large rectangular piece of wax/parchment paper. Place the mixture on one side of the paper and then fold the paper over to press down on top.

3. Chill in the refrigerator for an hour or more, then cut into sixteen bars and serve. Store bars in the refrigerator for up to a week or freeze for up to a few months.

Nutritional Analysis (per serving): Calories: 150 | Protein: 5g | Carbohydrates: 13g | Fat: 10g | Saturated Fat: 0.5g | Cholesterol: 0mg | Sodium: 10mg | Fiber: 2g | PCF Ratio: 12-31-57 | Exchange Approx.: 1 Starch, ½ High-Fat Meat, ½ Fat

OATMEAL RAISIN PANCAKES

YIELDS 12 PANCAKES; SERVING SIZE: 2 PANCAKES

2 cups oat flour

½ cup old-fashioned rolled oats

2 teaspoons baking powder

2 packed tablespoons brown sugar

½ teaspoon ground cinnamon

½ cup liquid egg whites

2 cups skim milk or other nondairy milk

1 teaspoon vanilla extract

½ cup raisins

Cooking spray

Making Your Own Oat Flour

Don't have oat flour on hand? You can make your own by simply grinding oats to a fine powder in a blender or food processor.

1. Combine the flour, oats, baking powder, brown sugar, and cinnamon together in a medium bowl.

2. Pour the egg whites, milk, and vanilla into a large bowl and whisk together. Add the flour mixture to the liquid, whisking rapidly until a smooth, thin batter is formed. Stir in the raisins and mix well. Allow the batter to thicken for about 10–15 minutes for best results.

3. Add about ¼ cup batter for each pancake to a skillet coated with cooking spray and cook on high heat for 1–2 minutes on each side. Repeat with ¼ cup mixture eleven more times for a total of twelve small to medium pancakes.

Nutritional Analysis (per serving): Calories: 230 | Protein: 8g | Carbohydrates: 41g | Fat: 3g | Saturated Fat: 0g | Cholesterol: 0mg | Sodium: 260mg | Fiber: 5g | PCF Ratio: 15-74-11 | Exchange Approx.: 1½ Starches, ¾ Fruit, ½ Other Carbohydrate

MORNING GLORY PANCAKES

**YIELDS 12 PANCAKES; SERVING SIZE:
2 PANCAKES**

2 cups oat flour

2 teaspoons baking powder

2 packed tablespoons brown sugar

1 teaspoon ground cinnamon

½ cup liquid egg whites

2 cups skim milk or other nondairy milk

1 teaspoon vanilla extract

¼ cup grated zucchini

¼ cup grated apple, skin on or peeled

¼ cup grated carrot

2 tablespoons shredded unsweetened coconut

¼ cup chopped walnuts

Cooking spray

1. Combine the flour, baking powder, brown sugar, and cinnamon together in a medium bowl.

2. Pour the egg whites, milk, and vanilla into a large bowl and whisk together. Add the flour mixture to the liquid, whisking rapidly until a smooth, thin batter is formed. Stir in the grated zucchini, apple, carrot, coconut, and walnuts and mix well. Allow the batter to thicken for about 10–15 minutes for best results.

3. Add about ¼ cup batter for each pancake to a skillet coated with cooking spray and cook on high heat for 1–2 minutes on each side. Repeat with ¼ cup mixture eleven more times for a total of twelve small to medium pancakes.

Nutritional Analysis (per serving): Calories: 200 | Protein: 6g | Carbohydrates: 32g | Fat: 4g | Saturated Fat: 1g | Cholesterol: 0mg | Sodium: 100mg | Fiber: 4g | PCF Ratio: 10-63-27 | Exchange Approx.: 1 Starch, ¼ Fruit, ¼ Vegetable, ½ Other Carbohydrate, 1 Fat

PEANUT BUTTER PANCAKES

YIELDS 12 PANCAKES; SERVING SIZE: 2 PANCAKES

2 cups oat flour

2 teaspoons baking powder

2 tablespoons plus 2 teaspoons (packed) brown sugar

½ cup liquid egg whites

2 cups skim milk or other nondairy milk

1 teaspoon vanilla extract

¼ cup creamy peanut butter

Cooking spray

1. Combine the flour, baking powder and brown sugar together in a medium bowl.

2. Pour the egg whites, milk, vanilla, and peanut butter into a large bowl and whisk together. Add the flour mixture to the liquid, whisking rapidly until a smooth, thin batter is formed. Allow the batter to thicken for about 10–15 minutes for best results.

3. Add ¼ cup batter for each pancake to a skillet coated with cooking spray and cook on high heat for 1–2 minutes on each side. Repeat with ¼ cup mixture eleven more times for a total of twelve small to medium pancakes.

Nutritional Analysis (per serving): Calories: 300 | Protein: 10g | Carbohydrates: 30g | Fat: 14g | Saturated Fat: 1g | Cholesterol: 0mg | Sodium: 180mg | Fiber: 4g | PCF Ratio: 13-44-43 | Exchange Approx.: 2 Starches, 1 High-Fat Meat, 1 Fat

GINGERBREAD PANCAKES

YIELDS 12 PANCAKES; SERVING SIZE: 2 PANCAKES

2 cups oat flour

2 teaspoons baking powder

2 packed tablespoons brown sugar

½ teaspoon ground ginger

1 teaspoon pumpkin pie spice

2 teaspoons molasses

½ cup unsweetened applesauce

½ cup liquid egg whites

1 cup skim milk or other nondairy milk

1 teaspoon vanilla extract

Cooking spray

1. Combine the flour, baking powder, brown sugar, ginger, and pie spice together in a medium bowl.

2. Pour the molasses, applesauce, egg whites, milk, and vanilla into a large bowl and whisk together. Add the flour mixture to the liquid, whisking rapidly until a smooth, thin batter is formed. Allow the batter to thicken for about 10–15 minutes for best results.

3. Add about ¼ cup batter for each pancake to a skillet coated with cooking spray and cook on high heat for 1–2 minutes on each side. Repeat with ¼ cup mixture eleven more times for a total of twelve small to medium pancakes.

Nutritional Analysis (per serving): Calories: 160 | Protein: 4g | Carbohydrates: 26g | Fat: 3g | Saturated Fat: 0g | Cholesterol: 0mg | Sodium: 70mg | Fiber: 4g | PCF Ratio: 12-72-16 | Exchange Approx.: 1 Starch, ½ Fat, ¾ Other Carbohydrate

PUMPKIN PANCAKES

YIELDS 12 PANCAKES; SERVING SIZE: 2 PANCAKES

2 cups oat flour

2 teaspoons baking powder

2 packed tablespoons brown sugar

½ teaspoon pumpkin pie spice

½ cup liquid egg whites

1⅓ cups skim milk or other nondairy milk

½ cup canned or fresh cooked pumpkin purée (not pumpkin pie filling)

Cooking spray

1. Combine the flour, baking powder, brown sugar, and pie spice together in a medium bowl.

2. Pour the egg whites, milk, and pumpkin into a large bowl and whisk together. Add the flour mixture to the liquid, whisking rapidly until a smooth, thin batter is formed. Allow the batter to thicken for about 10–15 minutes for best results.

3. Add ¼ cup batter for each pancake to a skillet coated with cooking spray and cook on high heat for 1–2 minutes on each side. Repeat with ¼ cup mixture eleven more times for a total of twelve small to medium pancakes.

Nutritional Analysis (per serving): Calories: 150 | Protein: 5g | Carbohydrates: 23g | Fat: 3g | Saturated Fat: 0g | Cholesterol: 0mg | Sodium: 80mg | Fiber: 4g | PCF Ratio: 14-68-18 | Exchange Approx.: 1 Starch, ¼ Vegetable, ½ Other Carbohydrate, ½ Fat

SLOW-COOKER PUMPKIN APPLE OATS

YIELDS 4 CUPS; SERVING SIZE: 1 CUP

1 cup old-fashioned rolled oats

1½ cups water

2 cups unsweetened almond milk or skim milk

½ cup canned or fresh cooked pumpkin purée (not pumpkin pie filling)

1 cup peeled, chopped apples

3 or 4 packed tablespoons brown sugar

1 teaspoon vanilla extract

½ teaspoon pumpkin pie spice

1 teaspoon ground cinnamon

Dash of salt (optional)

Combine all the ingredients in a small to medium slow cooker, such as a 3-quart size, and heat on low for 3–5 hours depending on desired consistency.

Nutritional Analysis (per serving): Calories: 200 | Protein: 3g | Carbohydrates: 36g | Fat: 3g | Saturated Fat: 0g | Cholesterol: 0mg | Sodium: 55mg | Fiber: 5g | PCF Ratio: 7-68-25 | Exchange Approx.: 2 Starches, ¼ Fruit, ½ Fat

CARROT CAKE YOGURT

SERVES 1

6 ounces vanilla nonfat yogurt (Greek style or regular)

¼ cup finely grated carrot

1 tablespoon chopped raisins

1 tablespoon chopped walnuts

1 dash each ground cinnamon, ground nutmeg, and ground ginger (optional)

Mix all the ingredients in a small bowl and serve.

Nutritional Analysis (per serving): Calories: 250 | Protein: 14g | Carbohydrates: 38g | Fat: 5g | Saturated Fat: 0.5g | Cholesterol: 0mg | Sodium: 25mg | Fiber: 2g | PCF Ratio: 22-60-18 | Exchange Approx.: ¼ Fruit, 1 Skim Milk, ¼ Vegetable, 1 Other Carbohydrate, 1 Lean Meat, ½ Fat

CARROT ZUCCHINI SPICE MUFFINS

YIELDS 12 MUFFINS; SERVING SIZE: 1 MUFFIN

2 cups old-fashioned rolled oats

¾ cup all-purpose or oat flour

1 teaspoon baking powder

½ teaspoon baking soda

2 teaspoons ground cinnamon

3 large overripe bananas, peeled and mashed

6 tablespoons liquid egg whites

6 packed tablespoons brown sugar

¼ cup skim or other nondairy milk

1 tablespoon vanilla extract

½ cup finely grated carrot

½ cup finely grated zucchini

½ cup finely grated apple

Cooking spray

Pump Up the Protein in These Muffins

Adding 6 tablespoons of unflavored protein powder to this recipe will increase the protein to 7g per serving, adding 1 Lean Meat exchange. Simply mix it in with the dry ingredients while making the recipe. Decrease baking time by 2–5 minutes.

1. Preheat oven to 350°F.

2. Combine the oats, oat flour, baking powder, baking soda, and cinnamon in a small bowl.

3. In a large bowl, beat together the mashed banana, egg whites, brown sugar, milk, and vanilla. Stir in the carrots, zucchini, and apple.

4. Gradually add the dry ingredients to the wet mixture just enough to combine ingredients. Do not overmix. Spoon into muffin tins coated with cooking spray.

5. Bake on the bottom rack of the oven for about 30–35 minutes until top is lightly browned and firm. Cool in muffin tin for at least 10 minutes before removing. Store these moist muffins in the refrigerator.

Nutritional Analysis (per serving): Calories: 140 | Protein: 3g | Carbohydrates: 29g | Fat: 1.5g | Saturated Fat: 0g | Cholesterol: 0mg | Sodium: 120mg | Fiber: 3g | PCF Ratio: 10-80-10 | Exchange Approx.: 2 Starches

BANANA WALNUT MUFFINS

YIELDS 12 MUFFINS; SERVING SIZE: 1 MUFFIN

2 cups old-fashioned rolled oats

¾ cup all-purpose or oat flour

1 teaspoon baking powder

½ teaspoon baking soda

3 large overripe bananas, peeled and mashed

6 tablespoons liquid egg whites

¼ cup packed brown sugar

¼ cup skim or other nondairy milk

1 tablespoon vanilla extract

⅓ cup finely chopped walnuts

Cooking spray

1. Preheat oven to 350°F.

2. Combine the oats, oat flour, baking powder, and baking soda in a small bowl.

3. In a large bowl, beat together the mashed banana, egg whites, brown sugar, milk, and vanilla.

4. Gradually add the dry ingredients to the wet mixture just enough to combine ingredients. Do not overmix.

5. Stir in the walnuts and spoon into muffin tins coated with cooking spray.

6. Bake on the bottom rack of the oven for about 30–35 minutes until top is lightly browned and firm. Cool in muffin tin for at least 10 minutes before removing. Store these moist muffins in the refrigerator.

Nutritional Analysis (per serving): Calories: 140 | Protein: 4g | Carbohydrates: 24g | Fat: 3.5g | Saturated Fat: 0g | Cholesterol: 0mg | Sodium: 115mg | Fiber: 3g | PCF Ratio: 10-68-22 | Exchange Approx.: 1½ Starches, ½ Fat

GARDEN MEDLEY FRITTATA

SERVES 4; SERVING SIZE: ¼ FRITTATA

1 tablespoon olive oil

½ cup chopped red bell pepper

¼ cup chopped onion

½ cup chopped zucchini

1 cup chopped mushrooms

1 cup spinach

2 cups liquid egg whites

2 tablespoons crumbled goat cheese

2 tablespoons chopped fresh basil

Alternative to Using an Ovenproof Skillet

If you don't have an oven-safe skillet, you can cook the vegetables in a regular pan. Then pour the egg mixture into a baking dish and add the cooked vegetables, as well as the goat cheese and basil, and just bake it all in that dish. If you use this method, add 5–10 minutes to the baking time and check to make sure the egg is fully cooked before serving.

1. Preheat oven to 450°F.

2. Coat an 8" ovenproof skillet with the olive oil and warm on medium heat. Add the peppers and onions and sauté for 3–5 minutes. Put in the zucchini and mushrooms and sauté a few more minutes until tender. Stir in the spinach and cook for another minute until it starts to wilt.

3. Pour the egg whites over the vegetables, sprinkle with cheese and basil, and cook on medium heat for about 5 minutes until the egg starts to set and the edges start to brown a bit.

4. Remove from heat and bake in the oven for 10–15 minutes until the egg is firm and fully cooked throughout.

Nutritional Analysis (per serving): Calories: 100 | Protein: 9g | Carbohydrates: 6g | Fat: 4g | Saturated Fat: 1g | Cholesterol: 5mg | Sodium: 140mg | Fiber: 1g | PCF Ratio: 36-22-42 | Exchange Approx.: 1 Lean Meat, 1 Fat

SKILLET POTATOES

YIELDS 3 CUPS; SERVING SIZE: ½ CUP

1 teaspoon olive oil

1 cup sliced red bell pepper

¾ cup diced white onion

½ cup corn (fresh, canned, or frozen thawed)

2 medium precooked and cubed baked potatoes, skins on

½ cup diced tomato

Salt and pepper to taste

Red pepper flakes (optional)

1. Coat a large skillet or pan with the olive oil. Put in the peppers and sauté for a few minutes on medium heat. Add the onions and corn and sauté a few more minutes until just before browned.

2. Fold the cooked potato into the mixture along with the tomatoes and heat the entire mixture, stirring frequently until lightly browned, another 4–5 minutes.

3. Use salt and pepper to taste. Red pepper flakes can be added for more spice.

Nutritional Analysis (per serving): Calories: 90 | Protein: 2g | Carbohydrates: 20g | Fat: 1g | Saturated Fat: 0g | Cholesterol: 0mg | Sodium: 5mg | Fiber: 2g | PCF Ratio: 9-81-10 | Exchange Approx.: 1 Starch, 1 Vegetable

PUMPKIN OAT LOAF

**YIELDS 1 LARGE LOAF, 12 SLICES;
SERVING SIZE: 1 SLICE**

Cooking spray

1⅓ cups whole-wheat pastry flour or regular whole-wheat flour

½ teaspoon baking soda

¼ teaspoon baking powder

½ teaspoon pumpkin pie spice

½ teaspoon ground cinnamon

⅓ cup old-fashioned rolled oats

2 tablespoons canola oil

⅔ cup packed brown sugar

1 egg

½ cup canned fresh-cooked pumpkin purée (not pumpkin pie filling)

1 cup chopped apples, peeled or skins on

½ cup dried cranberries

½ cup chopped walnuts

1. Preheat oven to 350°F. Coat a 9" × 4" × 3" pan with cooking spray.

2. Combine the flour, baking soda, baking powder, pumpkin pie spice, cinnamon, and oats in a medium-sized bowl and mix well.

3. In a larger bowl, beat together the oil, brown sugar, egg, and pumpkin until smooth. Add the dry ingredients gradually in small amounts and mix until dry ingredients are incorporated, yet not overmixed.

4. Fold in the apples, cranberries, and walnuts and pour batter into the prepared loaf pan. Bake for 35–40 minutes or until a toothpick comes out mostly clean.

Nutritional Analysis (per serving): Calories: 190 | Protein: 4g | Carbohydrates: 30g | Fat: 6g | Saturated Fat: 0g | Cholesterol: 0mg | Sodium: 75mg | Fiber: 3g | PCF Ratio: 8-63-29 | Exchange Approx.: 2 Starches, 1 Fat

BANANA BLUEBERRY OAT LOAF

**YIELDS 1 LARGE LOAF, 12 SLICES;
SERVING SIZE: 1 SLICE**

Cooking spray

1 cup whole-wheat pastry flour (or regular whole-wheat flour will do too)

⅔ cup quick oats

½ teaspoon baking soda

¼ teaspoon baking powder

4 ounces light coconut milk

⅔ cup brown sugar

¼ cup egg substitute or egg whites

1 extra-large very ripe banana, peeled and mashed

¾ cup blueberries

1. Preheat oven to 350°F. Coat a 9" × 4" × 3" loaf pan with cooking spray.

2. In a medium-sized bowl, combine the flour, oats, baking soda, and baking powder.

3. In a larger bowl, beat together the coconut milk, brown sugar, egg substitute/whites, and banana. Gradually add the dry ingredients until they are mixed in completely and the batter is a smooth consistency, but avoid overmixing. Fold in the blueberries.

4. Pour batter into the loaf pan and bake for 45–50 minutes or until a toothpick comes out mostly clean.

Nutritional Analysis (per serving): Calories: 125 | Protein: 2g | Carbohydrates: 27g | Fat: 1g | Saturated Fat: 0g | Cholesterol: 0mg | Sodium: 83mg | Fiber: 2g | PCF Ratio: 6-87-7 | Exchange Approx.: 1½ Starches

BANANA ALMOND CHAI SMOOTHIE

SERVES 1

1 cup unsweetened vanilla almond milk or skim milk

1 chai tea bag

1 medium frozen banana, peeled and cut into chunks

1 tablespoon almond butter

1 teaspoon vanilla extract

1. Warm the milk in a saucepan to just before boiling and add tea bag. Remove from heat and allow the tea bag to steep for at least 10 minutes. Then remove tea bag, pour milk into a heatproof container, and let cool in the refrigerator. (This can be done overnight as well.)

2. Once cooled, add the milky tea, banana chunks, almond butter, and vanilla extract to a blender and process until smooth.

Nutritional Analysis (per serving): Calories: 250 | Protein: 6g | Carbohydrates: 33g | Fat: 12g | Saturated Fat: 0g | Cholesterol: 0mg | Sodium: 180mg | Fiber: 6g | PCF Ratio: 9-51-40 | Exchange Approx.: 1½ Fruits, 1 Skim Milk, 1 Medium-Fat Meat

TRIPLE B (BLACKBERRY, BANANA, BASIL) SMOOTHIE

SERVES 1

½ cup unsweetened vanilla almond milk or skim milk

½ cup blackberries

2 teaspoons chopped fresh basil

½ medium frozen banana, peeled and cut into chunks

Add all the ingredients to a blender and process until smooth.

Nutritional Analysis (per serving): Calories: 100 | Protein: 2g | Carbohydrates: 21g | Fat: 2g | Saturated Fat: 0g | Cholesterol: 0mg | Sodium: 90mg | Fiber: 6g | PCF Ratio: 8-76-16 | Exchange Approx.: 1 Fruit, ½ Skim Milk

STRAWBERRY BANANA SNACK SMOOTHIE

SERVES 1

½ cup unsweetened vanilla almond milk or skim milk

2 large strawberries, cut into chunks and frozen

½ medium banana, peeled, cut into chunks, and frozen

Add all the ingredients to a blender and process until smooth.

Nutritional Analysis (per serving): Calories: 80 | Protein: 1g | Carbohydrates: 17g | Fat: 2g | Saturated Fat: 0g | Cholesterol: 0mg | Sodium: 90mg | Fiber: 3g | PCF Ratio: 6-76-18 | Exchange Approx.: ¾ Fruit, ½ Skim Milk

SWEET AND SPICY YOGURT

SERVES 1

6 ounces plain nonfat yogurt

2 packed teaspoons brown sugar

¼ teaspoon ground ginger

¼ teaspoon ground cinnamon

Make This Recipe to Grab and Go

Use a 6-ounce container of yogurt for this recipe, add all the ingredients, and mix in the container itself to take with you as a quick breakfast or snack.

Put all of the ingredients in a small bowl and mix well.

Nutritional Analysis (per serving): Calories: 120 | Protein: 9g | Carbohydrates: 20g | Fat: 0g | Saturated Fat: 0g | Cholesterol: 0mg | Sodium: 140mg | Fiber: 0g | PCF Ratio: 30-70-0 | Exchange Approx.: 1 Skim Milk, ¼ Other Carbohydrate

BASIC WHITE BREAD

YIELDS 2 LARGE LOAVES; SERVING SIZE: 1 SLICE

5–6 cups flour

1 package (2½ teaspoons) active dry yeast

¼ cup warm water

2 tablespoons sugar

1¾ cups warm potato water or plain water

2 tablespoons shortening

1 tablespoon sea salt

Nonstick spray

1. Place ⅓ of flour in large bowl and set aside. Mix yeast with ¼ cup warm water in another bowl, stirring well. Add sugar and potato water to yeast. Add mixture to flour; stir well. Set aside 5 minutes to allow yeast to proof.

2. Stir; cut in shortening using a pastry blender or your hands. Stir in salt and as much of remaining flour as possible. Dough has enough flour when it's still somewhat sticky to the touch, yet pulls away from side of bowl as it's stirred. Turn out dough onto lightly floured work surface. Knead for 8–10 minutes until smooth and elastic, adding flour as necessary. Dough will take on an almost glossy appearance once it's been kneaded sufficiently.

3. Transfer dough to bowl treated with nonstick spray. Cover with damp cloth; place in warm, draft-free area. Allow to rise until doubled in volume, about 1–1½ hours.

4. Punch dough down and let rise a second time until almost doubled in bulk.

5. Treat two 9" × 5" bread pans with nonstick spray. Punch dough down again; divide into two loaves. Shape loaves; place in bread pans. Cover and let rise until almost doubled.

6. Preheat oven to 350°F. Bake 20–30 minutes until golden brown. Remove from pans and allow to cool on rack.

Nutritional Analysis (per serving): Calories: 77 | Protein: 2g | Carbohydrates: 15g | Fat: 1g | Saturated Fat: 0g | Cholesterol: 0mg | Sodium: 175mg | Fiber: 1g | PCF Ratio: 11-79-10 | Exchange Approx.: 1 Starch

FIBER-ENRICHED CHEDDAR BREAD

YIELDS 1 LOAF (12 SLICES); SERVING SIZE: 1 SLICE

1½ cups warm water

1 package (2½ teaspoons) active dry yeast

2½ teaspoons salt

½ cup wheat bran

3 cups bread flour

⅔ cup grated reduced-fat Cheddar cheese

1 tablespoon grated Parmesan cheese

Cornmeal for cookie sheet

1. Combine water, yeast, and salt in mixer bowl or food processor. Add remaining ingredients; mix well using dough hook or dough attachment until very soft dough is formed.

2. Transfer dough to large, loosely covered bowl; allow to rise at room temperature for 2 hours. Dough can be used after rising but is much easier to handle after it has been refrigerated several hours or overnight.

3. When ready to bake, sprinkle a light dusting of flour on top of dough. With floured hands, remove dough from bowl; shape into round loaf.

4. Place dough on cookie sheet or pizza peel liberally covered with cornmeal. Allow dough to rise at room temperature for 45 minutes.

5. Preheat oven to 450°F with baking or pizza stone placed in center rack of oven. Before transferring dough to hot stone, slash dough across top using floured sharp knife. Slide dough onto hot baking stone; place shallow pan of hot water on lower rack of oven to create steam underneath bread.

6. Bake for 40 minutes or until bread is deeply browned and has a hardened crust. Remove to a cooling rack; allow to cool before slicing.

Nutritional Analysis (per serving): Calories: 141 | Protein: 6g | Carbohydrates: 25g | Fat: 1g | Saturated Fat: 0g | Cholesterol: 2mg | Sodium: 546mg | Fiber: 1g | PCF Ratio: 19-73-8 | Exchange Approx.: 1½ Starches

GOLDEN RAISIN BREAD

YIELDS 1 LOAF (12 SLICES); SERVING SIZE: 1 SLICE

1½ cups warm water

2½ teaspoons active dry yeast

2½ teaspoons salt

⅓ cup wheat germ

1 cup whole-wheat flour

2 cups bread flour

2 tablespoons honey

1 teaspoon ground cinnamon

½ cup golden raisins

1 tablespoon egg whites

½ tablespoon water

1. Combine water, yeast, and salt in mixer bowl or food processor. Using dough hook or dough attachment for food processor, add in remaining ingredients except egg whites and water; mix well until very soft dough is formed.

2. Transfer dough to loosely covered large bowl; allow to rise at room temperature for 2 hours. Dough can be used after rising; however, it is much easier to handle after it has been refrigerated several hours or overnight.

3. When ready to bake, lightly grease 9" × 4" × 3" loaf pan. Scoop dough out of bowl with wet hands (this makes it easier to handle); shape into elongated loaf and place in loaf pan. Allow dough to rise for 1 hour.

4. Preheat oven to 375°F. In a small bowl, mix together 1 tablespoon egg whites and ½ tablespoon water to make an egg wash.

5. Brush loaf with egg wash and bake on middle rack of preheated oven. Place shallow pan of hot water on the lower rack to create steam under bread.

6. Bake for 45–50 minutes until bread is golden brown. Cool in pan for 10 minutes, then remove to wire rack. Allow bread to cool completely before slicing.

Nutritional Analysis (per serving): Calories: 163 | Protein: 6g | Carbohydrates: 34g | Fat: 1g | Saturated Fat: 0g | Cholesterol: 0mg | Sodium: 497mg | Fiber: 3g | PCF Ratio: 13-82-5 | Exchange Approx.: 1½ Starches, ½ Fruit

WHOLE-WHEAT BREAD

YIELDS 2 LOAVES; SERVING SIZE: 1 SLICE

1 package (2½ teaspoons) active dry yeast

2 cups warm water

3 cups unbleached all-purpose or bread flour

2 tablespoons sugar

½ cup hot water

2 teaspoons salt

½ cup brown sugar

3 tablespoons shortening

3 cups whole-wheat flour

History Lesson

The sponge process of making bread was more popular years ago, when foodstuffs were less processed and the quality of yeast was less reliable. The yeast works in a batter and the dough rises only once. The sponge process produces a loaf that is lighter but coarser grained.

1. Add yeast to 2 cups warm water. Stir in all-purpose flour and sugar; beat until smooth, either by hand or with mixer. Set in warm place to proof until it becomes foamy and bubbly, up to 1 hour.

2. Combine ½ cup hot water, salt, brown sugar, and shortening; stir. Allow to cool to lukewarm. (Stirring sugar until it's dissolved should be sufficient to cool water; test to be sure, as adding liquid that's too warm can kill yeast.) Add to bubbly flour mixture. Stir in whole-wheat flour; beat until smooth, but do not knead.

3. Divide dough into two lightly greased loaf pans. Cover; set in warm place until doubled in size. Preheat oven to 350°F; bake for 50 minutes.

Nutritional Analysis (per serving): Calories: 86 | Protein: 2g | Carbohydrates: 17g | Fat: 1g | Saturated Fat: 0g | Cholesterol: 0mg | Sodium: 118mg | Fiber: 1g | PCF Ratio: 10-77-13 | Exchange Approx.: 1 Starch

BREAD MACHINE WHITE BREAD

YIELDS 1 LARGE LOAF; SERVING SIZE: 1 SLICE

1¼ cups skim milk

2 tablespoons nonfat milk powder

1 tablespoon olive or canola oil

1 teaspoon sea salt

1 tablespoon granulated sugar

4 cups unbleached all-purpose or bread flour

1 package (2½ teaspoons) active dry yeast

Add ingredients to bread machine in order recommended by manufacturer, being careful yeast doesn't come in contact with salt.

Nutritional Analysis (per serving): Calories: 90 | Protein: 3g | Carbohydrates: 17g | Fat: 1g | Saturated Fat: 0g | Cholesterol: 1mg | Sodium: 106mg | Fiber: 1g | PCF Ratio: 13-79-8 | Exchange Approx.: 1 Starch

HONEY OAT BRAN BREAD

YIELDS 1 LARGE LOAF; SERVING SIZE: 1 SLICE

1¼ cups skim milk

2 tablespoons nonfat buttermilk powder

1 tablespoon olive or canola oil

1 medium egg

1 cup oat bran

1 teaspoon sea salt

½ cup whole-wheat flour

2½ cups unbleached all-purpose or bread flour

1 tablespoon honey

1 package (2½ teaspoons) active dry yeast

Use light-crust setting on your bread machine; add ingredients in order recommended by manufacturer. Be careful yeast doesn't come in contact with salt.

Nutritional Analysis (per serving): Calories: 86 | Protein: 3g | Carbohydrates: 16g | Fat: 1g | Saturated Fat: 0g | Cholesterol: 8mg | Sodium: 109mg | Fiber: 1g | PCF Ratio: 15-72-13 | Exchange Approx.: 1 Starch

7-GRAIN BREAD

YIELD: 1 LARGE LOAF; SERVING SIZE: 1 SLICE

1¼ cups skim milk

2 tablespoons nonfat milk powder

1 tablespoon olive or canola oil

¾ cup dry 7-grain cereal

½ cup oat bran

1 teaspoon sea salt

2¼ cups unbleached all-purpose or bread flour

½ cup whole-wheat flour

1 tablespoon honey

1 package (2½ teaspoons) dry yeast

Lactose-Free Bread

When cooking for someone who is lactose intolerant, substitute equal amounts of water or soymilk for any milk called for in bread recipes.

Add ingredients to bread machine in order recommended by manufacturer; be careful that yeast doesn't come in contact with salt. Bake on whole-wheat bread setting.

Nutritional Analysis (per serving): Calories: 82 | Protein: 3g | Carbohydrates: 15g | Fat: 1g | Saturated Fat: 0g | Cholesterol: 8mg | Sodium: 108mg | Fiber: 1g | PCF Ratio: 14-73-12 | Exchange Approx.: 1 Starch

MULTIGRAIN CORNBREAD

SERVES 16; SERVING SIZE: 1 SLICE

Nonstick cooking spray

1 egg

2 tablespoons egg whites

3 tablespoons butter, melted

1½ cups low-fat buttermilk

1 teaspoon vanilla extract

1¾ cups cornmeal

¾ cup whole-wheat pastry flour

1 tablespoon ground flaxseed

3 tablespoons Splenda Granulated

1 tablespoon sugar

4 teaspoons baking powder

½ teaspoon baking soda

Pinch salt

Don't Have Buttermilk?

When baking, soured milk is a good substitution for buttermilk. To replace 1 cup of buttermilk in a recipe, stir 1 tablespoon of white vinegar or fresh lemon juice into 1 cup of milk. Let the milk stand for 5 minutes or until milk thickens.

1. Preheat oven to 375°F. Spray 8" × 8" square baking pan with nonstick cooking spray.

2. In medium bowl, whisk together egg, egg whites, butter, buttermilk, and vanilla. Set aside.

3. In larger bowl, combine cornmeal, flour, flaxseed, Splenda, sugar, baking powder, baking soda, and salt; mix well.

4. Make well in center of dry ingredients; pour in buttermilk mixture. Mix gently with spoon until all dry ingredients are moistened; do not overmix.

5. Spoon batter into prepared pan. Bake for 25–30 minutes or until center springs back when lightly touched. Cool on wire rack before slicing into pieces.

Nutritional Analysis (per serving): Calories: 124 | Protein: 4g | Carbohydrates: 20g | Fat: 3g | Saturated Fat: 1g | Cholesterol: 16mg | Sodium: 220mg | Fiber: 2g | PCF Ratio: 12-65-23 | Exchange Approx.: 1 Starch, ½ Fat

CHEDDAR CORNBREAD

YIELDS 1 LARGE LOAF; SERVING SIZE: 1 SLICE

1¼ cups water

1 tablespoon honey

3 tablespoons butter

¼ cup nonfat milk powder

1 package (2½ teaspoons) active dry yeast

2½ cups unbleached all-purpose or bread flour

1 cup yellow cornmeal

1½ teaspoons sea salt

⅔ cup grated Cheddar cheese

1. Use light-crust setting on bread machine. Add all ingredients except cheese in order suggested by bread machine manual. Process on basic bread cycle according to manufacturer's directions.

2. At beeper (or end of first kneading), add cheese. Finish cooking.

Nutritional Analysis (per serving): Calories: 102 | Protein: 3g | Carbohydrates: 16g | Fat: 3g | Saturated Fat: 2g | Cholesterol: 8mg | Sodium: 172mg | Fiber: 1g | PCF Ratio: 13-63-24 | Exchange Approx.: 1 Starch, ½ Fat

COTTAGE CHEESE BREAD

YIELDS 1 LARGE LOAF; SERVING SIZE: 1 SLICE

¼ cup water

1 cup nonfat cottage cheese

2 tablespoons butter

1 egg

1 tablespoon sugar

¼ teaspoon baking soda

1 teaspoon salt

3 cups unbleached all-purpose or bread flour

1 package (2½ teaspoons) active dry yeast

Why Breads Need Salt

Salt is only used in bread to enhance the flavor. If salt comes directly in contact with yeast before yeast has had a chance to begin to work, it can hinder the action of the yeast. Keep that in mind when adding ingredients to your bread machine.

Add ingredients to bread machine in order recommended by manufacturer, being careful yeast doesn't come in contact with salt. Check bread machine at "beep" to make sure dough is pulling away from sides of pan and forming a ball. Add water or flour if needed. (Note: You do not want dough to be overly dry.) Bake at white bread setting, light crust.

Nutritional Analysis (per serving): Calories: 76 | Protein: 3g | Carbohydrates: 13g | Fat: 1g | Saturated Fat: 1g | Cholesterol: 11mg | Sodium: 114mg | Fiber: 1g | PCF Ratio: 16-68-16 | Exchange Approx.: 1 Starch

HAWAIIAN-STYLE BREAD

**YIELDS 1 LARGE LOAF, 24 SLICES;
SERVING SIZE: 1 SLICE**

1 egg

½ cup pineapple juice or ⅛ cup frozen
  pineapple juice concentrate and ⅜ cup
  water

¾ cup water

2 tablespoons butter

1 teaspoon vanilla extract

½ teaspoon ground ginger

1 teaspoon salt

1½ cups unbleached bread flour

2⅛ cups unbleached all-purpose flour

¼ cup sugar

2 tablespoons nonfat milk powder

1 package (2½ teaspoons) active dry yeast

Unless instructions for bread machine differ, add
ingredients in order listed here. Use light-crust setting.

Nutritional Analysis (per serving): Calories: 89 | Protein:
2g | Carbohydrates: 17g | Fat: 1g | Saturated Fat:
1g | Cholesterol: 11mg | Sodium: 103mg | Fiber: 1g | PCF Ratio:
11-75-14 | Exchange Approx.: 1 Starch

FIBER-ENRICHED BANANA BREAD

**YIELDS 1 LARGE LOAF, 12 SLICES;
SERVING SIZE: 1 SLICE**

Nonstick cooking spray

½ cup buttermilk

¼ cup wheat bran

1 cup mashed ripe banana

1 egg

¼ cup egg whites

2 tablespoons canola oil

1 teaspoon vanilla extract

2 tablespoons honey

1¼ cups whole-wheat pastry flour

½ cup all-purpose flour

⅓ cup Splenda Granulated

1 teaspoon baking soda

1½ teaspoons baking powder

½ teaspoon salt

1. Preheat oven to 375°F. Spray 9" × 4" × 3" loaf pan with nonstick cooking spray.

2. Place buttermilk and wheat bran in medium bowl; allow wheat bran to soak 10 minutes. Stir in banana, egg, egg whites, oil, vanilla, and honey.

3. In larger bowl, sift together flours, Splenda, baking soda, baking powder, and salt; add dry ingredients to banana mixture. Using a large spoon, stir just until dry ingredients are moistened; do not overmix.

4. Spoon batter into prepared loaf pan. Bake for 45 minutes or until top is lightly browned and inserted toothpick comes out clean. Cool in pan for 10 minutes before removing to wire rack.

Nutritional Analysis (per serving): Calories: 65 | Protein: 5g | Carbohydrates: 29g | Fat: 4g | Saturated Fat: 1g | Cholesterol: 22mg | Sodium: 348mg | Fiber: 4g | PCF Ratio: 12-67-21 | Exchange Approx.: 1 Starch, ½ Fruit, 1 Fat

WHOLE-WHEAT ZUCCHINI BREAD

**YIELDS 4 MINI LOAVES, 20 SLICES
(5 SLICES PER MINI LOAF); SERVING SIZE:
1 SLICE**

Cooking spray

2 eggs

2 tablespoons egg whites

½ cup honey

2 cups shredded zucchini

⅔ cup unsweetened applesauce

⅓ cup canola oil

2 teaspoons vanilla extract

2 cups whole-wheat pastry flour

1 cup all-purpose flour

¼ cup Splenda Granulated

1 teaspoon salt

2 teaspoons baking powder

1 teaspoon baking soda

2 teaspoons ground cinnamon

½ teaspoon ground nutmeg

⅓ cup toasted sunflower seeds

Variations

For variations to this recipe, ⅓ cup dried cranberries, currants, raisins, or chopped nuts can be added in place of the sunflower seeds.

1. Preheat oven to 350°F. Spray four mini loaf pans with cooking spray.

2. In large mixing bowl, beat eggs and egg whites until foamy. Mix in honey, zucchini, applesauce, canola oil, and vanilla.

3. In separate mixing bowl, sift together whole-wheat flour, all-purpose flour, Splenda, salt, baking powder, baking soda, cinnamon, and nutmeg.

4. Gradually add dry ingredients to zucchini mixture; mix until all ingredients are combined, but do not overmix. Stir in sunflower seeds.

5. Divide batter evenly into prepared mini loaf pans. Bake for 35–40 minutes or until tops are browned and inserted toothpick comes out clean.

6. Remove pans to wire rack and cool for 10 minutes before removing from pans. Cool completely before slicing.

Nutritional Analysis (per serving): Calories: 178 | Protein: 4g | Carbohydrates: 29g | Fat: 6g | Saturated Fat: 1g | Cholesterol: 25mg | Sodium: 243mg | Fiber: 3g | PCF Ratio: 9-63-28 | Exchange Approx.: 1½ Starches, 1 Fat

APPLESAUCE BUCKWHEAT MUFFINS

YIELDS 12 MUFFINS; SERVING SIZE: 1 MUFFIN

Nonstick cooking spray

1 cup buttermilk

½ cup unsweetened applesauce

¼ cup canola oil

1 egg

2 tablespoons egg whites

2 tablespoons maple syrup

1 teaspoon vanilla extract

1¼ cups whole-wheat pastry flour

¾ cup light buckwheat flour

¼ cup Splenda Granulated

1½ teaspoons baking powder

1½ teaspoons baking soda

¼ teaspoon salt

2 teaspoons ground cinnamon

¼ teaspoon ground allspice

Crisp Topping (optional):

1 tablespoon Splenda Brown Sugar Blend

¼ teaspoon cinnamon

¼ cup oats

2 teaspoons ground flaxseed

1 tablespoon whole-wheat pastry flour

1 tablespoon butter, melted

1. Preheat oven to 375°F. Prepare muffin pan with nonstick cooking spray.

2. In medium bowl, whisk together buttermilk, applesauce, oil, egg, egg whites, maple syrup, and vanilla.

3. In separate bowl, sift together whole-wheat flour, buckwheat flour, Splenda, baking powder, baking soda, salt, and spices. Gradually add dry ingredients to liquid mixture; mix just enough to combine ingredients. Do not overmix. Spoon batter evenly into prepared muffin pan.

4. In small bowl, mix together all ingredients for Crisp Topping. Sprinkle evenly on top of each muffin.

5. Bake for 20–25 minutes or until center of muffin springs back when lightly touched. Cool in muffin tin for 5 minutes before removing to wire rack.

Nutritional Analysis (per muffin, with Crisp Topping): Calories: 182 | Protein: 5g | Carbohydrates: 27g | Fat: 7g | Saturated Fat: 1g | Cholesterol: 24mg | Sodium: 302mg | Fiber: 3g | PCF Ratio: 11-56-34 | Exchange Approx.: 1 Starch, ½ Fruit, 1 Fat

PEAR WALNUT MUFFINS

12 MUFFINS; SERVING SIZE: 1 MUFFIN

Nonstick cooking spray

1 cup buttermilk

3 tablespoons canola oil

1 egg

2 tablespoons egg whites

⅔ cup peeled and chopped pears

2 tablespoons honey

1¼ cups whole-wheat pastry flour

¾ cup all-purpose flour

3 tablespoons Splenda Granulated

1½ teaspoons baking powder

1½ teaspoons baking soda

¼ teaspoon salt

1 teaspoon ground cinnamon

¼ teaspoon ground ginger

⅓ cup chopped walnuts

Crisp Topping (optional):

1 tablespoon Splenda Brown Sugar Blend

Pinch ground ginger

¼ cup oats

2 teaspoons ground flaxseed

1 tablespoon whole-wheat pastry flour

1 tablespoon butter, melted

1. Preheat oven to 375°F. Prepare muffin pan with nonstick cooking spray.

2. In medium bowl, whisk together buttermilk, oil, egg, egg whites, pears, and honey.

3. In separate bowl, sift together whole-wheat flour, all-purpose flour, Splenda, baking powder, baking soda, salt, spices, and walnuts. Gradually add dry ingredients to liquid mixture; stir just enough to combine ingredients. Do not overmix. Spoon batter evenly into prepared muffin pan.

4. In small bowl, mix together all ingredients for Crisp Topping. Sprinkle evenly on top of each muffin.

5. Bake for 20–25 minutes or until center of muffin springs back when lightly touched. Cool in muffin tin for 5 minutes before removing to wire rack.

Nutritional Analysis (per muffin, with Crisp Topping): Calories: 195 | Protein: 5g | Carbohydrates: 27g | Fat: 8g | Saturated Fat: 1g | Cholesterol: 24mg | Sodium: 289mg | Fiber: 3g | PCF Ratio: 11-54-35 | Exchange Approx.: 1 Starch, ½ Fruit, 1 Fat

MILK BISCUITS

3 cups unbleached all-purpose flour

1 teaspoon salt

1½ teaspoons baking soda

1 tablespoon cream of tartar

1 teaspoon baking powder

½ cup butter

1⅓ cups milk

Healthy Substitutions

Despite the downside of all the butter, the upside is these biscuits are so rich you won't even notice they don't contain sugar. Consult your dietitian if you are on a diet to control cholesterol. You can substitute ¼ cup nonfat yogurt for half of the butter in this recipe.

1. Preheat oven to 400°F. For quick mixing, use food processor. Just add all ingredients at once; pulse until just blended. Be careful not to overprocess, as biscuits won't be as light.

2. To mix by hand, sift together dry ingredients. Cut in butter using pastry blender or fork until mixture resembles coarse crumbs. Add milk; stir until mixture pulls away from sides of bowl.

3. Use 1 heaping tablespoon for each biscuit, dropping dough onto greased baking sheets. (You can also try pan liners, such as parchment.) Bake until golden brown, about 20–30 minutes.

Nutritional Analysis (per serving): Calories: 98 | Protein: 2g | Carbohydrates: 13g | Fat: 4g | Saturated Fat: 3g | Cholesterol: 11mg | Sodium: 205mg | Fiber: 0g | PCF Ratio: 9-53-38 | Exchange Approx.: 1 Starch, ½ Fat

ANGELIC BUTTERMILK BATTER BISCUITS

**YIELDS 24 BISCUITS; SERVING SIZE:
1 BISCUIT**

3 tablespoons nonfat buttermilk powder

2 tablespoons granulated sugar

¾ cup warm water

1 tablespoon active dry yeast

2½ cups unbleached all-purpose flour

½ teaspoon sea salt

½ teaspoon baking powder

¼ cup unsalted butter

¼ cup nonfat plain yogurt

Nonstick cooking spray

Why Breads Need Sugar

Bread recipes need sugar or a sweetener, like honey, to "feed" the yeast. This helps the yeast work, which in turn helps the bread rise.

1. Put buttermilk powder, sugar, and warm water in food processor; process until mixed. Sprinkle yeast over top; pulse once or twice to mix. Allow mixture to sit at room temperature for about 5 minutes or until yeast begins to bubble. Add all remaining ingredients to food processor; pulse until mixed, being careful not to overprocess dough.

2. Preheat oven to 400°F; drop 1 heaping teaspoon per biscuit onto baking sheet treated with nonstick spray. Set in warm place; allow biscuits to rise for about 15 minutes.

3. Bake biscuits for 12–15 minutes.

Nutritional Analysis (per serving): Calories: 74 | Protein: 2g | Carbohydrates: 12g | Fat: 2g | Saturated Fat: 1g | Cholesterol: 6mg | Sodium: 55mg | Fiber: 1g | PCF Ratio: 11-64-26 | Exchange Approx.: 1 Starch

ORANGE DATE BREAD

**YIELDS 2 LARGE LOAVES; SERVING SIZE:
1 SLICE**

Nonstick cooking spray

2 tablespoons frozen orange juice
concentrate

2 tablespoons grated orange zest

¾ cup pitted chopped dates

½ cup brown sugar

¼ cup granulated sugar

1 cup plain nonfat yogurt

1 egg

1¼ cups all-purpose flour

¾ cup whole-wheat flour

1 teaspoon baking soda

1 teaspoon baking powder

½ teaspoon salt

1 tablespoon vegetable oil

1 teaspoon vanilla extract

Are Your Eyes Bigger Than Your Stomach?

Use mini loaf pans. It's much easier to
arrive at the number of servings in the
form of a full slice when you use smaller
loaf pans. There's a psychological advan-
tage to getting a full rather than half slice.

1. Preheat oven to 350°F. Spray four mini loaf pans with
nonstick cooking spray.

2. In food processor, process orange juice concentrate,
orange zest, dates, sugars, yogurt, and egg until mixed.
(This will cut dates into smaller pieces, too.) Add remaining
ingredients; pulse until mixed, scraping down side of bowl
if necessary.

3. Divide mixture between the pans. Spread the mixture so
each pan has an even layer. Bake for 15–20 minutes or until
a toothpick inserted into center of loaf comes out clean.

4. Cool bread in pans on wire rack for 10 minutes. Remove
bread to rack and cool to room temperature.

Nutritional Analysis (per serving): Calories: 79 | Protein:
2g | Carbohydrates: 16g | Fat: 1g | Saturated Fat:
0g | Cholesterol: 8mg | Sodium: 130mg | Fiber: 1g | PCF Ratio:
9-80-10 | Exchange Approx.: 1 Starch

CHAPTER 3

APPETIZERS

CUCUMBER SLICES WITH SMOKED SALMON CREAM

YIELDS ABOUT ½ CUP; SERVING SIZE: 1 TEASPOON

2 or 3 cucumbers

1 ounce smoked salmon

8 ounces room temperature Neufchâtel cheese

½ tablespoon lemon juice

½ teaspoon freshly ground pepper

Dried dill (optional)

1. Cut cucumbers into ¼" slices. Place on paper towels to drain while you prepare salmon cream.

2. Combine smoked salmon, Neufchâtel, lemon juice, and pepper in food processor; blend until smooth.

3. Fit a pastry bag with tip; spoon salmon cream into the bag. Pipe 1 teaspoon of salmon cream atop each cucumber slice. Garnish with dried dill if desired.

Nutritional Analysis (per serving): Calories: 27 | Protein: 1g | Carbohydrates: 0.5g | Fat: 2g | Saturated Fat: 1g | Cholesterol: 7mg | Sodium: 50mg | Fiber: .07g | PCF Ratio: 17-8-75 | Exchange Approx.: ½ Fat

FLAXSEED OIL–FORTIFIED SALSA DIP

YIELDS ABOUT 1 CUP; SERVING SIZE: 1 TABLESPOON

⅛ cup flaxseed oil

½ cup mild salsa

1 teaspoon freeze-dried chives

1 teaspoon dried basil

Pinch of sea salt

¼ cup chopped onion

Blend all ingredients together in food processor or blender for a smooth dip; otherwise, mix thoroughly with a fork.

Nutritional Analysis (per serving): Calories: 18 | Protein: 0g | Carbohydrates: 1g | Fat: 2g | Saturated Fat: 0g | Cholesterol: 0mg | Sodium: 49mg | Fiber: 0g | PCF Ratio: 5-17-78 | Exchange Approx.: 3 servings equals 1 Fat

LEMON TAHINI VEGETABLE DIP

YIELDS ABOUT 5 CUPS; SERVING SIZE: 1 TABLESPOON

1 cup sesame seeds

¼ cup lemon juice

1 cup water

2 tablespoons ground flaxseed

1 teaspoon garlic powder

⅛ teaspoon cider vinegar

1 teaspoon sea salt

Put all ingredients in food processor; blend until smooth.

Nutritional Analysis (per serving): Calories: 26 | Protein: 1g | Carbohydrates: 1g | Fat: 2g | Saturated Fat: 0g | Cholesterol: 0mg | Sodium: 61mg | Fiber: 1g | PCF Ratio: 16-11-73 | Exchange Approx.: ½ Fat

GARLIC AND FETA CHEESE DIP

YIELDS 1½ CUPS; SERVING SIZE: 1 TABLESPOON

1 clove dry-roasted garlic

½ cup crumbled feta cheese

4 ounces softened cream cheese

¼ cup real mayonnaise

¼ teaspoon dried basil

¼ teaspoon dried cilantro or oregano

⅛ teaspoon dried dill

⅛ teaspoon dried thyme

1. To dry-roast garlic: Preheat oven to 350°F; lightly spray small covered baking dish with nonstick spray. Slice off ½" from top of each garlic head; rub off any loose skins, being careful not to separate cloves. Place in baking dish, cut-side up (if roasting more than 1 head, arrange in dish so they don't touch). Cover and bake until the garlic cloves are very tender when pierced, about 30–45 minutes. Roasted garlic heads will keep in refrigerator 2–3 days.

2. In food processor, combine all ingredients; process until thoroughly mixed. Cover and chill until ready to serve with assorted vegetables.

3. Note: This dip is somewhat high in fat if you use regular cream cheese, whereas nonfat cream cheese would lower the total fat in this recipe by 38 grams. People on a salt-restricted diet need to check with their dietitians about using nonfat cream cheese because it's much higher in sodium.

Nutritional Analysis (per serving): Calories: 11 | Protein: 0g | Carbohydrates: 0g | Fat: 1g | Saturated Fat: 1g | Cholesterol: 0mg | Sodium: 22mg | Fiber: 0g | PCF Ratio: 9-10-80 | Exchange Approx.: 1 Free Condiment

SPICY ALMOND DIP

YIELDS ABOUT ½ CUP: SERVING SIZE: 1 TABLESPOON

¼ cup ground raw almonds

2 teaspoons Worcestershire sauce

½ teaspoon honey

½ teaspoon chili powder

1 teaspoon poppy seeds

½ teaspoon onion powder

⅛ cup water

Pinch of black pepper

Put all ingredients in food processor; blend until smooth.

Nutritional Analysis (per serving): Calories: 23 | Protein: 1g | Carbohydrates: 1g | Fat: 2g | Saturated Fat: 0g | Cholesterol: 0mg | Sodium: 148mg | Fiber: 0g | PCF Ratio: 12-25-63 | Exchange Approx.: ½ Fat

ARTICHOKE DIP

YIELDS ABOUT 1 CUP: SERVING SIZE: 1½ TABLESPOONS

1 cup artichoke hearts, drained

1 tablespoon chopped red onion

1 tablespoon chopped sun-dried tomatoes

1 tablespoon low-fat mayonnaise

1 tablespoon reduced-fat sour cream

2 teaspoons grated Parmesan cheese

1 teaspoon lemon juice

½ teaspoon minced garlic

1 tablespoon olive oil

Variation

For a variation on this recipe, you can use ¼ cup roasted red peppers instead of sun-dried tomatoes.

Put all ingredients in food processor; blend until smooth. Chill before serving.

Nutritional Analysis (per serving): Calories: 47 | Protein: 1g | Carbohydrates: 4g | Fat: 3g | Saturated Fat: 1g | Cholesterol: 1mg | Sodium: 129mg | Fiber: 2g | PCF Ratio: 11-33-56 | Exchange Approx.: 1 Vegetable, ½ Fat

EASY ONION DIP

**YIELDS 2 CUPS; SERVING SIZE:
1½ TABLESPOONS**

1 cup nonfat yogurt

1 cup reduced-fat sour cream

2 tablespoons onion flakes

½ teaspoon salt

¼ teaspoon lemon pepper

1 teaspoon dried dill

Mix all ingredients together. Refrigerate for 2–3 hours in covered container before serving.

Nutritional Analysis: Calories: 50 | Protein: 2g | Carbohydrates: 4g | Fat: 3g | Saturated Fat: 2g | Cholesterol: 10mg | Sodium: 147mg | Fiber: 8g | PCF Ratio: 17-30-53 | Exchange Approx.: ½ Fat

FRENCH ONION SOUP DIP

**YIELDS ABOUT 1¾ CUPS; SERVING SIZE:
1 TABLESPOON**

1 cup chopped sweet onion

2 tablespoons reduced (double-strength) beef broth

1 tablespoon grated Parmesan cheese

1 cup nonfat cottage cheese

Guilt-Free Flavors

Adjust the flavor of dips or spreads without adding calories by adding onion or garlic powder or your choice of herbs.

1. Put onion and beef broth in a microwave-safe dish. Cover and microwave on high 1 minute; stir. Continue to microwave on high in 30-second intervals until onion is transparent. Stir in Parmesan cheese. Set aside and allow to cool.

2. In blender, process cottage cheese until smooth. Mix into onion mixture. Serve warm or refrigerate until needed and serve cold.

Nutritional Analysis (per serving): Calories: 7 | Protein: 1g | Carbohydrates: 1g | Fat: 0g | Saturated Fat: 0g | Cholesterol: 1mg | Sodium: 11mg | Fiber: 0g | PCF Ratio: 61-28-11 | Exchange Approx.: 1 Free Condiment

HORSERADISH DIP

**YIELDS 1¾ CUPS; SERVING SIZE:
1 TABLESPOON**

1 cup nonfat cottage cheese

1 tablespoon olive oil

½ cup nonfat plain yogurt

3 tablespoons prepared horseradish

1 teaspoon lemon juice

Optional seasonings to taste: onion
powder, cumin, sea salt, ginger

Combine all ingredients in blender or food processor; process until smooth.

Nutritional Analysis (per serving): Calories: 12 | Protein: 1g | Carbohydrates: 1g | Fat: 1g | Saturated Fat: 0g | Cholesterol: 0mg | Sodium: 9mg | Fiber: 0g | PCF Ratio: 39-21-40 | Exchange Approx.: 1 Free Condiment

HERBED YOGURT CHEESE SPREAD

YIELDS ABOUT 1½ CUPS; SERVING SIZE: 4 TABLESPOONS

1½ cups plain nonfat yogurt

1 tablespoon minced scallion

1 tablespoon minced fresh parsley

1 teaspoon minced garlic

2 tablespoons minced roasted red pepper

¼ teaspoon salt

Pinch of ground cayenne pepper

Get Your Calcium!

Yogurt is one of the top sources of calcium, a vital mineral for bone health. Yogurt cheese is very easy to make and can often be substituted in dip (or other) recipes that call for cream cheese. Cream cheese, unlike yogurt, contains mostly fat and is not a significant source of calcium or protein.

1. Prepare yogurt cheese in advance: Line fine mesh strainer with a coffee filter. Place plain yogurt in filter; set strainer over a bowl. Cover and refrigerate for 8 hours or overnight. When all fluid has drained, it should be consistency of softened cream cheese.

2. Add scallions, parsley, garlic, red pepper, salt, and cayenne. Mix well and refrigerate.

3. Serve with crackers or raw vegetables.

Nutritional Analysis (per serving): Calories: 36 | Protein: 4g | Carbohydrates: 5g | Fat: 0g | Saturated Fat: 0g | Cholesterol: 1mg | Sodium: 146mg | Fiber: 0g | PCF Ratio: 41-56-3 | Exchange Approx.: ½ Milk

GARBANZO DIP

YIELDS ABOUT 2 CUPS; SERVING SIZE: 1 TABLESPOON

3 cups cooked garbanzo (or other white beans) beans

½ teaspoon ground cumin

1 tablespoon lemon juice

1 tablespoon dried parsley

¼ teaspoon dried basil

1 teaspoon onion powder

¼ teaspoon garlic powder

1 tablespoon honey

Combine all ingredients in food processor or blender; process until smooth. Add 1 teaspoon of water or bean broth if you need to thin the dip.

Nutritional Analysis (per serving): Calories: 24 | Protein: 4g | Carbohydrates: 5g | Fat: 0g | Saturated Fat: 0g | Cholesterol: 0mg | Sodium: 1mg | Fiber: 1g | PCF Ratio: 25-73-2 | Exchange Approx.: ½ Very Lean Meat

ZESTY ALMOND SPREAD

YIELDS ABOUT ¼ CUP; SERVING SIZE: 1 TABLESPOON

30 unsalted almonds

2 teaspoons honey

1 teaspoon chili powder

¼ teaspoon garlic powder

Pinch of sea salt (optional)

Place all ingredients in food processor or blender; process to desired consistency.

Nutritional Analysis (per serving, without salt): Calories: 50 | Protein: 2g | Carbohydrates: 4g | Fat: 4g | Saturated Fat: 1g | Cholesterol: 0mg | Sodium: 1mg | Fiber: 1g | PCF Ratio: 11-28-61 | Exchange Approx.: 1 Fat

HERBED CHEESE SPREAD

YIELDS ABOUT 1 CUP; SERVING SIZE: 1 TABLESPOON

2 teaspoons chopped fresh parsley leaves

2 teaspoons chopped fresh chives

1 teaspoon chopped fresh thyme

½ teaspoon freshly ground black pepper

½ cup nonfat cottage cheese

4 ounces room temperature Neufchâtel cheese

Toasted Nut Garnish

Herbed Cheese Spread is good on garlic toast sprinkled with a few toasted pine nuts, sunflower seeds, sesame seeds, or other chopped nuts. Toast nuts in small skillet in single layer. Over low heat, toast until lightly golden, stirring often to prevent burning, for 3–4 minutes. Cool on paper towels.

Place herbs in food processor; pulse until chopped. Add cheeses; process until smooth.

Nutritional Analysis (per serving): Calories: 20 | Protein: 1g | Carbohydrates: 0.5g | Fat: 2g | Saturated Fat: 1g | Cholesterol: 5mg | Sodium: 26mg | Fiber: 0g | PCF Ratio: 27-6-67 | Exchange Approx.: ¼ Skim Milk or 1 Free Condiment

EASY OLIVE SPREAD

YIELDS ABOUT 3 CUPS; SERVING SIZE: 1 TABLESPOON

1 cup black olives

3 cloves garlic

1 tablespoon chopped fresh flat-leaf parsley

1 tablespoon chopped fresh basil

2 teaspoons minced lemon zest

Freshly ground black pepper to taste

½ cup nonfat cottage cheese

2 tablespoons cream cheese

1 tablespoon real mayonnaise

Delicious Substitutions

Substitute marinated mushrooms or artichoke hearts for olives in this recipe.

1. Combine olives, garlic, parsley, basil, lemon zest, and black pepper in food processor; pulse until chopped. Transfer to a bowl and set aside.

2. Add cottage cheese, cream cheese, and mayonnaise to blender or food processor; process until smooth. Fold cheese mixture into chopped olive mixture.

Nutritional Analysis (per serving): Calories: 15 | Protein: 1g | Carbohydrates: 1g | Fat: 1g | Saturated Fat: 0.5g | Cholesterol: 1mg | Sodium: 56mg | Fiber: 0g | PCF Ratio: 17-19-64 | Exchange Approx.: 1 Free Condiment

MUSHROOM CAVIAR

YIELDS ABOUT 3 CUPS; SERVING SIZE: 1 TABLESPOON

1½ cups ¼"-cubed portobello mushrooms

1½ cups ¼"-cubed white button mushrooms

¼ cup chopped scallions

4 cloves dry-roasted garlic (see Garlic and Feta Cheese Dip in this chapter for dry-roasting instructions)

1 teaspoon fresh lemon juice

½ teaspoon balsamic vinegar

1 tablespoon extra-virgin olive oil

½ teaspoon chopped fresh thyme (optional)

Sea salt and freshly ground black pepper to taste (optional)

Pseudo Sauté

When onions and scallions are sautéed in butter or oil, they go through a caramelization process that doesn't occur when they're steamed. To create this flavor without increasing fat in a recipe, transfer steamed vegetables to nonstick wok or skillet (coated with nonstick spray or a small portion of oil called for in recipe) and sauté until extra moisture evaporates.

1. Place mushrooms and chopped scallion in microwave-safe bowl; cover and microwave on high 1 minute. Rotate bowl; microwave in 30-second intervals until tender.

2. Transfer scallions and mushrooms to food processor. (Reserve any liquid to use for thinning if necessary.) Pulse several times to chop mixture, scraping down sides of bowl as needed. Add remaining ingredients; pulse until mixed. Place in small crock or serving bowl; serve warm with toasted bread. Refrigerated leftovers will last a few days.

Nutritional Analysis (per serving): Calories: 9 | Protein: 0g | Carbohydrates: 1g | Fat: 1g | Saturated Fat: 0g | Cholesterol: 0mg | Sodium: 1mg | Fiber: 0g | PCF Ratio: 11-32-57 | Exchange Approx.: 1 Free Condiment

GLUTEN-FREE SESAME SEED CRACKERS

**YIELDS 36 CRACKERS; SERVING SIZE:
1 CRACKER**

1½ cups spelt flour

1 cup sesame seeds

¼ cup arrowroot

1 tablespoon olive or vegetable oil

3 tablespoons nonfat yogurt

¼ cup nonfat dry milk

½ teaspoon Ener-G Baking Powder
  (aluminum-free)

⅔ teaspoon sea salt (optional)

½ cup water

Nonstick cooking spray

1. Preheat oven to 400°F. Mix all ingredients except water and spray; add ½ cup water a little at a time to form a soft dough-like consistency. Be careful not to work the dough too much; you do not want to knead spelt flour.

2. On floured surface, use rolling pin to roll dough to ⅛" thick. Use cookie cutter to cut into shapes; place on cookie sheet treated with nonstick spray. (Or use a pizza cutter to crosscut the dough into square- or rectangular-shaped crackers.) Prick each cracker with a fork. Bake about 12 minutes or until golden brown. Store cooled crackers in airtight container.

Nutritional Analysis (per serving): Calories: 50 | Protein: 2g | Carbohydrates: 5g | Fat: 3g | Saturated Fat: 1g | Cholesterol: 0mg | Sodium: 5mg | Fiber: 1g | PCF Ratio: 15-38-47 | Exchange Approx.: ½ Starch

ASIAN GINGERED ALMONDS

YIELDS 1 CUP; SERVING SIZE:
1 TABLESPOON

2 teaspoons unsalted butter

1 tablespoon Bragg Liquid Aminos

1 teaspoon ground ginger

1 cup slivered almonds

Nonstick cooking spray

Good Fat!

Almonds and many other nuts fall within the good fats category because they are low in unhealthy saturated fats.

1. Preheat oven to 350°F. In microwave-safe bowl, mix butter, Bragg Liquid Aminos, and ginger. Microwave on high 30 seconds or until butter is melted; blend well.

2. Spread almonds on shallow baking sheet treated with nonstick spray. Bake for 12–15 minutes or until light gold, stirring occasionally.

3. Pour seasoned butter over almonds; stir to mix. Bake for an additional 5 minutes. Store in airtight containers in cool place.

Nutritional Analysis (per serving): Calories: 58 | Protein: 2g | Carbohydrates: 2g | Fat: 5g | Saturated Fat: 1g | Cholesterol: 1mg | Sodium: 44mg | Fiber: 1g | PCF Ratio: 14-12-74 | Exchange Approx.: 1½ Fats

ANTIPASTO ROLL-UPS

YIELDS 8 ROLLS; SERVING SIZE: 1 ROLL

1 large eggplant, cut into 8 (⅛"-thick) rounds

1 red bell pepper, halved and seeded

Cooking spray

2–3 tablespoons chopped fresh basil

8 black or green olives, halved

1 reduced-fat string cheese stick, halved and sliced into eight strips

8 pieces thin-sliced nitrate-free salami

Mustard (optional)

8 toothpicks

1. Preheat oven to 425°F. Add the eggplant and bell peppers to a large baking sheet coated with cooking spray and roast on the top rack for 15 minutes. Flip the veggies over and roast for another 15 minutes or until lightly browned. Remove from oven and let cool. Cut the cooled peppers into eight squares.

2. Assemble each roll as follows: lay down one piece of eggplant and top with one salami piece, one red pepper square, a few bits of basil, a strip of cheese, and two halves of an olive. Add a dollop of mustard if desired and then roll up and place a toothpick through the center. Repeat seven more times for a total of eight roll-ups.

Nutritional Analysis (per serving): Calories: 70 | Protein: 3g | Carbohydrates: 5g | Fat: 4g | Saturated Fat: 1.5g | Cholesterol: 15mg | Sodium: 180mg | Fiber: 3g | PCF Ratio: 16-30-54 | Exchange Approx.: 1 Vegetable, 1 Fat

5-MINUTE NACHOS FOR ONE

SERVES 1

1 ounce unsalted tortilla chips

⅓ cup canned, drained low-sodium pinto beans

1 ounce shredded cheese

1 tablespoon finely chopped avocado

1 tablespoon diced tomato (or prepared salsa/pico de gallo)

1 tablespoon finely chopped black olives

1. Spread the chips on a microwave-safe plate and top with the beans.

2. Sprinkle with the cheese and microwave for 45–60 seconds until the cheese is melted and the beans are warm.

3. Garnish with avocado, tomato, and olives and serve.

Nutritional Analysis (per serving): Calories: 310 | Protein: 15g | Carbohydrates: 38g | Fat: 12g | Saturated Fat: 4.5g | Cholesterol: 20mg | Sodium: 510mg | Fiber: 8g | PCF Ratio: 19-48-33 | Exchange Approx.: 2 Starches, 1 Medium-Fat Meat, 1 Fat

GREEK CUCUMBER BOATS

YIELDS 8 BOATS; SERVING SIZE: 1 BOAT

5 tablespoons hummus or Baba Ghanoush (see recipe in this chapter)

4 Persian cucumbers, ends trimmed, peeled, halved, and seeded (to make eight boats)

4 teaspoons chopped kalamata olives

4 teaspoons crumbled reduced-fat feta cheese

4 teaspoons finely diced tomato

Spoon about 2 teaspoons hummus into each cucumber half, then sprinkle with ½ teaspoon each of olives, cheese, and tomatoes and serve.

Nutritional Analysis (per serving): Calories: 35 | Protein: 1g | Carbohydrates: 4g | Fat: 1.5g | Saturated Fat: 0g | Cholesterol: 0mg | Sodium: 100mg | Fiber: 1g | PCF Ratio: 13-41-46 | Exchange Approx.: ½ Vegetable, ½ Fat

QUINOA-STUFFED MUSHROOMS

YIELDS 12 MUSHROOMS; SERVING SIZE: 1 MUSHROOM

1 teaspoon olive oil

3 tablespoons finely chopped white onion

2 slices turkey bacon, diced

½ cup cooked quinoa

2 tablespoons vegetable or chicken broth

¼ teaspoon garlic powder

3 tablespoons light cream cheese

12 large button mushrooms, stems removed

4 tablespoons shredded Parmesan cheese

1. Preheat oven to 375°F.

2. Coat a small pan with 1 teaspoon olive oil and add the onions and turkey bacon. Sauté on medium heat for 3–4 minutes until softened. Add the cooked quinoa, broth, and garlic powder and cook for another 3–4 minutes, stirring frequently. Remove from the heat, let cool, and transfer to a small bowl. Stir in the cream cheese.

3. Place the mushrooms on a baking sheet and divide/add the filling to them. Bake for 15 minutes until starting to brown.

4. Remove from oven, top with Parmesan cheese, and bake for another 2–3 minutes until cheese is melted and lightly toasted.

Nutritional Analysis (per serving): Calories: 40 | Protein: 2g | Carbohydrates: 3g | Fat: 2.5g | Saturated Fat: 1g | Cholesterol: 5mg | Sodium: 85mg | Fiber: 0g | PCF Ratio: 21-29-50 | Exchange Approx.: 1 Vegetable, ½ Fat

MEDITERRANEAN GRILLED EGGPLANT STACKS

YIELDS 4 STACKS; SERVING SIZE: 1 STACK

2 red bell peppers, sliced in half lengthwise, cored, and seeded

1 large eggplant, sliced into 12 (¼") rounds

Cooking spray

8 small green or black olives, sliced

2 teaspoons chopped walnuts

¼ cup hummus

4 large fresh basil leaves

4 teaspoons crumbled reduced-fat feta cheese

1. Preheat oven to 425°F. Cut each of the pepper halves into four squares to yield a total of eight squares from each pepper, sixteen altogether.

2. Coat a large baking sheet with cooking spray and arrange the pepper and eggplant on it. Roast on the top rack of the oven about 15 minutes until starting to soften and brown. Remove from the oven, flip the slices over, and return to the oven to roast again for another 5–7 minutes; then let cool.

3. Assemble the stacks as follows: Start with one round of eggplant, spread with 1 teaspoon hummus, top with two pepper squares and one basil leaf. Then add another eggplant round on top. Spread this second eggplant round with 1 teaspoon hummus, add two pepper squares and two sliced olives. Place the third and final eggplant round on top, spread with 1 teaspoon hummus, and sprinkle on 1 teaspoon feta cheese and ½ teaspoon walnuts to complete the stack. Repeat this process three more times for a total of four eggplant-and-pepper stacks.

Nutritional Analysis (per serving): Calories: 100 | Protein: 3g | Carbohydrates: 15g | Fat: 4g | Saturated Fat: 0g | Cholesterol: 0mg | Sodium: 210mg | Fiber: 7g | PCF Ratio: 12-55-33 | Exchange Approx.: 2 Vegetables, 1 Fat

THREE-MUSHROOM MINI PIZZAS

YIELDS 10 MINI PIZZAS; SERVING SIZE: 1 PIZZA

1 teaspoon olive oil

2 garlic cloves, finely chopped (to yield 2 teaspoons)

¼ cup diced red onion

1 cup chopped shiitake mushrooms

1 cup chopped portobello mushrooms

1 cup chopped white button mushrooms

1 tablespoon chicken or vegetable broth

Cooking spray

10 mini pita circles, preferably whole wheat

3 tablespoons plus 1 teaspoon chopped fresh basil

5 tablespoons crumbled goat cheese

3 tablespoons plus 1 teaspoon finely shredded Parmesan cheese

1. Preheat oven to 375°F. Coat a large pan or skillet with the teaspoon olive oil and sauté the garlic and onion on medium-high heat for a few minutes until lightly browned. Add the mushrooms plus the tablespoon broth and cook for 3–5 minutes, stirring often until mushrooms are soft.

2. Put the ten mini pitas on a large baking sheet coated with cooking spray. To each pita add 1 heaping tablespoon of the mushroom/onion mixture, then 1 teaspoon chopped basil, and finish with ½ tablespoon goat cheese.

3. Bake for 10 minutes, remove from oven, and sprinkle each with 1 teaspoon Parmesan and continue to bake for a few more minutes until the cheese is melted.

Nutritional Analysis (per serving): Calories: 107 | Protein: 5g | Carbohydrates: 15g | Fat: 3g | Saturated Fat: 1g | Cholesterol: 5mg | Sodium: 250mg | Fiber: 2g | PCF Ratio: 23-52-25 | Exchange Approx.: 1 Starch, ½ Fat

PORTOBELLO MEXICAN PIZZAS

YIELDS 6 PIZZAS; SERVING SIZE: 1 PIZZA

6 large portobello mushrooms (about 4"–5" in diameter)

Cooking spray

1 teaspoon olive oil

1 cup diced white onion

2 cups chopped red bell pepper

1 (15-ounce) can black beans, rinsed well

1 cup corn (fresh, canned, or frozen thawed)

½ cup canned diced tomatoes

1 tablespoon ground cumin

1–2 teaspoons chili powder

¼ teaspoon garlic powder

¾ cup shredded reduced-fat Cheddar cheese

1–2 tablespoons chopped fresh cilantro (optional)

1. Preheat oven to 350°F. Rinse the mushrooms well, cut out the stems (without creating a hole in the bottom), pat dry, and place on a baking sheet coated with cooking spray, stem-side up. Bake for about 15 minutes.

2. While the mushrooms are baking, add the teaspoon oil, onions, and peppers to a medium-sized pan and sauté on medium heat for about 5 minutes until lightly browned and tender. Put in the beans, corn, tomatoes, and spices and heat for another 5–7 minutes, stirring occasionally; then set aside.

3. Remove the mushrooms from the oven and drain/blot any excess moisture. Add ½ cup of the filling to each mushroom.

4. Place the filled mushrooms back in the oven and bake for 15 minutes. Remove again from oven, sprinkle each with 2 tablespoons cheese, and bake for another 2–3 minutes until cheese is slightly melted. Garnish with chopped cilantro on top if desired.

Nutritional Analysis (per serving): Calories: 180 | Protein: 11g | Carbohydrates: 26g | Fat: 3g | Saturated Fat: 0.5g | Cholesterol: 10mg | Sodium: 490mg | Fiber: 7g | PCF Ratio: 20-50-30 | Exchange Approx.: 1 Starches, 2 Vegetables, ½ Medium-Fat Meat, ½ Fat

QUICK BRUSCHETTA SALAD FOR ONE

SERVES 1

1 Roma tomato, chopped

1 low-fat string cheese stick, cut into small cubes or slices

2 or 3 fresh basil leaves, chopped

Dash of balsamic vinegar

Salt and pepper to taste

Combine all the ingredients in a small bowl.

Nutritional Analysis (per serving): Calories: 70 | Protein: 7g | Carbohydrates: 4g | Fat: 3g | Saturated Fat: 0.5g | Cholesterol: 10mg | Sodium: 180mg | Fiber: 1g | PCF Ratio: 40-22-38 | Exchange Approx.: 1 Vegetable, 1 Lean Meat, ¼ Fat

NUTTY FRUIT AND CHEESE BITES

YIELDS 6 "BITES"; SERVING SIZE: 1 BITE

1 medium apple, cored and cut into 6 slices

2 tablespoons spreadable light Swiss cheese or light cream cheese

1 tablespoon dried cranberries

1 tablespoon chopped walnuts or pecans

Spread 1 teaspoon of the cheese on top of each apple slice. Then divide and sprinkle the cranberries and nuts on top of each slice.

Nutritional Analysis (per serving): Calories: 60 | Protein: 2g | Carbohydrates: 9g | Fat: 2.5g | Saturated Fat: 0.5g | Cholesterol: 0mg | Sodium: 160mg | Fiber: 1g | PCF Ratio: 13-50-37 | Exchange Approx.: ½ Fruit, ½ Fat

BABA GHANOUSH

YIELDS ABOUT 2 CUPS; SERVING SIZE: 2 TABLESPOONS

1 medium to large eggplant

4 garlic cloves

2 tablespoons lemon juice

2 tablespoons nonfat Greek yogurt

1 tablespoon sesame oil

Fun Serving Suggestions

This creamy low-calorie dip is great served with cut-up veggies and whole-wheat crackers, as a spread in sandwiches, and even added atop salads.

1. Preheat oven to 425°F.

2. Rinse and pierce eggplant several times with a fork. Roast whole on a baking sheet until tender when pierced with a knife, about 45–60 minutes. Add garlic cloves to baking sheet for the last 15 minutes that eggplant is cooking to roast them as well.

3. Remove the garlic cloves and eggplant from the oven and let cool for 20–30 minutes.

4. Halve the eggplant and scoop out the flesh. Chop up the garlic. Add the eggplant, chopped garlic, lemon juice, yogurt, and sesame oil to a blender or food processor and purée until smooth. Store dip in the refrigerator in an airtight container for a few days.

Nutritional Analysis (per serving): Calories: 15 | Protein: 1g | Carbohydrates: 1g | Fat: 1g | Saturated Fat: 0g | Cholesterol: 0mg | Sodium: 0mg | Fiber: 1g | PCF Ratio: 20-20-60 | Exchange Approx.: ½ Vegetable

SPINACH AND GOAT CHEESE QUESADILLAS

YIELDS 2 QUESADILLAS; SERVING SIZE: ½ QUESADILLA

2 teaspoons olive oil, divided

⅓ cup chopped white onion

½ cup corn (fresh, canned, or frozen thawed)

¼ teaspoon chili powder

¼ teaspoon garlic powder

¼ teaspoon ground cumin

3 cups fresh spinach, rinsed well and patted dry

1 tablespoon water

4 corn tortillas

¼ cup crumbled goat cheese

Chopped avocado, fat-free sour cream, and salsa (optional, for garnish)

1. Coat a large-sized pan with 1 teaspoon olive oil and warm on medium heat. Add the onions and sauté for a few minutes until lightly browned.

2. Then add the corn, chili powder, garlic powder, and cumin and sauté for 2–3 minutes. Put in the spinach, sauté for 1 minute, sprinkle with 1 tablespoon water, and heat for another few minutes until the spinach is slightly wilted.

3. Remove spinach/corn mixture from the pan and set aside in a dish. Coat the pan again with another teaspoon of olive oil and place on high heat. Put two tortillas in the pan, divide the spinach/corn filling between them, and top each with half of the goat cheese. Place the other two tortillas on top of each. Heat one side for 5–7 minutes or until lightly browned. Flip over and heat another 5 minutes on the second side. Cut the two quesadillas into halves and top with chopped avocado, fat-free sour cream, and salsa if desired.

Nutritional Analysis (per serving): Calories: 127 | Protein: 6g | Carbohydrates: 17g | Fat: 3.5g | Saturated Fat: 2g | Cholesterol: 10mg | Sodium: 175mg | Fiber: 3g | PCF Ratio: 19-57-24 | Exchange Approx.: 1 Starch, ½ Vegetable, ½ Fat

VEGGIE POT STICKERS

YIELDS 12 POT STICKERS; SERVING SIZE: 1 POT STICKER

1 tablespoon plus 1 teaspoon sesame oil

1 clove garlic, finely chopped

1 teaspoon finely chopped fresh ginger

¼ cup chopped green onion

½ cup chopped celery

½ cup chopped or shredded carrots

½ cup canned, rinsed, drained, and chopped water chestnuts

1 tablespoon low-sodium soy sauce

1 cup chopped napa cabbage

½ cup chopped mushrooms

12 wonton wrappers

Additional Ways to Cook Your Pot Stickers

For a softer pot sticker you can steam them for a few minutes on each side in a pan filled with ¼"–½" of boiling water, with a lid on. Another way to cook the wontons is to bake them at 350°F on a baking sheet for about 7–10 minutes on each side.

1. Coat a large skillet or wok with 1 tablespoon sesame oil; add the garlic, ginger, and onions and sauté for a few minutes until slightly browned. Put in the celery, carrot, and water chestnuts and sauté for another 3–4 minutes.

2. Add the soy sauce, cabbage, and mushrooms and sauté for 3–5 minutes until all the vegetables are slightly softened. Spoon them onto a dish and let cool for a few minutes.

3. Remove the wonton wrappers from the package and lay them out on a clean cutting board. Spoon 1 heaping tablespoon of the mixture onto one side of each wrapper. Wet all the edges with water (using your fingers), fold over the wrapper to make a triangle, and pinch closed all along the edges.

4. Add the remaining 1 teaspoon of sesame oil to the skillet on high heat and add the filled wontons; heat about 3–5 minutes on each side until lightly browned and slightly crispy.

Nutritional Analysis (per serving): Calories: 45 | Protein: 1g | Carbohydrates: 6g | Fat: 1.5g | Saturated Fat: 0g | Cholesterol: 0mg | Sodium: 85mg | Fiber: 0g | PCF Ratio: 9-53-38 | Exchange Approx.: ½ Starch

PORTOBELLO AND SAUSAGE PIZZAS

SERVES 2; SERVING SIZE: 1 PIZZA

2 large portobello mushrooms (about 4"–5" in diameter), rinsed, stems removed, patted dry

Cooking spray

1 teaspoon olive oil

½ cup sliced precooked turkey or chicken sausage

2 tablespoons diced white onion

⅓ cup chopped red bell pepper

1 teaspoon diced garlic

2 tablespoons chopped black olives

2 cups torn fresh spinach

1 tablespoon water

2 tablespoons tomato sauce (optional)

2 tablespoons chopped fresh basil

4 tablespoons cheese (mozzarella, feta, goat, Parmesan all work well)

1. Preheat oven to 350°F. Place the mushrooms on a baking sheet coated with cooking spray, stem-side up. Bake for about 15 minutes.

2. While the mushrooms are baking, add the oil, sausage, onions, peppers, and garlic to a medium pan and sauté on medium heat for about 4–6 minutes until lightly browned/tender. Then add the olives and spinach and sprinkle with the 1 tablespoon water and heat for another 2–4 minutes, stirring occasionally. Set aside.

3. Remove the mushrooms from the oven and drain/blot any excess moisture. Spread each with 1 tablespoon sauce (if desired) and top with the sausage/veggie mixture and fresh basil, dividing it between the two. Place the filled mushrooms back in the oven and bake for 10–12 minutes. Remove from the oven once more, sprinkle each with 2 tablespoons cheese, and bake for another 2–3 minutes until cheese is slightly melted.

Nutritional Analysis (per serving): Calories: 210 | Protein: 18g | Carbohydrates: 14g | Fat: 11g | Saturated Fat: 3g | Cholesterol: 30mg | Sodium: 580mg | Fiber: 4g | PCF Ratio: 31-17-52 | Exchange Approx.: 2½ Vegetables, 2 Medium-Fat Meats

PRESTO PIZZA QUESADILLA

SERVES 1

1 small whole-wheat tortilla

¼ cup low-sodium marinara sauce

2 tablespoons grated low-fat mozzarella cheese

1 teaspoon chopped fresh basil

1 teaspoon chopped black olives

1. Lay the tortilla on a clean flat surface. Spread one half with the marinara sauce and sprinkle that same half with the rest of the ingredients. Fold the plain half over.

2. Microwave on high for 45 seconds–1 minute or heat in a small nonstick pan on medium heat for a few minutes on each side until cheese is melted.

Nutritional Analysis (per serving): Calories: 200 | Protein: 9g | Carbohydrates: 28g | Fat: 7g | Saturated Fat: 2.5g | Cholesterol: 10mg | Sodium: 400mg | Fiber: 4g | PCF Ratio: 17-54-29 | Exchange Approx.: 2 Starches, ½ Medium-Fat Meat, ½ Fat

TOMATO BASIL MINI WRAPS

YIELDS 4 WRAPS; SERVING SIZE: 1 WRAP

4 tablespoons light cream cheese

4 small whole-wheat tortillas

4 Roma tomatoes, thinly sliced into rounds

4 teaspoons chopped fresh basil

1. Spread 1 tablespoon cream cheese per tortilla to evenly coat. Place the sliced tomatoes in the middle, dividing them evenly between the four tortillas.

2. Sprinkle each with a teaspoon of chopped basil and roll up.

Nutritional Analysis (per serving): Calories: 170 | Protein: 6g | Carbohydrates: 24g | Fat: 6g | Saturated Fat: 2.5g | Cholesterol: 10mg | Sodium: 370mg | Fiber: 3g | PCF Ratio: 14-55-31 | Exchange Approx.: 1½ Starches, 1 Fat

EGGPLANT BRUSCHETTA

YIELDS 8 ROUNDS; SERVING SIZE: 1 ROUND

Cooking spray

1 eggplant, cut into 8 (½"–1") rounds

1½ cups chopped tomato

3 tablespoons chopped fresh basil

2 teaspoons olive oil

¼ teaspoon crushed garlic (½ or 1 clove chopped)

Veggie Bruschetta Alternatives

Instead of eggplant, you can use grilled zucchini or yellow squash sliced lengthwise as the base of this recipe. The cooking time in the oven should be reduced. One tablespoon balsamic vinegar can also be substituted for oil to decrease fat and add different flavor.

1. Preheat oven to 425°F. Coat a large baking sheet with cooking spray and arrange eggplant slices on it. Roast on the top rack of the oven about 15 minutes until starting to soften and brown. Remove from the oven, flip the slices over, and return to the oven to roast again for another 5–7 minutes. Set aside to cool and pat dry any moisture.

2. Mix the chopped tomato, basil, olive oil, and garlic in a small bowl.

3. Top the eggplant with the tomato mixture, dividing it between the eight grilled slices.

Nutritional Analysis (per serving): Calories: 35 | Protein: 1g | Carbohydrates: 5g | Fat: 1.5g | Saturated Fat: 0g | Cholesterol: 0mg | Sodium: 0mg | Fiber: 3g | PCF Ratio: 11-57-32 | Exchange Approx.: 1 Vegetable, ¼ Fat

WHITE BEAN AND ARTICHOKE SPREAD

YIELDS 1²/₃ CUPS; SERVING SIZE: ¹/₃ CUP

1 (14-ounce) can white kidney beans, rinsed well

6 tablespoons low-sodium vegetable broth

2 tablespoons nonfat Greek yogurt

²/₃ cup (about 4 hearts) chopped cooked artichoke hearts

1 clove garlic, diced

A Few Tips for Easier Preparation

Cut minutes off the prep time of this recipe by using precooked artichokes canned in water and substituting ¼–½ teaspoon crushed garlic for the fresh garlic clove.

1. Add half the rinsed beans and 3 tablespoons broth to a blender and blend for 1 minute. Then add the other half of the beans and remaining 3 tablespoons of broth to the blender and blend for another minute.

2. Put in the Greek yogurt, artichokes, and garlic and blend until a smooth, thick mixture is formed. Store dip in the refrigerator in an airtight container for a few days.

Nutritional Analysis (per serving): Calories: 97 | Protein: 7g | Carbohydrates: 17g | Fat: 0g | Saturated Fat: 0g | Cholesterol: 0mg | Sodium: 230mg | Fiber: 7g | PCF Ratio: 30-70-0 | Exchange Approx.: 1 Starch, ½ Lean Meat

TOASTED PITA CROUTONS

SERVES 4; SERVING SIZE: ¼ OF RECIPE

Cooking spray

1 whole-wheat pita bread, cut into
    1" cubes

1 teaspoon olive oil

½ teaspoon dried oregano

¼ teaspoon garlic powder

Salt and pepper to taste

1. Preheat oven to 350°F. Prepare a small baking sheet with cooking spray and add the pita cubes. Drizzle with the olive oil and toss to coat.

2. In a small dish combine the oregano and garlic powder and sprinkle them evenly over the pita cubes.

3. Bake for 7–10 minutes on one side until lightly browned. Turn over and bake for another 5–7 minutes. Remove from oven and add salt/pepper to taste if desired. Keep in an airtight container in the fridge if not served immediately.

Nutritional Analysis (per serving): Calories: 45 | Protein: 2g | Carbohydrates: 9g | Fat: 0g | Saturated Fat: 0g | Cholesterol: 0mg | Sodium: 105mg | Fiber: 1g | PCF Ratio: 20-80-0 | Exchange Approx.: ½ Starch

SPICY FRUIT DIP

YIELDS ABOUT 1 CUP; SERVING SIZE: 2 TABLESPOONS

1 cup nonfat Greek yogurt

1½ tablespoons honey

2 tablespoons pineapple juice

⅛ teaspoon vanilla or almond extract

⅛ teaspoon ground ginger

Liven Up Your Fruit

Serve this dip with milder fruits like apples and pears to kick them up and give them some spice.

Combine all of the ingredients in a small bowl. Chill and serve or store in the refrigerator in an airtight container for a few days.

Nutritional Analysis (per serving): Calories: 30 | Protein: 3g | Carbohydrates: 5g | Fat: 0g | Saturated Fat: 0g | Cholesterol: 0mg | Sodium: 10mg | Fiber: 0g | PCF Ratio: 40-60-0 | Exchange Approx.: ½ Other Carbohydrate

APPLE CINNAMON YOGURT DIP

YIELDS ABOUT 1 CUP; SERVING SIZE: 2 TABLESPOONS

1 cup nonfat Greek yogurt

½ cup applesauce

1 tablespoon honey

⅛ teaspoon vanilla extract

⅛ teaspoon ground cinnamon

Dips Aren't Just for Veggies!

Jazz up your fruit salad by adding a serving of this creamy complement on top. Sprinkle with 1 tablespoon chopped nuts to add some crunch and 1 Healthy Fat exchange.

Combine all of the ingredients in a small bowl. Chill and serve or store in the refrigerator in an airtight container for a few days.

Nutritional Analysis (per serving): Calories: 35 | Protein: 3g | Carbohydrates: 6g | Fat: 0g | Saturated Fat: 0g | Cholesterol: 0mg | Sodium: 10mg | Fiber: 0g | PCF Ratio: 35-65-0 | Exchange Approx.: ½ Other Carbohydrate

TOASTED PUMPKIN SEEDS

SERVES 8; SERVING SIZE: ¼ CUP

2 cups pumpkin seeds, scooped from fresh pumpkin

1 tablespoon olive, peanut, or canola oil

Sea salt (optional)

1. Rinse pumpkin seeds, removing all pulp and strings; spread in single layer on large baking sheet. Let air-dry for at least 3 hours.

2. Preheat oven to 375°F. Drizzle oil over seeds and lightly sprinkle with salt if using. (Alternative method would be to put dried pumpkin seeds in a plastic bag and add oil. Seal bag; toss to mix.) Toss; spread out in single layer.

3. Bake for 15–20 minutes until lightly browned and toasted. Stir the seeds occasionally during the baking to allow for even browning. Remove hulls to eat.

Nutritional Analysis (per serving, without salt): Calories: 202 | Protein: 9g | Carbohydrates: 6g | Fat: 18g | Saturated Fat: 3g | Cholesterol: 0mg | Sodium: 6mg | Fiber: 1g | PCF Ratio: 16-11-73 | Exchange Approx.: 1 Lean Meat, 3 Fats

SNACK MIX

6 cups mixed cereal (such as a mixture of unsweetened bran, oat, rice, and wheat cereals)

1 cup mini bow-knot pretzels

⅔ cup dry-roasted peanuts

⅛ cup (2 tablespoons) butter, melted

⅛ cup (2 tablespoons) olive, canola, or peanut oil

1 tablespoon Homemade Worcestershire Sauce (see recipe in Chapter 6)

¼ teaspoon garlic powder

Tabasco sauce or other liquid hot pepper sauce to taste (optional)

Tip

The nutritional analysis will depend on the type of fat and cereals used in the recipe, most notably regarding the PCF ratio.

1. Preheat oven to 300°F. In large bowl, combine cereals, pretzels, and peanuts.

2. In another bowl, combine butter, oil, Worcestershire, garlic powder, and Tabasco if using. Pour over cereal mixture; toss to coat evenly.

3. Spread mixture on large baking sheet; bake for 30–40 minutes, stirring every 10 minutes until crisp and dry. Cool and store in airtight container. Serve at room temperature.

Nutritional Analysis (per serving, on average): Calories: 125 | Protein: 3g | Carbohydrates: 16g | Total Fat: 5g | Cholesterol: 4mg | Sodium: 201mg | Fiber: 2g | PCF Ratio: variable | Exchange Approx.: 1 Starch, 1 Fat

TORTILLA CHIPS

SERVES 1

1 nonfat corn tortilla

Spray olive oil

Sea salt to taste (optional)

Seasoning blend of your choice to taste

Tip

When you buy tortillas, look for a brand made with only cornmeal, water, and lime juice. Nutritional analysis and exchange approximations will depend on the brand of tortillas and amount of oil you use.

1. Preheat oven to 400°F. Spray both sides of tortilla with olive oil. Season lightly with sea salt or any seasoning blend.

2. Bake tortilla on cookie sheet until crisp and beginning to brown, 2–5 minutes depending on thickness of tortilla. Break tortilla into large pieces.

Nutritional Analysis (per serving): Calories: 81 | Protein: 1g | Carbohydrates: 14g | Fat: 5g | Saturated Fat: 1g | Cholesterol: 0mg | Sodium: 30mg | Fiber: 1g | PCF Ratio: 5-54-41 | Exchange Approx.: 1 Starch, ½ Fat

BLACK OLIVE MOCK CAVIAR

YIELDS 1¼ CUPS; SERVING SIZE: 1 TABLESPOON

1 (5¾-ounce) can chopped black olives

1 (4-ounce) can chopped green chili peppers

1 cup diced fresh or canned (no salt added) tomato

2 tablespoons chopped green onions

1 clove garlic, minced

1 tablespoon extra-virgin olive oil

1 teaspoon red wine vinegar

Pinch of sugar

½ teaspoon freshly ground black pepper

In medium-sized mixing bowl, mix together all ingredients. Cover; chill overnight. Serve cold or at room temperature.

Nutritional Analysis (per serving): Calories: 21 | Protein: 0g | Carbohydrates: 1g | Fat: 2g | Saturated Fat: 0g | Cholesterol: 0mg | Sodium: 85mg | Fiber: 0g | PCF Ratio: 3-25-73 | Exchange Approx.: 1 Free Condiment or ½ Fat

ALMOND SPREAD

**YIELDS ½ CUP; SERVING SIZE:
1 TABLESPOON**

¼ cup ground raw almonds

2 teaspoons honey

4 teaspoons water

Pinch of salt (optional)

Toasted Almond Seasoning

Add extra flavor to salads, rice dishes, or vegetables by sprinkling toasted almonds over top. Toast ½ cup ground raw almonds in nonstick skillet over low heat, stirring frequently until they reach a light brown color. Store cooled almonds in airtight container in cool, dry place. This low-sodium substitute has only 16 calories per teaspoon, PCF ratio of 14-12-74, and counts as ½ Fat exchange approximation.

In blender, combine all ingredients; process until smooth.

Nutritional Analysis (per serving, without salt): Calories: 30 | Protein: 1g | Carbohydrates: 3g | Fat: 2g | Saturated Fat: 0g | Cholesterol: 0mg | Sodium: 0mg | Fiber: 1g | PCF Ratio: 11-34-56 | Exchange Approx.: ½ Fat

ASIAN POPCORN

SERVES 1

4 cups air-popped popcorn

Nonstick or butter-flavored cooking spray

1 teaspoon Bragg Liquid Aminos or low-sodium soy sauce

2 teaspoons fresh lemon juice

1 teaspoon five-spice powder

¼ teaspoon ground coriander

¼ teaspoon garlic powder

Keeping Snacks in Stock

Because there are no oils to go rancid, air-popped popcorn will keep for weeks if you store it in an airtight container. Pop a large batch and keep some on hand for later. Flavor it according to your taste, and you'll have a warm, healthy snack.

1. Preheat oven to 250°F. Spread popcorn on nonstick cookie sheet; lightly coat with nonstick or butter-flavored cooking spray.

2. Mix together all remaining ingredients. Drizzle over popcorn; lightly toss to coat evenly. Bake for 5 minutes, toss popcorn and rotate pan, and bake for an additional 5 minutes. Serve warm.

Nutritional Analysis (per serving): Calories: 129 | Protein: 3g | Carbohydrates: 26g | Fat: 1g | Saturated Fat: 0g | Cholesterol: 0mg | Sodium: 221mg | Fiber: 5g | PCF Ratio: 14-77-9 | Exchange Approx.: 1 Starch, 1 Free Condiment

ZUCCHINI WITH CHEESE SPREAD

SERVES 8: SERVING SIZE: 1 TABLESPOON

⅓ cup softened fat-free cream cheese

¼ cup finely chopped red bell pepper

2 teaspoons dried parsley

¼ teaspoon onion powder

¼ teaspoon dried Italian seasoning

2 drops red pepper sauce

1 large green zucchini, peeled and cut into ¼" slices

1 green onion, thinly sliced

1. Mix the ingredients except zucchini and green onion until well blended.

2. Spread 1–2 teaspoons of cream cheese mixture onto each slice of zucchini; place on serving platter. Sprinkle with green onion; cover and refrigerate for 1 hour or until firm.

Nutritional Analysis (per serving): Calories: 38 | Protein: 4g | Carbohydrates: 4g | Fat: 0g | Saturated Fat: 0g | Cholesterol: 2mg | Sodium: 140mg | Fiber: 2g | PCF Ratio: 42-43-15 | Exchange Approx.: 1 Vegetable, ½ Fat

CREAMY FRUIT CUP

SERVES 1

4 ounces (half small container) nonfat plain yogurt

1 tablespoon unsweetened applesauce

1 teaspoon lemon juice

½ cup cubed fresh or frozen cantaloupe

¼ cup cubed or sliced apple

6 seedless red or green grapes

Grated lemon zest (optional)

Just Juice?

Fruit and fruit juice provide healthy nutrients and, in most cases, fiber, too. That's the good news. The downside is they also convert quickly to glucose. For that reason, many people can only consume them as part of a meal, rather than alone as a snack.

1. Mix together yogurt, applesauce, and lemon juice in a small bowl; in another small bowl, add all the fruit and toss to combine. Drizzle dressing over mixed fruit. (If you prefer a sweeter dressing, you can add another tablespoon of applesauce or blend in 2 teaspoons of low-sugar apple jelly without increasing the number of fruit exchanges; adjust calorie count accordingly.)

2. Sprinkle lemon zest over top of dressing.

Nutritional Analysis (per serving, without additional applesauce or jelly): Calories: 128 | Protein: 7g | Carbohydrates: 26g | Fat: 1g | Saturated Fat: 0g | Cholesterol: 0mg | Sodium: 89mg | Fiber: 2g | PCF Ratio: 19-77-3 | Exchange Approx.: ½ Skim Milk, 1½ Fruits

CHAPTER 4

SOUPS AND STEWS

VEGETABLE BROTH

YIELDS ABOUT 2½ QUARTS; SERVING SIZE: ¾ CUP

4 carrots, peeled and chopped

2 celery stalks and leaves, chopped

1 green bell pepper, seeded and chopped

2 medium zucchini, chopped

1 small onion, chopped

1 cup chopped fresh spinach

2 cups chopped leeks

½ cup chopped scallions

1 cup chopped green beans

1 cup chopped parsnips

2 bay leaves

2 cloves garlic, crushed

Sea salt and freshly ground black pepper (optional)

3 quarts water

Perpetual Broth

The easiest way to create vegetable broth is to keep a container in the freezer for saving liquid from cooked vegetables. Vegetable broth makes a great addition to sauces, soups, and many other recipes. Substitute it for meat broth in most recipes or use instead of water for cooking pasta, rice, and other grains.

1. Place all ingredients in large pot; bring to a boil. Reduce heat; cover pot and simmer 30 minutes or until vegetables are tender. Discard bay leaves.

2. Use slotted spoon to transfer vegetables to different pot; mix with some of broth for 1 Free exchange vegetable soup. Freeze mixture in single-serving containers to keep on hand for a quick, heat-in-the-microwave snack.

3. Or if you prefer, you can strain remaining vegetables from broth; purée in blender or food processor and return to broth to add dietary fiber and body. Cool and freeze until needed.

Nutritional Analysis (per serving): Calories: 10 | Protein: 0g | Carbohydrates: 2g | Fat: 0g | Saturated Fat: 0g | Cholesterol: 0mg | Sodium: 8mg | Fiber: 1g | PCF Ratio: 11-85-4 | Exchange Approx.: 1 Free Vegetable

BEEF BROTH: EASY SLOW-COOKER METHOD

YIELDS ABOUT 3 CUPS BROTH; SERVING SIZE: ½ CUP

1 pound lean round steak

1 onion, chopped

2 carrots, peeled and chopped

2 celery stalks and leaves, chopped

1 bay leaf

4 sprigs parsley

6 black peppercorns

¼ cup dry white wine

4 cups water

Trade Secrets

Some chefs swear that a hearty beef broth requires oven-roasted bones. Place bones on a roasting tray and bake in 425°F oven for 30–60 minutes. Blot fat from bones before adding to rest of broth ingredients. You may need to reduce amount of water in your slow cooker, which will produce a more concentrated broth.

1. Cut beef into several pieces; add to slow cooker with all other ingredients. Use high setting until mixture reaches a boil, then reduce heat to low. Allow to simmer covered overnight or up to 16 hours.

2. Remove beef and drain on paper towels to absorb any fat. Save for use in another recipe. Strain broth, discarding vegetables. (You don't want to eat vegetables cooked directly with the beef because they will have absorbed too much of the residual fat.) Put broth in a covered container and refrigerate for several hours or overnight; this allows time for fat to congeal on top of broth. Remove hardened fat and discard. (When you remove fat from broth, the exchange approximation for it will be 1 Free exchange.) Broth will keep in refrigerator for a few days. Freeze any you won't use within that time.

Nutritional Analysis (per serving): Calories: 58 | Protein: 9g | Carbohydrates: 0g | Fat: 2g | Saturated Fat: 1g | Cholesterol: 27mg | Sodium: 14mg | Fiber: 0g | PCF Ratio: 65-0-35 | Exchange Approx.: 1 Lean Meat

CHICKEN BROTH: EASY SLOW-COOKER METHOD

YIELDS ABOUT 4 CUPS; SERVING SIZE: ½ CUP

1 small onion, peeled and chopped

2 carrots, peeled and chopped

2 celery stalks and leaves, chopped

1 bay leaf

4 sprigs parsley

6 black peppercorns

¼ cup dry white wine

2 pounds chicken pieces, skin removed

4 cups water

Reduced Broth

Reducing broth is the act of boiling it to decrease the amount of water so you're left with a richer broth. Canned chicken broth won't reduce as easily through boiling as a homemade broth will. The broth from this recipe will be richer than what most recipes call for, so unless you need reduced broth, thin it with water as needed. Assuming you remove the fat from the broth, it will be a Free exchange.

1. Add all ingredients except water to slow cooker. The chicken pieces and vegetables should be loosely layered and fill no more than ¾ of slow cooker. Add enough water to just cover ingredients; cover slow cooker. Use high setting until mixture almost reaches a boil, then reduce heat to low. Allow to simmer overnight or up to 16 hours, checking occasionally and adding more water if necessary.

2. Remove chicken pieces and drain on paper towels to absorb any fat. Allow to cool; remove meat from bones. Strain vegetables from broth and discard. (You don't want to eat vegetables cooked directly with chicken because they will have absorbed too much of the residual fat.) Put broth in a covered container; refrigerate for several hours or overnight, allowing fat to congeal on top. Remove hardened fat and discard.

3. To separate broth into small amounts for use when you steam vegetables or potatoes, fill up an ice cube tray with broth. Let freeze, then remove cubes from tray and store in labeled freezer bag. Common ice cube trays allow for ⅛ cup or 2 tablespoons of liquid per section.

Nutritional Analysis (per serving): Calories: 67 | Protein: 9g | Carbohydrates: 0g | Fat: 3g | Saturated Fat: 1g | Cholesterol: 24mg | Sodium: 22mg | Fiber: 0g | PCF Ratio: 53-0-47 | Exchange Approx.: ½ Very Lean Meat, ½ Lean Meat

FISH STOCK

YIELDS 4 CUPS; SERVING SIZE: 1 CUP

4 cups fish heads, bones, and trimmings
  (approximately 1 pound)

2 stalks celery and leaves, chopped

1 onion, chopped

1 carrot, peeled and chopped

1 bay leaf

4 sprigs fresh parsley

Sea salt and pepper to taste (optional)

Tip

To make stock from shellfish, simply substitute shrimp, crab, or lobster shells for the fish heads and bones.

1. Use your own fish trimmings (saved in bag in the freezer) or ask the butcher at your local fish market or supermarket for fish trimmings. Wash the trimmings well.

2. In a stockpot, combine all ingredients; add enough water to cover everything by 1" or so. Bring to a boil over high heat; reduce heat to low. Skim off foam that rises to top. Cover and simmer 20 minutes.

3. Remove from heat; strain through a sieve, discarding all solids. Refrigerate or freeze.

Nutritional Analysis (per serving): Calories: 40 | Protein: 5g | Carbohydrates: 0g | Fat: 2g | Saturated Fat: 1g | Cholesterol: 2mg | Sodium: Variable | Fiber: 0g | PCF Ratio: 55-0-45 | Exchange Approx.: 1 Very Lean Meat

LENTIL SOUP WITH HERBS AND LEMON

SERVES 4; SERVING SIZE: ¼ RECIPE

1 cup lentils, soaked overnight in 1 cup water

6 cups low-fat, reduced-sodium chicken broth

1 carrot, sliced

1 stalk celery, sliced

1 yellow onion, thinly sliced

2 teaspoons olive oil

1 tablespoon dried tarragon

½ teaspoon dried oregano

Sea salt and black pepper to taste (optional)

1 tablespoon lemon juice

4 thin slices of lemon

Believe It or Not!

Put a fork at the bottom of the pan when you cook a pot of beans. The beans will cook in half the time.

1. Drain and rinse lentils. Add lentils and broth to pot over medium heat; bring to a boil. Reduce heat and simmer until tender, approximately 15 minutes. (If you did not presoak the lentils, increase cooking time by about 15 minutes.)

2. While lentils are cooking, sauté carrot, celery, and onion in oil for 8 minutes or until onion is golden brown. Remove from heat and set aside.

3. When lentils are tender, add vegetables, tarragon, oregano, and salt and pepper if using; cook for 2 minutes. Stir in lemon juice. Ladle into four serving bowls; garnish with lemon slices.

Nutritional Analysis (per serving): Calories: 214 | Protein: 15g | Carbohydrates: 34g | Fat: 3g | Saturated Fat: 1g | Cholesterol: 0mg | Sodium: 353mg | Fiber: 16g | PCF Ratio: 27-61-12 | Exchange Approx.: 1 Lean Meat, 2 Starches, 1 Vegetable

LENTIL-VEGETABLE SOUP

SERVES 4; SERVING SIZE: ¼ RECIPE

5 cups water or your choice of broth

1 medium sweet potato, peeled and chopped

1 cup uncooked lentils

2 medium onions, chopped

¼ cup barley

2 tablespoons dried parsley

2 carrots, sliced

1 celery stalk, chopped

2 teaspoons ground cumin

Combine all ingredients in soup pot; simmer until lentils are soft, about 1 hour.

Nutritional Analysis (per serving, with water): Calories: 273 | Protein: 16g | Carbohydrates: 53g | Fat: 1g | Saturated Fat: 0g | Cholesterol: 0mg | Sodium: 34mg | Fiber: 19g | PCF Ratio: 23-74-3 | Exchange Approx.: 1 Very Lean Meat, 3 Starches, 1 Vegetable

COLD ROASTED RED PEPPER SOUP

SERVES 4; SERVING SIZE: ¼ RECIPE

1 teaspoon olive oil

½ cup chopped onion

3 roasted red bell peppers, seeded and chopped

3¼ cups low-fat, reduced-sodium chicken broth

½ cup nonfat plain yogurt

½ teaspoon sea salt (optional)

4 sprigs fresh basil (optional)

1. Heat saucepan over medium-high heat. Add olive oil; sauté onion until transparent. Add peppers and broth. Bring to a boil; reduce heat and simmer for 15 minutes. Remove from heat; purée in blender or food processor until smooth.

2. Allow to cool. Stir in yogurt and salt if using; chill well in refrigerator. Garnish the soup with fresh basil sprigs if desired.

Nutritional Analysis (per serving, without salt): Calories: 73 | Protein: 5g | Carbohydrates: 9g | Fat: 4g | Saturated Fat: 1g | Cholesterol: 3mg | Sodium: 404mg | Fiber: 3g | PCF Ratio: 21-39-40 | Exchange Approx.: ½ Fat, ½ Starch

TOMATO-VEGETABLE SOUP

SERVES 6; SERVING SIZE: ⅙ RECIPE

1 tablespoon olive oil

2 teaspoons minced garlic

⅔ teaspoon ground cumin

2 carrots, chopped

2 stalks celery, diced

1 medium onion, chopped

⅔ cup unsalted tomato paste

½ teaspoon red pepper flakes

2 cups canned unsalted peeled tomatoes, with juice

⅔ teaspoon chopped fresh oregano

3 cups low-fat, reduced-sodium chicken broth

3 cups fat-free beef broth

2 cups diced potatoes

2 cups shredded cabbage

½ cup green beans

½ cup fresh or frozen corn kernels

½ teaspoon freshly cracked black pepper

¼ cup lime juice or balsamic vinegar

1. Heat olive oil in large stockpot; sauté garlic, cumin, carrot, and celery 1 minute. Add onion; cook until transparent.

2. Stir in tomato paste; sauté until it begins to brown.

3. Add remaining ingredients except for lime juice or vinegar. Bring to a boil; reduce heat and simmer for 20–30 minutes, adding additional broth or water if needed. Just before serving, add lime juice or balsamic vinegar.

Nutritional Analysis (per serving): Calories: 158 | Protein: 5g | Carbohydrates: 31g | Fat: 3g | Saturated Fat: 1g | Cholesterol: 0mg | Sodium: 349mg | Fiber: 5g | PCF Ratio: 12-72-16 | Exchange Approx.: 1½ Starches, 1 Vegetable

NUTTY GREEK SNAPPER SOUP

SERVES 4; SERVING SIZE: ¼ RECIPE

1-pound (16 ounces) red snapper fillet

2 large cucumbers, peeled, halved, seeded, and cut into 1" pieces

4 green onions, chopped

4 cups nonfat plain yogurt

1 cup packed fresh parsley, basil, cilantro, arugula, and chives, mixed

3 tablespoons lime juice

Salt and pepper to taste (optional)

¼ cup chopped walnuts

Herb sprigs for garnish (optional)

Tip

You can make this soup using leftover fish or substitute halibut, cod, or sea bass for the snapper.

1. Rinse red snapper fillet and pat dry with paper towels. Broil fillet until opaque through the thickest part, about 4 minutes on each side depending on the thickness of fillet. Let cool. (Alternatives would be to steam or poach the fillet.)

2. Put half of cucumber with green onions in bowl of food processor; pulse to coarsely chop. Transfer to a large bowl.

3. Add remaining cucumber, yogurt, and fresh herbs to food processor; process until smooth and frothy. (Alternatively, you can grate cucumbers, finely mince green onion and herbs, and stir together with yogurt in large bowl.) Stir in lime juice and season with salt and pepper to taste if using. Cover and refrigerate for at least 1 hour or up to 8 hours; the longer the soup cools, the more the flavors will mellow.

4. While soup cools, break cooled red snapper fillet into large chunks, discarding skin and any bones. Ladle chilled soup into shallow bowls and add red snapper. Sprinkle chopped walnuts over soup, garnish with herb sprigs if using, and serve.

Nutritional Analysis (per serving): Calories: 309 | Protein: 39g | Carbohydrates: 25g | Fat: 6g | Saturated Fat: 1g | Cholesterol: 46mg | Sodium: 240mg | Fiber: 2g | PCF Ratio: 50-33-17 | Exchange Approx.: 4 Lean Meats, 1 Skim Milk, 1 Vegetable

MINESTRONE SOUP GENOESE STYLE

SERVES 6; SERVING SIZE: ⅙ RECIPE

4 cloves garlic, minced

2 tablespoons chopped fresh basil

¼ teaspoon salt

2 tablespoons olive oil

1 ounce grated Romano cheese

2 cups shredded cabbage

1 cup diced zucchini

1 cup (cut into 1" pieces) green beans

1 cup peeled and chopped potatoes

2 cups cooked navy beans

½ cup chopped celery

¼ cup fresh or frozen peas

1 tablespoon tomato paste

3 cups water

Salt and pepper to taste

Tip

Make extra garlic paste (using first five ingredients and step 1) and keep refrigerated. You'll have instant garlic-cheese flavor on hand for soups, sauces, garlic bread, and pasta dishes. Garlic paste keeps in the refrigerator for up to 2 weeks.

1. Combine garlic, basil, and salt. Add olive oil and Romano cheese; mix well into a paste and set aside. (Using a mortar and pestle works very well.)

2. Combine cabbage, zucchini, green beans, potatoes, cooked navy beans, celery, peas, tomato paste, and water in a 4–6-quart soup pot.

3. Bring to a boil; reduce heat and simmer for 45–60 minutes or until tender.

4. Mix garlic paste into soup; simmer an additional 5 minutes. Season with salt and pepper to taste and serve.

Nutritional Analysis (per serving): Calories: 201 | Protein: 9g | Carbohydrates: 29g | Fat: 6g | Saturated Fat: 2g | Cholesterol: 5mg | Sodium: 271mg | Fiber: 6g | PCF Ratio: 17-56-27 | Exchange Approx.: 1½ Starches, 1 Vegetable, 1 Fat

BROCCOLI AND WHOLE-GRAIN PASTA SOUP

SERVES 6; SERVING SIZE: ⅙ RECIPE

1–3 slices bacon, cut into 1" pieces

1 tablespoon chopped onion

2 cloves garlic, minced

1 tablespoon tomato paste

3 cups water

1 cup peeled and cubed eggplant

¾ teaspoon salt

¼ teaspoon pepper

½ teaspoon dried oregano

8 ounces broccoli florets

1 cup cooked al dente whole-grain pasta shells

1 ounce grated Romano cheese

1. Place bacon, onion, and garlic in a 4-quart soup pot; brown.

2. Add tomato paste, water, eggplant, salt, pepper, and oregano. Bring to a boil; reduce heat and simmer for 20 minutes or until eggplant is soft cooked.

3. Add broccoli florets; simmer for 5 minutes until broccoli is tender but still slightly crisp. Add cooked pasta.

4. Serve soup immediately with a sprinkling of grated cheese.

Nutritional Analysis (per serving): Calories: 86 | Protein: 6g | Carbohydrates: 10g | Fat: 3g | Saturated Fat: 1g | Cholesterol: 9mg | Sodium: 185mg | Fiber: 2g | PCF Ratio: 25-43-32 | Exchange Approx.: ½ Starch, 1 Vegetable, 1 Fat

WHITE BEAN AND ESCAROLE SOUP

SERVES 6; SERVING SIZE: ⅙ RECIPE

1 cup dry navy beans

3 cups water

1 cup chopped onion

½ cup peeled and chopped potato

1 clove garlic, minced

3 ounces Canadian bacon, cut in ½" cubes

2½ cups water

½ teaspoon salt

¼ teaspoon pepper

1 teaspoon vegetable oil

8 ounces coarsely chopped escarole

Slow-Cooker Method

This soup can also be prepared using a slow cooker. Soak beans as described in step 1; drain. Add beans, onion, potatoes, garlic, Canadian bacon, and 2½ cups water to slow cooker. Cook for 8–10 hours. At end of cooking, add escarole; simmer for 5–10 minutes until escarole is wilted and tender. Add salt and pepper to taste.

1. Place dry beans and 3 cups of water in medium saucepan. Bring to a boil; remove from heat. Allow beans to soak several hours or overnight.

2. Drain beans; place in pressure cooker with onion, potatoes, garlic, Canadian bacon, 2½ cups water, salt, pepper, and vegetable oil. Close cover securely, place pressure regulator on vent pipe, and cook for 30 minutes with pressure regulator rocking slowly. (If using an electric pressure cooker, follow manufacturer instructions.) Let pressure drop on its own.

3. Add chopped escarole; simmer for 5–10 minutes until escarole is wilted and cooked tender.

Nutritional Analysis (per serving): Calories: 163 | Protein: 11g | Carbohydrates: 27g | Fat: 2g | Saturated Fat: 0g | Cholesterol: 7mg | Sodium: 349mg | Fiber: 9g | PCF Ratio: 26-64-10 | Exchange Approx.: 1½ Starches, ½ Vegetable, 1½ Very Lean Meats, 2 Fats

FRESH TOMATO BASIL SOUP

SERVES 6; SERVING SIZE: ⅙ RECIPE

1 tablespoon butter

¼ cup chopped onion

4 cups (2 pounds) crushed tomatoes

¼ cup loosely chopped fresh basil leaves

1 cup low-sodium chicken broth

2 ounces reduced-fat (Neufchâtel) cream cheese

Freshly ground pepper to taste

Easy Measures

Consider freezing broth in an ice cube tray. Most ice cube tray sections hold ⅛ cup (2 tablespoons) of liquid. Once broth is frozen, you can transfer cubes to freezer bag or container. This makes it easy to measure out the amount you need for recipes.

1. Melt butter in soup pot. Add onions; sauté until soft. Add crushed tomato, basil, and chicken broth.

2. Bring to a boil. Reduce heat; cook for another 15 minutes. Remove from heat; stir in cream cheese until melted.

3. Transfer to food processor or blender; purée until smooth. Depending on size of processor or blender, you may need to purée a partial portion at a time. Add ground pepper to taste.

Nutritional Analysis (per serving): Calories: 87 | Protein: 3g | Carbohydrates: 12g | Fat: 4g | Saturated Fat: 2g | Cholesterol: 10mg | Sodium: 449mg | Fiber: 3g | PCF Ratio: 13-50-37 | Exchange Approx.: 2 Vegetables, 1 Fat

WINTER SQUASH AND RED PEPPER SOUP

SERVES 6; SERVING SIZE: ⅙ RECIPE

1 large winter squash, halved and seeded
   (to yield 3½ cups cooked)

1 tablespoon olive oil

1 cup chopped onions

1 tablespoon chopped garlic

4 ounces roasted red pepper

3 cups low-sodium chicken broth

½ cup dry white wine

2 teaspoons sugar

1 teaspoon ground cinnamon

½ teaspoon ground ginger

1 tablespoon reduced-fat sour cream
   (optional)

1. Preheat oven to 400°F. Place squash face-down on oiled 9" × 13" glass baking dish; bake for 50–60 minutes or until squash is cooked tender. When cool enough to handle, scoop squash out of skins and set aside.

2. In large nonstick skillet, heat olive oil. Add onions and garlic; sauté until tender and continue to cook until the onions are soft and have turned brown (caramelized).

3. Add roasted pepper and chicken broth; simmer for another 16 minutes.

4. Add cooked winter squash, white wine, sugar, cinnamon, and ginger; simmer for another 5 minutes.

5. Transfer to food processor or blender; purée until smooth. Depending on size of processor or blender, you may need to purée a partial portion at a time. If desired, stir in reduced-fat sour cream and serve.

Nutritional Analysis (per serving, without sour cream): Calories: 137 | Protein: 3g | Carbohydrates: 24g | Fat: 3g | Saturated Fat: 1g | Cholesterol: 0mg | Sodium: 445mg | Fiber: 6g | PCF Ratio: 10-70-20 | Exchange Approx.: 1 Starch, 1 Vegetable, ½ Fat

VEGETABLE AND BEAN CHILI

SERVES 8; SERVING SIZE: 1/8 RECIPE

4 teaspoons olive oil

2 cups chopped onions

1/2 cup green bell pepper, seeded and chopped

3 cloves garlic, chopped

1 small jalapeño pepper, finely chopped (include the seeds if you like the chili extra hot)

1 tablespoon chili powder

1 teaspoon ground cumin

1 (28-ounce) can unsalted tomatoes, chopped and undrained

2 zucchini, peeled and chopped

2 (15-ounce) cans unsalted kidney beans, rinsed

1 tablespoon chopped semisweet chocolate

3 tablespoons chopped fresh cilantro

1. Heat heavy pot over moderately high heat. Add olive oil, onions, bell pepper, garlic, and jalapeño; sauté until vegetables are softened, about 5 minutes. Add chili powder and cumin; sauté for 1 minute, stirring frequently to mix well.

2. Add tomatoes with juice and zucchini; bring to a boil. Lower heat and simmer partially covered for 15 minutes, stirring occasionally.

3. Stir in beans and chocolate; simmer, stirring occasionally, for additional 5 minutes or until beans are heated through and chocolate is melted. Stir in cilantro and serve.

Nutritional Analysis (per serving): Calories: 205 | Protein: 12g | Carbohydrates: 35g | Fat: 3g | Saturated Fat: 1g | Cholesterol: 0mg | Sodium: 156mg | Fiber: 13g | PCF Ratio: 22-65-13 | Exchange Approx.: 1 Lean Meat, 2 Starches, 1 Vegetable

RICH AND CREAMY SAUSAGE-POTATO SOUP

SERVES 2; SERVING SIZE: ½ RECIPE

1 teaspoon olive oil

½ teaspoon butter

½ cup chopped onion, steamed

1 clove dry-roasted garlic (see Garlic and Feta Cheese Dip recipe in Chapter 3 for dry-roasting instructions)

1 ounce crumbled cooked Mock Chorizo (see recipes in Chapter 9)

¼ teaspoon celery seed

2 Yukon gold potatoes, peeled and diced into 1" pieces

½ cup fat-free chicken broth

1½ cups Mock Cream (see recipe in Chapter 6)

1 teaspoon white wine vinegar

1 teaspoon vanilla extract

Fresh parsley, to taste (optional)

Sea salt and freshly ground black pepper, to taste (optional)

Skim the Fat

You can remove fat from soups and stews by dropping ice cubes into the pot. The fat will cling to the cubes as you stir. Be sure to take out the cubes before they melt. Fat also clings to lettuce leaves; simply sweep them over the top of the soup. Discard ice cubes or leaves when done.

1. In saucepan, heat olive oil and butter over medium heat. Add onion, roasted garlic, chorizo, celery seed, and potatoes; sauté until heated.

2. Add chicken broth; bring to a boil. Cover saucepan, reduce heat, and maintain simmer for 10 minutes or until potatoes are tender. Add Mock Cream and heat.

3. Remove pan from burner and stir in vinegar and vanilla. Add optional seasonings to taste.

Nutritional Analysis (per serving): Calories: 326 | Protein: 17g | Carbohydrates: 53g | Fat: 6g | Saturated Fat: 2g | Cholesterol: 19mg | Sodium: 259mg | Fiber: 3g | PCF Ratio: 20-64-16 | Exchange Approx.: 1 Fat, ½ Medium-Fat Meat, 1 Starch, 1½ Skim Milks, 1 Vegetable

CHICKEN CORN CHOWDER

SERVES 10; SERVING SIZE: 1/10 RECIPE

Nonstick cooking spray

1 pound boneless skinless chicken breast, cut into chunks

1 medium onion, chopped

1 red bell pepper, diced

1 large potato, diced

2 (16-ounce) cans low-fat, reduced-sodium chicken broth

1 (8¾-ounce) can unsalted cream-style corn

½ cup all-purpose flour

2 cups skim milk

4 ounces diced Cheddar cheese

½ teaspoon sea salt

Freshly ground pepper to taste

½ cup processed bacon bits

Tip

To trim down the fat in this recipe, use a reduced-fat cheese, such as Cabot Sharp Light or Cabot Sharp Extra Light Cheddar.

1. Spray large soup pot with nonstick cooking spray; heat on medium setting until hot. Add chicken, onion, and bell pepper; sauté over medium heat until chicken is browned and vegetables are tender. Stir in potatoes and broth; bring to a boil. Reduce heat and simmer covered for 20 minutes. Stir in corn.

2. Blend flour and milk in bowl; gradually stir into pot. Increase heat to medium; cook until mixture comes to a boil, then reduce heat and simmer until soup is thickened, stirring constantly. Add cheese; stir until melted and blended in. Add salt and pepper to taste and sprinkle with bacon bits before serving.

Nutritional Analysis (per serving): Calories: 193 | Protein: 17g | Carbohydrates: 21g | Fat: 5g | Saturated Fat: 3g | Cholesterol: 39mg | Sodium: 155mg | Fiber: 2g | PCF Ratio: 22-36-42 | Exchange Approx.: 1½ Very Lean Meats, ½ Starch, 1 Vegetable, ½ Skim Milk, ½ High-Fat Meat

SALMON CHOWDER

SERVES 4; SERVING SIZE: ¼ RECIPE

1 (7½-ounce) can unsalted salmon

2 teaspoons butter

1 medium onion, chopped

2 stalks celery, chopped

1 sweet green pepper, seeded and chopped

1 clove garlic, minced

4 carrots, peeled and diced

4 small potatoes, peeled and diced

1 cup fat-free chicken broth

1 cup water

½ teaspoon cracked black pepper

½ teaspoon dill seed

1 cup diced zucchini

1 cup Mock Cream (see recipe in Chapter 6)

1 (8¾-ounce) can unsalted cream-style corn

Freshly ground black pepper to taste

½ cup chopped fresh parsley (optional)

1. Drain and flake salmon; discard liquid.

2. In large nonstick saucepan, melt butter over medium heat; sauté onion, celery, green pepper, garlic, and carrots, stirring often until tender, about 5 minutes.

3. Add potatoes, broth, water, cracked black pepper, and dill seed; bring to boil. Reduce heat, cover, and simmer for 20 minutes or until potatoes are tender.

4. Add zucchini; simmer covered for another 5 minutes.

5. Add salmon, Mock Cream, corn, and ground black pepper; cook over low heat just until heated through. Just before serving, add parsley if desired.

Nutritional Analysis (per serving): Calories: 364 | Protein: 20g | Carbohydrates: 61g | Fat: 6g | Saturated Fat: 2g | Cholesterol: 28mg | Sodium: 199mg | Fiber: 7g | PCF Ratio: 22-65-14 | Exchange Approx.: ½ Fat, 2 Starches, 2 Lean Meats, 2 Vegetables, ½ Skim Milk

SWEET AND SPICY ACORN SQUASH SOUP

YIELDS 5 CUPS; SERVING SIZE: 1 CUP

1 medium to large acorn squash (to yield 3 cups cooked acorn squash)

½ tablespoon butter or margarine

1 cup peeled and chopped apple

3 cups low-sodium vegetable or chicken broth

1 packed tablespoon brown sugar

1 teaspoon ground cumin

Salt and pepper to taste

1. Preheat the oven to 375°F. Roast acorn squash whole for 40–45 minutes until the outside is starting to brown, the skin is soft, and it is easily pierced with a fork or knife.

2. Allow the squash to cool for 10 minutes, then carefully cut in half (watch for trapped hot steam inside). Scoop out the seeds and then set aside 3 cups of cooked squash.

3. While the squash is cooling, add the ½ tablespoon butter/margarine to a large pot and put in the apple. Warm on medium heat, stirring occasionally for about 5–7 minutes until it is lightly browned and softened. Put the squash, broth, brown sugar, and cumin in the pot and simmer on low heat for 10–15 minutes.

4. Remove from heat and allow to cool. Carefully transfer the soup to a food processor or blender and purée until smooth. Depending on the size of your food processor or blender, you may need to purée a partial portion at a time.

5. Put the puréed mixture back in the pot and warm on low heat for about 5 minutes, stirring frequently to prevent the thick soup from spattering. Add salt and pepper to taste.

Nutritional Analysis (per serving): Calories: 90 | Protein: 1g | Carbohydrates: 21g | Fat: 1.5g | Saturated Fat: 0g | Cholesterol: 0mg | Sodium: 350mg | Fiber: 5g | PCF Ratio: 4-84-12 | Exchange Approx.: 1 Starch, ¼ Fruit

FRESH ROASTED PUMPKIN PARMESAN SOUP

YIELDS 4 CUPS; SERVING SIZE: 1 CUP

1 average-sized pie pumpkin (to yield
   3 cups fresh roasted pumpkin)

3½ cups low-sodium chicken or vegetable
   broth

½ teaspoon garlic powder

⅓ cup grated Parmesan cheese

1. Preheat the oven to 400°F. Roast the pumpkin whole on a baking sheet for 40–60 minutes. (The actual time will vary based on the oven's actual temperature, the moistness of the pumpkin, and its size. You will know it's done when a knife slips into the flesh very easily.) Carefully cut in half (watch for trapped hot steam inside). Scoop out the seeds and then set aside 3 cups of cooked pumpkin.

2. Add the broth to a large pot and bring to a boil on high heat. Add the pumpkin and garlic powder and reduce heat to medium-low. Simmer for a few minutes.

3. Remove from heat and let cool. Stir in the Parmesan cheese and carefully transfer the soup to a food processor or blender and purée until smooth. Depending on the size of your food processor or blender, you may need to purée a partial portion at a time.

4. Put the puréed mixture back in the pot and warm for about 5 minutes on low heat, stirring frequently to prevent the thick soup from spattering.

Nutritional Analysis (per serving): Calories: 80 | Protein: 4g | Carbohydrates: 12g | Fat: 3g | Saturated Fat: 0g | Cholesterol: 10mg | Sodium: 260mg | Fiber: 3g | PCF Ratio: 19-53-28 | Exchange Approx.: ¾ Starch, ½ Medium-Fat Meat

VEGGIE CABBAGE SOUP

YIELDS 10 CUPS; SERVING SIZE: 2 CUPS

1 teaspoon olive oil

2 cups chopped carrots

2 cups chopped celery

1 cup chopped onion

2 cups chopped cabbage

1 (15-ounce) can diced tomatoes

4 cups low-sodium chicken or vegetable broth

½–1 teaspoon garlic powder

2 teaspoons sweet paprika

1. Add the olive oil, carrots, celery, and onion to a large pot and sauté on medium heat for 3–5 minutes, stirring frequently.

2. Add the cabbage, tomatoes, broth, garlic powder, and paprika and bring to a boil, then reduce the heat and simmer for at least 12–15 minutes until all the veggies are tender.

Nutritional Analysis (per serving): Calories: 80 | Protein: 4g | Carbohydrates: 14g | Fat: 2g | Saturated Fat: 0g | Cholesterol: 0mg | Sodium: 360mg | Fiber: 4g | PCF Ratio: 5-69-16 | Exchange Approx.: 3 Vegetables

TOMATO MUSHROOM SOUP

YIELDS 9 CUPS; SERVING SIZE: 1 CUP

1 teaspoon olive oil, divided

1 cup chopped onion

1 tablespoon chopped garlic

5 cups sliced button or cremini mushrooms

1 cup tomato sauce

4 cups Low Sodium V8 juice

1 (14-ounce) can fire-roasted tomatoes

1 teaspoon dried oregano

Black pepper (optional)

Chopped fresh basil (optional)

1. Add ½ teaspoon of olive oil, the onions, and garlic to a large pot and sauté for 3–5 minutes on medium heat until lightly browned. Add the other ½ teaspoon of olive oil and the mushrooms and sauté for another 5 minutes until softened.

2. Put in the tomato sauce, V8, canned tomatoes, and oregano; bring to a boil and then simmer for another 5–10 minutes. Add black pepper to taste and garnish with chopped fresh basil if desired.

Nutritional Analysis (per serving): Calories: 60 | Protein: 3g | Carbohydrates: 12g | Fat: 0.5g | Saturated Fat: 0g | Cholesterol: 0mg | Sodium: 290mg | Fiber: 2g | PCF Ratio: 20-79-1 | Exchange Approx.: 2½ Vegetables

VERSATILE CHICKEN VEGETABLE SOUP

YIELDS 14 CUPS; SERVING SIZE: 1 CUP

1 teaspoon olive oil

2 cups chopped carrots

2 cups chopped celery

1 cup chopped onion

2 cups sliced mushrooms

3 cups cooked and cubed chicken breast

8 cups low-sodium chicken broth

¼ teaspoon garlic powder

1 teaspoon of your favorite low-sodium seasoning blend

More Versions and Variations:

Some tasty add-ins to this recipe are a few handfuls of raw spinach or one 14-ounce can of tomatoes (which adds 2g carbohydrates/serving), or add a whole-grain starch like 2 cups cooked brown rice, 2 cups cooked whole-wheat pasta, or 3 cups corn (which will add 6 grams of carbohydrates/serving).

1. Add the olive oil, carrots, celery, and onion to a large pot and sauté on medium heat for 5–7 minutes, stirring frequently.

2. Add the mushrooms, cooked chicken, and broth and bring to a light boil; then reduce the heat, add garlic powder and desired seasoning, and simmer for at least 10–15 minutes until veggies are tender.

Nutritional Analysis (per serving): Calories: 80 | Protein: 11g | Carbohydrates: 4g | Fat: 1.5g | Saturated Fat: 0g | Cholesterol: 25mg | Sodium: 85mg | Fiber: 1g | PCF Ratio: 55-25-20 | Exchange Approx.: 1 Vegetable, 1½ Very Lean Meats

SIMPLE BROCCOLI SOUP

YIELDS 4 CUPS; SERVING SIZE: 1 CUP

4 cups chopped broccoli

1 teaspoon olive oil

3 or 4 finely chopped fresh garlic cloves

½ cup chopped white or yellow onion

3 cups chicken or vegetable broth

1 tablespoon grated Parmesan cheese

Salt, pepper, and garlic powder (optional)

1. Steam the broccoli by boiling it in a pan in ½" of water or in a Pyrex dish in ½" of water in the microwave for 3–4 minutes until tender when pierced with a fork.

2. Add the olive oil to a large pot with the garlic and onions and sauté them on medium-high heat until lightly browned/tender, about 2–4 minutes. Put in the broth and cooked broccoli and bring to a boil; then reduce to low heat and simmer for 3–5 minutes.

3. Remove from heat and let cool. Carefully transfer the soup to a food processor or blender and purée until smooth. Depending on the size of your food processor or blender, you may need to purée a partial portion at a time.

4. Put the puréed mixture back in the pot and add the Parmesan cheese, along with salt, pepper, and garlic powder to taste. Warm on low heat for 5–10 minutes, stirring frequently to prevent the thick soup from spattering.

Nutritional Analysis (per serving): Calories: 50 | Protein: 2g | Carbohydrates: 6g | Fat: 2g | Saturated Fat: 0g | Cholesterol: 0mg | Sodium: 140mg | Fiber: 2g | PCF Ratio: 16-48-36 | Exchange Approx.: 1 Vegetable, ½ Fat

CELERY SOUP

YIELDS 4 CUPS; SERVING SIZE: 1 CUP

1 teaspoon olive oil, divided

½ cup chopped white or yellow onion

1 teaspoon finely chopped fresh garlic

4 cups chopped celery

3 cups low-sodium chicken or vegetable broth

Black pepper (optional)

Spicing Up Your Soup

This soup, along with many others in this chapter, is a simple, clean recipe that you can enhance with your signature flavors. Add a dash of cumin and/or curry to make things more exotic, or put in a pinch of chili powder and/or red pepper for some spice. A sprinkle of Parmesan cheese is a great way to garnish as well.

1. Add ½ teaspoon of olive oil to a large pot along with the onions and garlic and sauté them on medium heat until lightly browned, about 3–4 minutes.

2. Put in the other ½ teaspoon of olive oil plus the chopped celery and sauté some more, stirring frequently for another 5–7 minutes.

3. Add the broth, bring to a boil, then reduce to low heat and simmer for 10–12 minutes until the celery is tender.

4. Remove from heat and let cool. Carefully transfer the soup to a food processor or blender and purée until smooth. Depending on the size of your food processor or blender, you may need to purée a partial portion at a time.

5. Put the puréed soup back in the pot and warm on low heat for 5–7 minutes, stirring frequently to prevent the thick soup from spattering. Add pepper to taste.

Nutritional Analysis (per serving): Calories: 45 | Protein: 3g | Carbohydrates: 7g | Fat: 1.5g | Saturated Fat: 0.5g | Cholesterol: 0mg | Sodium: 190mg | Fiber: 1g | PCF Ratio: 9-64-27 | Exchange Approx.: 1½ Vegetables

ROASTED ZUCCHINI AND GARLIC SOUP

YIELDS 5 CUPS; SERVING SIZE: 1 CUP

Cooking spray

1 pound zucchini (about 4 or 5 medium-large), sliced into ¼"-thick strips

4 whole garlic cloves

⅓ cup sliced onion

3 cups low-sodium chicken or vegetable broth

Salt and pepper to taste

1. Preheat oven to 425°F.

2. Place the zucchini, garlic, and onions on a large baking sheet coated with cooking spray and roast until tender, about 15 minutes each side. Remove from oven and let cool for 15–20 minutes.

3. Chop up the cooked zucchini, garlic, and onions and add half of them plus 1 cup broth to a food processor or blender and purée until smooth. Add the remaining portion and another cup of broth and blend until smooth.

4. Pour the mixture into a medium- or large-sized pot and add the last cup of broth and salt and pepper to taste; warm on medium heat, stirring occasionally, about 5–7 minutes.

Nutritional Analysis (per serving): Calories: 35 | Protein: 2g | Carbohydrates: 6g | Fat: 0g | Saturated Fat: 0g | Cholesterol: 0mg | Sodium: 90mg | Fiber: 2g | PCF Ratio: 16-76-8 | Exchange Approx.: 1¼ Vegetables

CARROT LENTIL SOUP

YIELDS 7 CUPS; SERVING SIZE: 1 CUP

1 teaspoon olive oil

1 cup chopped carrots

1 cup chopped celery

1 cup chopped white onion

3 cups cooked lentils

4 cups low-sodium chicken or vegetable broth

1 teaspoon dried oregano

½ teaspoon garlic powder

Time-Saving Tip

To cut preparation time use store-bought precooked lentils that are available in the can or vacuum packed. Rinse well in a colander before adding.

1. Coat a large pot with the olive oil and put in the carrots, celery, and onions; sauté on medium heat until just before tender, about 7–10 minutes.

2. Add the cooked lentils, broth, oregano, and garlic powder and bring to a light boil. Reduce to low heat and simmer about 10 minutes until warmed through.

Nutritional Analysis (per serving): Calories: 120 | Protein: 7g | Carbohydrates: 21g | Fat: 1g | Saturated Fat: 0g | Cholesterol: 0mg | Sodium: 220mg | Fiber: 9g | PCF Ratio: 25-69-6 | Exchange Approx.: 1 Starch, 1 Vegetable, 1 Lean Meat

WHITE BEAN SPINACH AND MUSHROOM SOUP

YIELDS 6 CUPS; SERVING SIZE: 1 CUP

1 teaspoon olive oil

¾ cup chopped white onion

4 cups chopped mushrooms, such as cremini or button

1 (14-ounce) can white beans, rinsed well

4 cups low-sodium chicken or vegetable broth

1 teaspoon garlic powder

1 teaspoon black pepper

4 cups chopped fresh spinach

1. Coat a large pot with the olive oil and put in the onions and mushrooms; sauté on medium heat until just before tender, about 7–10 minutes.

2. Add the canned beans, broth, garlic powder, and pepper and bring to a light boil.

3. Reduce to low heat, add the spinach, and simmer for about 5–7 minutes until warmed through.

Nutritional Analysis (per serving): Calories: 100 | Protein: 5g | Carbohydrates: 17g | Fat: 1g | Saturated Fat: 0g | Cholesterol: 0mg | Sodium: 200mg | Fiber: 6g | PCF Ratio: 22-70-8 | Exchange Approx.: ½ Starch, 1½ Vegetables, ½ Very Lean Meat

EASY BORSCHT

YIELDS 6 CUPS; SERVING SIZE: 1 CUP

1 teaspoon olive oil

¾ cup chopped onions

¾ cup sliced carrots

¾ cup thinly sliced celery

3 cups chopped cooked fresh or canned beets (regular, not pickled)

1 cup shredded cabbage

4 cups low-sodium chicken or vegetable broth

Salt and pepper (optional)

1. Coat a large pot with the olive oil and put in the onions, carrots, and celery. Sauté on medium heat until just before tender, about 7–10 minutes.

2. Add the cooked beets, cabbage, and broth and bring to a light boil. Reduce to low heat and simmer about 10–12 minutes until warmed through. Add salt and pepper to taste.

Nutritional Analysis (per serving): Calories: 60 | Protein: 2g | Carbohydrates: 13g | Fat: 1g | Saturated Fat: 0g | Cholesterol: 0mg | Sodium: 150mg | Fiber: 3g | PCF Ratio: 11-77-12 | Exchange Approx.: 2½ Vegetables

QUICK PUMPKIN COCONUT SOUP

YIELDS 6 CUPS; SERVING SIZE: 1 CUP

2 (15-ounce) cans pumpkin purée

1 (15-ounce) can low-sodium chicken or vegetable broth

1 teaspoon curry powder

½ teaspoon ground cumin

¼ teaspoon salt

½ cup light coconut milk

1. Add the pumpkin, broth, spices, and salt to a large pot and let simmer on medium-low heat for 10 minutes, stirring occasionally to produce a thick and smooth consistency.

2. Stir in the coconut milk and simmer for another 3–5 minutes until warmed through.

Nutritional Analysis (per serving): Calories: 45 | Protein: 1g | Carbohydrates: 9g | Fat: 1g | Saturated Fat: 1g | Cholesterol: 0mg | Sodium: 150mg | Fiber: 2g | PCF Ratio: 11-86-3 | Exchange Approx.: ½ Starch

LOW-CAL GARDEN SOUP

YIELDS 8 CUPS; SERVING SIZE: 1 CUP

1 teaspoon olive oil

¾ cup chopped white onion

1½ cups chopped celery

1½ cups chopped carrots

1½ cups chopped zucchini

1½ cups cut green beans

½ teaspoon garlic powder

1 teaspoon dried oregano

4 cups chicken or vegetable broth

1 (14-ounce) can stewed tomatoes

Chopped fresh basil (optional, to garnish)

1. Coat a large-sized pot with the olive oil and put in the onions, carrots, and celery; sauté on medium heat until just before tender, about 10 minutes.

2. Add the rest of the veggies, garlic powder, oregano, broth, and canned tomatoes and bring to a light boil. Reduce to low heat and simmer until the veggies are tender, about 10–15 minutes. Garnish with chopped basil if desired.

Nutritional Analysis (per serving): Calories: 60 | Protein: 2g | Carbohydrates: 12g | Fat: 1g | Saturated Fat: 0g | Cholesterol: 0mg | Sodium: 230mg | Fiber: 3g | PCF Ratio: 10-78-12 | Exchange Approx.: 2½ Vegetables

MUSHROOM SOUP

YIELDS 7 CUPS; SERVING SIZE: 1 CUP

9 cups chopped various mushrooms (such as cremini, button, portobello)

2 teaspoons olive oil, divided

¾ cup chopped white onion

¼ cup chopped green onion

4 cups low-sodium chicken or vegetable broth

1 teaspoon garlic powder

¼ cup chopped fresh basil

2 tablespoons white wine

½ cup fat-free half-and-half

1. Put 2 cups of mushrooms aside. Use 1 teaspoon of olive oil to coat a large pan. Add the onions and 7 cups of the mushrooms and sauté on medium heat for 7–10 minutes until they are soft and browned.

2. In a separate large pot, add the broth and the garlic powder and place on medium heat. Put the cooked mushrooms/onions in the pot of broth and simmer for 5 minutes. Turn off heat, add the fresh basil, and set aside to cool.

3. While the broth mixture is cooling, coat the large pan again with the remaining 1 teaspoon olive oil and add the last 2 cups of the mushrooms and sauté on medium heat for 5–7 minutes until mushrooms are soft and browned; set aside.

4. Carefully transfer the cooled mushroom and broth mixture from the pot to a food processor or blender. Depending on the size of your food processor or blender, you may need to purée a partial portion at a time.

5. Put the puréed mixture back in the pot, add the cooked mushrooms and white wine, and warm on low heat for a few minutes, stirring frequently to prevent the thick soup from spattering. Add the fat-free half-and-half and simmer for 3–5 minutes on low heat until uniformly heated.

Nutritional Analysis (per serving): Calories: 60 | Protein: 3g | Carbohydrates: 9g | Fat: 1g | Saturated Fat: 0g | Cholesterol: 0mg | Sodium: 90mg | Fiber: 1g | PCF Ratio: 21-63-16 | Exchange Approx.: 2½ Vegetables

TRIPLE TOMATO BISQUE

YIELDS 10 CUPS; SERVING SIZE: 1 CUP

1 teaspoon olive oil

⅔ cup chopped shallots

1⅓ cups diced fresh tomatoes

2 tablespoons sun-dried tomatoes

1 teaspoon dried oregano

1 teaspoon garlic powder

4 cups chicken or vegetable broth

1 (28-ounce) can crushed tomatoes

¼ cup chopped fresh basil

½ cup fat-free half-and-half

1. Add the olive oil to a large pot; put in the shallots, fresh tomatoes, sun-dried tomatoes, oregano, and garlic powder and sauté for a few minutes on medium heat until soft. Pour in the broth and canned tomatoes and simmer for 5–10 minutes.

2. Remove the tomato broth mixture from heat, let cool, and add the fresh basil. Carefully transfer the soup to a food processor or blender and purée until smooth. Depending on the size of your food processor or blender, you may need to purée a partial portion at a time.

3. Put the puréed mixture back in the saucepan and warm on low heat, stirring frequently (to prevent the thick soup from spattering.) Add the fat-free half-and-half and simmer for 5 minutes on low heat until warmed through.

Nutritional Analysis (per serving): Calories: 60 | Protein: 2g | Carbohydrates: 10g | Fat: 0g | Saturated Fat: 0g | Cholesterol: 0mg | Sodium: 190mg | Fiber: 2g | PCF Ratio: 17-75-8 | Exchange Approx.: 2 Vegetables

SUMMER VEGETABLE STEW

YIELDS 10 CUPS; SERVING SIZE: 1 CUP

1 teaspoon olive oil

1 cup chopped turkey or chicken sausage

1 or 2 cloves garlic, diced

1 cup chopped white onion

1 cup chopped or shredded carrots

1 cup chopped celery

1 cup chopped zucchini

1 cup chopped yellow squash

1 cup chopped green beans (fresh or frozen thawed)

1 cup chopped mushrooms

1 cup chopped broccoli florets

1 cup chopped red bell pepper

1 cup chopped canned artichokes (water-packed variety)

½ cup corn (fresh, canned, or frozen thawed)

1 (14-ounce) can crushed tomatoes

1 (14-ounce) can low-sodium chicken or vegetable broth

½ cup rinsed canned kidney beans

Chopped black olives (optional)

Chopped fresh basil (optional)

Grated Parmesan cheese (optional)

Customizing This Soup

Not a fan of one of the veggies in the recipe? Then double any of the existing or substitute 1–2 cups of another, such as cauliflower, eggplant, or spinach. If you want to keep this completely vegetarian, then replace the chicken/turkey sausage with veggie sausage or cubed tofu.

1. Coat a large pot with the olive oil and put in the chopped sausage, garlic, onions, carrots, and celery; sauté on medium heat until just before tender, about 7–10 minutes.

2. Add the rest of the veggies, canned tomatoes, broth, and beans and bring to a light boil. Reduce to low heat and simmer until the veggies are tender, about 7–10 minutes.

3. Garnish with olives, fresh basil, and Parmesan cheese.

Nutritional Analysis (per serving): Calories: 120 | Protein: 7g | Carbohydrates: 16g | Fat: 4g | Saturated Fat: 1g | Cholesterol: 20mg | Sodium: 290mg | Fiber: 6g | PCF Ratio: 21-57-22 | Exchange Approx.: ¼ Starch, 2 Vegetables, 1 Medium-Fat Meat

DOUBLE CORN TORTILLA SOUP

YIELDS 4 CUPS, 4 SERVINGS; SERVING SIZE: 1¾ CUPS WITH ¼ OF TORTILLA STRIP TOPPING

3 corn tortillas

1 (28-ounce) can crushed tomatoes

4 cups low-sodium chicken or vegetable broth

1½ teaspoons chili powder

½ teaspoon crushed garlic (or 1 clove garlic, chopped)

½ teaspoon ground cumin

1 teaspoon olive oil

1 cup corn (fresh, canned, or frozen thawed)

½ cup chopped white or yellow onion

2 cups shredded carrots

½ cup diced avocado (optional)

1 tablespoon chopped fresh cilantro (optional)

1 lime, cut into quarters (optional)

Light sour cream or nonfat plain yogurt (optional)

Making This Soup a Meal

This version is vegetarian, but cooked cubed or shredded chicken or even turkey breast can be added to make it heartier and to pump up the protein.

1. Preheat oven to 350°F. Thinly slice two of the corn tortillas into ¼"-thin strips and bake for about 10 minutes or until crispy. Set aside.

2. Put the canned tomatoes, broth, chili powder, garlic, and cumin in a large pot. Break the remaining tortilla into bits and add as well. Bring to a light boil, then simmer for a few minutes until the tortilla is tender. Remove from heat and let cool.

3. Coat a separate pan with the olive oil and add the corn, onion, and carrot. Sauté on medium heat until tender, about 5 minutes, and then set aside.

4. Carefully pour the cooled tomato broth mixture into a food processor or blender and purée until smooth. Depending on the size of your food processor or blender, you may need to purée a partial portion at a time.

5. Put the blended mixture back in the pot, toss in the cooked carrots/corn/onion mixture, and simmer for 5 minutes until uniformly heated.

6. Serve sprinkled with tortilla strips. Garnish with avocado, chopped cilantro, a lime wedge, and a spoonful of light sour cream or plain nonfat yogurt (if desired).

Nutritional Analysis (per serving): Calories: 200 | Protein: 6g | Carbohydrates: 39g | Fat: 2g | Saturated Fat: 0g | Cholesterol: 0mg | Sodium: 480mg | Fiber: 8g | PCF Ratio: 11-79-10 | Exchange Approx.: 2 Starches, 2 Vegetables

CURRIED CARROT SOUP

YIELDS 7 CUPS; SERVING SIZE 1 CUP

7 cups washed, peeled, and sliced carrots

1 teaspoon olive oil

½ cup chopped white onion

4 cups chicken or vegetable broth

2 teaspoons curry powder

½ cup light coconut milk

1. Put the carrots in a pot of water or steam them in a large microwave in a microwave- safe dish filled with 1" of water on high for about 8 minutes or until very tender. Drain the liquid after cooking.

2. Coat a medium-sized pot with the olive oil, add the onions, and sauté on high heat for a few minutes until just before browned. Add the cooked carrots to the pot and pour in the broth. Sprinkle in the curry powder and heat until just before boiling, about 5 minutes.

3. Remove from heat and let cool. Then carefully transfer the soup to a food processor or blender and purée until smooth. Depending on the size of your food processor or blender, you may need to purée one partial portion at a time.

4. Put the blended mixture back in the pot, add the coconut milk, and warm on low heat for about 5–7 minutes, stirring frequently to prevent the thick soup from spattering.

Nutritional Analysis (per serving): Calories: 80 | Protein: 1g | Carbohydrates: 16g | Fat: 2g | Saturated Fat: 1g | Cholesterol: 0mg | Sodium: 160mg | Fiber: 5g | PCF Ratio: 6-74-20 | Exchange Approx.: 3 Vegetables

EASY CORN SOUP

YIELDS 6 CUPS; SERVING SIZE: 1 CUP

1 teaspoon olive oil

4 cups sliced mushrooms

½ cup chopped green onion

1 teaspoon crushed garlic or 1 or 2 cloves chopped

¼ teaspoon ground ginger

2 (14-ounce) cans low-sodium cream-style corn

1 (14-ounce) can chicken or vegetable broth

1. Coat a medium-sized pot with the olive oil and add the mushrooms, green onion, garlic, and ginger. Sauté them until slightly soft, about 5–7 minutes.

2. Add creamed corn and broth and stir well. Simmer for 10 minutes until warmed through.

Nutritional Analysis (per serving): Calories: 90 | Protein: 2g | Carbohydrates: 19g | Fat: 1g | Saturated Fat: 0g | Cholesterol: 0mg | Sodium: 95mg | Fiber: 3g | PCF Ratio: 10-79-11 | Exchange Approx.: ¾ Starch, 1 Vegetable

RUSTIC VEGGIE SOUP

YIELDS 10 CUPS; SERVING SIZE: 2 CUPS

1 teaspoon olive oil

2 slices turkey bacon, diced

1 cup chopped onion

1 cup sliced carrots

1 cup chopped celery

1 cup quartered Brussels sprouts

2 cups chopped broccoli

2 cups chopped cremini mushrooms

1 cup chopped yellow squash

7 cups low-sodium vegetable or chicken broth

1. Coat a large pot with the olive oil and put in the turkey bacon, onions, carrots, and celery; sauté until just before tender, about 7–10 minutes.

2. Add in the rest of the veggies and broth and bring to a light boil. Reduce to low heat and simmer until the veggies are tender, about 15 minutes.

Nutritional Analysis (per serving): Calories: 110 | Protein: 5g | Carbohydrates: 16g | Fat: 2g | Saturated Fat: 0g | Cholesterol: 10mg | Sodium: 350mg | Fiber: 5g | PCF Ratio: 20-63-17 | Exchange Approx.: 3 Vegetables, ½ Lean Meat

CONDENSED CREAM OF MUSHROOM SOUP

YIELDS EQUIVALENT OF 1 (10.75-OUNCE) CAN

¾ cup finely chopped fresh mushrooms

½ cup water

⅛ cup Ener-G Pure Potato Flour

1 teaspoon chopped onion (optional)

1 tablespoon chopped celery (optional)

Potato Flour Substitute?

Instant mashed potatoes can replace potato flour; however, the amount needed will vary according to the brand of potatoes. Also, you'll need to consider other factors such as added fats and hydrogenated oils.

1. In a microwave-safe covered container, microwave mushrooms and water (and onion and celery if using) 2 minutes or until tender. (About ¾ cup chopped mushrooms will yield ½ cup steamed ones.) Reserve any resulting liquid; add enough water to equal 1 cup.

2. Place all ingredients in a blender; process. The thickness of soup concentrate will vary according to how much moisture remains in mushrooms. If necessary, add 1–2 tablespoons of water to achieve a paste. (Low-sodium canned mushrooms work in this recipe, but the nutritional analysis assumes fresh mushrooms are used. Adjust sodium content accordingly.)

Nutritional Analysis (per recipe): Calories: 92 | Protein: 3g | Carbohydrates: 21g | Fat: 1g | Saturated Fat: 0g | Cholesterol: 0mg | Sodium: 13mg | Fiber: 3g | PCF Ratio: 12-84-4 | Exchange Approx.: Will depend on serving size and preparation method

CONDENSED CREAM OF CHICKEN SOUP, MINOR'S BASE METHOD

YIELDS EQUIVALENT OF 1 (10.75-OUNCE) CAN

1 cup water

¾ teaspoon Minor's Low Sodium Chicken Base

¼ cup Ener-G Pure Potato Flour

Condensed Cream of Chicken Soup with Regular Chicken Broth

For the equivalent of 1 (10.75-ounce) can of condensed chicken soup, blend 1 cup reduced-fat canned chicken broth with ¼ cup Ener-G Pure Potato Flour. Will last refrigerated for 3 days. Nutritional Analysis: Calories: 181; Protein: 7.6g; Carbohydrates: 34g; Fat: 1.5g; Saturated Fat: 0.4g; Cholesterol: 0mg; Sodium: 785mg; Fiber: 2.4g; PCF Ratio: 17-76-7; Exchange Approx.: Will depend on serving size and preparation method.

Place all ingredients in blender; process until well blended.

Nutritional Analysis (per recipe): Calories: 158 | Protein: 4g | Carbohydrates: 35g | Fat: 1g | Saturated Fat: 0g | Cholesterol: 1mg | Sodium: 162mg | Fiber: 2g | PCF Ratio: 9-88-3 | Exchange Approx.: Will depend on serving size and preparation method

CONDENSED CREAM OF CELERY SOUP

YIELDS EQUIVALENT OF 1 (10.75-OUNCE) CAN

½ cup steamed chopped celery

½ cup water

⅛ cup Ener-G Pure Potato Flour

1. In a microwave-safe covered container, microwave celery in water for 2 minutes or until tender. Do not drain any resulting liquid. If necessary, add enough water to bring celery and liquid to 1 cup total.

2. Place all ingredients in blender; process. Use immediately or store in a covered container in refrigerator for use within 3 days. Thickness of concentrate will depend on how much moisture remains in celery; add 1–2 tablespoons of water if necessary to achieve a paste.

Nutritional Analysis (per recipe): Calories: 85 | Protein: 2g | Carbohydrates: 20g | Fat: 0g | Saturated Fat: 0g | Cholesterol: 0mg | Sodium: 79mg | Fiber: 2g | PCF Ratio: 9-89-2 | Exchange Approx.: Will depend on serving size and preparation method

CONDENSED CREAM OF POTATO SOUP

YIELDS EQUIVALENT OF 1 (10.75-OUNCE) CAN

½ cup peeled diced potatoes

½ cup water

1 tablespoon Ener-G Pure Potato Flour

Tip

The Nutritional Analysis for this recipe assumes you'll use the entire tablespoon of Ener-G Pure Potato Flour; however, the amount needed will depend on the amount of starch in the potatoes you use. For example, new potatoes will require more potato flour than larger, Idaho-style potatoes.

1. Place potatoes and water in covered microwave-safe bowl; microwave on high 4–5 minutes until potatoes are fork-tender.

2. Pour potatoes and water in blender, being careful of steam. Remove vent from blender lid; process until smooth. Add potato flour 1 teaspoon at a time while blender is running.

Nutritional Analysis (per recipe): Calories: 103 | Protein: 2g | Carbohydrates: 24g | Fat: 0g | Saturated Fat: 0g | Cholesterol: 0mg | Sodium: 9mg | Fiber: 2g | PCF Ratio: 8-91-1 | Exchange Approx.: Will depend on serving size and preparation method

CONDENSED TOMATO SOUP

YIELDS EQUIVALENT OF 1 (10.75-OUNCE) CAN

1 cup peeled chopped tomato, with juice

Additional tomato juices (if necessary)

¼ teaspoon baking soda

⅛ cup Ener-G Pure Potato Flour

Direct Preparation

If you'll be making the soup immediately after you prepare the condensed soup recipe, you can simply add your choice of the additional 1 cup of liquid (such as skim milk, soymilk, or water) to the blender and use that method to mix the milk and soup concentrate together. Pour the combined mixture into your pan or microwave-safe dish.

1. Place tomato in microwave-safe bowl; microwave on high 2–3 minutes until tomato is cooked. Add additional tomato juices if necessary to bring mixture back up to 1 cup.

2. Add baking soda; stir vigorously until bubbling stops.

3. Pour cooked tomato mixture into blender; add potato flour 1 tablespoon at a time, processing until well blended.

Nutritional Analysis (per serving): Calories: 136 | Protein: 4g | Carbohydrates: 31g | Fat: 1g | Saturated Fat: 0g | Cholesterol: 0mg | Sodium: 352mg | Fiber: 4g | PCF Ratio: 11-83-6 | Exchange Approx.: Will depend on serving size and preparation method

CONDENSED CHEESE SOUP

YIELDS EQUIVALENT OF 1 (10.75-OUNCE) CAN

½ cup water

⅛ cup Ener-G Pure Potato Flour

¼ cup nonfat cottage cheese

½ cup shredded American, Cheddar, or Colby cheese

Be Aware of Your Exchanges

When using any soup preparation method, you'll need to add the appropriate exchange approximations for each serving amount (usually ¼ of the total) of whatever condensed soup you make. For example, broth-based soups like chicken and cream of mushroom or celery would be a Free exchange; cream of potato soup would add 1 Carbohydrate/Starch.

Place water, potato flour, and cottage cheese in blender; process until well blended. Stir in shredded cheese. Cheese will melt as casserole is baked, prepared in microwave, or cooked on stovetop according to recipe instructions.

Nutritional Analysis (per recipe): Calories: 315 | Protein: 20g | Carbohydrates: 18g | Fat: 18g | Saturated Fat: 11g | Cholesterol: 56mg | Sodium: 384mg | Fiber: 1g | PCF Ratio: 26-23-51 | Exchange Approx.: Will depend on serving size and preparation method

SOUP PREPARATION METHOD

SERVES 4; SERVING SIZE: ¼ RECIPE

Any previous condensed soup recipe

1 cup skim milk

1. To use any of the homemade condensed soup recipes as soup, add condensed soup and 1 cup of skim milk (or soymilk or water) to a pan. Stir using a spoon or whisk to blend. Cook over medium heat for 10 minutes until mixture begins to simmer.

2. Season according to taste.

   Nutritional Analysis (per serving, with skim milk): Additional Calories: 21 | Protein: 2g | Carbohydrates: 3g | Fat: 0g | Saturated Fat: 0g | Cholesterol: 1mg | Sodium: 32mg | Fiber: 0g | PCF Ratio: 39-56-5 | Exchange Approx.: 1 Low-Fat Milk for entire pot of soup; divide accordingly per serving

EGGPLANT AND TOMATO STEW

SERVES 4; SERVING SIZE: ¼ RECIPE

2 eggplants, trimmed but left whole

2 teaspoons olive oil

1 medium-sized Spanish onion, chopped

1 teaspoon chopped garlic

2 cups cooked or canned chopped unsalted tomatoes, with liquid

1 teaspoon hot pepper sauce, to taste (optional)

Ketchup, to taste (optional)

Nonfat plain yogurt, to taste (optional)

Fresh parsley sprigs, to taste (optional)

1. Preheat oven to 400°F.

2. Roast eggplants on baking sheet until soft, about 45 minutes. Remove all meat from eggplants.

3. In large sauté pan, heat oil; sauté onions and garlic. Add eggplant and all other ingredients except yogurt and parsley. Remove from heat and transfer to food processor; pulse until it becomes creamy.

4. Serve at room temperature, garnished with a dollop of yogurt and parsley if desired.

   Nutritional Analysis (per serving): Calories: 135 | Protein: 4g | Carbohydrates: 26g | Fat: 3g | Saturated Fat: 1g | Cholesterol: 0mg | Sodium: 22mg | Fiber: 9g | PCF Ratio: 12-69-19 | Exchange Approx.: ½ Fat, 4 Vegetables

HEARTY BEEF STEW

SERVES 4; SERVING SIZE: ¼ RECIPE

1 tablespoon olive oil

12 ounces beef round, cut into 1" cubes

1 cup chopped onion

2 cups 1"-cubed potatoes

½ cup 1"-diced carrots

1 cup green beans

½ cup peeled and 1"-diced turnip

1 tablespoon chopped fresh parsley

¼ teaspoon Tabasco

1 cup Low Sodium V8 juice

¼ teaspoon salt

1 tablespoon all-purpose flour (optional)

¼ cup water (optional)

Slow-Cook Method for Beef Stew

If you don't have a pressure cooker, you can make this recipe in a slow cooker. First, heat olive oil in skillet. Dredge meat in 1–2 tablespoons flour; add to skillet and brown. Transfer to slow cooker; add onions, V8, potatoes, carrots, green beans, turnip, salt, parsley, and Tabasco. Cook on low 4–6 hours.

1. Heat olive oil in pressure cooker and brown meat. Add onions, potatoes, carrots, green beans, turnip, parsley, Tabasco, V8 juice, and salt.

2. Close cover securely; place pressure regulator on vent pipe and cook 10–12 minutes with pressure regulator rocking slowly. (Or follow manufacturer instructions for your pressure cooker). Cool down pressure cooker at once (nonelectric pressure cookers).

3. If desired, make paste of 1 tablespoon flour and ¼ cup water; stir into stew to thicken. Heat and stir liquid until thickened.

Nutritional Analysis (per serving): Calories: 326 | Protein: 26g | Carbohydrates: 32g | Fat: 10g | Saturated Fat: 3g | Cholesterol: 88mg | Sodium: 335mg | Fiber: 4g | PCF Ratio: 32-39-28 | Exchange Approx.: 3 Lean Meats, 1 Starch, 3 Vegetables

MOROCCAN STEW

YIELDS 7 CUPS; SERVING SIZE: 1 CUP

1½ teaspoons curry powder

1½ teaspoons ground cumin

1½ teaspoons ground cinnamon

¼ teaspoon garlic powder

¼ teaspoon ground turmeric

1 (28-ounce) can crushed tomatoes

1 teaspoon olive oil

¼ cup chopped white onion

2 cups sliced carrots

2 cups sliced zucchini

2 cups peeled and ½"-cubed eggplant

1 (14-ounce) can chickpeas, rinsed well

1. Combine the spices and canned tomatoes and set aside.

2. Coat a large pot with the olive oil and put in the onions and carrots; sauté until just before tender, about 5–10 minutes.

3. Add the zucchini, eggplant, canned tomatoes/spice mixture, and chickpeas and bring to a light boil. Reduce to low heat and simmer until the veggies are tender, about 12–15 minutes.

Nutritional Analysis (per serving): Calories: 140 | Protein: 6g | Carbohydrates: 26g | Fat: 2g | Saturated Fat: 0g | Cholesterol: 0mg | Sodium: 380mg | Fiber: 4g | PCF Ratio: 17-72-11 | Exchange Approx.: 1 Starch, 2 Vegetables, ¼ Lean Meat

SAVORY FISH STEW

SERVES 6; SERVING SIZE: ⅙ RECIPE

1 tablespoon olive oil

1 onion, finely chopped

½ cup dry white wine

3 large tomatoes, chopped

2 cups low-sodium chicken broth

8 ounces clam juice

3 cups fresh spinach

1 pound halibut fillets, cut into 1" pieces

White pepper to taste

1 tablespoon chopped fresh cilantro

1. Place a large pan over medium heat. Add oil to the pan and sauté onions for 2–3 minutes. Add wine to deglaze the pan. Scrape the pan to loosen small bits of onion.

2. Add tomatoes and cook for 3–4 minutes, then add broth and clam juice to the pan. Stir in spinach and allow to wilt while continuing to stir.

3. Season fish with pepper. Place fish in the pan and cook for 5–6 minutes until opaque. Mix in cilantro before serving.

Nutritional Analysis (per serving): Calories: 230 | Protein: 14g | Carbohydrates: 11g | Fat: 14g | Saturated Fat: 2.5g | Cholesterol: 35mg | Sodium: 290mg | Fiber: 2g | PCF Ratio: 25-20-55 | Exchange Approx.: 1½ Vegetable, 2 Medium Fat Meat, 1 Fat

CHAPTER 5

SALADS AND SALAD DRESSINGS

MINTED LENTIL AND TOMATO SALAD

SERVES 6; SERVING SIZE: ⅙ RECIPE

1 cup dry lentils

2 cups water

½ cup chopped onion

2 teaspoons minced garlic

¼ cup chopped celery

½ cup chopped green pepper

½ cup finely chopped parsley

2 tablespoons finely chopped fresh mint or
  2 teaspoons dried

¼ cup lemon juice

¼ cup olive oil

½ teaspoon salt

1 cup diced fresh tomato

1. Place lentils and water in medium-sized saucepan; bring to a quick boil. Reduce heat; cover and cook on low 15–20 minutes or until tender. Drain and transfer to medium bowl.

2. Add onion, garlic, celery, green pepper, parsley, and mint; mix well.

3. In small bowl, whisk together lemon juice, olive oil, and salt. Pour into lentils; mix well. Cover and refrigerate several hours.

4. Before serving, mix in diced tomatoes.

Nutritional Analysis: Calories: 136 | Protein: 4g | Carbohydrates: 11g | Fat: 9g | Saturated Fat: 1g | Cholesterol: 0mg | Sodium: 211mg | Fiber: 4g | PCF Ratio: 10-31-59 | Exchange Approx.: ½ Starch, 1 Vegetable, ½ Lean Meat, 2 Fats

MARINATED ROASTED PEPPERS AND EGGPLANT

SERVES 4; SERVING SIZE: ¼ RECIPE

1 large eggplant, sliced into ¼"-thick rounds

4 tablespoons olive oil, divided

1 pound sweet red peppers, roasted

1 tablespoon balsamic vinegar

1 tablespoon finely chopped onion

1 teaspoon oregano

Freshly ground pepper

Variations

You can use zucchini or yellow squash in place of eggplant. Other herb choices for the marinade include basil, thyme, or savory. Use marinated vegetables on top of tossed salads or grilled London broil.

1. Brush eggplant slices with 2 tablespoons olive oil; place on grill. Grill on both sides for about 5 minutes each until softened. Remove from grill and place in container. Add roasted peppers to container.

2. Prepare marinade by whisking together balsamic vinegar, remaining 2 tablespoons olive oil, chopped onion, oregano, and pepper; pour over vegetables. Cover and refrigerate.

Nutritional Analysis (per serving): Calories: 179 | Protein: 2g | Carbohydrates: 14g | Fat: 14g | Saturated Fat: 2g | Cholesterol: 0mg | Sodium: 5mg | Fiber: 6g | PCF Ratio: 5-29-66 | Exchange Approx.: 3 Vegetables, 3 Fats

SPINACH SALAD WITH POMEGRANATE

SERVES 6; SERVING SIZE: ⅙ RECIPE

1 pound fresh spinach, washed, drained, and loosely chopped

½ cup very thinly sliced red onion

8 ounces fresh tomatoes, cut into ½" wedges

⅓ cup chopped walnuts

½ teaspoon salt

¼ cup lemon juice

1½ tablespoons olive oil

¼ cup pomegranate seeds

For a Different Twist: Toasted Almond Seasoning

Add an extra flavor dimension to salads, rice dishes, or vegetables by sprinkling toasted almonds over the top. Toast ½ cup chopped raw almonds in a nonstick skillet over low heat, stirring frequently until they are a light brown color. Store the cooled almonds in an airtight container in a cool, dry place. This low-sodium substitute has only 16 calories per teaspoon, has a PCF ratio of 14-12-74, and counts as a ½ Fat exchange approximation.

1. Add spinach, onions, tomato, and walnuts to a large bowl; toss lightly.

2. In small bowl, whisk together salt, lemon juice, and olive oil. Drizzle over salad; toss lightly.

3. Garnish salad with pomegranate seeds.

Nutritional Analysis (per serving): Calories: 107 | Protein: 4g | Carbohydrates: 8g | Fat: 8g | Saturated Fat: 1g | Cholesterol: 0mg | Sodium: 259mg | Fiber: 3g | PCF Ratio: 13-26-61 | Exchange Approx.: 1 Vegetable, 2 Fats

WARM CARROT AND RAISIN SALAD

YIELDS 2½ CUPS; SERVING SIZE: ½ CUP

2 tablespoons fresh orange juice

1 teaspoon honey

⅛ teaspoon ground cinnamon

1 teaspoon olive oil

2½ cups shredded or matchstick carrots

2 tablespoons currants or raisins

1. In a small bowl, mix the orange juice, honey, and cinnamon.

2. Coat a small or medium pan with the olive oil, add the carrots, and sauté 3–5 minutes until lightly browned.

3. Pour the orange juice mixture over the carrots. Add the currants or raisins and cook for another few minutes until warmed through.

Nutritional Analysis (per serving): Calories: 50 | Protein: 1g | Carbohydrates: 10g | Fat: 1g | Saturated Fat: 0g | Cholesterol: 0mg | Sodium: 40mg | Fiber: 2g | PCF Ratio: 5-77-18 | Exchange Approx.: ¼ Fruit, 1 Vegetable

CURRY CHICKEN SALAD

YIELDS 3½ CUPS; SERVING SIZE: ½ CUP

2 cups cooked chicken

¾ cup chopped celery

½ cup sliced apples

2 tablespoons golden raisins

2 tablespoons chopped cashews

½ cup nonfat Greek yogurt

¼ cup light mayonnaise

½ teaspoon rice vinegar

¾ teaspoon curry powder

1. Put the chicken, celery, apples, raisins, and cashews in a medium bowl.

2. In a smaller bowl, combine the yogurt, mayonnaise, vinegar, and curry powder and pour over the chicken mixture. Mix well. Serve chilled.

Nutritional Analysis (per serving): Calories: 130 | Protein: 14g | Carbohydrates: 7g | Fat: 4.5g | Saturated Fat: 1g | Cholesterol: 35mg | Sodium: 135mg | Fiber: 1g | PCF Ratio: 49-14-37 | Exchange Approx.: ¼ Fruit, 1½ Lean Meats, ½ Fat

TOMATO AND CUCUMBER SALAD WITH MINT

SERVES 6; SERVING SIZE: ⅙ RECIPE

2 cucumbers, peeled and cut into ½"-wide pieces

⅓ cup red wine vinegar

1 teaspoon sugar

½ teaspoon salt

2 cups chopped tomatoes

⅔ cup chopped red onion

¼ cup chopped fresh mint

2 tablespoons olive oil

1. Place cucumbers in medium bowl. Add vinegar, sugar, and salt; stir. Let stand at room temperature for 15 minutes.

2. Add tomatoes, red onion, mint, and olive oil; toss lightly to blend.

Nutritional Analysis (per serving): Calories: 68 | Protein: 1g | Carbohydrates: 7g | Fat: 5g | Saturated Fat: 1g | Cholesterol: 0mg | Sodium: 202mg | Fiber: 1g | PCF Ratio: 5-32-63 | Exchange Approx.: 1 Vegetable, 1 Fat

TABBOULEH

SERVES 6; SERVING SIZE: ⅙ RECIPE

1 cup boiling water

½ cup bulgur wheat

1 cup packed and finely chopped fresh parsley

⅓ cup finely chopped fresh mint

½ cup finely chopped red onion

1 cup chopped cucumber

¼ cup lemon juice

¼ cup olive oil

½ teaspoon salt

Freshly ground pepper to taste

1 cup chopped fresh tomato

2 cups leaf lettuce (optional)

Parsley . . . Not Just a Garnish

Parsley is a key ingredient in tabbouleh and many other Middle Eastern dishes. Parsley is low in calories and packed with vitamin C, iron, and other trace minerals. Add it liberally to all salads.

1. In small bowl, pour boiling water over bulgur wheat; let stand 20 minutes.

2. When bulgur is softened, drain and squeeze out any excess water using a colander lined with cheesecloth.

3. Combine parsley, mint, onion, cucumber, and bulgur wheat. Add lemon juice, olive oil, salt, and ground pepper; mix well.

4. Cover and refrigerate at least 3 hours.

5. Just before serving, add chopped tomatoes; toss lightly. Serve as is or on bed of leaf lettuce.

Nutritional Analysis (per serving): Calories: 144 | Protein: 3g | Carbohydrates: 15g | Fat: 9g | Saturated Fat: 1g | Cholesterol: 0mg | Sodium: 212mg | Fiber: 4g | PCF Ratio: 7-38-55 | Exchange Approx.: ½ Starch, 1 Vegetable, 2 Fats

TOMATOES STUFFED WITH QUINOA SALAD

SERVES 6; SERVING SIZE: 1 TOMATO

½ cup quinoa

1 cup water

6 large (3 pounds) tomatoes

1½ cups peeled and finely diced cucumber

⅓ cup chopped fresh parsley

¼ cup chopped fresh mint

½ cup finely chopped red onion

3 tablespoons crumbled feta cheese

2 tablespoons lemon juice

3 tablespoons olive oil

1. Rinse quinoa in fine mesh strainer before cooking. To cook: place quinoa and water in small saucepan; bring to a boil. Reduce heat; cover and cook until all water is absorbed, about 15 minutes. Cool.

2. Prepare tomatoes: remove caps and hollow out, leaving shell about ½" thick.

3. In mixing bowl, combine quinoa, cucumbers, parsley, mint, red onion, and feta cheese.

4. Mix lemon juice and olive oil together; pour over quinoa and vegetables.

5. Stuff tomatoes with mixture and serve.

Nutritional Analysis (per serving): Calories: 180 | Protein: 5g | Carbohydrates: 24g | Fat: 9g | Saturated Fat: 2g | Cholesterol: 4mg | Sodium: 78mg | Fiber: 4g | PCF Ratio: 11-49-40 | Exchange Approx.: ½ Starch, 2½ Vegetables, 2½ Fats

CUCUMBERS WITH MINTED YOGURT

SERVES 8; SERVING SIZE: ⅛ RECIPE

1 cup nonfat plain yogurt

1 clove garlic, finely chopped

¼ teaspoon ground cumin

1 teaspoon lemon zest

½ cup chopped fresh mint

1 tablespoon lemon juice

¼ teaspoon salt

4 cups peeled, seeded, and chopped cucumbers

1. Combine yogurt, garlic, cumin, lemon zest, mint, lemon juice, and salt in blender or food processor; blend until smooth.

2. Add yogurt mixture to cucumbers; mix. Chill before serving.

Nutritional Analysis (per serving): Calories: 31 | Protein: 2g | Carbohydrates: 4g | Fat: 1g | Saturated Fat: 0g | Cholesterol: 2mg | Sodium: 52mg | Fiber: 1g | PCF Ratio: 27-56-17 | Exchange Approx.: 1 Vegetable

WILTED LETTUCE WITH A HEALTHIER DIFFERENCE

SERVES 1

Nonstick spray

½ teaspoon olive oil

¼ cup chopped red onion

1½ cups tightly packed loose-leaf lettuce

¼ teaspoon lemon juice or your choice of vinegar

½ teaspoon extra-virgin olive oil, walnut oil, or almond oil

Dried herbs of your choice, such as thyme or parsley, to taste (optional)

Pinch of sugar, to taste (optional)

Pinch of toasted sesame seeds or grated Parmesan cheese, to taste (optional)

Adventuresome Additions

Dried cranberries or other dried fruit are delicious in wilted lettuce dishes; the addition of diced apples or pineapple makes a perfect wilted greens accompaniment for pork.

1. In heated nonstick skillet treated with nonstick spray, add ½ teaspoon of olive oil and the red onion. Sauté until onion is almost transparent; add greens. Sauté greens until warmed and wilted.

2. In salad bowl, whisk lemon juice with ½ teaspoon extra-virgin olive oil. Add pinch of herbs and sugar if using; whisk into oil mixture. Add wilted greens; toss with dressing. Top salad with pinch of toasted sesame seeds or Parmesan cheese if desired. Serve immediately.

Nutritional Analysis (per serving): Calories: 71 | Protein: 2g | Carbohydrates: 7g | Fat: 5g | Saturated Fat: 1g | Cholesterol: 0mg | Sodium: 9mg | Fiber: 2g | PCF Ratio: 8-34-57 | Exchange Approx.: 2 Free Vegetables, 1 Fat

GREEN BEAN AND MUSHROOM SALAD

SERVES 4; SERVING SIZE: ¼ RECIPE

2 cups fresh small green beans, ends trimmed

1½ cups sliced fresh mushrooms

½ cup chopped red onion

3 tablespoons extra-virgin olive, canola, or corn oil

1 tablespoon balsamic or red wine vinegar

1 clove garlic, minced

½ teaspoon sea salt (optional)

¼ teaspoon freshly ground pepper (optional)

1. Cook green beans in large pot of unsalted boiling water for 5 minutes. Drain in colander; immediately plunge into bowl of ice water to stop cooking process and retain bright green color of the beans.

2. Once beans are cool, drain and place in large bowl. If you'll be serving salad immediately, add mushrooms and onions to bowl; toss to mix. (Otherwise, chill beans separately and add to salad immediately before serving.)

3. To make dressing, combine oil and vinegar in small bowl. Whisk together with garlic; pour over salad. Toss lightly; season with salt and pepper if desired. Serve immediately.

Nutritional Analysis (per serving): Calories: 131 | Protein: 2g | Carbohydrates: 9g | Fat: 10g | Saturated Fat: 1g | Cholesterol: 0mg | Sodium: 4mg | Fiber: 3g | PCF Ratio: 7-26-67 | Exchange Approx.: 2 Fats, 2 Vegetables

MANDARIN SNAP PEA SALAD

SERVES 8; SERVING SIZE: 1/8 RECIPE

3/4 pound snap peas, cut into 1/2" pieces

1 cup canned, drained mandarin oranges

1 1/2 cups canned, rinsed, and drained kidney beans

1 cup thinly sliced red onion

1/2 cup chopped fresh parsley

2 cups chopped cabbage

1/3 cup Poppy Seed Dressing

Poppy Seed Dressing

1/2 cup red wine vinegar

1/4 cup orange juice

3 tablespoons lemon juice

1/2 cup canola oil

1 teaspoon Splenda Brown Sugar Blend

1 teaspoon dry mustard

1 teaspoon salt

1 tablespoon poppy seeds

1. In medium bowl, combine snap peas, mandarin oranges, kidney beans, onions, parsley, and cabbage.

2. To make dressing, combine all dressing ingredients in covered jar; shake to mix. Store in refrigerator.

3. Mix in Poppy Seed Dressing; refrigerate several hours before serving.

Nutritional Analysis (per serving, without dressing): Calories: 76 | Protein: 4g | Carbohydrates: 16g | Fat: 0g | Saturated Fat: 0g | Cholesterol: 0mg | Sodium: 344mg | Fiber: 4g | PCF Ratio: 19-78-3 | Exchange Approx.: 1/2 Starch, 1 Vegetable, 1/2 Lean Meat, 1/2 Fat

Nutritional Analysis (per 1-ounce (1 1/2 tablespoons) serving): Calories: 68g | Protein: 0g | Carbohydrates: 9g | Fat: 7g | Saturated Fat: 1g | Cholesterol: 0mg | Sodium: 148mg | Fiber: 0g | PCF Ratio: 1-9-90 | Exchange Approx.: 1 1/2 Fats

BROCCOLI-CAULIFLOWER SLAW

SERVES 8; SERVING SIZE: ⅛ RECIPE

4 cups raw broccoli florets

4 cups raw cauliflower florets

½ cup real mayonnaise

1 cup cottage cheese, 1% fat

3 tablespoons tarragon vinegar

1 tablespoon balsamic vinegar

⅛ cup packed brown sugar

3 tablespoons sliced red onion

Tip

Substituting cottage cheese for some mayonnaise cuts fat and calories considerably. Cut them even more by using nonfat cottage cheese and nonfat mayonnaise.

1. Put broccoli and cauliflower in food processor; pulse-process to consistency of shredded cabbage. Pour into a bowl.

2. Place remaining ingredients in food processor; process until smooth. Pour resulting dressing over broccoli-cauliflower mixture; stir. Chill until ready to serve.

Nutritional Analysis (per serving): Calories: 117 | Protein: 6g | Carbohydrates: 13g | Fat: 5g | Saturated Fat: 1g | Cholesterol: 0mg | Sodium: 46mg | Fiber: 1g | PCF Ratio: 19-42-39 | Exchange Approx.: 1 Misc. Carbohydrate, 1 Fat

ZESTY FETA AND OLIVE SALAD

SERVES 4; SERVING SIZE: ¼ RECIPE

2 ounces crumbled feta cheese

1 small red onion, diced

½ cup chopped celery

½ cup diced cucumber

1 clove garlic, minced

1 teaspoon lemon zest

1 teaspoon orange zest

1 cup halved very small cherry tomatoes

½ cup mix of pitted and sliced green and kalamata olives

1 tablespoon extra-virgin olive oil

2 tablespoons minced fresh Italian parsley

2 teaspoons minced fresh oregano

1 teaspoon minced fresh mint

1 tablespoon minced fresh cilantro (optional)

Large romaine or butter lettuce leaves

Freshly ground black pepper

1. In a large bowl, place feta, onion, celery, cucumber, garlic, lemon zest, orange zest, tomatoes, and olives; mix.

2. Add olive oil and fresh herbs; toss again.

3. Arrange lettuce leaves on four salad plates; spoon feta salad on top. Top with pepper and serve.

Nutritional Analysis (per serving): Calories: 109 | Protein: 3g | Carbohydrates: 6g | Fat: 8g | Saturated Fat: 3g | Cholesterol: 132mg | Sodium: 326mg | Fiber: 2g | PCF Ratio: 11-22-66 | Exchange Approx.: 1 Vegetable, 2 Fats

AVOCADO AND PEACH SALAD

SERVES 4; SERVING SIZE: ¼ RECIPE

⅛ cup water

⅛ cup frozen orange juice concentrate

1 clove garlic, crushed

1 teaspoon rice wine vinegar

1 tablespoon extra-virgin olive oil

½ teaspoon vanilla extract

1½ cups tightly packed baby arugula

2 tablespoons tarragon leaves

1 avocado, peeled, pitted, and diced

1 peach, peeled, pitted, and diced

½ cup thinly sliced Vidalia onion

Kosher or sea salt and freshly ground black
    pepper to taste (optional)

Experiment Sensibly

When it comes to new herbs and spices,
err on the side of caution. Not sure
whether or not you like a seasoning? Mix
all other ingredients together and test a
bite of salad with pinch of herb or spice
before adding it to entire recipe.

1. In measuring cup, whisk water, orange juice concentrate, garlic, vinegar, oil, and vanilla together until well mixed.

2. Prepare salad by arranging layers of arugula and tarragon; then add avocado, peach, and onions and drizzle with prepared orange juice vinaigrette. Season with salt and pepper if desired and serve.

Nutritional Analysis (per serving, without salt): Calories: 160 | Protein: 2g | Carbohydrates: 15g | Fat: 11g | Saturated Fat: 2g | Cholesterol: 0mg | Sodium: 11mg | Fiber: 4g | PCF Ratio: 6-35-59 | Exchange Approx.: 3 Fats, 1 Free Vegetable, ½ Fruit

ORANGE-AVOCADO SLAW

SERVES 10; SERVING SIZE: 1/10 RECIPE

¼ cup orange juice

½ teaspoon curry powder

⅛ teaspoon ground cumin

¼ teaspoon sugar

1 teaspoon white wine vinegar

1 tablespoon olive oil

1 avocado, peeled, pitted, and chopped

5 cups broccoli slaw mix

Sea salt and freshly ground black pepper to taste (optional)

1. In bowl, whisk together orange juice, curry powder, cumin, sugar, and vinegar. Add oil in stream, whisking until emulsified.

2. In large bowl, toss avocado with slaw mix; drizzle with vinaigrette. Chill until ready to serve. Season with salt and pepper if desired.

Nutritional Analysis (per serving, without salt): Calories: 60 | Protein: 2g | Carbohydrates: 5g | Fat: 5g | Saturated Fat: 1g | Cholesterol: 0mg | Sodium: 14mg | Fiber: 2g | PCF Ratio: 11-27-62 | Exchange Approx.: 1 Fat, ½ Free Vegetable

TACO SALAD

SERVES 8; SERVING SIZE: 1/8 RECIPE

1 recipe Vegetable and Bean Chili (see recipe in Chapter 4)

8 cups tightly packed salad greens

2 cups shredded Cheddar cheese

8 ounces nonfat corn chips

Nonstarchy Free-exchange vegetables of your choice, such as chopped celery, onion, or banana or jalapeño peppers (optional)

1. Prepare Vegetable and Bean Chili.

2. Divide salad greens between eight large bowls. Top with chili, Cheddar cheese, corn chips, and vegetables or peppers if using.

Nutritional Analysis (per serving): Calories: 426 | Protein: 23g | Carbohydrates: 58g | Fat: 13g | Saturated Fat: 7g | Cholesterol: 30mg | Sodium: 380mg | Fiber: 13g | PCF Ratio: 21-53-26 | Exchange Approx.: 1 Lean Meat, 1 High-Fat Meat, 3 Starches, 2 Vegetables

HONEY DIJON TUNA SALAD

SERVES 1

¼ cup canned drained tuna

½ cup diced celery

¼ cup diced onion

¼ cup seeded and diced red or green pepper

4 ounces (½ small container) nonfat plain yogurt

1 teaspoon Dijon mustard

1 teaspoon lemon juice

¼ teaspoon honey

1 tablespoon raisins

1 cup tightly packed iceberg lettuce or other salad greens

1. Use fork to flake tuna into bowl. Add all other ingredients except lettuce; mix well. Serve on lettuce or greens.

2. Alternate serving suggestion: Mix with ½ cup chilled, cooked pasta before dressing salad greens. Adds 1 Starch exchange choice.

Nutritional Analysis (per serving): Calories: 194 | Protein: 22g | Carbohydrates: 24g | Fat: 1g | Saturated Fat: 0g | Cholesterol: 0mg | Sodium: 575mg | Fiber: 4g | PCF Ratio: 45-49-6 | Exchange Approx.: 1 Lean Meat, 2 Vegetables, ½ Fruit, ½ Skim Milk

SPINACH SALAD WITH APPLE-AVOCADO DRESSING

¼ cup unsweetened apple juice

1 teaspoon (or up to 1 tablespoon) cider vinegar

1 clove garlic, minced

1 teaspoon Bragg Liquid Aminos or soy sauce

½ teaspoon Homemade Worcestershire Sauce (see recipe in Chapter 6)

2 teaspoons olive oil

1 avocado, peeled, seeded, and chopped

2½ cups tightly packed spinach and other salad greens

½ cup thinly sliced red onion

½ cup sliced radishes

½ cup bean sprouts

Salads Don't Have to Be Fat-Free

Unless on a calorie-restricted diet, fat-free may not be the best choice—consult your dietitian. Studies show women who consume up to 41.7 grams of vegetable fat a day have up to 22 percent less chance of developing type 2 diabetes. Vegetable oils—combined with a diet rich in fish, fruits, vegetables, whole grains, and nuts—are much healthier than using chemically created fat-free foods and are believed to prevent certain cancers, too.

1. In blender or food processor, combine juice, vinegar (the amount of which will depend on how you like your dressing), garlic, Liquid Aminos, Worcestershire, oil, and avocado; process until smooth.

2. In large bowl, toss greens, onions, radishes, and bean sprouts. Pour dressing over salad; toss again.

Nutritional Analysis (per serving): Calories: 122 | Protein: 2g | Carbohydrates: 8g | Fat: 10g | Saturated Fat: 1g | Cholesterol: 0mg | Sodium: 90mg | Fiber: 3g | PCF Ratio: 7-25-68 | Exchange Approx.: 2½ Fats, 1 Free Vegetable

GREEK PASTA SALAD

SERVES 4; SERVING SIZE: ¼ RECIPE

1 tablespoon lemon juice

3 tablespoons olive oil

1 teaspoon dried oregano

1 teaspoon Dijon mustard

1 clove garlic, minced

2 cups cooked pasta

1 cup slivered blanched almonds

1 cup sliced cucumber

1 cup diced fresh tomato

½ cup chopped red onion

½ cup Greek olives

2 ounces crumbled feta cheese

1½ cups romaine lettuce leaves

Sweet and Savory Side Salad

For one serving of easy, versatile salad or simple dressing over salad greens, mix ¾ cup shredded carrots, ¼ cup diced celery, 1 tablespoon raisins, and 1 teaspoon frozen pineapple juice concentrate.

Nutritional Analysis: Calories: 31; Protein: 0.5g; Carbohydrates: 7.6g; Fat: 0.1g; Saturated Fat: 0.01g; Cholesterol: 0mg; Sodium: 15mg; Fiber: 1g; PCF Ratio: 6-92-2; Exchange Approx.: ½ Fruit, 1 Free Vegetable, 1 Vegetable.

1. In large salad bowl, whisk lemon juice with olive oil, oregano, mustard, and garlic. Cover and refrigerate 1 hour or up to 12 hours.

2. Immediately before serving, toss pasta with almonds, cucumbers, tomatoes, onions, olives, and feta cheese. Serve over lettuce, top with dressing, and toss to combine.

Nutritional Analysis (per serving): Calories: 420 | Protein: 12g | Carbohydrates: 31g | Fat: 29g | Saturated Fat: 5g | Cholesterol: 13mg | Sodium: 312mg | Fiber: 6g | PCF Ratio: 11-28-61 | Exchange Approx.: 1 Medium-Fat Meat, 1 Meat Substitute, 1 Free Vegetable, 1½ Starches, 4 Fats

GOLDEN RAISIN SMOKED TURKEY SALAD

**YIELDS 4 GENEROUS-SIZED SALADS;
SERVING SIZE: 1 SALAD**

4 cups chopped broccoli

2 cups chopped cauliflower

3 shallots, chopped

1⅓ cups golden raisins

1 cup 1% cottage cheese

¼ cup real mayonnaise

¼ cup firm silken tofu

3 tablespoons tarragon vinegar

1 tablespoon balsamic vinegar

¼ cup brown sugar

¼ pound (4 ounces) chopped smoked
    turkey breast

Freshly ground pepper (optional)

4 cups salad greens

Tip

Because of the smoked turkey, this salad is high in sodium. If you're on a sodium-restricted diet, substitute regular cooked turkey or chicken breast. Punch up the flavor by adding 1 teaspoon Bragg Liquid Aminos or Homemade Worcestershire Sauce (see recipe in Chapter 6).

1. Combine broccoli, cauliflower, and shallots in large bowl; stir in raisins.

2. In blender or food processor, mix together cottage cheese, mayonnaise, tofu, vinegars, and brown sugar until smooth.

3. Add turkey to broccoli mixture; add dressing and toss. Season with freshly ground pepper to taste. Chill until ready to serve over salad greens.

Nutritional Analysis (per serving): Calories: 355 | Protein: 21g | Carbohydrates: 62g | Fat: 8g | Saturated Fat: 2g | Cholesterol: 19mg | Sodium: 723mg | Fiber: 4g | PCF Ratio: 21-61-18 | Exchange Approx.: 1 Very Lean Meat, 1 Lean Meat, 1½ Vegetables, 3 Fats, 1 Fruit, 1 Misc. Carbohydrate

RAINBOW POTATO SALAD

SERVES 6; SERVING SIZE: ⅙ RECIPE

2 pounds (6 medium) red potatoes, washed and scrubbed

⅓ cup finely chopped carrots

¼ cup finely chopped onion

¼ cup finely chopped green pepper

¼ cup finely chopped yellow or red bell pepper

2 tablespoons red wine vinegar

2 tablespoons lemon juice

¼ teaspoon celery seed

1 teaspoon sugar

½ teaspoon salt

2 tablespoons light mayonnaise

1. Place whole potatoes in pot and cover with water. Boil over medium heat for about 20 minutes until potatoes are cooked. Drain; set aside to cool.

2. Combine carrots, onion, peppers, vinegar, lemon juice, celery seed, sugar, and salt in small bowl; mix. Cover and refrigerate for 2–3 hours.

3. After vegetables have marinated, add light mayonnaise; mix well.

4. Cut potatoes (with skins on) into ½" cubes.

5. In large bowl, combine potatoes and vegetables; mix well.

Nutritional Analysis (per serving): Calories: 146 | Protein: 5g | Carbohydrates: 29g | Fat: 2g | Saturated Fat: 0g | Cholesterol: 0mg | Sodium: 615mg | Fiber: 5g | PCF Ratio: 12-77-11 | Exchange Approx.: 1½ Starches

POTATO AND SNOW PEA SALAD

SERVES 8; SERVING SIZE: ⅛ RECIPE

2 pounds (6 medium) red potatoes, washed and scrubbed

3 slices bacon, cut into ½" pieces

½ cup chopped onion

¾ pound snow peas, cut into ½" pieces

½ teaspoon salt

¼ cup apple cider vinegar

1. Place whole potatoes in pot; cover with water. Boil over medium heat for 20 minutes until potatoes are cooked. Drain and chill. Once chilled, cut into ½" cubes.

2. Place bacon in nonstick frying pan with onions; fry for 3–4 minutes until crisp. There should be a light coating of fat in pan from bacon. If there is excess fat, pour off before going to step 3.

3. Add snow peas; toss with bacon and onion mixture for 2 minutes. Remove from heat.

4. Dissolve salt into cider vinegar; mix into snow pea mixture.

5. In large bowl, combine potatoes and snow peas; mix well.

Nutritional Analysis (per serving): Calories: 139 | Protein: 5g | Carbohydrates: 28g | Fat: 1g | Saturated Fat: 0g | Cholesterol: 3mg | Sodium: 223mg | Fiber: 3g | PCF Ratio: 13-78-9 | Exchange Approx.: 1 Starch, 1 Vegetable, ½ Fat

SUMMER SALAD

SERVES 6; SERVING SIZE: ⅙ RECIPE

2 cups snap peas, cut into 1" pieces

2 cups ½"-cubed summer squash

½ cup chopped carrots

3 tablespoons minced mushrooms

2 cups chopped cucumbers

¼ cup thinly sliced onion

2 tablespoons canola oil

2 tablespoons balsamic vinegar

¼ teaspoon salt

¼ teaspoon dried thyme

¼ teaspoon dried marjoram

Tip

Add the oil-and-vinegar dressing just before serving. Minimize the exposure of vinegar to certain vegetables such as snap peas and green beans to retain their bright colors.

1. Combine snap peas, squash, carrots, and mushrooms; steam for 2–3 minutes until crisp-tender. Cool and refrigerate.

2. When cooled, add cucumbers and onions.

3. Whisk together canola oil, balsamic vinegar, salt, thyme, and marjoram. Pour over vegetables; toss lightly. Serve.

Nutritional Analysis (per serving): Calories: 73 | Protein: 2g | Carbohydrates: 7g | Fat: 5g | Saturated Fat: 1g | Cholesterol: 0mg | Sodium: 109mg | Fiber: 2g | PCF Ratio: 9-36-55 | Exchange Approx.: 1½ Vegetables, 1 Fat

ROASTED EGGPLANT SALAD

YIELDS 4 CUPS; SERVING SIZE: ½ CUP

Cooking spray

2 large eggplants, cut into ¼" rounds and then quartered

¼ cup hummus

1 tablespoon balsamic vinegar

¼ cup fat-free feta cheese

¼ cup chopped walnuts

Fresh basil leaves (optional)

1. Preheat oven to 425°F. Coat a large baking sheet with cooking spray and arrange the eggplant quarters on it.

2. Roast on the top rack of the oven about 10 minutes until starting to soften and brown. Remove from the oven, flip the eggplant over, and return to the oven for another 5–7 minutes. Let cool.

3. Whisk the hummus and vinegar together in a small bowl.

4. Put the cooled eggplant in a medium-sized bowl; add the hummus dressing, feta, and walnuts and mix well. Garnish with fresh basil if desired.

Nutritional Analysis (per serving): Calories: 80 | Protein: 3g | Carbohydrates: 10g | Fat: 4g | Saturated Fat: 0.5g | Cholesterol: 0mg | Sodium: 100mg | Fiber: 5g | PCF Ratio: 14-46-40 | Exchange Approx.: 1½ Vegetables, 1 Fat

APRICOT, ARUGULA, AND ALMOND SALAD

SERVES 1

1 packed cup of arugula

1 large apricot

7 almonds, finely chopped

1 tablespoon crumbled goat cheese

Dressing of choice

1. Wash and dry the arugula and apricot. Loosely chop the arugula and cut the apricot into ½" cubes. Add them to a medium-sized bowl. Top with the almonds and goat cheese.

2. Toss with desired dressing and serve.

Nutritional Analysis (per serving, not including dressing): Calories: 100 | Protein: 4g | Carbohydrates: 7g | Fat: 7g | Saturated Fat: 2g | Cholesterol: 10mg | Sodium: 110mg | Fiber: 2g | PCF Ratio: 14-25-61 | Exchange Approx.: ¼ Vegetable, ½ Fruit, 1½ Fats

KALE COLESLAW

YIELDS 6 CUPS; SERVING SIZE: 1 CUP

2½ cups shredded kale

2½ cups shredded cabbage

¼ cup light mayonnaise

¾ cup low-fat buttermilk or plain low-fat kefir

2 tablespoons seasoned rice vinegar

1 teaspoon sugar

¼ cup sunflower seeds

1. Put the kale and cabbage in a medium-sized bowl. In a smaller bowl, whisk together the mayonnaise, buttermilk/kefir, rice vinegar, and sugar until smooth.

2. Pour the dressing into the bowl of cabbage/kale, add the sunflower seeds, and mix well.

Nutritional Analysis (per serving): Calories: 90 | Protein: 4g | Carbohydrates: 9g | Fat: 6g | Saturated Fat: 1g | Cholesterol: 5mg | Sodium: 220mg | Fiber: 2g | PCF Ratio: 15-36-49 | Exchange Approx.: 1 Vegetable, ¼ Other Carbohydrate, 1 Fat

THREE-BEAN SALAD WITH BLACK-EYED PEAS AND TOMATOES

YIELDS 6 CUPS; SERVING SIZE: ½ CUP

1 (15-ounce) can kidney beans, drained and rinsed

1 (15-ounce) can garbanzo beans, drained and rinsed

1 (15-ounce) can black-eyed peas, drained and rinsed

2 cups cooked, cooled, and chopped green beans

1 cup reduced-fat Italian or balsamic vinaigrette dressing

1 teaspoon dried oregano

1½ tablespoons olive oil

Salt and pepper (optional)

1 cup halved grape tomatoes

1. Combine the kidney beans, garbanzo beans, black-eyed peas, and green beans in a large bowl.

2. In a smaller bowl, whisk the dressing, oregano, and olive oil together and pour over the beans. Mix well until evenly coated. Add salt and pepper to taste and place in the fridge to chill and marinate at least 30–60 minutes before serving. Garnish with the halved tomatoes just before serving.

Nutritional Analysis (per serving): Calories: 130 | Protein: 5g | Carbohydrates: 22g | Fat: 2.5g | Saturated Fat: 0g | Cholesterol: 0mg | Sodium: 290mg | Fiber: 6g | PCF Ratio: 16-68-16 | Exchange Approx.: 1 Starch, 1 Vegetable, ½ Fat

QUADRUPLE-BERRY SPINACH SALAD

SERVES 4; SERVING SIZE: ¼ RECIPE

4 heaping cups of fresh spinach, washed and patted dry

¼ cup blueberries

¼ cup raspberries

¼ cup blackberries

¼ cup chopped strawberries

¼ cup slivered almonds

¼ cup crumbled goat cheese

Dressing of choice

Add the spinach and berries to a medium-sized bowl. Top with the goat cheese and almonds, toss with desired dressing, and serve.

Nutritional Analysis (per serving, not including dressing): Calories: 100 | Protein: 4g | Carbohydrates: 8g | Fat: 5g | Saturated Fat: 2g | Cholesterol: 10mg | Sodium: 95mg | Fiber: 3g | PCF Ratio: 15-34-51 | Exchange Approx.: ½ Fruit, 1 Vegetable, 1 Fat

LEMON RAISIN BRUSSELS SPROUTS SALAD

YIELDS 8 CUPS; SERVING SIZE: 1 CUP

Cooking spray

8 cups trimmed and halved Brussels sprouts

¼ cup olive oil

¼ cup lemon juice

¼ cup raisins

¼ cup walnuts

1. Preheat oven to 350°F. Coat a baking sheet with cooking spray, add the Brussels sprouts, and roast for 20–30 minutes (turning them halfway through) until lightly browned and tender but still slightly firm when pierced with a fork. Let cool and set aside.

2. In a medium bowl, whisk together the olive oil and lemon juice.

3. Once cooled, chop up the Brussels sprouts and add them along with the raisins and walnuts to the bowl with the dressing. Mix well until evenly coated.

Nutritional Analysis (per serving): Calories: 150 | Protein: 4g | Carbohydrates: 15g | Fat: 10g | Saturated Fat: 1.5g | Cholesterol: 0mg | Sodium: 25mg | Fiber: 4g | PCF Ratio: 9-38-53 | Exchange Approx.: ¼ Fruit, 1½ Vegetables, 2 Fats

ROASTED BRUSSELS SPROUTS SALAD WITH CRANBERRIES AND ALMONDS

YIELDS 8 CUPS; SERVING SIZE: 1 CUP

8 cups trimmed and halved Brussels sprouts

Cooking spray

3 tablespoons olive oil

1 tablespoon Dijon mustard

1 tablespoon pure maple syrup

2 tablespoons dried cranberries

2 tablespoons slivered almonds

1. Preheat oven to 350°F. Coat a baking sheet with cooking spray, place the Brussels sprouts on it, and roast for 20–30 minutes (turning them halfway through) until lightly browned and tender but still slightly firm when pierced with a fork. Let cool and set aside.

2. In a medium bowl, whisk together the olive oil, mustard, and maple syrup. Chop up the cooled Brussels sprouts and add them along with the cranberries and almonds to the bowl with dressing. Mix well until evenly coated with dressing.

Nutritional Analysis (per serving): Calories: 110 | Protein: 3g | Carbohydrates: 12g | Fat: 6g | Saturated Fat: 1g | Cholesterol: 0mg | Sodium: 65mg | Fiber: 4g | PCF Ratio: 11-40-49 | Exchange Approx.: 1½ Vegetables, ¼ Other Carbohydrate, 1 Fat

VEGETARIAN ANTIPASTO SALAD

YIELDS ABOUT 8 CUPS; SERVING SIZE: 1 CUP

1 cup halved marinated mushrooms

1 cup chopped canned artichokes

1 cup chopped roasted red peppers

½ cup sliced black olives

1 cup cubed light mozzarella cheese

½ cup chopped fresh basil

4 cups chopped romaine lettuce

Dressing of your choice

Calorie-Cutting Tips

To keep calories low, try to find the veggies packed/marinated in water or vinegar. If you select the ones packed in oil, simply rinse them before using.

Toss all of the ingredients in a large bowl and serve.

Nutritional Analysis (per serving, not including dressing): Calories: 80 | Protein: 5g | Carbohydrates: 9g | Fat: 3.5g | Saturated Fat: 1g | Cholesterol: 5mg | Sodium: 480mg | Fiber: 3g | PCF Ratio: 24-41-35 | Exchange Approx.: 1½ Vegetables, ½ Lean Meat, ½ Fat

TANGY PINEAPPLE COLESLAW

**YIELDS 6 SERVINGS; SERVING SIZE:
½ CUP**

¼ cup nonfat Greek yogurt

¼ cup light mayonnaise

¼ cup finely chopped canned pineapple
(packed in its own juice)

2 tablespoons pineapple juice (from the
canned pineapple)

2½ cups shredded cabbage

½ cup shredded carrots

In a medium bowl, combine the yogurt, mayonnaise, pineapple, and pineapple juice. Put in the cabbage and carrots and mix well until evenly covered with the dressing.

Nutritional Analysis (per serving): Calories: 60 | Protein: 1g | Carbohydrates: 6g | Fat: 3.5g | Saturated Fat: 0.5g | Cholesterol: 0mg | Sodium: 85mg | Fiber: 1g | PCF Ratio: 11-47-42 | Exchange Approx.: ¼ Fruit, ½ Vegetable, ½ Fat

WATERMELON AND FETA SALAD

YIELDS 4 CUPS; SERVING SIZE: 1 CUP

4 cups ½"-cubed watermelon

2 tablespoons fresh chopped basil

4 tablespoons white balsamic vinegar

2 tablespoons water

2 teaspoons honey

Squeeze of fresh lemon juice

¼ cup reduced-fat feta cheese

1. Put the watermelon into a medium bowl.

2. In a smaller bowl, whisk together the basil, vinegar, water, honey, and lemon. Pour over the watermelon. Mix well to evenly coat. Sprinkle with cheese and lightly stir.

Nutritional Analysis (per serving): Calories: 80 | Protein: 2g | Carbohydrates: 19g | Fat: 1g | Saturated Fat: 1g | Cholesterol: 5mg | Sodium: 125mg | Fiber: 1g | PCF Ratio: 10-80-10 | Exchange Approx.: 1 Fruit, ½ Medium-Fat Meat

CUCUMBER DILL SALAD

YIELDS 2 CUPS; SERVING SIZE: ½ CUP

2 Persian cucumbers, peeled and sliced into very thin rounds

6 tablespoons nonfat Greek yogurt

1 teaspoon seasoned rice vinegar

½ teaspoon dill, fresh or dried

¼ teaspoon garlic powder

Combine all of the ingredients in a small bowl.

Nutritional Analysis (per serving): Calories: 20 | Protein: 2g | Carbohydrates: 3g | Fat: 0g | Saturated Fat: 0g | Cholesterol: 0mg | Sodium: 35mg | Fiber: 0g | PCF Ratio: 53-44-3 | Exchange Approx.: ½ Vegetable

BEET AND WALNUT SALAD

SERVES 4; SERVING SIZE: ¼ RECIPE

4 cups salad greens

1 cup chopped beets (canned and rinsed, or fresh cooked and cooled)

2 tablespoons chopped walnuts

2 tablespoons goat cheese

Maple Mustard Vinaigrette (see recipe in this chapter)

Combine all of the ingredients in a large bowl and toss with the dressing.

Nutritional Analysis (per serving, not including the dressing): Calories: 65 | Protein: 2g | Carbohydrates: 5g | Fat: 3.5g | Saturated Fat: 1g | Cholesterol: 5mg | Sodium: 100mg | Fiber: 2g | PCF Ratio: 15-36-49 | Exchange Approx.: 1 Vegetable, ¾ Fat

BROCCOLI SALAD

YIELDS 5 CUPS; SERVING SIZE: ½ CUP

½ cup nonfat Greek yogurt

½ cup light mayonnaise

2 tablespoons seasoned rice vinegar

1 tablespoon sugar

5 cups chopped raw broccoli

¼ cup raisins, dried currants, or dried cranberries

¼ cup chopped nuts, such as cashews, pecans, or almonds

1. In a medium bowl, combine the yogurt, mayonnaise, vinegar, and sugar. Stir in the broccoli, dried fruit, and nuts.

2. Mix well until evenly coated with the dressing.

Nutritional Analysis (per serving): Calories: 80 | Protein: 2g | Carbohydrates: 9g | Fat: 4.5g | Saturated Fat: 0.5g | Cholesterol: 0mg | Sodium: 160mg | Fiber: 2g | PCF Ratio: 11-41-48 | Exchange Approx.: 1½ Vegetables, 1 Fat

CHOPPED MEXICAN SALAD WITH CILANTRO LIME DRESSING

YIELDS 10 CUPS; SERVING SIZE: 2 CUPS

4 cups chopped romaine lettuce

1 cup shredded red cabbage

1 cup shredded carrots

1 cup diced cucumber

1 cup diced tomato

1 cup corn (fresh, frozen thawed, or canned rinsed)

1 cup canned rinsed black beans

½ cup shredded low-fat cheese

2 tablespoons olive oil

3 tablespoons low-fat buttermilk

2 tablespoons finely chopped cilantro

1 tablespoon lime juice

1 teaspoon rice vinegar

1 teaspoon ground cumin

Another Choice of Dressing

If you don't have all the dressing ingredients on hand, an alternative is to spice up your favorite Italian or ranch dressing by adding a dash of ground cumin, a squeeze of lime juice, and/or 1–2 tablespoons of your favorite salsa.

1. Combine the lettuce, cabbage, carrots, cucumber, tomato, corn, beans, and cheese in a large bowl.

2. In a small bowl, whisk the olive oil, buttermilk, cilantro, lime juice, rice vinegar, and cumin together. Pour over the salad and toss to coat.

Nutritional Analysis (per serving): Calories: 180 | Protein: 8g | Carbohydrates: 19g | Fat: 9g | Saturated Fat: 2.5g | Cholesterol: 10mg | Sodium: 200mg | Fiber: 5g | PCF Ratio: 16-42-42 | Exchange Approx.: 1 Starch, 1 Vegetable, ½ Medium-Fat Meat, 1 Fat

GRILLED PEAR AND TOASTED WALNUT SALAD WITH HERBES DE PROVENCE

YIELDS 5 CUPS; SERVING SIZE: 1 CUP

3 teaspoons olive oil, divided

2 medium pears, cored and cut vertically into ¼" wedges

2 tablespoons chopped walnuts

2 tablespoons white balsamic vinegar

1 tablespoon Dijon mustard

1 tablespoon honey

3 tablespoons water

½ teaspoon herbes de Provence

5 lightly packed cups field greens

1. Coat a medium pan with 1 teaspoon olive oil, add the pears, and warm on medium-high heat until the slices are lightly browned, about 5–8 minutes each side. Remove the pears from the pan and set aside. Add the walnuts to the pan and toast for a few minutes on high heat and add to the pears to cool.

2. In a small bowl, whisk together the vinegar, the remaining 2 teaspoons oil, mustard, honey, water, and herbes de Provence.

3. Put the greens in a large salad bowl. Add the pears and the nuts, pour in the dressing, and mix well.

Nutritional Analysis (per serving): Calories: 120 | Protein: 1g | Carbohydrates: 19g | Fat: 5g | Saturated Fat: 0.5g | Cholesterol: 0mg | Sodium: 95mg | Fiber: 4g | PCF Ratio: 5-60-35 | Exchange Approx.: 1 Fruit, ½ Vegetable, 1 Fat

SESAME SEAWEED SALAD

YIELDS 3 CUPS; SERVING SIZE: ½ CUP

½ cup dry wakame seaweed (to yield 2 cups rehydrated)

½ cup sliced cucumber, skin on

½ cup shredded carrot

½ cup cooked and shelled edamame

1 tablespoon sesame seeds

2 tablespoons sesame oil

¼ cup seasoned rice vinegar

1 teaspoon low-sodium soy sauce

½ teaspoon brown sugar

1 or 2 dashes red pepper flakes (optional)

1. Rehydrate and soften the seaweed by soaking it in cold water for about 3–5 minutes, then rinse and pat dry. Toss the seaweed, cucumber, carrots, edamame, and sesame seeds in a medium bowl.

2. In a small bowl, whisk together the sesame oil, rice vinegar, soy sauce, brown sugar, and red pepper flakes

3. Add the dressing to the bowl with the seaweed salad and toss until evenly coated

Nutritional Analysis (per serving): Calories: 80 | Protein: 3g | Carbohydrates: 6g | Fat: 6g | Saturated Fat: 0.5g | Cholesterol: 0mg | Sodium: 310mg | Fiber: 1g | PCF Ratio: 12-26-62 | Exchange Approx.: 1 Vegetable, ¼ Other Carbohydrate, 1 Fat

MAPLE MUSTARD VINAIGRETTE

**YIELDS 4 HEAPING TABLESPOONS;
SERVING SIZE: 1 HEAPING TABLESPOON**

2 tablespoons pure maple syrup

2 tablespoons white balsamic vinegar

2 teaspoons olive oil

2 tablespoons honey Dijon mustard

1 tablespoon water

Combine all of the ingredients in a small bowl and whisk together until smooth. Store unused dressing in an airtight container in the refrigerator for a few days.

Nutritional Analysis (per serving): Calories: 70 | Protein: 0g | Carbohydrates: 9g | Fat: 2.5g | Saturated Fat: 0g | Cholesterol: 0mg | Sodium: 35mg | Fiber: 0g | PCF Ratio: 0-64-36 | Exchange Approx.: ½ Other Carbohydrate, ½ Fat

HONEY VANILLA VINAIGRETTE

**YIELDS ABOUT 10 TABLESPOONS;
SERVING SIZE: 1 TABLESPOON**

½ cup seasoned rice vinegar

1 tablespoon olive oil

2 tablespoons honey

1 teaspoon vanilla extract

Whisk all the ingredients in a small bowl. Store unused dressing in an airtight container in the refrigerator for a few days.

Nutritional Analysis (per serving): Calories: 35 | Protein: 0g | Carbohydrates: 5g | Fat: 1.5g | Saturated Fat: 0g | Cholesterol: 0mg | Sodium: 190mg | Fiber: 0g | PCF Ratio: 0-60-40 | Exchange Approx.: ¼ Other Carbohydrate, ¼ Fat

STRAWBERRY VINAIGRETTE

YIELDS 1½ CUPS; SERVING SIZE: 2 TABLESPOONS

½ cup balsamic vinegar

½ cup chopped fresh strawberries

3 tablespoons olive oil

¼ cup water

4 teaspoons sugar or honey

Few dashes of pepper (optional)

Put all of the ingredients in a blender or food processor and blend on high speed for about 30 seconds or until smooth. Store unused dressing in an airtight container in the refrigerator for a few days.

Nutritional Analysis (per serving): Calories: 40 | Protein: 0g | Carbohydrates: 5g | Fat: 2.5g | Saturated Fat: 0g | Cholesterol: 0mg | Sodium: 0mg | Fiber: 0g | PCF Ratio: 1-34-65 | Exchange Approx.: ¼ Other Carbohydrate, ½ Fat

3-INGREDIENT BBQ RANCH

YIELDS 14 TABLESPOONS; SERVING SIZE: 2 TABLESPOONS

½ cup plain low-fat kefir

2 tablespoons light mayonnaise

¼ cup BBQ sauce

Add all of the ingredients to a small bowl and whisk together. Store unused dressing in an airtight container in the refrigerator for a few days.

Nutritional Analysis (per serving): Calories: 30 | Protein: 0g | Carbohydrates: 5g | Fat: 1g | Saturated Fat: 0g | Cholesterol: 0mg | Sodium: 140mg | Fiber: 0g | PCF Ratio: 0-65-35 | Exchange Approx.: ¼ Other Carbohydrate

TANGY BALSAMIC DRESSING

YIELDS 10 TABLESPOONS; SERVING SIZE: 1 TABLESPOON

¼ cup olive oil

¼ cup balsamic vinegar

2 tablespoons lemon juice

Salt and pepper (optional)

Whisk together all the ingredients in a small bowl. Store unused dressing in an airtight container in the refrigerator for a few days.

Nutritional Analysis (per serving): Calories: 55 | Protein: 0g | Carbohydrates: 1.5g | Fat: 5.5g | Saturated Fat: 1g | Cholesterol: 0mg | Sodium: 70mg | Fiber: 0g | PCF Ratio: 0-10-90 | Exchange Approx.: 1 Fat

CREAMY FETA VINAIGRETTE

YIELDS ABOUT ⅔ CUP; SERVING SIZE: 1 TABLESPOON

½ cup plain low-fat yogurt

1 tablespoon lemon juice

1 tablespoon olive oil

1½ ounces feta cheese

2 teaspoons mint

½ packet Splenda (optional)

Freshly ground pepper to taste

Process all ingredients in food processor or blender. Chill before serving.

Nutritional Analysis (per serving): Calories: 31 | Protein: 1g | Carbohydrates: 1g | Fat: 2g | Saturated Fat: 1g | Cholesterol: 4mg | Sodium: 57mg | Fiber: 0g | PCF Ratio: 17-17-66 | Exchange Approx.: ½ Fat

RASPBERRY TARRAGON VINAIGRETTE

**YIELDS ¾ CUP; SERVING SIZE:
1 TABLESPOON**

2 cups lightly mashed raspberries

2 tablespoons honey

2 cups red wine vinegar

¼ cup raspberry vinegar (see step 1)

½ cup olive oil

2 teaspoons lemon juice

½ tablespoon finely chopped tarragon

Salt and pepper to taste

1. To make raspberry vinegar, combine 2 cups raspberries, 2 tablespoons honey, and 2 cups red wine vinegar in nonstick saucepan. Simmer uncovered for 10 minutes; cool. Place in 1-quart jar; store at room temperature for 3 weeks. Strain vinegar from berries; pour strained vinegar into an empty wine bottle. Cork or cap.

2. Combine raspberry vinegar, olive oil, lemon juice, tarragon, and salt and pepper in a covered jar; shake thoroughly.

Nutritional Analysis (per serving): Calories: 120 | Protein: 0g | Carbohydrates: 9g | Fat: 9g | Saturated Fat: 1g | Cholesterol: 0mg | Sodium: 0mg | Fiber: 0g | PCF Ratio: 0-33-67 | Exchange Approx.: 2 Fats

BUTTERMILK DRESSING

**YIELDS ABOUT ⅔ CUP; SERVING SIZE:
1 TABLESPOON**

½ cup plain nonfat yogurt

1 tablespoon buttermilk powder

1 teaspoon prepared mustard

¼ teaspoon cider vinegar

1 tablespoon light brown sugar

¼ teaspoon paprika

⅛ teaspoon hot red pepper sauce (optional)

¼ teaspoon salt (optional)

Place all ingredients in jar; put lid on and shake vigorously until mixed. Refrigerate any unused portions. May be kept in refrigerator up to 3 days.

Nutritional Analysis (per serving, without salt): Calories: 14 | Protein: 1g | Carbohydrates: 3g | Fat: 0g | Saturated Fat: 0g | Cholesterol: 0mg | Sodium: 18mg | Fiber: 0g | PCF Ratio: 25-71-5 | Exchange Approx.: 1 Free

BLUE CHEESE DRESSING

YIELDS 6 TABLESPOONS; SERVING SIZE: 1 TABLESPOON

2 tablespoons Mock Cream (see recipe in Chapter 6)

1 tablespoon cottage cheese

1 tablespoon real mayonnaise

½ teaspoon lemon juice

½ teaspoon honey

1 tablespoon plus 2 teaspoons crumbled blue cheese

Put Mock Cream, cottage cheese, mayonnaise, lemon juice, and honey in blender; process until smooth. Fold in blue cheese.

Nutritional Analysis (per serving): Calories: 24 | Protein: 1g | Carbohydrates: 1g | Fat: 2g | Saturated Fat: 1g | Cholesterol: 3mg | Sodium: 52mg | Fiber: 0g | PCF Ratio: 21-23-57 | Exchange Approx.: ½ Fat

DIJON VINAIGRETTE

YIELDS ABOUT 5 TABLESPOONS; SERVING SIZE: 1 TABLESPOON

1 tablespoon Dijon mustard

½ teaspoon sea salt

½ teaspoon freshly ground black pepper

1 tablespoon red wine vinegar

3 tablespoons virgin olive oil

The Vinegar-Oil Balancing Act

The easiest way to tame too much vinegar is to add some vegetable oil. Because oil adds fat, the better alternative is to start with less vinegar and add it gradually until you arrive at a flavor you prefer.

Put all ingredients in small bowl; use wire whisk or fork to mix.

Nutritional Analysis (per serving): Calories: 74 | Protein: 0g | Carbohydrates: 1g | Fat: 8g | Saturated Fat: 1g | Cholesterol: 0mg | Sodium: 266mg | Fiber: 0g | PCF Ratio: 1-2-97 | Exchange Approx.: 2 Fats

TANGY LEMON-GARLIC TOMATO DRESSING

YIELDS ABOUT ¾ CUP; SERVING SIZE: 1 TABLESPOON

1 tablespoon ground flaxseed

2 cloves garlic

⅛ cup cider vinegar

⅛ teaspoon freshly ground pepper

1 small tomato, chopped

¼ teaspoon celery seed

1 tablespoon lemon juice

¼ cup water

Place all ingredients in blender; blend until smooth.

Nutritional Analysis (per serving): Calories: 7 | Protein: 0g | Carbohydrates: 1g | Fat: 1g | Saturated Fat: 0g | Cholesterol: 0mg | Sodium: 1mg | Fiber: 1g | PCF Ratio: 14-44-42 | Exchange Approx.: ½ Free

CASHEW-GARLIC RANCH DRESSING

YIELDS ABOUT ¾ CUP; SERVING SIZE: 1 TABLESPOON

¼ cup raw cashews or ⅛ cup cashew butter without salt

½ cup water

½ teaspoon stone-ground mustard

1½ tablespoons chili sauce

½ teaspoon horseradish

1 teaspoon Bragg Liquid Aminos or tamari sauce

1 clove garlic

1½ teaspoons honey

⅛ teaspoon pepper

1. Process cashews and water in blender or food processor until creamy.

2. Add remaining ingredients; mix well. Refrigerate for 30 minutes.

Nutritional Analysis (per serving): Calories: 21 | Protein: 1g | Carbohydrates: 2g | Fat: 2g | Saturated Fat: 0g | Cholesterol: 0mg | Sodium: 14mg | Fiber: 0g | PCF Ratio: 10-33-57 | Exchange Approx.: ½ Fat

LEMON-ALMOND DRESSING

YIELDS ABOUT ⅔ CUP; SERVING SIZE: 1 TABLESPOON

¼ cup raw almonds

1 tablespoon lemon juice

¼ cup water

1½ teaspoons honey

¼ teaspoon lemon pepper

½" slice (1" diameter) peeled ginger

¼ clove garlic

1½ teaspoons chopped fresh chives or ½ teaspoon dried chives

1½ teaspoons chopped fresh sweet basil or ½ teaspoon dried basil

Salad: Undressed

Make a quick salad without dressing by mixing chopped celery, onion, and other vegetables such as cucumbers or zucchini. Add low-salt seasoning or toss vegetables with Bragg Liquid Aminos or low-sodium soy sauce and serve over salad greens.

Put all ingredients in food processor or blender; process until smooth.

Nutritional Analysis (per serving): Calories: 25 | Protein: 1g | Carbohydrates: 2g | Fat: 2g | Saturated Fat: 0g | Cholesterol: 0mg | Sodium: 0mg | Fiber: 1g | PCF Ratio: 12-27-61 | Exchange Approx.: ½ Fat

CHAPTER 6

SALSAS, SAUCES, AND SPICES

QUICK TOMATO SAUCE

SERVES 8; SERVING SIZE: 1/8 RECIPE

2 pounds very ripe tomatoes

2 tablespoons extra-virgin olive oil

2 cloves garlic, minced

1/2 teaspoon ground cumin

2 large sprigs fresh thyme or 1/2 teaspoon dried thyme

1 bay leaf

Kosher or sea salt and freshly ground black pepper to taste (optional)

3 tablespoons total chopped fresh basil, oregano, tarragon, and parsley or cilantro, or a combination of all the listed herbs to taste; if using dried herbs, reduce the amount to 1 tablespoon

Remember . . .

The addition of 1/4 teaspoon granulated sugar to tomato sauce helps cut the acidity of the tomatoes without affecting the exchange approximations for the recipe.

1. Peel and seed tomatoes; chop with knife or food processor.

2. Heat large skillet; add olive oil. Reduce heat to low; sauté garlic and cumin.

3. Add tomatoes, thyme, bay leaf, salt, and pepper if using. If using dried herbs, add now. Simmer uncovered over medium heat 8–10 minutes, stirring often; reduce heat to maintain a simmer if necessary. Simmer until tomatoes are soft and sauce has thickened, about 30 minutes. Discard bay leaf and thyme sprigs; adjust seasoning to taste. If using fresh herbs, add just before serving.

Nutritional Analysis (per serving, without salt): Calories: 40 | Protein: 1g | Carbohydrates: 6g | Fat: 2g | Saturated Fat: 0g | Cholesterol: 0mg | Sodium: 10mg | Fiber: 1g | PCF Ratio: 9-49-42 | Exchange Approx.: 1 Vegetable, 1/2 Fat

BASIC TOMATO SAUCE

YIELDS ABOUT 5 CUPS; SERVING SIZE: ¼ CUP

2 tablespoons olive oil

2 cups coarsely chopped yellow onion

½ cup sliced carrots

2 cloves garlic, minced

4 cups canned Italian plum tomatoes with juice

1 teaspoon dried oregano

1 teaspoon dried basil

¼ teaspoon sugar

Kosher or sea salt and freshly ground black pepper to taste (optional)

Dash of ground anise seed (optional)

Culinary Antacids

Stir in 2 teaspoons Smucker's Low Sugar Concord Grape Reduced Sugar Jelly to tame hot chili or acidic sauces such as tomato sauce. You won't really notice the flavor of the jelly, and it will do a great job of reducing any tart, bitter, or acidic tastes in your sauce.

1. Heat olive oil in large, deep skillet or saucepan over medium-high heat. Add onions, carrots, and garlic; sauté until onions are transparent. (For a richer-tasting sauce, allow onions to caramelize or reach a light golden brown.)

2. Purée tomatoes in food processor.

3. Add the puréed tomatoes, oregano, basil, and sugar to onion mixture along with salt, pepper, and anise if using. Simmer partially covered for 45 minutes.

4. If you prefer a smoother sauce, process sauce in food processor again.

Nutritional Analysis (per serving, without salt): Calories: 37 | Protein: 1g | Carbohydrates: 5g | Fat: 2g | Saturated Fat: 0g | Cholesterol: 0mg | Sodium: 9mg | Fiber: 1g | PCF Ratio: 9-55-36 | Exchange Approx.: 1½ Vegetables

FRESH GARDEN TOMATO SAUCE

SERVES 12; SERVING SIZE: 1/12 RECIPE

3 tablespoons olive oil

1 cup chopped celery

1 cup finely chopped onion

1 cup chopped green (or sweet red) pepper

2 cloves garlic, crushed

8 cups peeled and crushed fresh tomatoes

1 (5-ounce) can tomato paste

1 cup grated zucchini

1 tablespoon chopped fresh oregano

1 tablespoon chopped fresh basil

½ teaspoon crushed red pepper

½ cup dry red wine

Tip

Don't waste unused tomato paste left in can. Spoon out tablespoon-sized portions and place on plastic wrap or in sandwich baggies. Seal packages and store in freezer. When you need tomato paste in a recipe, add frozen paste directly to sauce; no need to defrost.

1. In large heavy saucepan or Dutch oven, heat oil. Add celery, onion, and peppers; sauté 5 minutes. Add crushed garlic; sauté additional 2 minutes.

2. Add crushed tomatoes, tomato paste, zucchini, oregano, basil, and red pepper. Bring to a boil; reduce heat and simmer 2–3 hours.

3. Add wine during last 30 minutes of cooking.

Nutritional Analysis (per serving): Calories: 154 | Protein: 6g | Carbohydrates: 26g | Fat: 5g | Saturated Fat: 1g | Cholesterol: 0mg | Sodium: 867mg | Fiber: 6g | PCF Ratio: 15-61-25 | Exchange Approx.: 5 Vegetables, 1 Fat

CARIBBEAN KIWI SALSA

SERVES 6; SERVING SIZE: ⅙ RECIPE

1 cup peeled and chopped kiwi

1 cup chopped pineapple

1 cup peeled and chopped mango

⅓ cup chopped red onion

1 cup chopped red bell pepper

⅓ cup cooked black beans

3 tablespoons chopped fresh cilantro

2 tablespoons lime juice

½ teaspoon chili powder

Dash ground cayenne pepper

1. Mix all ingredients together in medium bowl.

2. Chill at least 2 hours before serving.

Nutritional Analysis (per serving): Calories: 79 | Protein: 2g | Carbohydrates: 19g | Fat: 0g | Saturated Fat: 0g | Cholesterol: 0mg | Sodium: 28mg | Fiber: 3g | PCF Ratio: 9-87-5 | Exchange Approx.: 1 Fruit, ½ Vegetable

ZESTY BLACK BEAN SALSA

SERVES 10; SERVING SIZE: ¹⁄₁₀ RECIPE

1 cup chopped red onion

¼ cup chopped fresh cilantro

¼ cup chopped fresh parsley

3 tablespoons chopped jalapeño

1½ cups cooked black beans

4 cups chopped tomato

3 tablespoons lime juice

2 tablespoons olive oil

1. Place onion, cilantro, parsley, and jalapeño in food processor; chop finely.

2. In medium bowl, combine onion mixture, black beans, and tomatoes.

3. In small bowl, whisk together lime juice and olive oil. Pour over ingredients; mix well.

4. Chill well before serving.

Nutritional Analysis (per serving): Calories: 91 | Protein: 4g | Carbohydrates: 13g | Fat: 3g | Saturated Fat: 0g | Cholesterol: 0mg | Sodium: 125mg | Fiber: 4g | PCF Ratio: 15-55-30 | Exchange Approx.: ½ Starch, 1 Vegetable, ½ Fat

FRESH PEACH-MANGO SALSA

SERVES 6; SERVING SIZE: ⅙ RECIPE

1 cup peeled and ¼"-cubed mango

1 peach, peeled, pitted, and cut into
   ¼" pieces

1 cup finely chopped red onion

1 cup cucumber, peeled and cut into
   ¼" pieces

1 tablespoon balsamic vinegar

1 tablespoon lime juice

1 teaspoon chili powder

½ teaspoon ground cumin

1 tablespoon chopped fresh cilantro

1 tablespoon chopped fresh parsley

¼ teaspoon salt

1. Mix all ingredients together in medium bowl.

2. Chill at least 4 hours before serving.

Nutritional Analysis (per serving): Calories: 45 | Protein: 1g | Carbohydrates: 10g | Fat: 1g | Saturated Fat: 0g | Cholesterol: 0mg | Sodium: 104mg | Fiber: 2g | PCF Ratio: 9-82-9 | Exchange Approx.: ½ Fruit

SALSA WITH A KICK

YIELDS ABOUT 2 CUPS; SERVING SIZE: 1 TABLESPOON

2 teaspoons ground flaxseed

4 medium tomatoes, chopped

1 clove garlic, chopped

½ small onion

½ tablespoon cider vinegar

¼ teaspoon Tabasco sauce

⅛ teaspoon ground cayenne pepper

1 tablespoon chopped fresh cilantro

Friendly Fat and Fiber

In addition to providing fiber, ground flax-seed is a rich source of omega-3 and omega-6 essential fatty acids. The oil is low in saturated fat and therefore a heart-healthy choice. Just remember that flax-seed oil must be refrigerated or it will go rancid.

Place all ingredients in blender or food processor; process briefly until blended but not smooth.

Nutritional Analysis (per serving): Calories: 5 | Protein: 0g | Carbohydrates: 1g | Fat: 0g | Saturated Fat: 0g | Cholesterol: 0mg | Sodium: 2mg | Fiber: 0g | PCF Ratio: 14-65-21 | Exchange Approx.: 3 tablespoons equals 1 Free Condiment

AVOCADO-CORN SALSA

SERVES 4; SERVING SIZE: ¼ RECIPE

1 cup blanched fresh or frozen thawed corn kernels

1 small banana pepper, seeded and chopped

¼ cup diced red radishes

⅛ cup thinly sliced green onion

1 avocado, pitted, peeled, and diced

1 tablespoon lime juice

½ teaspoon white wine vinegar

1 teaspoon extra-virgin olive oil

¼ teaspoon dried oregano

Dash of ground cumin

Dash of Tabasco sauce

1. Combine corn, banana pepper, radish, and green onion in medium bowl.

2. In another bowl, combine half of diced avocado and lime juice; stir to thoroughly coat.

3. In blender, combine other half of avocado, vinegar, oil, oregano, cumin, and Tabasco; process until smooth. Pour over corn mixture; stir.

4. Add avocado mixture. Serve immediately.

Nutritional Analysis (per serving): Calories: 133 | Protein: 2g | Carbohydrates: 14g | Fat: 9g | Saturated Fat: 1g | Cholesterol: 0mg | Sodium: 10mg | Fiber: 4g | PCF Ratio: 7-37-56s | Exchange Approx.: ½ Starch/Vegetable, 2 Fats

ROASTED CORN SALSA

SERVES 6; SERVING SIZE: ⅙ RECIPE

2 ears corn

1½ cups skinned and chopped fresh
   tomatoes

½ cup chopped red onion

3 tablespoons finely chopped jalapeño
   pepper

1 tablespoon rice wine vinegar

¼ cup chopped roasted red pepper

1½ tablespoons chopped fresh cilantro

1 teaspoon finely chopped garlic

1 tablespoon lime juice

½ teaspoon ground cumin

2 teaspoons red wine vinegar

1. Husk corn and place on grill. Cook for about 10–12 minutes until lightly browned and tender. Set aside to cool.

2. Combine tomatoes, onion, jalapeño, rice wine vinegar, red pepper, cilantro, garlic, lime juice, cumin, and red wine vinegar.

3. When corn has cooled, cut kernels off cobb and add to tomato mixture.

Nutritional Analysis (per serving): Calories: 104 | Protein: 4g | Carbohydrates: 24g | Fat: 1g | Saturated Fat: 0g | Cholesterol: 0mg | Sodium: 77mg | Fiber: 3g | PCF Ratio: 12-80-8 | Exchange Approx.: 1 Starch, ½ Vegetable

PINEAPPLE-CHILI SALSA

SERVES 4; SERVING SIZE: ¼ RECIPE

½ cup unsweetened diced pineapple

½ cup roughly chopped papaya, peach, or mango

1 small poblano chili pepper, diced

¼ cup chopped red bell pepper

¼ cup chopped yellow bell pepper

1 tablespoon fresh key lime or fresh lime juice

¼ cup chopped red onion

Combine all ingredients in bowl; toss to mix.

Nutritional Analysis (per serving): Calories: 29 | Protein: 1g | Carbohydrates: 7g | Fat: 0g | Saturated Fat: 0g | Cholesterol: 0mg | Sodium: 2mg | Fiber: 1g | PCF Ratio: 8-87-5 | Exchange Approx.: ½ Fruit

CRANBERRY ORANGE RELISH

SERVES 12; SERVING SIZE: ½ CUP

16 ounces fresh cranberries

1½ cups orange sections

2 teaspoons grated orange zest

¼ cup brown sugar

⅓ cup Splenda Granulated

1 teaspoon ground cinnamon

1. Chop cranberries and orange sections in food processor using pulse setting until coarsely chopped. Transfer to saucepan.

2. Bring cranberry mixture, orange zest, brown sugar, and Splenda to boil over medium heat. Cook 2 minutes.

3. Remove from heat; stir in cinnamon. Chill before serving.

Nutritional Analysis (per serving): Calories: 62 | Protein: 0g | Carbohydrates: 16g | Fat: 0g | Saturated Fat: 0g | Cholesterol: 0mg | Sodium: 3mg | Fiber: 2g | PCF Ratio: 3-96-1 | Exchange Approx.: 1 Fruit

HORSERADISH MUSTARD

YIELDS ¾ CUP; SERVING SIZE: 1 TEASPOON

¼ cup dry mustard

2½ tablespoons prepared horseradish

1 teaspoon sea salt

¼ cup white wine vinegar

1 tablespoon olive oil

Ground cayenne pepper to taste (optional)

Combine ingredients in food processor or blender; process until smooth. Pour into decorative jar; store in refrigerator.

Nutritional Analysis (per serving): Calories: 10 | Protein: 0g | Carbohydrates: 1g | Fat: 1g | Saturated Fat: 0g | Cholesterol: 0mg | Sodium: 68mg | Fiber: 0g | PCF Ratio: 12-25-63 | Exchange Approx.: 1 Free Condiment

ALMOND HONEY MUSTARD

YIELDS ABOUT ½ CUP; SERVING SIZE: 1 TEASPOON

¼ cup unsalted almond butter

2 teaspoons mustard

1 teaspoon honey

2 tablespoons lemon juice

½ teaspoon garlic powder

Pinch of ground cumin (optional)

Pinch of sea salt (optional)

Add all ingredients to food processor or blender; process until smooth.

Nutritional Analysis (per serving, without cumin and salt): Calories: 21 | Protein: 1g | Carbohydrates: 1g | Fat: 2g | Saturated Fat: 1g | Cholesterol: 0mg | Sodium: 6mg | Fiber: 0g | PCF Ratio: 9-19-72 | Exchange Approx.: ½ Fat

PICCALILLI

**YIELDS 2 QUARTS; SERVING SIZE:
2 TABLESPOONS**

1 cup diced green tomatoes

1½ cups diced cabbage

1 cup diced white onions

1 cup diced cauliflower

1 cup diced cucumber

½ cup diced red pepper

½ cup diced green pepper

¼ cup pickling salt

1½ cups apple cider vinegar or white
  vinegar

¾ cup sugar

½ teaspoon ground turmeric

1 teaspoon ground ginger

1½ teaspoons dried mustard

1½ teaspoons mustard seed

1 teaspoon celery seed

Sachet of pickling spices

Pickled whole onions to taste (optional)

Comparative Analysis

Omitting both sugar and pickling salt
makes this recipe even better for you, with
one-third the calories, less than half the
carbohydrates, a PCF ratio of 12-84-4, and
an exchange approximation of ½ Free
Vegetable.

1. Layer vegetables in bowl with pickling salt. Store in refrigerator overnight to remove moisture from vegetables.

2. Drain and rinse vegetables. (Rinsing will remove much of the salt; however, if sodium is a concern, you can omit it altogether.)

3. To make marinade, combine vinegar, sugar, turmeric, ginger, dried mustard, mustard seed, celery seed, and pickling spice sachet in large, noncorrosive stockpot. Bring ingredients to boil; boil for 2 minutes. Add vegetables; boil for an additional 10 minutes.

4. Remove pickling spice sachet and add pickled onions if you are using them; boil for another 2 minutes.

5. Remove from heat and allow to cool. Pack vegetables in jars, then fill with pickling liquid until vegetables are covered. Store covered glass jars in refrigerator. Serve chilled as a relish or on deli sandwiches.

Nutritional Analysis (per serving, without salt): Calories: 13 | Protein: 0g | Carbohydrates: 3g | Fat: 0g | Saturated Fat: 0g | Cholesterol: 0mg | Sodium: 1mg | Fiber: 0g | PCF Ratio: 4-94-1 | Exchange Approx.: ½ Misc. Carbohydrate

PEPPER AND CORN RELISH

4 banana or jalapeño peppers, seeded and chopped

⅓ cup frozen thawed corn

⅓ cup chopped red onion

⅛ teaspoon ground coriander

2 teaspoons lime juice

Freshly ground black pepper to taste

Tip

For a colorful mild relish, use a combination of 2 tablespoons chopped green bell pepper and an equal amount of chopped red pepper in place of the jalapeño peppers.

Toss peppers in bowl with remaining ingredients. Relish can be served immediately or chilled and served the next day.

Nutritional Analysis (per serving): Calories: 39 | Protein: 2g | Carbohydrates: 9g | Fat: 1g | Saturated Fat: 0g | Cholesterol: 0mg | Sodium: 7mg | Fiber: 2g | PCF Ratio: 14-78-8 | Exchange Approx.: ½ Starch

CRANBERRY-RAISIN CHUTNEY

**YIELDS ABOUT 3 CUPS; SERVING SIZE:
1 TABLESPOON**

1 cup diced onions

1 cup peeled diced apples

1 cup diced bananas

1 cup diced peaches

¼ cup raisins

¼ cup dry white wine

¼ cup dried cranberries

¼ cup apple cider vinegar

1 teaspoon brown sugar

Sea salt and freshly ground black pepper
to taste (optional)

Tip

This chutney is also good if you substitute other dried fruit for the raisins or cranberries.

In large saucepan, combine all ingredients. Cook over low heat for about 1 hour, stirring occasionally. Cool completely. Can be kept for 1 week in refrigerator or in freezer for 3 months, or canned using same sterilizing method you'd use to can mincemeat.

Nutritional Analysis (per serving, without salt): Calories: 14 | Protein: 0g | Carbohydrates: 3g | Fat: 0g | Saturated Fat: 0g | Cholesterol: 0mg | Sodium: 1mg | Fiber: 0g | PCF Ratio: 4-93-3 | Exchange Approx.: 1 Free Condiment

PLUM SAUCE

YIELDS 1¼ CUPS; SERVING SIZE: 1 TABLESPOON

1 cup plum jam

2 teaspoons grated lemon zest

1 tablespoon lemon juice

1 tablespoon rice wine vinegar

½ teaspoon ground ginger

½ teaspoon crushed anise seeds

¼ teaspoon dry mustard

¼ teaspoon ground cinnamon

⅛ teaspoon ground cloves

⅛ teaspoon hot pepper sauce

1. Heat plum jam in small saucepan over medium heat until melted.

2. Stir in remaining ingredients. Bring the mixture to a boil; lower heat and simmer for 1 minute, stirring constantly. Use cooled sauce as meat seasoning or a dip for eggrolls.

Nutritional Analysis (per serving): Calories: 29 | Protein: 0g | Carbohydrates: 8g | Fat: 0g | Saturated Fat: 0g | Cholesterol: 0mg | Sodium: 0mg | Fiber: 0g | PCF Ratio: 0-100-0 | Exchange Approx.: ½ Fruit

ROASTED RED PEPPER AND PLUM SAUCE

**YIELDS 2 CUPS; SERVING SIZE:
1 TABLESPOON**

1 large roasted red pepper

½ pound apricots, quartered and pitted

¾ pound plums, quartered and pitted

1⅓ cups apple cider vinegar

⅔ cup water

⅓ cup white sugar

½ cup brown sugar

2 tablespoons corn syrup

2 tablespoons fresh grated ginger

1 teaspoon salt

1 tablespoon toasted mustard seeds

4 scallions, chopped (white part only)

1 teaspoon minced garlic

½ teaspoon ground cinnamon

1. Place all ingredients together in large pot; bring to a boil. Reduce heat; simmer covered for 30 minutes.

2. Uncover and simmer for 1 hour.

3. Place in blender or food processor; process to desired consistency. Can be stored in refrigerator for 4–6 weeks.

Nutritional Analysis (per serving): Calories: 38 | Protein: 0g | Carbohydrates: 10g | Fat: 1g | Saturated Fat: 0g | Cholesterol: 0mg | Sodium: 76mg | Fiber: 1g | PCF Ratio: 3-95-2 | Exchange Approx.: ½ Misc. Carbohydrate

HOMEMADE WORCESTERSHIRE SAUCE

**YIELDS 1 CUP; SERVING SIZE:
1 TABLESPOON**

1½ cups cider vinegar

¼ cup plum jam

1 tablespoon blackstrap molasses

1 clove garlic, crushed

⅛ teaspoon chili powder

⅛ teaspoon ground cloves

Pinch of ground cayenne pepper

¼ cup chopped onion

½ teaspoon ground allspice

⅛ teaspoon dry mustard

1 teaspoon Bragg Liquid Aminos

Combine all ingredients in large saucepan; stir until mixture boils. Lower heat; simmer uncovered for 1 hour, stirring occasionally. Store in covered jar in refrigerator.

Nutritional Analysis (per serving): Calories: 14 | Protein: 0g | Carbohydrates: 4g | Fat: 0g | Saturated Fat: 0g | Cholesterol: 0mg | Sodium: 15mg | Fiber: 0g | PCF Ratio: 3-97-0 | Exchange Approx.: 1 Free Condiment

PESTO SAUCE

YIELDS ABOUT 3 CUPS; SERVING SIZE: 1 TABLESPOON

¾ cup pine nuts

4 cups tightly packed basil leaves

½ cup freshly grated Parmesan cheese

3 large garlic cloves, minced

¼ teaspoon salt

1 teaspoon freshly ground black pepper

½ cup extra-virgin olive oil

1. Preheat oven to 350°F. Spread pine nuts on baking sheet. Bake for about 5 minutes; stir. Continue to bake for 10 minutes until nuts are golden brown and highly aromatic, stirring occasionally. Let nuts cool completely; chop finely.

2. Fill medium-sized heavy saucepan halfway with water. Place over medium heat; bring to a boil. Next to pot, place large bowl filled with water and ice. Using tongs, dip a few basil leaves into boiling water. Blanch for 3 seconds; quickly remove from boiling water and place in ice water. Repeat process until all basil has been blanched, adding ice to water as needed. Drain basil in colander and pat dry with a towel.

3. In blender or food processor, combine basil, pine nuts, cheese, garlic, salt, pepper, and all but 1 tablespoon olive oil; process until smooth and uniform. Pour into airtight container and add remaining olive oil to top to act as protective barrier. Pesto can be stored in refrigerator for up to 5 days.

4. To freeze pesto, place it in a tightly sealed container. To freeze small amounts of pesto, pour into ice cube trays and freeze until solid. Once frozen, you can remove the pesto cubes and place them in sealed freezer bags.

Nutritional Analysis (per serving): Calories: 37 | Protein: 1g | Carbohydrates: 1g | Fat: 4g | Saturated Fat: 1g | Cholesterol: 1mg | Sodium: 14mg | Fiber: 0g | PCF Ratio: 10-6-85 | Exchange Approx.: 1 Fat

HONEY AND CIDER GLAZE

SERVES 4; SERVING SIZE: ¼ RECIPE

3 tablespoons cider or apple juice

½ teaspoon honey

1 teaspoon lemon juice

1 teaspoon Bragg Liquid Aminos

½ teaspoon grated lemon zest

Spice Tea Chicken Marinade

Steep four orange or lemon spice tea bags in 2 cups boiling water for 4 minutes. Dissolve 1 teaspoon honey into the tea, pour it over four chicken pieces, and marinate in the refrigerator for 30 minutes. Occasionally turn and baste any exposed portions of chicken. Pour the tea into the roasting pan to provide moisture—discard it after cooking.

1. Preheat oven to 375°F. Combine cider or apple juice, honey, lemon juice, Liquid Aminos, and zest in microwave-safe bowl; microwave on high 30 seconds. Stir until honey is dissolved.

2. Arrange chicken pieces on rack placed in roasting pan or broiling pan. Brush or spoon 1 teaspoon of glaze over top of each piece. Cook for 15 minutes, then baste with the glaze. Cook for 10 minutes, baste again, then return to oven for 5 minutes or until chicken registers 165°F. Allow chicken to sit 5 minutes before serving.

Nutritional Analysis (per serving, glaze only): Calories: 10 | Protein: 0g | Carbohydrates: 2g | Fat: 0g | Saturated Fat: 0g | Cholesterol: 0mg | Sodium: 55mg | Fiber: 0g | PCF Ratio: 9-90-1 | Exchange Approx.: 1 Free Condiment

GINGERED PEACH SAUCE

SERVES 4; SERVING SIZE: ½ CUP

2 teaspoons olive oil

1 tablespoon chopped shallot

2 teaspoons grated fresh ginger

⅓ cup dry white wine

1 small peach, peeled and diced

1 tablespoon frozen unsweetened orange juice concentrate

1 teaspoon Bragg Liquid Aminos

½ teaspoon cornstarch

1. Heat olive oil in nonstick skillet over medium heat; sauté shallot and ginger. Add wine; simmer until reduced by half. Add peach, orange juice concentrate, and Bragg Liquid Aminos; return to simmer, stirring occasionally.

2. In separate container, mix cornstarch with a tablespoon of sauce; stir to create a slurry, mixing well to remove any lumps. Add slurry to sauce; simmer for 5–7 minutes until mixture thickens. Transfer to blender or food processor; process until smooth.

Nutritional Analysis (per serving): Calories: 54 | Protein: 1g | Carbohydrates: 5g | Fat: 2g | Saturated Fat: 1g | Cholesterol: 0mg | Sodium: 57mg | Fiber: 1g | PCF Ratio: 5-47-48 | Exchange Approx.: ½ Fat, 1 Fruit

MOCK CREAM

YIELDS 1¼ CUPS; SERVING SIZE: 2 TABLESPOONS

1 cup skim milk

¼ cup nonfat dry milk

Comparative Analysis

Using 1¼ cups heavy cream would give you the following breakdown: Calories: 515; Protein: 3g; Carbohydrates: 4g; Fat: 55g; Saturated Fat: 34g; Cholesterol: 205mg; Sodium: 56mg; Fiber: 0g; PCF Ratio: 2-3-95; Exchange Approx.: 11 Fats.

Process ingredients in blender until mixed. Use as a substitute for heavy cream.

Nutritional Analysis (per recipe): Calories: 147 | Protein: 14g | Carbohydrates: 21g | Fat: 1g | Saturated Fat: 1g | Cholesterol: 8mg | Sodium: 221mg | Fiber: 0g | PCF Ratio: 39-57-3 | Exchange Approx.: 1½ Skim Milks

MOCK WHITE SAUCE

YIELDS ABOUT 1 CUP; SERVING SIZE: ½ CUP

1 tablespoon unsalted butter

1 tablespoon flour

¼ teaspoon sea salt

Pinch of white pepper

1 cup Mock Cream (see recipe in this chapter)

1. In medium-sized heavy nonstick saucepan, melt butter over very low heat. Butter should gently melt; you do not want it to bubble and turn brown. While butter is melting, mix together flour, salt, and white pepper in small bowl.

2. Once butter is melted, add flour mixture; stir constantly. (A heat-safe flat-bottom spoon safe for nonstick pans works well for this.) Once mixture thickens and starts to bubble, about 2 minutes, slowly pour in some Mock Cream; stir until blended with roux. Add a little more Mock Cream; stir until blended. Add remaining Mock Cream; continue cooking, stirring constantly to make sure sauce doesn't stick to bottom of pan. Once sauce begins to steam and appears just about to boil, reduce heat and simmer until sauce thickens, about 3 minutes.

Nutritional Analysis (per recipe): Calories: 61 | Protein: 2g | Carbohydrates: 6g | Fat: 3g | Saturated Fat: 2g | Cholesterol: 9mg | Sodium: 190mg | Fiber: 0g | PCF Ratio: 20-36-44 | Exchange Approx.: ½ Fat, ½ Skim Milk

FAT-FREE ROUX

YIELDS ENOUGH TO THICKEN 1 CUP OF LIQUID; SERVING SIZE: ¼ CUP

1 tablespoon cornstarch

2 tablespoons wine

Serving Options

Make this roux with red wine for a defatted beef broth gravy. Use white wine for chicken or seafood gravy or sauce.

1. Whisk ingredients together until well blended, making sure there are no lumps.

2. To use as thickener for 1 cup of broth, heat broth until it reaches a boil. Slowly whisk roux into broth; return to a boil. Reduce heat; simmer, stirring constantly until mixture thickens enough to coat back of spoon. (A gravy or sauce made in this manner will thicken more as it cools. It's important to bring a cornstarch slurry to a boil; this helps it thicken and removes the starchy taste.)

Nutritional Analysis (per serving, roux only): Calories: 13 | Protein: 0g | Carbohydrates: 2g | Fat: 0g | Saturated Fat: 0g | Cholesterol: 0mg | Sodium: 1mg | Fiber: 0g | PCF Ratio: 1-99-0 | Exchange Approx.: 1 Free

MADEIRA SAUCE

SERVES 4; SERVING SIZE: ¼ CUP

2 teaspoons olive oil

1 clove garlic, crushed

1 tablespoon chopped shallot

1 teaspoon unsalted tomato paste

⅓ cup Madeira

¼ cup shellfish, vegetable, or chicken broth

1 tablespoon lemon juice

2 teaspoons Mock Cream (see recipe in this chapter)

2 teaspoons unsalted butter

Salt and freshly ground black pepper (optional)

1. Heat olive oil in nonstick saucepan over medium heat. Add garlic and shallot; sauté for 3 minutes until translucent.

2. Add tomato paste; sauté 30 seconds, stirring as needed.

3. Add Madeira, broth, lemon juice, and Mock Cream; simmer for 5 minutes until mixture is reduced by half. Whisk in butter to form an emulsion. Keep the sauce warm until needed, being careful not to let it boil or become too cold after the butter has been added. (Optional: Strain sauce and season with salt and pepper.)

Nutritional Analysis (per serving): Calories: 56 | Protein: 0g | Carbohydrates: 2g | Fat: 4g | Saturated Fat: 2g | Cholesterol: 5mg | Sodium: 3mg | Fiber: 0g | PCF Ratio: 2-14-84 | Exchange Approx.: 1 Fat, ½ Vegetable

MOCK BÉCHAMEL SAUCE

YIELDS 1 CUP; SERVING SIZE: ¼ CUP

1 egg

1 cup Mock Cream (see recipe in this chapter)

1 teaspoon unsalted butter

1. In quart-sized or larger microwave-safe bowl, whisk egg into Mock Cream until well blended. Microwave on high for 1 minute; whisk mixture again. Microwave on high for 30 seconds; whisk again. Microwave on high for another 30 seconds; whisk again. (Strain mixture if there appears to be any cooked egg solids; this seldom occurs if mixture is whisked at intervals specified.)

2. Allow the mixture to cool slightly; whisk in butter.

Nutritional Analysis (per serving): Calories: 53 | Protein: 4g | Carbohydrates: 4g | Fat: 2g | Saturated Fat: 1g | Cholesterol: 51mg | Sodium: 58mg | Fiber: 0g | PCF Ratio: 32-32-36 | Exchange Approx.: ½ Fat, ½ Skim Milk

PEANUT SAUCE

YIELDS ABOUT 1 CUP; SERVING SIZE: 1 TABLESPOON

¼ cup creamy peanut butter

¼ cup light coconut milk

¼ cup water

1 tablespoon soy sauce

1 tablespoon rice vinegar

2 teaspoons sesame oil

2 teaspoons lime juice

1 teaspoon brown sugar

Pinch of fresh or ground ginger

½ teaspoon red pepper flakes (optional)

Combine all of the ingredients in a small bowl. Whisk together until a smooth consistency is reached.

Nutritional Analysis (per serving): Calories: 35 | Protein: 0g | Carbohydrates: 2g | Fat: 3g | Saturated Fat: 0g | Cholesterol: 0mg | Sodium: 105mg | Fiber: 0g | PCF Ratio: 12-17-71 | Exchange Approx.: ¾ Fat

MOCK CAULIFLOWER SAUCE

SERVES 4; SERVING SIZE: ½ CUP

2 cups chopped cauliflower

¼ cup diced Spanish onion

1 clove dry-roasted garlic (see Garlic and Feta Cheese Dip recipe in Chapter 3 for dry-roasting instructions) or ½ clove crushed garlic

1 tablespoon dry white wine

Freshly ground white pepper to taste

2 tablespoons Mock Cream (see recipe in this chapter)

Tip

If you use frozen cauliflower to make Mock Cauliflower Sauce, be sure to thaw and drain it first. Otherwise, there will be too much moisture and the resulting sauce will be too thin.

1. Add cauliflower, onion, garlic, and white wine to microwave-safe bowl; cover and microwave on high for 5 minutes or until cauliflower is tender and onions are transparent. (Microwave on high for additional 1-minute intervals if necessary.)

2. Pour vegetable-wine mixture into blender or food processor, being careful not to burn yourself on steam. Season with white pepper and add Mock Cream; process until smooth.

Nutritional Analysis (per serving): Calories: 27 | Protein: 2g | Carbohydrates: 5g | Fat: 1g | Saturated Fat: 0g | Cholesterol: 0mg | Sodium: 16mg | Fiber: 2g | PCF Ratio: 24-66-10 | Exchange Approx.: 1 Vegetable

ALMOND YOGURT APPLESAUCE

YIELDS 12 TABLESPOONS; SERVING SIZE: 2 TABLESPOONS

½ cup vanilla Greek yogurt

4 teaspoons almond butter

4 teaspoons unsweetened applesauce

2 tablespoons milk

2–4 drops almond extract

Dash of cinnamon

Saucy Serving Suggestions

This sauce is a great higher-protein, lower-sugar alternative to syrup for pancakes, waffles, and French toast.

Put all of the ingredients in a small bowl and mix well. Store unused dressing in an airtight container in the refrigerator for a few days.

Nutritional Analysis (per serving): Calories: 35 | Protein: 3g | Carbohydrates: 2g | Fat: 2g | Saturated Fat: 0g | Cholesterol: 0mg | Sodium: 10mg | Fiber: 0g | PCF Ratio: 30-20-50 | Exchange Approx.: ½ Lean Meat, ½ Fat

BANANA CREAM CHEESE

SERVES 1

1 tablespoon reduced-fat cream cheese

⅓ of a very ripe peeled medium banana

Mash the banana well with a fork in a small bowl. Stir in the cream cheese and mix well. Serve immediately.

Nutritional Analysis (per serving): Calories: 70 | Protein: 2g | Carbohydrates: 10g | Fat: 2.5g | Saturated Fat: 1.5g | Cholesterol: 10mg | Sodium: 50mg | Fiber: 1g | PCF Ratio: 11-57-12 | Exchange Approx.: ¾ Fruit, ½ Fat

STRAWBERRY CREAM CHEESE

SERVES 1

2 tablespoons whipped light cream cheese

2 tablespoons finely diced fresh strawberries

¼ teaspoon honey

Put the cream cheese in a small bowl. Add the berries and mix/mash well until they are mostly blended; stir in the honey. Serve immediately.

Nutritional Analysis (per serving): Calories: 80 | Protein: 1g | Carbohydrates: 4g | Fat: 5g | Saturated Fat: 3.5g | Cholesterol: 20mg | Sodium: 65mg | Fiber: 0g | PCF Ratio: 6-19-75 | Exchange Approx.: ¼ Fruit, 1 Fat

SIMPLE BUT DELICIOUS APPLESAUCE

YIELDS 3 CUPS; SERVING SIZE: ½ CUP

1½ cups water

7 cups peeled, cored, and cut (chopped into 1" chunks) apples

Tips for Maximizing and Adding Flavor

Sweet and soft apples such as Gala, Fuji, McIntosh, and Cortland varieties work best in this recipe. If you would like to add more sweetness, stir in 1–2 teaspoons maple syrup or brown sugar, and you can also add a dash or two of cinnamon and a splash of vanilla for additional flavor.

1. Bring the water to a boil on high heat in a large pot. Add the apples and reduce to medium-low heat and simmer, stirring occasionally until apples are very tender, about 10–15 minutes.

2. Transfer the apples to a colander, drain excess water, and then put them into a medium bowl. Mash with a fork until desired consistency is reached.

Nutritional Analysis (per serving): Calories: 80 | Protein: 0g | Carbohydrates: 20g | Fat: 0g | Saturated Fat: 0g | Cholesterol: 0mg | Sodium: 0mg | Fiber: 4g | PCF Ratio: 2-96-2 | Exchange Approx.: 1⅓ Fruits

LEMONY CREAM CHEESE SPREAD

YIELDS 12 TABLESPOONS; SERVING SIZE: 1 TABLESPOON

1 (8-ounce) tub light cream cheese

4 teaspoons powdered sugar

2 tablespoons fresh lemon juice

Serving Suggestions

This recipe is a cross between a frosting and a spread. It's great for serving with muffins or quick breads and is a nice lower-sugar frosting for desserts.

Put all the ingredients in a medium bowl and mix well by hand or with an electric mixer. Store unused spread in an airtight container in the refrigerator for up to a week.

Nutritional Analysis (per serving): Calories: 50 | Protein: 3g | Carbohydrates: 2g | Fat: 3g | Saturated Fat: 2g | Cholesterol: 10mg | Sodium: 60mg | Fiber: 0g | PCF Ratio: 23-20-57 | Exchange Approx.: ¼ Other Carbohydrate, ½ Fat

LEMON CUMIN MAYO

YIELDS 12 TABLESPOONS; SERVING SIZE: 1 TABLESPOON

½ cup nonfat Greek yogurt

¼ cup light mayo

1 or 2 squeezes of fresh lemon juice

½ teaspoon ground cumin

Salt and pepper to taste (optional)

A Dip or a Sauce?

This works great as a spread for sandwiches or even as a dip for veggies.

Add all of the ingredients to a small bowl and mix well. Store unused portions in an airtight container in the refrigerator for up to a week.

Nutritional Analysis (per serving, without salt): Calories: 15 | Protein: 1g | Carbohydrates: 1g | Fat: 1g | Saturated Fat: 0g | Cholesterol: 0mg | Sodium: 40mg | Fiber: 0g | PCF Ratio: 20-20-60 | Exchange Approx.: ⅓ Fat

EASY FRUIT YOGURT

SERVES 2; SERVING SIZE: ½ CUP

1 cup nonfat plain Greek yogurt

2 tablespoons lower-sugar jam

Ways to Use This Yogurt

Add this yogurt to fruit salad, mix it in with cottage cheese, or serve it over your favorite high-fiber cereal to add protein and delicious flavor.

Put the yogurt into a small dish, spoon in the jam, and stir well.

Nutritional Analysis (per serving): Calories: 90 | Protein: 11g | Carbohydrates: 10g | Fat: 0g | Saturated Fat: 0g | Cholesterol: 0mg | Sodium: 40mg | Fiber: 0g | PCF Ratio: 46-54-0 | Exchange Approx.: 1 Skim Milk

EASY PUMPKIN PASTA SAUCE

YIELDS 2 CUPS; SERVING SIZE: ½ CUP

⅔ cup canned pumpkin

1⅓ cups jarred marinara sauce

Mix the pumpkin and marinara together in a small pot, heat, and serve. Store extra sauce in the refrigerator for a few days.

Nutritional Analysis (per serving): Calories: 45 | Protein: 1g | Carbohydrates: 9g | Fat: 1g | Saturated Fat: 0g | Cholesterol: 0mg | Sodium: 350mg | Fiber: 3g | PCF Ratio: 9-76-15 | Exchange Approx.: 2 Vegetables

CLASSIC PICO DE GALLO

YIELDS 5 CUPS; SERVING SIZE: ¼ CUP

3 large tomatoes, finely chopped

1 medium to large onion, finely chopped

2 Anaheim chili peppers, diced

½ cup finely chopped fresh cilantro

Juice of 1 lime

Juice of 1 lemon

Salt and pepper (optional)

Salsa Suggestions

This refreshing, easy, and healthy salsa makes a great accompaniment to fajitas, tacos, salads, and omelets. Mix it with a little avocado and you've got instant, delicious guacamole! If you like more spice, you can add jalapeño peppers as well.

Toss all of the ingredients in a medium-sized bowl and chill before serving. Store unused portions in an airtight container in the refrigerator for 1–2 days.

Nutritional Analysis (per serving): Calories: 10 | Protein: 0g | Carbohydrates: 2g | Fat: 0g | Saturated Fat: 0g | Cholesterol: 0mg | Sodium: 0mg | Fiber: 1g | PCF Ratio: 13-83-4 | Exchange Approx.: ½ Vegetable

CREAMY RED PEPPER AND TOMATO SAUCE

YIELDS 4 CUPS; SERVING SIZE: ½ CUP

1 tablespoon olive oil

⅔ cup chopped white onion

4 cloves garlic, chopped

4 cups chopped red bell pepper

1 (14-ounce) can diced tomatoes

4 tablespoons chopped fresh basil

½ cup fat-free half-and-half

¼ teaspoon salt (optional)

1. Coat a large pan with the olive oil; add the onions, garlic, and peppers and sauté on medium heat for 7–10 minutes until soft and browned. Then add the tomatoes to the pan and heat for another 3–5 minutes. Remove from heat, add the fresh basil, and let cool.

2. Carefully transfer the cooled tomato/pepper mixture from the pot to a food processor or blender and purée until smooth. Depending on the size of your food processor or blender, you may need to purée a partial portion at a time.

3. Put the blended mixture back in the pan, add the fat-free half-and-half, and simmer for 5 minutes on low heat until warmed through. Add salt if desired.

Nutritional Analysis (per serving, without salt): Calories: 60 | Protein: 2g | Carbohydrates: 9g | Fat: 2g | Saturated Fat: 0g | Cholesterol: 0mg | Sodium: 115mg | Fiber: 2g | PCF Ratio: 12-59-29 | Exchange Approx.: 1½ Vegetables, ½ Fat

CREAMY DIJON BASIL SAUCE

**YIELDS ABOUT 1 CUP; SERVING SIZE:
2 TABLESPOONS**

¼ cup finely chopped fresh basil

¼ cup grainy Dijon mustard

1 cup low-fat milk

Salt and pepper to taste

Put the chopped basil, Dijon mustard, and milk in a blender or food processor for about 1–2 minutes on high speed until puréed smooth. Add salt and pepper to taste.

Nutritional Analysis (per serving): Calories: 20 | Protein: 1g | Carbohydrates: 3g | Fat: 0g | Saturated Fat: 0g | Cholesterol: 0mg | Sodium: 200mg | Fiber: 0g | PCF Ratio: 23-63-14 | Exchange Approx.: ¼ Skim Milk

WHIPPED CINNAMON HONEY CREAM CHEESE

**YIELDS ABOUT 1 CUP; SERVING SIZE:
2 TABLESPOONS**

1 cup whipped cream cheese

4 teaspoons honey

½ teaspoon cinnamon

Add all the ingredients to a small bowl and mix well. Store unused portions in the refrigerator for up to a week.

Nutritional Analysis (per serving): Calories: 40 | Protein: 2g | Carbohydrates: 2g | Fat: 2.5g | Saturated Fat: 1.5g | Cholesterol: 5mg | Sodium: 50mg | Fiber: 0g | PCF Ratio: 21-26-53 | Exchange Approx.: ¼ Other Carbohydrate, ½ Fat

CHAPTER 7

PASTA, RICE, GRAINS, AND STARCHY VEGETABLES

FUSION LO MEIN

SERVES 6; SERVING SIZE: ⅙ RECIPE

2 tablespoons rice vinegar

2 tablespoons thawed pineapple-orange juice concentrate

2 teaspoons minced shallots

2 teaspoons lemon juice

1 teaspoon cornstarch

1 teaspoon Homemade Worcestershire Sauce (see recipe in Chapter 6)

1 teaspoon honey

2 cloves garlic, minced

Cooking spray

1 teaspoon olive oil

¾ cup chopped green onions

1 cup diagonally sliced (¼" thick) carrots

1 cup julienned yellow bell pepper

1 cup julienned red bell pepper

3 cups small broccoli florets

1 cup fresh bean sprouts

1½ cups cooked pasta

1. In food processor or blender, combine vinegar, juice concentrate, shallots, lemon juice, cornstarch, Worcestershire, honey, and garlic; process until smooth.

2. Heat wok or large nonstick skillet coated with cooking spray over medium-high heat until hot; add olive oil. Add onions; stir-fry 1 minute.

3. Add carrots, bell peppers, and broccoli; stir-fry another minute. Cover pan; cook 2 more minutes.

4. Add vinegar mixture and sprouts. Bring mixture to a boil; cook uncovered 30 seconds, stirring constantly.

5. Add cooked pasta; toss to mix.

Nutritional Analysis (per serving): Calories: 126 | Protein: 5g | Carbohydrates: 26g | Fat: 1g | Saturated Fat: 0g | Cholesterol: 0mg | Sodium: 35mg | Fiber: 4g | PCF Ratio: 14-77-9 | Exchange Approx.: 1 Starch, 1 Vegetable, ½ Fruit

ROASTED BUTTERNUT SQUASH PASTA

SERVES 4; SERVING SIZE: ¼ RECIPE

Nonstick spray

1 butternut squash, halved and seeded

4 teaspoons extra-virgin olive oil

1 clove garlic, minced

1 cup chopped red onion

2 teaspoons red wine vinegar

¼ teaspoon dried oregano

2 cups cooked pasta

Freshly ground black pepper (optional)

Tip

For added flavor, use roasted instead of raw garlic. Roasting garlic causes it to caramelize, adding a natural sweetness.

1. Preheat oven to 400°F. Using nonstick spray, coat one side of two pieces of heavy-duty foil large enough to wrap squash halves. Wrap squash in foil; place on a baking sheet. Bake 1 hour or until tender.

2. Scoop out baked squash flesh, discard rind, and roughly chop flesh. Add olive oil, garlic, and onion to nonstick skillet; sauté for about 5 minutes until onion is transparent. (Alternatively, put oil, garlic, and onion in covered microwave-safe dish; microwave on high 2–3 minutes.)

3. Remove pan from heat; stir in vinegar and oregano. Add squash; stir to coat in onion mixture. Add pasta; toss to mix. Season with freshly ground black pepper if desired.

Nutritional Analysis (per serving): Calories: 216 | Protein: 5g | Carbohydrates: 40g | Fat: 5g | Saturated Fat: 1g | Cholesterol: 0mg | Sodium: 8mg | Fiber: 2g | PCF Ratio: 9-70-21 | Exchange Approx.: 2 Starches, 1 Fat, ½ Vegetable

PASTA WITH ARTICHOKES

SERVES 4; SERVING SIZE: ¼ RECIPE

1 (10-ounce) package frozen artichoke hearts

1¼ cups water

1 tablespoon lemon juice

4 teaspoons olive oil

2 cloves garlic, minced

¼ cup drained and chopped sun-dried tomatoes packed in oil

¼ teaspoon red pepper flakes

2 teaspoons dried parsley

2 cups cooked pasta

¼ cup grated Parmesan cheese

Freshly ground black pepper to taste (optional)

Tip

You can decrease the amount of water to 3 tablespoons and add it with the artichokes and lemon juice to a covered microwave-safe dish. Microwave according to package directions; reserve all liquid. This results in a stronger lemon flavor, which compensates for the lack of salt in the recipe.

1. Cook artichokes in water and lemon juice according to package directions; drain, reserving ¼ cup of liquid. Cool artichokes; cut into quarters.

2. Heat olive oil in nonstick skillet over medium heat. Add garlic; sauté 1 minute. Reduce heat to low. Stir in artichokes and tomatoes; simmer 1 minute. Stir in reserved artichoke liquid, red pepper flakes, and parsley; simmer 5 minutes.

3. Pour artichoke sauce over pasta in a large bowl; toss gently to coat. Sprinkle with cheese and top with pepper if desired.

Nutritional Analysis (per serving): Calories: 308 | Protein: 10g | Carbohydrates: 47g | Fat: 9g | Saturated Fat: 2g | Cholesterol: 2mg | Sodium: 87mg | Fiber: 3g | PCF Ratio: 13-60-27 | Exchange Approx.: 1 Medium-Fat Meat, 2 Vegetables, 1 Starch, 2 Fats

PASTA WITH CREAMED CLAM SAUCE

SERVES 4; SERVING SIZE: ¼ RECIPE

1 (6½-ounce) can chopped clams

4 teaspoons olive oil

1 clove garlic, minced

1 tablespoon dry white wine or dry vermouth

½ cup Mock Cream (see recipe in Chapter 6)

¼ cup freshly grated Parmesan cheese

2 cups cooked pasta

Freshly ground black pepper to taste (optional)

1. Drain clams; reserve juice. Heat olive oil in large nonstick skillet. Add garlic and sauté 1 minute; stir in clams and sauté another minute. With slotted spoon, transfer clams to a bowl; cover to keep warm.

2. Add wine and reserved clam juice to skillet; bring to a boil and reduce by half. Lower heat and add Mock Cream; cook for about 2–3 minutes, being careful not to boil cream.

3. Stir in Parmesan cheese; continue to heat another minute, stirring constantly.

4. Add pasta; toss with sauce. Divide into four equal servings; serve immediately topped with freshly ground pepper if desired.

Nutritional Analysis (per serving): Calories: 226 | Protein: 15g | Carbohydrates: 24g | Fat: 7g | Saturated Fat: 2g | Cholesterol: 25mg | Sodium: 209mg | Fiber: 1g | PCF Ratio: 27-43-30 | Exchange Approx.: 1 Lean Meat, 1 Starch, 1 Fat, ½ Skim Milk

WHOLE-GRAIN NOODLES WITH CARAWAY CABBAGE

SERVES 6; SERVING SIZE: ⅙ RECIPE

2 tablespoons olive oil

½ cup chopped onion

2 cups coarsely chopped cabbage

1½ cups trimmed and halved Brussels sprouts

2 teaspoons caraway seed

1½ cups low-sodium chicken broth

¼ teaspoon freshly ground pepper

¼ teaspoon salt

6 ounces whole-grain noodles

1. Heat olive oil in large saucepan; sauté onions for about 5 minutes until translucent.

2. Add cabbage and Brussels sprouts; cook over medium heat 3 minutes.

3. Stir in caraway seed, broth, pepper, and salt; Cover and simmer 5–8 minutes until vegetables are crisp-tender.

4. Cook noodles in boiling water until tender; drain.

5. Mix noodles and vegetables together in a large bowl; serve.

Nutritional Analysis (per serving): Calories: 169 | Protein: 6g | Carbohydrates: 27g | Fat: 5g | Saturated Fat: 1g | Cholesterol: 0mg | Sodium: 250mg | Fiber: 5g | PCF Ratio: 14-60-26 | Exchange Approx.: 1 Starch, 1 Vegetable, 1 Fat

SQUASH AND BULGUR PILAF

SERVES 6; SERVING SIZE: ⅙ RECIPE

1 tablespoon olive oil

½ cup chopped onions

1 teaspoon minced garlic

1½ cups ½"-cubed yellow summer squash

1 cup bulgur wheat

1 tablespoon olive oil

2 cups low-sodium chicken broth

½ teaspoon ground cinnamon

¼ cup dried currants

¼ cup chopped walnuts

1. In large nonstick skillet, add olive oil, onions, garlic, yellow squash, and bulgur wheat and sauté until onions are tender, about 5 minutes.

2. Stir in chicken broth and cinnamon; heat to boiling. Reduce heat and simmer covered for 10 minutes.

3. Stir in currants; continue to simmer additional 15 minutes. Add walnuts just before serving.

Nutritional Analysis (per serving): Calories: 151 | Protein: 5g | Carbohydrates: 22g | Fat: 6g | Saturated Fat: 1g | Cholesterol: 0mg | Sodium: 190mg | Fiber: 5g | PCF Ratio: 13-54-32 | Exchange Approx.: 1 Starch, ½ Vegetable, 2 Fats

TUSCAN PASTA FAGIOLI

SERVES 6; SERVING SIZE: ⅙ RECIPE

2 tablespoons olive oil

⅓ cup chopped onion

3 cloves garlic, minced

½ pound tomatoes, peeled and chopped

5 cups low-sodium vegetable stock

¼ teaspoon freshly ground pepper

3 cups rinsed and drained canned cannellini beans

2½ cups whole-grain pasta shells

2 tablespoons grated Parmesan cheese

1. Heat olive oil in large pot; gently cook onions and garlic until soft but not browned. Add tomatoes, vegetable stock, and pepper.

2. Purée 1½ cups of cannellini beans in food processor or blender; add to stock. Cover and simmer 20–30 minutes.

3. While stock is simmering, cook pasta until al dente; drain. Add remaining beans and pasta to stock; heat through. Serve with Parmesan cheese.

Nutritional Analysis (per serving): Calories: 317 | Protein: 15g | Carbohydrates: 54g | Fat: 6g | Saturated Fat: 1g | Cholesterol: 2mg | Sodium: 248mg | Fiber: 11g | PCF Ratio: 18-65-17 | Exchange Approx.: 3 Starches, ½ Vegetable, 1 Fat

BROWN RICE AND VEGETABLE SAUTÉ

SERVES 4; SERVING SIZE: ¼ RECIPE

½ cup brown rice

1 cup water

1 tablespoon olive oil

½ cup chopped onions

1 cup chopped red bell peppers

1 teaspoon minced garlic

4 ounces sliced mushrooms

1 (12-ounce) package fresh bean sprouts

1 tablespoon reduced-sodium soy sauce

1 teaspoon fresh grated ginger

1. Add rice to water and bring to boil. Reduce heat; cover and simmer 35–40 minutes until cooked.

2. In large nonstick skillet or wok, heat olive oil. Add onions, red pepper, and garlic; cook until onion is translucent.

3. Add mushrooms, bean sprouts, and soy sauce; cook on low heat 3 minutes.

4. Add rice and ginger; mix ingredients. Cook on low additional 2–3 minutes.

Nutritional Analysis (per serving): Calories: 154 | Protein: 5g | Carbohydrates: 26g | Fat: 4g | Saturated Fat: 1g | Cholesterol: 0mg | Sodium: 352mg | Fiber: 3g | PCF Ratio: 12-64-24 | Exchange Approx.: 1 Starch, 1½ Vegetables, 1 Fat

HERBED QUINOA WITH SUN-DRIED TOMATOES

SERVES 6; SERVING SIZE: ⅙ RECIPE

½ tablespoon olive oil

¼ cup chopped onion

1 clove garlic, minced

1 cup quinoa

2 cups low-sodium chicken broth

½ cup sliced fresh mushrooms

6 sun-dried tomatoes, cut into ¼" pieces

1 teaspoon Italian-blend seasoning

Cooking Time for Quinoa

Quinoa takes no longer to cook than rice or pasta, usually about 15 minutes. You can tell quinoa is cooked when grains have turned from white to transparent and spiral-like germ has separated from seed.

1. In medium saucepan, heat olive oil; sauté onions and garlic.

2. Rinse quinoa in very fine mesh strainer before cooking. Add quinoa and broth to saucepan; bring to a boil for 2 minutes. Add mushrooms, sun-dried tomatoes, and Italian seasoning.

3. Reduce heat and cover. Cook 15 minutes or until all water is absorbed.

Nutritional Analysis (per serving): Calories: 119 | Protein: 5g | Carbohydrates: 21g | Fat: 2g | Saturated Fat: 0g | Cholesterol: 0mg | Sodium: 193mg | Fiber: 2g | PCF Ratio: 17-71-12 | Exchange Approx.: 1 Starch, ½ Very Lean Meat, 2 Fats

QUINOA WITH ROASTED VEGETABLES

SERVES 4; SERVING SIZE: ¼ RECIPE

⅔ cup chopped green pepper

½ cup chopped red pepper (mildly hot variety)

3 cups 1"-cubed eggplant

2 cloves garlic, finely chopped

1 tablespoon olive oil

¼ teaspoon ground cumin

½ cup quinoa

1 cup water

¼ teaspoon salt

Another Idea

Cook quinoa as outlined in steps 3 and 4. Combine with 3 cups of Oven-Roasted Ratatouille (see recipe in Chapter 8). Nutritional Analysis (for 1-cup serving): Calories: 162; Protein: 7g; Carbohydrates: 26g; Fat: 3g; Saturated Fat: 0g; Cholesterol: 1mg; Sodium: 202mg; Fiber: 4g; PCF Ratio: 13-69-18; Exchange Approx.: 1 Starch, 2 Vegetables, ½ Fat.

1. Preheat oven to 375°F. Combine peppers, eggplant, garlic, olive oil, and cumin in 2-quart baking dish. Cover and roast 20 minutes.

2. Remove cover; continue to roast in oven for about 30 minutes until vegetables are browned and cooked soft. Remove from oven; place cover back on.

3. Rinse quinoa in very fine mesh strainer before cooking. Bring water and salt to a boil; add quinoa and bring to a boil for 5 minutes. Cover, remove from heat, and let stand 15 minutes.

4. Once quinoa is cooked and all water is absorbed, add roasted vegetables and serve.

Nutritional Analysis (per serving): Calories: 120 | Protein: 4g | Carbohydrates: 9g | Fat: 4g | Saturated Fat: 0g | Cholesterol: 0mg | Sodium: 151mg | Fiber: 4g | PCF Ratio: 12-62-26 | Exchange Approx.: 1 Starch, 1 Vegetable, 2 Fats

KASHA-STUFFED RED PEPPERS

SERVES 4; SERVING SIZE: 1 PEPPER

1 cup kasha

1 egg white, lightly beaten

Nonstick cooking spray

2 cups low-sodium beef broth

4 ounces lean ground beef

1 cup finely chopped onion

5 ounces (½ package) frozen chopped spinach, thawed and drained

½ cup crumbled feta cheese

½ cup canned diced tomatoes

1 teaspoon dried oregano

⅛ teaspoon crushed red pepper

2 pounds (4 large) red bell peppers, tops removed and seeded

1½ cups water

Save the Tomato Juice

Most canned tomatoes are packed in juice or puréed tomato. When you open a can, save juices and add to recipes when liquids are called for. In this recipe, tomato juice from can could substitute for some water used to cook peppers in.

1. Preheat oven to 375°F.

2. Mix kasha and egg white together in small bowl. In large nonstick saucepan sprayed with nonstick cooking spray, add kasha; cook over high heat 2–3 minutes, stirring constantly, until kasha kernels are separated.

3. Add beef broth slowly. Reduce heat; cover and cook 7–10 minutes until kasha kernels are tender. Transfer to large bowl.

4. Brown beef in small nonstick skillet. Add onions; cook 2–3 minutes until slightly softened.

5. Add beef mixture and chopped spinach to cooked kasha; mix well. Stir in feta cheese, diced tomato, oregano, and crushed red pepper. Divide mixture equally; stuff each red pepper. Place peppers in 9" × 9" baking dish.

6. Pour water around peppers. Cover with foil; bake 60–75 minutes or until peppers are cooked.

Nutritional Analysis (per serving): Calories: 383 | Protein: 22g | Carbohydrates: 54g | Fat: 12g | Saturated Fat: 5g | Cholesterol: 40mg | Sodium: 387mg | Fiber: 11g | PCF Ratio: 22-53-25 | Exchange Approx.: 2 Starches, 4 Vegetables, 1½ Lean Meats, 2 Fats

RED AND WHITE BEAN SALAD

SERVES 8; SERVING SIZE: 1/8 RECIPE

2 cups cooked navy beans

2 cups cooked red beans

1 cup chopped arugula

1/4 cup lemon juice

3 tablespoons olive oil

1/4 teaspoon freshly ground pepper

1 cup thinly sliced red onion

8 ounces cherry tomatoes, cut in half

About Arugula

Arugula has several other names such as rocket, rugula, roquette, and rucola. It is sometimes found in baby greens or mesclun mixes. It has a nutty and peppery flavor, which can add interest to a salad or sandwich. Give arugula a try!

1. Combine beans together in medium bowl.

2. Whisk together arugula, lemon juice, olive oil, and pepper; pour over beans.

3. Add onions and toss lightly to mix. Let mixture refrigerate at least 3 hours.

4. Just before serving, toss in cherry tomatoes; mix lightly.

Nutritional Analysis (per serving): Calories: 86 | Protein: 8g | Carbohydrates: 27g | Fat: 6g | Saturated Fat: 1g | Cholesterol: 0mg | Sodium: 7mg | Fiber: 7g | PCF Ratio: 17-55-27 | Exchange Approx.: 1½ Starches, 1 Vegetable, ½ Very Lean Meat, 2 Fats

WHOLE-WHEAT COUSCOUS SALAD

SERVES 8; SERVING SIZE: 1/8 RECIPE

1 cup low-sodium chicken broth

1/4 cup dried currants

1/2 teaspoon ground cumin

3/4 cup whole-wheat couscous

1/4 cup olive oil

2 tablespoons lemon juice

1 cup chopped steamed (crisp-tender) broccoli

3 tablespoons pine nuts

1 tablespoon chopped fresh parsley

Aren't Currants Just Small Raisins?

Dried currants may look like miniature raisins, but they are actually quite different. Currants are berries from a shrub, not a vine, and there are red and black varieties. Black currants are rich in phytonutrients and antioxidants. They have twice the potassium of bananas and four times the vitamin C of oranges!

1. Combine chicken broth, currants, and cumin; bring to a boil. Remove from heat; stir in couscous. Cover and let sit until cool. Fluff couscous with fork 2 or 3 times during the cooling process.

2. Whisk together olive oil and lemon juice.

3. Add steamed broccoli and pine nuts to couscous. Pour oil and lemon juice over couscous; toss lightly. Garnish with chopped parsley.

Nutritional Analysis (per serving): Calories: 153 | Protein: 4g | Carbohydrates: 15g | Fat: 9g | Saturated Fat: 1g | Cholesterol: 0mg | Sodium: 85mg | Fiber: 2g | PCF Ratio: 9-38-52 | Exchange Approx.: 1 Starch, 2 Fats

BLUE CHEESE PASTA

SERVES 4; SERVING SIZE: ½ CUP

2 teaspoons olive oil

1 clove garlic, minced

½ cup nonfat cottage cheese

2 ounces crumbled blue cheese

Skim milk as needed (optional)

2 cups cooked pasta

¼ cup freshly grated Parmesan cheese

Freshly ground black pepper (optional)

1. Heat olive oil in large nonstick skillet. Add garlic; sauté 1 minute. Lower heat; stir in cottage cheese and cook for 2 minutes.

2. Add blue cheese; stir to combine. Thin sauce with a little skim milk if necessary.

3. Toss sauce with pasta; divide into four equal servings. Top each serving with a tablespoon of Parmesan cheese and freshly ground black pepper if desired.

Nutritional Analysis (per serving): Calories: 213 | Protein: 12g | Carbohydrates: 21g | Fat: 9g | Saturated Fat: 4g | Cholesterol: 17mg | Sodium: 317mg | Fiber: 1g | PCF Ratio: 23-39-37 | Exchange Approx.: ½ High-Fat Meat, ½ Very Lean Meat, ½ Lean Meat, 1 Starch, ½ Fat

CRANBERRY ALMOND RICE

YIELDS ABOUT 2 CUPS; SERVING SIZE: ⅓ CUP

2 cups cooked brown rice

1 teaspoon butter or margarine

¼ cup slivered almonds

¼ cup dried cranberries

⅓ cup unsweetened almond milk

1. Cook rice according to package directions and set aside.

2. Put the butter/margarine in a medium-sized pot and add the nuts and cranberries. Toast on low heat for 5–8 minutes.

3. Add the rice and stir in the almond milk to evenly coat. Heat for another 2–4 minutes until warmed through.

Nutritional Analysis (per serving): Calories: 130 | Protein: 2g | Carbohydrates: 24g | Fat: 3.5g | Saturated Fat: 0.5g | Cholesterol: 0mg | Sodium: 15mg | Fiber: 2g | PCF Ratio: 7-71-22 | Exchange Approx.: 1 Starch, 1 Fat

PASTA WITH TUNA ALFREDO SAUCE

SERVES 4; SERVING SIZE: ½ CUP

1 cup nonfat cottage cheese

1 tablespoon skim milk

2 teaspoons olive oil

1 clove garlic, minced

2 (6-ounce) cans tuna packed in water, drained

⅛ cup (2 tablespoons) dry white wine

¼ cup freshly grated Parmesan cheese

2 cups cooked pasta

Freshly ground black pepper to taste (optional)

1. Process cottage cheese and skim milk in food processor or blender until smooth. Set aside.

2. Heat olive oil in large nonstick skillet. Add garlic; sauté 1 minute. Stir in tuna; sauté another minute.

3. Add wine to skillet; bring to a boil. Lower heat; add cottage cheese mixture. Cook for about 5 minutes, being careful not to let it boil.

4. Stir in Parmesan; continue to heat 1 minute, stirring constantly.

5. Add pasta; toss with sauce. Divide into four equal servings; serve immediately topped with freshly ground pepper if desired.

Nutritional Analysis (per serving): Calories: 278 | Protein: 33g | Carbohydrates: 21g | Fat: 5g | Saturated Fat: 2g | Cholesterol: 32mg | Sodium: 401mg | Fiber: 1g | PCF Ratio: 50-31-18 | Exchange Approx.: 1½ Very Lean Meats, 1½ Lean Meats, 1½ Carbohydrates/Starches

BLACK BEAN AND QUINOA SKILLET

YIELDS 6 CUPS; SERVING SIZE: ½ CUP

3 cups cooked quinoa

1 teaspoon olive oil

1 cup finely chopped red bell pepper

¼ cup finely chopped Anaheim chili pepper

¼ cup finely chopped white onion

1 (15-ounce) can black beans, rinsed well

1 cup corn (fresh, canned, or frozen thawed)

1 tablespoon lime juice

½ tablespoon ground cumin

1–2 tablespoons chopped fresh cilantro

Salt and pepper (optional)

Optional garnishes: chopped tomato, avocado, light sour cream, low-fat cheese, additional lime juice and cilantro

1. Cook quinoa according to package directions.

2. Add the teaspoon olive oil to a large pan, put in the peppers and onion, and sauté on medium-high heat until slightly soft, about 3–5 minutes. Then add the black beans, corn, lime juice, cumin, and cilantro and heat another 5 minutes, stirring frequently.

3. Mix in the cooked quinoa and heat for another 3–5 minutes. Add salt and pepper to taste and serve warm with optional garnishes if desired.

Nutritional Analysis (per serving, without salt): Calories: 110 | Protein: 4g | Carbohydrates: 18g | Fat: 1.5g | Saturated Fat: 0g | Cholesterol: 0mg | Sodium: 300mg | Fiber: 3g | PCF Ratio: 18-51-31 | Exchange Approx.: 1 Starch, ½ Lean Meat

MEDITERRANEAN QUINOA SALAD

YIELDS 3 CUPS; SERVING SIZE: ½ CUP

1 cup cooked quinoa

1 cup cooked lentils

1 tablespoon olive oil

1 tablespoon balsamic vinegar

1 tablespoon lemon juice

¼ teaspoon garlic powder

1–2 tablespoons chopped fresh basil

1 cup peeled and chopped cucumber

2 tablespoons chopped kalamata or black olives

2 tablespoons reduced-fat feta cheese

Salt and pepper (optional)

1. Add the olive oil, vinegar, lemon juice, garlic powder, and chopped basil to a small bowl and whisk together.

2. In a medium bowl, toss together the cooked quinoa and lentils, cucumber, and olives. Stir in the olive oil dressing and feta cheese; add salt and pepper if desired.

Nutritional Analysis (per serving, without salt): Calories: 110 | Protein: 5g | Carbohydrates: 14g | Fat: 4g | Saturated Fat: 0.5g | Cholesterol: 0mg | Sodium: 130mg | Fiber: 4g | PCF Ratio: 18-50-32 | Exchange Approx.: 1 Starch, ¾ Fat

CURRY ORZO AND VEGETABLES

YIELDS 5 CUPS; SERVING SIZE: 1 CUP

1 cup dry whole-wheat orzo

1 cup chicken or vegetable broth

1 cup chopped carrots

2 cups chopped cauliflower florets

1 teaspoon olive oil

½–¾ teaspoon curry powder

¼ teaspoon garlic powder

2 tablespoons golden raisins

Chopped cashews (optional)

1. Cook orzo by boiling 1 quart of water, adding the orzo, and simmering for about 10–15 minutes until tender; drain.

2. Add the broth, carrots, and cauliflower to a large saucepan; cover with the lid and simmer on medium heat until the veggies are slightly tender, about 5 minutes.

3. Once cooked, add the orzo to the pan with the vegetables; stir in the olive oil, curry powder, garlic powder, and raisins and heat for another 3–5 minutes. Serve warm or chilled topped with chopped cashews if desired.

Nutritional Analysis (per serving): Calories: 80 | Protein: 3g | Carbohydrates: 16g | Fat: 1g | Saturated Fat: 0g | Cholesterol: 0mg | Sodium: 70mg | Fiber: 4g | PCF Ratio: 13-77-10 | Exchange Approx.: ¾ Starch, 1 Vegetable

ORZO WITH ZUCCHINI, OLIVES, AND FETA

YIELDS 3½ CUPS; SERVING SIZE: ½ CUP

1 cup dry whole-wheat orzo

1 teaspoon plus 1 tablespoon olive oil, divided

2 cups sliced zucchini

¼ cup chopped black olives

¼ cup chopped fresh basil

1 tablespoon lemon juice

¼ teaspoon garlic powder

¼ cup reduced-fat feta cheese

1. Cook orzo by boiling 1 quart of water, adding the orzo, and simmering for about 10–15 minutes until tender; drain.

2. Add 1 teaspoon olive oil to a medium-sized pan, put in zucchini, and sauté on medium heat for about 3–5 minutes until slightly tender. Stir in the olives and basil and remove from heat.

3. In a small bowl, whisk together 1 tablespoon olive oil, the lemon juice, and the garlic powder.

4. Add the cooked/drained orzo and the zucchini mixture together to a medium-sized bowl. Stir in the olive oil and lemon dressing and feta cheese and serve at room temperature or cold.

Nutritional Analysis (per serving): Calories: 90 | Protein: 3g | Carbohydrates: 13g | Fat: 3g | Saturated Fat: 0.5g | Cholesterol: 0mg | Sodium: 75mg | Fiber: 3g | PCF Ratio: 13-57-30 | Exchange Approx.: ½ Starch, 1 Vegetable, ½ Fat

GRILLED VEGETABLE PASTA SALAD

YIELDS 8 CUPS; SERVING SIZE: 1 CUP

1 cup broccoli florets

1 cup button mushrooms

1 red bell pepper, cut lengthwise into ¼" strips

1 zucchini, cut lengthwise into ¼" strips

1 yellow squash, cut lengthwise into ¼" strips

½ large eggplant or 1 small, cut into ¼"-thick rounds

4 cups cooked whole-wheat pasta

¼ cup corn (fresh, canned, or frozen thawed)

½ cup chopped kalamata or black olives

¼ cup olive oil

2 tablespoons balsamic vinegar

3 tablespoons chopped fresh basil

1. Preheat the grill on high. Skewer the broccoli and mushrooms or place them on foil. Grill the broccoli and mushroom skewers along with the red pepper, zucchini, squash, and eggplant on high heat, about 5–7 minutes on each side until lightly browned. Set aside to cool.

2. Put the cooked pasta into a medium-sized bowl. Chop up the cooled grilled vegetables into 1" cubes and add to the bowl. Add in the corn and olives.

3. In a small bowl, whisk together the oil, vinegar, and basil and pour over the pasta and vegetables; mix well

Nutritional Analysis (per serving): Calories: 220 | Protein: 5g | Carbohydrates: 28g | Fat: 9g | Saturated Fat: 1g | Cholesterol: 0mg | Sodium: 100mg | Fiber: 5g | PCF Ratio: 9-53-38 | Exchange Approx.: 1½ Starches, 1½ Vegetables, 1½ Fats

SPINACH AND WALNUT GNOCCHI

YIELDS 3 CUPS; SERVING SIZE: ½ CUP

2 cups cooked gnocchi, preferably whole wheat

1 teaspoon olive oil

½ cup finely chopped shallots

2 or 3 garlic cloves, finely chopped

6 cups fresh spinach

½ cup chicken or vegetable broth

¼ cup white wine

3 tablespoons chopped walnuts

3 tablespoons grated Parmesan cheese

Chopped fresh basil (optional)

1. Coat a large pan with the olive oil; add the shallots and garlic and brown on medium heat for about 3 minutes. Add the spinach, broth, and wine and heat until spinach is slightly wilted. Stir in the cooked gnocchi and heat for another few minutes until warmed though.

2. Top with nuts and cheese and serve. Garnish with fresh chopped basil if desired.

Nutritional Analysis (per serving): Calories: 220 | Protein: 7g | Carbohydrates: 31g | Fat: 5g | Saturated Fat: 1.5g | Cholesterol: 10mg | Sodium: 370mg | Fiber: 3g | PCF Ratio: 14-61-25 | Exchange Approx.: 1½ Starches, 1 Vegetable, 1 Fat

EASY PASTA SAUSAGE TOSS

SERVES 4; SERVING SIZE: ¼ RECIPE

2 cups cooked penne or fusilli pasta

8 ounces fully cooked chicken or turkey sausage, chopped into ¼"-thick rounds

1 tablespoon olive oil

1 (8-ounce) package sliced mushrooms

1 cup chopped canned artichokes

2 cups fresh baby spinach

¼ cup chopped olives

¼ cup chopped fresh basil

½ teaspoon crushed garlic

Grated Parmesan cheese (optional)

1. Brown the sausage in a large pan coated with the olive oil on medium-high heat for a few minutes.

2. Add the mushrooms and artichokes and heat for another few minutes. Put in the cooked pasta plus the spinach, olives, basil, and garlic and warm through on medium heat for 3–4 minutes. Sprinkle with Parmesan cheese if desired.

Nutritional Analysis (per serving): Calories: 250 | Protein: 16g | Carbohydrates: 25g | Fat: 10g | Saturated Fat: 2g | Cholesterol: 45mg | Sodium: 400mg | Fiber: 6g | PCF Ratio: 24-40-36 | Exchange Approx.: 1 Starch, 2 Vegetables, 1½ Medium-Fat Meats

SOUTHWESTERN PASTA PRIMAVERA

YIELDS 8 CUPS, SERVING SIZE: 1 CUP

3 cups cooked whole-wheat pasta

1 teaspoon olive oil

1 cup chopped white onion

1 cup chopped red bell pepper

2 cups sliced zucchini

1 cup canned black beans, rinsed well

1 cup corn (fresh, canned or frozen
  thawed)

1 (14-ounce) can stewed tomatoes

1 tablespoon ground cumin

1 tablespoon chili powder

Low-fat shredded cheese (optional)

Chopped fresh cilantro (optional)

1. Coat a large pan with the olive oil, add the onions and bell peppers, and sauté on medium heat for 3–4 minutes until lightly browned. Then add the zucchini, black beans, corn, tomatoes, cumin, and chili powder. Simmer for 5–7 minutes, stirring occasionally.

2. Rinse and drain the cooked pasta and stir it into the pan with the vegetable/tomato mixture. Cook for another 2–3 minutes until warmed through. Garnish with cheese and chopped cilantro if desired.

Nutritional Analysis (per serving): Calories: 160 | Protein: 6g | Carbohydrates: 30g | Fat: 2g | Saturated Fat: 0g | Cholesterol: 0mg | Sodium: 300mg | Fiber: 5g | PCF Ratio: 15-78-7 | Exchange Approx.: 1½ Starches, 1½ Vegetables

PASTA WITH CHICKEN, SUN-DRIED TOMATOES, AND ARTICHOKES

SERVES 6; SERVING SIZE: ⅙ RECIPE

3 cups cooked whole-wheat pasta

2 large or 4 small chicken breasts

1 tablespoon plus 1 teaspoon olive oil

½ cup diced shallots

2 cloves garlic

3 cups broccoli florets

⅓ cup sun-dried tomatoes

1 (14-ounce) can low-sodium chicken broth

1 cup white wine

⅓ cup chopped black or kalamata olives

⅓ cup chopped fresh basil

Grated Parmesan cheese (optional)

1. Brown the chicken in a skillet coated with 1 tablespoon olive oil for 6–7 minutes on each side until no longer pink in the center. Let the cooked chicken cool, cut into cubes, and set aside.

2. Add 1 teaspoon olive oil, shallots, and garlic to the skillet and sauté on medium heat for 3–4 minutes until lightly browned. Then add the broccoli, sun-dried tomatoes, half of the chicken broth, and half of the white wine and simmer for another 5–7 minutes.

3. Put the cooked pasta and the browned chicken in the pan with the broccoli and tomato mixture along with the rest of the chicken broth and wine and sprinkle with chopped olives and basil. Cook for another 2–3 minutes until warmed through. Sprinkle with Parmesan cheese if desired.

Nutritional Analysis (per serving): Calories: 290 | Protein: 22g | Carbohydrates: 30g | Fat: 7g | Saturated Fat: 1g | Cholesterol: 40mg | Sodium: 150mg | Fiber: 5g | PCF Ratio: 29-43-28 | Exchange Approx.: 1 Starch, 2 Vegetables, 2 Lean Meats, 1 Fat

COCONUT CASHEW RICE

YIELDS 2 CUPS; SERVING SIZE: ⅓ CUP

2 cups cooked brown rice

1 teaspoon butter or margarine

¼ cup chopped cashews

¼ cup golden raisins

⅓ cup light coconut milk

1. Coat a medium-sized pot with the butter/margarine, add the nuts and raisins, and toast on low heat for 5–8 minutes.

2. Add the rice and stir in the coconut milk to evenly coat. Heat for another few minutes and serve.

Nutritional Analysis (per serving): Calories: 150 | Protein: 3g | Carbohydrates: 24g | Fat: 4.5g | Saturated Fat: 1.5g | Cholesterol: 0mg | Sodium: 50mg | Fiber: 2g | PCF Ratio: 7-65-28 | Exchange Approx.: 1 Starch, ½ Fruit, 1 Fat

CILANTRO RICE

YIELDS 2 CUPS; SERVING SIZE: ⅓ CUP

2 cups cooked brown rice

2 teaspoons lime juice

2 teaspoons olive oil

1 tablespoon chopped fresh cilantro

Put the brown rice in a small bowl. Add the lime juice, olive oil, and cilantro. Stir well and serve.

Nutritional Analysis (per serving): Calories: 90 | Protein: 1g | Carbohydrates: 19g | Fat: 2g | Saturated Fat: 0g | Cholesterol: 0mg | Sodium: 0mg | Fiber: 1g | PCF Ratio: 6-77-17 | Exchange Approx.: 1 Starch

FIESTA RICE

YIELDS 4½ CUPS; SERVING SIZE: ½ CUP

3 cups cooked brown rice

1 teaspoon olive oil

¼ cup diced white onion

¼ cup diced yellow, red, or orange bell pepper

1 cup chicken or vegetable broth

1 cup canned stewed tomatoes

¼ cup corn (fresh, frozen thawed, or canned rinsed)

¼ teaspoon chili powder

1. Coat a medium-sized pot with the olive oil and warm on medium-high heat. Put in the onions and peppers and sauté for 4–5 minutes until softened.

2. Add the broth, tomatoes, corn, and chili powder and mix well. Stir in the cooked rice and heat 5–7 minutes until warmed through.

Nutritional Analysis (per serving): Calories: 100 | Protein: 1g | Carbohydrates: 23g | Fat: 1g | Saturated Fat: 0g | Cholesterol: 0mg | Sodium: 90mg | Fiber: 2g | PCF Ratio: 7-85-8 | Exchange Approx.: 1½ Starches

WHOLE-WHEAT DUMPLINGS

YIELDS 2 CUPS; SERVING SIZE: ½ CUP

1 cup whole-wheat pastry flour

½ cup egg substitute or liquid egg whites

2 tablespoons water

½ teaspoon salt

1. Combine all of the ingredients in a small bowl and mix with a whisk or a spoon until a thick dough is formed. Refrigerate for 20 minutes.

2. Bring a medium-sized pot of water to a boil and drop the dough in teaspoonfuls into the boiling water; using a knife to cut away the teaspoonfuls is helpful.

3. Once all the dough has been put into the water, reduce to medium-low heat and simmer for 4–7 minutes until dumplings are firm yet tender when pierced with a fork.

Nutritional Analysis (per serving): Calories: 130 | Protein: 6g | Carbohydrates: 24g | Fat: 0g | Saturated Fat: 0g | Cholesterol: 0mg | Sodium: 350mg | Fiber: 4g | PCF Ratio: 15-77-8 | Exchange Approx.: 1½ Starches

EDAMAME SUCCOTASH

YIELDS 7 CUPS; SERVING SIZE: 1 CUP

2 tablespoons butter or margarine, divided

2 tablespoons diced red onion

1 cup chopped red pepper

1 cup sweet corn (fresh, canned, or frozen thawed)

2 cups shelled and cooked edamame

Salt and pepper (optional)

1. Coat a large pan with 1 tablespoon of the butter/margarine and add the onions and red pepper. Sauté until slightly tender, about 5 minutes.

2. Throw in the corn and edamame, add the remaining 1 tablespoon butter/margarine, and sauté for another 5–7 minutes. Add salt and pepper to taste if desired.

Nutritional Analysis (per serving, without salt): Calories: 110 | Protein: 6g | Carbohydrates: 9g | Fat: 5g | Saturated Fat: 2g | Cholesterol: 10mg | Sodium: 70mg | Fiber: 1g | PCF Ratio: 22-33-45 | Exchange Approx.: ½ Starch, ½ Vegetable, ½ Very Lean Meat, ½ Fat

SWEET AND SMOKY SWEET POTATO SLICES

YIELDS 4 CUPS; SERVING SIZE: ½ CUP

3 or 4 sweet potatoes, peel on, scrubbed, and cut into very thin ⅛"-thick slices (to yield 5 cups)

2 tablespoons olive oil

2 packed teaspoons brown sugar

1 tablespoon smoked paprika

½ teaspoon sea salt

1. Preheat oven to 375°F.

2. Put the sweet potato slices in a medium bowl, add the olive oil, and mix well to coat.

3. In a separate small dish combine the brown sugar, smoked paprika, and salt. Sprinkle this mixture over the sweet potatoes; mix well.

4. Bake for 25–30 minutes (flipping them once halfway through the baking) until lightly browned and starting to crisp.

Nutritional Analysis (per serving): Calories: 110 | Protein: 1g | Carbohydrates: 18g | Fat: 3.5g | Saturated Fat: 0.5g | Cholesterol: 0mg | Sodium: 190mg | Fiber: 3g | PCF Ratio: 5-66-29 | Exchange Approx.: 1 Starch, ½ Fat

BROCCOLI SMASHED POTATOES

YIELDS 4 CUPS; SERVING SIZE: ½ CUP

1½ pounds new potatoes

2 cups broccoli florets

½ cup fat-free half-and-half

½–1 teaspoon garlic powder

2 tablespoons grated Parmesan cheese

¼ cup diced fresh chives

Salt and pepper (optional)

1. Wash and scrub potatoes and boil them in a large pot of water until soft when pierced with a fork, about 25–30 minutes.

2. Meanwhile, cook the broccoli until tender by either boiling it in a pot of water or steaming in a Pyrex dish in ½" of water for about 3–4 minutes until soft.

3. Drain and cool the cooked potatoes and broccoli and place them in a large bowl. Mash them together with a fork.

4. In a small bowl, whisk the half-and-half, garlic powder, Parmesan cheese, and chives together and pour them into the bowl with potatoes and broccoli. Continue to mash until desired consistency is reached. Add salt and pepper to taste if desired.

Nutritional Analysis (per serving, without salt): Calories: 80 | Protein: 3g | Carbohydrates: 17g | Fat: 0.5g | Saturated Fat: 0g | Cholesterol: 0mg | Sodium: 60mg | Fiber: 2g | PCF Ratio: 15-78-7 | Exchange Approx.: 1 Starch, ¼ Vegetable

CHERRY PECAN SWEET POTATO SALAD

YIELDS 3 CUPS; SERVING SIZE: ½ CUP

2 cups cooked, cooled, cubed sweet
    potato

1 cup pitted chopped cherries

¼ cup chopped pecans

2 tablespoons maple syrup

1 tablespoon olive oil

Combine all of the ingredients in a medium bowl and serve.

Nutritional Analysis (per serving): Calories: 150 | Protein: 2g | Carbohydrates: 23g | Fat: 6g | Saturated Fat: 0.5g | Cholesterol: 0mg | Sodium: 25mg | Fiber: 3g | PCF Ratio: 5-61-34 | Exchange Approx.: 1 Starch, ½ Other Carbohydrate, 1 Fat

SUMMER CORN SALAD

YIELDS 2½ CUPS; SERVING SIZE: ½ CUP

2 cups cooked corn (fresh, canned, or
    frozen thawed)

½ cup diced roasted bell pepper

1 tablespoon olive oil

1 teaspoon lemon juice

1 teaspoon lime juice

1–2 teaspoons chopped cilantro

Salt and pepper to taste (optional)

1. Add the corn and the peppers to a medium bowl.

2. In a separate small bowl, mix the olive oil, lemon juice, and lime juice.

3. Pour the dressing over the corn and peppers, sprinkle with chopped cilantro, and mix well. Add salt and pepper to taste if desired.

Nutritional Analysis (per serving, without salt): Calories: 80 | Protein: 1g | Carbohydrates: 12g | Fat: 3g | Saturated Fat: 0g | Cholesterol: 0mg | Sodium: 10mg | Fiber: 2g | PCF Ratio: 5-60-33 | Exchange Approx.: ¾ Starch, ½ Fat

SOUTHWESTERN SWEET POTATO SKILLET

YIELDS 3 CUPS; SERVING SIZE: ½ CUP

1 tablespoon olive oil

½ cup diced green or red bell pepper

⅓ cup diced white onion

2 medium sweet potatoes, cooked and cubed to yield about 2 cups

1 cup sliced white mushrooms

½ cup cooked or canned beans, such as kidney, black, or pinto

½ cup diced fresh or canned tomato

½ teaspoon garlic powder

½ teaspoon paprika

¼ teaspoon chili powder

Optional garnishes: diced avocado, turkey bacon bits, low-fat cheese

1. Add the olive oil to a large skillet, put in the peppers and onion, and sauté for a few minutes on medium heat until starting to brown and soften.

2. Add the potato, mushrooms, beans, tomatoes, and spices and heat for another 7–10 minutes until lightly browned and warmed through.

3. Garnish with diced avocado, turkey bacon bits, and cheese if desired.

Nutritional Analysis (per serving): Calories: 80 | Protein: 3g | Carbohydrates: 16g | Fat: 1g | Saturated Fat: 0g | Cholesterol: 0mg | Sodium: 65mg | Fiber: 4g | PCF Ratio: 15-80-5 | Exchange Approx.: 1 Starch

CHAPTER 8

VEGETABLE SIDES

Green Beans in
Tomato Sauce
278

Italian-Inspired Green
Beans
278

Soy Basil Grilled
Asparagus
279

Sesame Asparagus
279

Zucchini Home Fries
280

Grilled Cumin
Cauliflower
280

Zucchini "Noodles"
281

Lemon Walnut
Broccoli
282

Baked Carrot Fries
282

Maple-Glazed Carrots
with Cranberries and
Walnuts
283

Cauliflower with
Olives and Peppers
284

Honey-Roasted
Carrots
284

Cauliflower "Rice"
285

HEALTHY ONION RINGS

SERVES 4; SERVING SIZE: ¼ CUP

1 cup (¼" thick) yellow onion slices

½ cup flour

½ cup nonfat plain yogurt

½ cup bread crumbs

Nonstick cooking spray

Sea salt and freshly ground black pepper
to taste (optional)

1. Preheat oven to 350°F. Dredge onion slices in flour; shake off any excess. Dip onions in yogurt; dredge through bread crumbs.

2. Prepare baking sheet with nonstick cooking spray. Arrange onion rings on pan; bake 15–20 minutes. Place under broiler additional 2 minutes to brown. Season with salt and pepper if desired.

Nutritional Analysis (per serving, without salt): Calories: 111 | Protein: 4g | Carbohydrates: 22g | Fat: 1g | Saturated Fat: 0g | Cholesterol: 1mg | Sodium: 255mg | Fiber: 1g | PCF Ratio: 16-80-4 | Exchange Approx.: 1 Vegetable, 1 Starch

SWEET POTATO CRISPS

SERVES 2; SERVING SIZE: ½ RECIPE

1 small sweet potato or yam

Nonstick spray

1 teaspoon olive oil

Sea salt and freshly ground black pepper
to taste (optional)

1. Preheat oven to 400°F. Scrub sweet potato and pierce flesh several times with fork. Place on microwave-safe plate; microwave 5 minutes on high. Remove from microwave; wrap in aluminum foil. Set aside 5 minutes.

2. Remove foil; peel and cut into French fries. Spread on baking sheet treated with nonstick spray; spritz with olive oil. Bake 10–15 minutes or until crisp. There's a risk that sweet potato strips will caramelize and burn; check often while cooking to ensure this doesn't occur. Lower oven temperature if necessary. Season with salt and pepper if desired.

Nutritional Analysis (per serving, without salt): Calories: 89 | Protein: 1g | Carbohydrates: 16g | Fat: 2g | Saturated Fat: 1g | Cholesterol: 0mg | Sodium: 7mg | Fiber: 9g | PCF Ratio: 6-70-24 | Exchange Approx.: 1 Starch, ½ Fat

OVEN-BAKED RED POTATOES

SERVES 4; SERVING SIZE: ¼ RECIPE

1 pound (16 ounces) small red potatoes, halved

¼ cup fresh lemon juice

1 teaspoon olive oil

1 teaspoon sea salt

¼ teaspoon freshly ground pepper

Remember the Roasting "Rack"

Use caution when roasting potatoes with meat: Potatoes will act like a sponge, soaking up fat. Your best option is to use lean cuts of meat and elevate them and vegetables above fat by putting a roasting rack in pan or making a "bridge" with celery to elevate meat. Discard celery when done.

Preheat oven to 350°F. Arrange potatoes in 13" × 9" ovenproof casserole dish. Combine remaining ingredients; pour over potatoes. Bake 30–40 minutes or until potatoes are tender, turning 3 or 4 times to baste.

Nutritional Analysis (per serving): Calories: 120 | Protein: 2g | Carbohydrates: 26g | Fat: 1g | Saturated Fat: 0g | Cholesterol: 0g | Sodium: 587mg | Fiber: 2g | PCF Ratio: 7-84-9 | Exchange Approx.: 1 Starch

BAKED FRENCH FRIES

SERVES 1

1 small white potato (3 ounces)

1 teaspoon olive oil

Nonstick spray

Sea salt and freshly ground black pepper
to taste (optional)

Get a Head Start

Speed up the time it takes to bake French
fries! First, cook potatoes in microwave
3–4 minutes in a covered microwave-safe
dish; allow to rest at least 1 minute. Dry
with paper towels if necessary; arrange on
baking sheet treated with nonstick spray.
Spray with flavored cooking spray or a few
spritzes of olive oil; bake at 400°F
5–8 minutes to crisp.

1. Preheat oven to 400°F. Wash, peel, and slice potato into French fry wedges. Wrap slices in paper towel to remove any excess moisture.

2. "Oil" potatoes by placing in plastic bag with olive oil. Close bag and shake until potatoes are evenly coated. Spread on baking sheet treated with nonstick spray; bake 5–10 minutes.

3. Remove pan from oven; quickly turn potatoes. Return pan to oven; bake another 10–15 minutes, depending on how crisp you prefer your fries. Season with salt and pepper if your diet allows additional sodium.

Nutritional Analysis (per serving, without salt): Calories: 119 | Protein: 2g | Carbohydrates: 18g | Fat: 5g | Saturated Fat: 1g | Cholesterol: 0mg | Sodium: 4mg | Fiber: 1g | PCF Ratio: 5-60-34 | Exchange Approx.: 1 Starch, 1 Fat

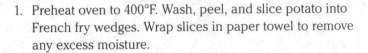

BAKED POTATO CHIPS

SERVES 1

1 small white potato (3 ounces)

Nonstick spray

1 teaspoon olive oil

Sea salt and freshly ground black pepper to taste (optional)

Tip

Nutritional allowance for this recipe allows for 1 teaspoon of olive oil. Even though you spritz potatoes with oil, remember chips have more surface area than fries. To cut more fat, eliminate oil (and Fat exchange) in Baked French Fries and Baked Potato Chips by using butter-flavored or olive oil cooking spray.

1. Preheat oven to 400°F. Wash, peel, and thinly slice potato. Wrap slices in paper towel to remove any excess moisture.

2. Spread potatoes on baking sheet treated with nonstick spray; spritz with olive oil. Bake 10–15 minutes depending on how crisp you prefer your fries. Season with salt and pepper if your diet allows additional sodium.

Nutritional Analysis (per serving, without salt): Calories: 119 | Protein: 2g | Carbohydrates: 18g | Fat: 5g | Saturated Fat: 1g | Cholesterol: 0mg | Sodium: 4mg | Fiber: 1g | PCF Ratio: 5-60-34 | Exchange Approx.: 1 Starch, 1 Fat

BROCCOLI RAAB WITH PINE NUTS

SERVES 4; SERVING SIZE: ¼ RECIPE

1 or 2 bunches broccoli raab (to yield ¾ pound)

1 tablespoon olive oil

4 cloves garlic, chopped

¼ cup chopped sun-dried tomatoes

2 tablespoons pine nuts

¼ teaspoon salt

¼ teaspoon crushed red pepper

Preventing Bitter Broccoli Raab

Broccoli raab and other leafy greens (mustard or collard greens) can have a bitter taste once cooked. Rather than add extra salt to offset bitterness, this recipe calls for blanching 2 minutes, which helps reduce bitterness. Blanching should be done as quickly as possible by starting with water at full rolling boil, then removing after 2 minutes of boiling. If allowed to cook too long, the boiling process will reduce amount of water-soluble nutrients found in vegetables.

1. Rinse broccoli raab well and trim stems. Loosely chop leafy parts, then blanch in 2 quarts boiling water 2 minutes. Drain well.

2. Heat olive oil in large skillet; add garlic. Sauté garlic 1–2 minutes; add cooked broccoli. Toss garlic and broccoli together well so that oil and garlic are mixed evenly.

3. Add remaining ingredients; cook additional 2–3 minutes until broccoli is tender.

Nutritional Analysis (per serving): Calories: 110 | Protein: 5g | Carbohydrates: 6g | Fat: 8g | Saturated Fat: 1g | Cholesterol: 0mg | Sodium: 229mg | Fiber: 4g | PCF Ratio: 18-20-62 | Exchange Approx.: 1 Vegetable, 1 Fat

SWEET POTATOES WITH ONIONS AND APPLE

SERVES 6; SERVING SIZE: ⅙ RECIPE

1 pound (about 2 large) sweet potatoes

½ teaspoon canola oil

1 cup thinly sliced onion

1 apple, peeled, cored, and chopped

½ cup low-sodium chicken broth

1. Wash and dry sweet potatoes; pierce skins several times with fork. Microwave on high 5–8 minutes or until tender.

2. While sweet potatoes are cooking, heat oil in large nonstick skillet over medium-high heat. Add onions; sauté until golden brown, about 10 minutes.

3. Add apple and chicken broth; cook until onions are tender and have caramelized.

4. Scoop cooked sweet potatoes from skins into microwaveable dish; mash lightly. Cover and microwave on high 1–2 minutes or until potatoes are heated. Top with sautéed onions and serve.

Nutritional Analysis (per serving): Calories: 127 | Protein: 2g | Carbohydrates: 28g | Fat: 1g | Saturated Fat: 0g | Cholesterol: 1mg | Sodium: 144mg | Fiber: 4g | PCF Ratio: 6-85-9 | Exchange Approx.: 1 Starch, ½ Vegetable

ROASTED-GARLIC MASHED POTATOES

SERVES 4; SERVING SIZE: ¼ RECIPE

4 cloves roasted garlic (see Garlic and Feta Cheese Dip in Chapter 3 for dry-roasting instructions)

1 small onion, chopped

¾ pound (12 ounces) peeled cooked potatoes

2 cups chopped cauliflower, steamed and drained

¼ cup buttermilk

⅛ cup nonfat cottage cheese

2 teaspoons unsalted butter

Sea salt and freshly ground black pepper to taste (optional)

Gravy Substitute

Instead of using gravy, sprinkle crumbled blue cheese or grated Parmesan over mashed potatoes. Just remember that cheese is a Meat exchange and adjust approximations accordingly.

Combine all ingredients; whip until fluffy. If potatoes or cauliflower are overly moist, add buttermilk gradually until whipped mixture reaches desired consistency. Combining steamed cauliflower with the potatoes allows you to increase the portion size without significantly changing the flavor of the mashed potatoes.

Nutritional Analysis (per serving, without salt): Calories: 126 | Protein: 4g | Carbohydrates: 23g | Fat: 2g | Saturated Fat: 1g | Cholesterol: 6mg | Sodium: 31mg | Fiber: 3g | PCF Ratio: 13-70-17 | Exchange Approx.: 1 Starch, 1 Vegetable, ½ Fat

FLUFFY BUTTERMILK MASHED POTATOES

SERVES 4; SERVING SIZE: ¼ RECIPE

¾ pound (12 ounces) peeled and boiled potatoes

¼ cup warm buttermilk

2 teaspoons unsalted butter

Sea salt and freshly ground black pepper to taste (optional)

1. Place potatoes in large bowl; partially mash.

2. Add warm buttermilk; mix well, mashing potatoes completely.

3. Stir in butter and salt and pepper if using. If you like your mashed potatoes creamy, add some of the potato water.

Nutritional Analysis (per serving, without salt): Calories: 97 | Protein: 2g | Carbohydrates: 18g | Fat: 2g | Saturated Fat: 1g | Cholesterol: 6mg | Sodium: 20mg | Fiber: 2g | PCF Ratio: 9-72-19 | Exchange Approx.: 1 Starch, ½ Fat

FRENCH TARRAGON GREEN BEANS

SERVES 4; SERVING SIZE: ¼ RECIPE

1½ tablespoons butter

¼ cup chopped red onion

½ pound fresh green beans

1 tablespoon finely chopped fresh tarragon

1. Melt butter in nonstick pan. Add onions; sauté until translucent.

2. Add green beans. Cover and steam 2–3 minutes.

3. Add tarragon; combine well. Steam an additional 2–3 minutes.

Nutritional Analysis (per serving): Calories: 59 | Protein: 0g | Carbohydrates: 5g | Fat: 3g | Saturated Fat: 1g | Cholesterol: 11mg | Sodium: 105mg | Fiber: 1g | PCF Ratio: 3-32-65 | Exchange Approx.: 1 Vegetable, 1 Fat

OVEN-ROASTED RATATOUILLE

SERVES 12; SERVING SIZE: 1/12 RECIPE

5 cups peeled and ½"-cubed eggplant

3 cups ½"-cubed yellow squash

½ pound green beans

½ cup chopped celery

1 cup chopped red onion

4 cloves garlic, chopped

1 (28-ounce) can diced tomatoes

1 tablespoon chopped fresh parsley

¼ teaspoon salt

½ teaspoon dried rosemary

½ teaspoon dried thyme

¼ cup olive oil

2 tablespoons balsamic vinegar

Swapping Fresh Herbs for Dried
If you do not have fresh herbs available, 1 teaspoon dried can be used in place of 1 tablespoon fresh.

1. Preheat oven to 375°F. In large Dutch oven or 9" × 13" baking dish, combine eggplant, yellow squash, green beans, celery, onion, garlic, tomatoes, parsley, salt, rosemary, thyme, and olive oil.

2. Roast uncovered in oven. Stir after 30 minutes, then continue roasting another 30 minutes or until vegetables are softened and lightly browned on top.

3. Remove from oven. Stir in balsamic vinegar and serve.

Nutritional Analysis (per serving): Calories: 87 | Protein: 2g | Carbohydrates: 11g | Fat: 5g | Saturated Fat: 1g | Cholesterol: 0mg | Sodium: 452mg | Fiber: 3g | PCF Ratio: 9-46-46 | Exchange Approx.: 2 Vegetables, 1 Fat

SESAME SNAP PEAS

SERVES 4; SERVING SIZE: ¼ RECIPE

½ tablespoon canola oil

10 ounces fresh snap peas

¼ cup thinly sliced scallions

1 tablespoon grated fresh ginger

2 teaspoons sesame oil

1 tablespoon sesame seeds

1. Heat canola oil in large nonstick skillet or wok.

2. Add snap peas, scallions, and ginger; stir-fry until peas are crisp-tender.

3. Stir in sesame oil and sesame seeds; toss lightly and serve.

Nutritional Analysis (per serving): Calories: 49 | Protein: 0g | Carbohydrates: 3g | Fat: 4g | Saturated Fat: 0g | Cholesterol: 0mg | Sodium: 149mg | Fiber: 0g | PCF Ratio: 2-27-72 | Exchange Approx.: 1 Vegetable, ½ Fat

AMISH-STYLE TURNIPS

SERVES 6; SERVING SIZE: ⅙ RECIPE

3 cups cooked and mashed turnips

1 slice whole-wheat bread

1 tablespoon melted butter

2 tablespoons Splenda Brown Sugar Blend

½ cup low-fat milk

1 egg

1. Preheat oven to 375°F.

2. Cook turnips in advance. If using fresh turnips, wash, peel, and cut into 1" cubes. Put in covered dish with ½ cup water; microwave on high 10–15 minutes until tender.

3. Place bread in food processor. Using pulse setting, process until bread is consistency of fine bread crumbs.

4. In medium bowl, mix together bread crumbs, melted butter, Splenda, milk, and egg. Add cooked turnip; mix well.

5. Turn mixture into greased casserole dish. Bake uncovered 30–35 minutes.

Nutritional Analysis (per serving): Calories: 80 | Protein: 2g | Carbohydrates: 12g | Fat: 3g | Saturated Fat: 2g | Cholesterol: 40mg | Sodium: 49mg | Fiber: 2g | PCF Ratio: 10-56-34 | Exchange Approx.: 1 Vegetable, ½ Starch, ½ Fat

SIMPLE SAUTÉED KALE

YIELDS 2 CUPS; SERVING SIZE: ½ CUP

6 packed cups torn or coarsely chopped kale leaves

3 teaspoons olive oil, divided

¼ cup low-sodium vegetable or chicken broth

Double the Recipe and the Flavor!

When doubling this recipe, it is useful to make the batches back to back rather than together since the kale takes up a lot of room initially in the pan. Great toppings for this dish include a little salt, pepper, crushed red pepper, garlic powder, or grated Parmesan cheese.

1. Wash and pat dry the kale. Remove the ribs and tear or chop the leaves.

2. Add 1½ teaspoons of olive oil to coat a large pan and warm on medium-high heat for 1 minute. Throw in the kale, pour the broth over, and cook for 5 minutes, stirring occasionally as it starts to soften. Remove cover, add the remaining 1½ teaspoons of olive oil, mix well, and heat for another 3–5 minutes.

Nutritional Analysis (per serving): Calories: 90 | Protein: 5g | Carbohydrates: 10g | Fat: 4.5g | Saturated Fat: 0g | Cholesterol: 0mg | Sodium: 55mg | Fiber: 2g | PCF Ratio: 20-40-40 | Exchange Approx.: 2 Vegetables, 1 Fat

GREEK-INSPIRED SAUTÉED SPINACH

YIELDS 4 CUPS; SERVING SIZE: 1 CUP

1 teaspoon olive oil

½ cup diced shallots

10 cups chopped fresh spinach, rinsed well

¼ cup water

½ cup finely diced kalamata or black olives

1 tablespoon pine nuts

4 tablespoons reduced-fat feta cheese (optional)

Making This Dish a Meal

This is a great side dish, or you can use it in many ways to make a meal. Serve it over ⅔ cup couscous or whole-grain pasta for a nice dish that will add 2 Starches. Add another vegetable serving by putting it in a grilled portobello for a Greek-style stuffed mushroom.

1. Coat a small or medium pan lightly with the olive oil and warm on medium heat.

2. Heat the shallots and sauté for a few minutes until lightly browned. Add half of the spinach, stir in ¼ cup water, and heat for about 1 minute until the spinach is slightly wilted.

3. Fold in the other half of the spinach, cover, and heat for another few minutes until the spinach is mostly cooked.

4. Stir in the olives and pine nuts until mixed well and warmed with the spinach for 1–2 minutes.

5. Serve sprinkled with 1 tablespoon cheese per serving if desired.

Nutritional Analysis (per serving): Calories: 110 | Protein: 4g | Carbohydrates: 11g | Fat: 6g | Saturated Fat: 1g | Cholesterol: 5mg | Sodium: 340mg | Fiber: 4g | PCF Ratio: 13-39-48 | Exchange Approx.: 2 Vegetables, ¼ Medium-Fat Meat, 1 Fat

BALSAMIC-ROASTED CAULIFLOWER WITH DATES AND PISTACHIOS

YIELDS 4 CUPS; SERVING SIZE: ½ CUP

7 cups cauliflower florets

1 tablespoon olive oil

1 tablespoon honey

3 tablespoons balsamic vinegar

Cooking spray

¼ cup pitted and chopped Medjool dates

¼ cup finely chopped pistachios

1. Preheat oven to 350°F. Put the cauliflower in a large bowl.

2. In a small bowl, whisk together the olive oil, honey, and vinegar.

3. Add the vinegar mixture to the bowl with the cauliflower and toss to coat. Then place it on a baking sheet coated with cooking spray and roast for 20 minutes, turning them halfway through until lightly browned and tender when pierced with a fork. In last few minutes of roasting sprinkle the dates and pistachios over the cauliflower to lightly toast them.

Nutritional Analysis (per serving): Calories: 90 | Protein: 3g | Carbohydrates: 12g | Fat: 4g | Saturated Fat: 0.5g | Cholesterol: 0mg | Sodium: 45mg | Fiber: 3g | PCF Ratio: 12-52-36 | Exchange Approx.: ¼ Fruit, 1 Vegetable, 1 Fat

MAPLE SPAGHETTI SQUASH WITH WALNUTS AND GOAT CHEESE

YIELDS 3 CUPS; SERVING SIZE: ½ CUP

1 (3–4-pound) spaghetti squash (to yield at least 3 cups cooked)

2 tablespoons olive oil

2 tablespoons maple syrup

3 tablespoons chopped walnuts

1 ounce crumbled goat cheese

Spaghetti Squash Stats

An average 4-pound spaghetti squash will yield about 4–5 cups, so you will need a little more than half that for this recipe.

1. Preheat the oven to 375°F. Cook the spaghetti squash by piercing it a few times with a fork, place in a shallow pan, and bake it whole for about 60 minutes. The squash is done once it is very soft when pierced with a knife.

2. Let the squash cool for 10 minutes, then cut in half, being careful of hot steam that may escape. Scoop out seeds and discard, then scoop out the flesh of the squash, which will be stringy like pasta, and set aside.

3. Add the olive oil and maple syrup to a medium-sized pan and warm on medium heat for 1–2 minutes. Put in 3 cups of the cooked spaghetti squash and sauté until almost warmed through, about 5–7 minutes. Sprinkle in the walnuts and mix well while continuing to cook for another 2–3 minutes until the squash is beginning to brown.

4. Transfer to a serving dish, top with the goat cheese, and serve.

Nutritional Analysis (per serving): Calories: 110 | Protein: 2g | Carbohydrates: 9g | Fat: 8g | Saturated Fat: 1.5g | Cholesterol: 0mg | Sodium: 30mg | Fiber: 1g | PCF Ratio: 5-31-64 | Exchange Approx.: ½ Starch, 1½ Fats

HONEY MUSTARD ROASTED CARROTS AND BRUSSELS SPROUTS

YIELDS 7 CUPS; SERVING SIZE: 1 CUP

3½ cups trimmed and quartered Brussels sprouts

3½ cups halved baby carrots

2 tablespoons olive oil, divided

Cooking spray

1 tablespoon maple syrup

2 tablespoons honey mustard

2 tablespoons finely chopped pecans

2 tablespoons chopped dried cranberries

1. Preheat oven to 350°F. Put the Brussels sprouts and carrots in a large bowl, add 1 tablespoon of the olive oil, and mix to coat. Then place the veggies on baking sheet coated with cooking spray and roast for 25–30 minutes, turning them halfway through until lightly browned and tender when pierced with a fork. Set aside and let cool.

2. In the large bowl, whisk together the remaining 1 tablespoon olive oil, maple syrup, and mustard. Throw in the Brussels sprouts, carrots, pecans, and cranberries and mix well until evenly coated with dressing. This dish can be served warm or cold.

Nutritional Analysis (per serving): Calories: 120 | Protein: 2g | Carbohydrates: 15g | Fat: 6g | Saturated Fat: 0g | Cholesterol: 0mg | Sodium: 60mg | Fiber: 3g | PCF Ratio: 8-50-42 | Exchange Approx.: 2 Vegetables, ½ Other Carbohydrate, 1 Fat

MAPLE BACON BRUSSELS SPROUTS

YIELDS 4½ CUPS; SERVING SIZE: ½ CUP

4 cups washed, stems trimmed, and halved Brussels sprouts

2 tablespoons olive oil, divided

1 cup chopped onion

1 cup (4 or 5 slices) chopped turkey bacon

2 tablespoons pure maple syrup, divided

1. Cook the Brussels sprouts until almost done. They can be cooked by either boiling them in a pot of water or steaming them in a Pyrex dish in ½" of water for about 4 minutes.

2. Meanwhile, coat a medium-sized pan with 1 tablespoon of the olive oil. Add the onion, turkey bacon, and 1 tablespoon of maple syrup and sauté until lightly browned, about 5–7 minutes.

3. Put in the cooked Brussels sprout halves, add the remaining 1 tablespoon each of olive oil and maple syrup, and continue to sauté until the Brussels sprouts are lightly browned and tender, about 5 minutes.

Nutritional Analysis (per serving): Calories: 80 | Protein: 4g | Carbohydrates: 8g | Fat: 4g | Saturated Fat: 0.5g | Cholesterol: 10mg | Sodium: 140mg | Fiber: 2g | PCF Ratio: 18-38-43 | Exchange Approx.: 1 Vegetable, ¼ Other Carbohydrate, 1 Fat

BALSAMIC-ROASTED BRUSSELS SPROUTS

YIELDS 5 CUPS; SERVING SIZE: 1 CUP

6 cups stems trimmed and quartered
  Brussels sprouts

1 tablespoon olive oil

1 tablespoon honey

2 tablespoons balsamic vinegar

Cooking spray

1. Preheat oven to 350°F. Put the Brussels sprouts in a large bowl.

2. In a small bowl, whisk together the olive oil, honey, and vinegar. Add the vinegar mixture to the bowl with the Brussels sprouts and toss to coat.

3. Place the Brussels sprouts on a baking sheet coated with cooking spray and roast for 25–30 minutes, turning them halfway through until lightly browned and tender when pierced with a fork.

Nutritional Analysis (per serving): Calories: 90 | Protein: 4g | Carbohydrates: 15g | Fat: 3g | Saturated Fat: 0g | Cholesterol: 0mg | Sodium: 30mg | Fiber: 4g | PCF Ratio: 15-57-28 | Exchange Approx.: 2 Vegetables, 1 Fat

SIMPLE ROASTED ASPARAGUS

SERVES 4; SERVING SIZE: ¼ RECIPE

Cooking spray

1 bunch (about 1½ pounds) rinsed and
  dried asparagus spears

½ tablespoon olive oil

⅛ teaspoon garlic powder

⅛ teaspoon salt

⅛ teaspoon pepper

1. Preheat oven to 400°F and coat a baking sheet with cooking spray.

2. Add the asparagus to the pan, drizzle with the oil, and sprinkle with the garlic powder, salt, and pepper.

3. Toss the spears by hand to make sure they are evenly coated and spread them out on the pan. Roast for 15–20 minutes, turning them every 5–7 minutes until tender.

Nutritional Analysis (per serving): Calories: 60 | Protein: 4g | Carbohydrates: 7g | Fat: 2g | Saturated Fat: 0g | Cholesterol: 0mg | Sodium: 75mg | Fiber: 4g | PCF Ratio: 25-49-26 | Exchange Approx.: 2 Vegetables

GREEN BEANS IN TOMATO SAUCE

YIELDS 5 CUPS; SERVING SIZE: ½ CUP

4 cups fresh or frozen thawed green beans

1 teaspoon olive oil

1 cup chopped onion

2 teaspoons chopped garlic

1 (15-ounce) can tomatoes

1 teaspoon sweet paprika

1. Cook greens beans al dente by boiling them in a pot of water for 7–10 minutes or steam in a microwave-safe dish in a small amount of water for 5 minutes, then drain.

2. Add the olive oil, onions, and garlic to a large pan and sauté for 3–4 minutes on medium-high heat until lightly browned.

3. Put in the canned tomatoes, paprika, and the cooked green beans. Cover and simmer, stirring occasionally for 10–15 minutes until warmed through.

Nutritional Analysis (per serving): Calories: 45 | Protein: 2g | Carbohydrates: 8g | Fat: 0.5g | Saturated Fat: 0g | Cholesterol: 0mg | Sodium: 70mg | Fiber: 2g | PCF Ratio: 15-71-14 | Exchange Approx.: 2 Vegetables

ITALIAN-INSPIRED GREEN BEANS

SERVES 4; SERVING SIZE: ¼ RECIPE

1 pound fresh green beans, trimmed and cut into 2" pieces

1 cup grape or cherry tomatoes

2 sticks cubed low-fat string cheese or ½ cup cubed low-fat mozzarella cheese

½ teaspoon dried oregano

1 teaspoon olive oil

1. Cook the greens beans al dente by boiling them in a pot of water for 7–10 minutes or steam in a microwave-safe dish in a small amount of water for 5 minutes, then drain.

2. Coat a medium-sized pan with the olive oil, add the tomatoes, and sauté on medium heat for 3–5 minutes until slightly softened.

3. Add the cooked green beans, sprinkle in the oregano, and cook for another 1–2 minutes. Let cool and toss in the cheese cubes.

Nutritional Analysis (per serving): Calories: 80 | Protein: 5g | Carbohydrates: 10g | Fat: 2.5g | Saturated Fat: 1g | Cholesterol: 0mg | Sodium: 100mg | Fiber: 4g | PCF Ratio: 25-50-25 | Exchange Approx.: 2 Vegetables, ½ Lean Meat

SOY BASIL GRILLED ASPARAGUS

SERVES 4; SERVING SIZE: ¼ RECIPE

1 pound asparagus, washed and trimmed about ¼"–½" from the bottom

¼ cup chopped fresh basil

1 teaspoon finely chopped garlic

½ cup low-sodium soy sauce

¼ teaspoon crushed red pepper

1. Add all the ingredients to a large zip-top bag or other sealable container, seal it, and shake well. Marinate in the fridge, preferably 4–6 hours.

2. Preheat a barbecue grill or a large nonstick pan on medium heat. Discard the marinade and add the asparagus. Heat 3–5 minutes on each side until lightly browned and slightly crispy on the edges.

Nutritional Analysis (per serving): Calories: 45 | Protein: 3g | Carbohydrates: 6g | Fat: 0g | Saturated Fat: 0g | Cholesterol: 0mg | Sodium: 290mg | Fiber: 2g | PCF Ratio: 35-62-3 | Exchange Approx.: 1½ Vegetables

SESAME ASPARAGUS

YIELDS 3 CUPS; SERVING SIZE: ½ CUP

3 cups rinsed and chopped (into 1" pieces) fresh asparagus

2 teaspoons sesame oil

2 teaspoons low-sodium soy sauce

¼ teaspoon crushed garlic or ½ clove, minced

1 teaspoon sesame seeds

1. Cook the asparagus until almost done by either boiling it in a pot of water or steaming it in a Pyrex dish in ½" of water for about 3–5 minutes.

2. Add sesame oil, soy sauce, and garlic to a medium-sized pan and set it to medium heat. Put in the asparagus and sauté 5–7 minutes until just before browned. Sprinkle with sesame seeds and serve.

Nutritional Analysis (per serving): Calories: 40 | Protein: 2g | Carbohydrates: 4g | Fat: 2g | Saturated Fat: 0g | Cholesterol: 0mg | Sodium: 125mg | Fiber: 2g | PCF Ratio: 20-40-40 | Exchange Approx.: 1 Vegetable, ¼ Fat

ZUCCHINI HOME FRIES

YIELDS 3½ CUPS; SERVING SIZE: ½ CUP

2 teaspoons olive oil, divided

1 red pepper, cut into ¼" cubes

1 green pepper, cut into ¼" cubes

½ cup diced white onion

4 zucchini, peeled and cut into ¼" cubes

½ teaspoon paprika

½ teaspoon chili powder

¼ teaspoon garlic powder

1. Add 1 teaspoon olive oil along with the peppers and onions to a large skillet and sauté on medium-high heat for 3–5 minutes.

2. Add the remaining 1 teaspoon of olive oil, the zucchini, and all the spices and sauté for another 3–5 minutes or until the veggies are lightly browned and slightly tender.

Nutritional Analysis (per serving): Calories: 40 | Protein: 1g | Carbohydrates: 5g | Fat: 1.5g | Saturated Fat: 0g | Cholesterol: 0mg | Sodium: 5mg | Fiber: 2g | PCF Ratio: 10-50-40 | Exchange Approx.: 1 Vegetable, ¼ Fat

GRILLED CUMIN CAULIFLOWER

SERVES 4; SERVING SIZE: ¼ RECIPE

3 cups cauliflower florets

Aluminum foil and cooking spray

1 tablespoon melted light margarine

½ teaspoon ground cumin, divided

Salt and pepper (optional)

1. Coat a large piece of aluminum foil with cooking spray. Put the cauliflower in the center and pour melted margarine over it, sprinkle with ¼ teaspoon cumin, and add salt and pepper (if desired). Fold over the sides of the foil to make a closed pouch and place on a heated barbecue grill.

2. Heat for 5 minutes, open (carefully since it will be hot and steam may escape), and turn each piece over.

3. Sprinkle with the remaining ¼ teaspoon cumin and heat for another 5 minutes until tender when pierced with a fork.

Nutritional Analysis (per serving): Calories: 20 | Protein: 1g | Carbohydrates: 4g | Fat: 0.5g | Saturated Fat: 0g | Cholesterol: 0mg | Sodium: 50mg | Fiber: 2g | PCF Ratio: 20-80-0 | Exchange Approx.: 1 Vegetable

ZUCCHINI "NOODLES"

YIELDS 4 CUPS; SERVING SIZE: 1 CUP

2 medium zucchini

Julienne peeler

1. Wash the zucchini well and cut about ½" off the top and the bottom.

2. Peel the zucchini lengthwise (like you would a carrot) using a julienne peeler. Try to peel as much off as possible until hitting the heavily seeded middle and there is too much resistance to peel further. One medium zucchini will make about 2 cups of "noodles."

3. The peeled zucchini comes out like thin spaghetti. If you use a regular peeler, the squash will be more like wide egg noodles. The zucchini noodles cook very quickly in a pan coated with olive oil or cooking spray, about 4–6 minutes on medium heat.

4. The zucchini can be served pasta-style with a favorite sauce or simply dressed with a bit of olive oil, fresh herbs, and grated Parmesan cheese. They can also be used raw in salads.

Nutritional Analysis (per serving): Calories: 20 | Protein: 2g | Carbohydrates: 4g | Fat: 0g | Saturated Fat: 0g | Cholesterol: 0mg | Sodium: 10mg | Fiber: 1g | PCF Ratio: 40-60-0 | Exchange Approx.: 1 Vegetable

LEMON WALNUT BROCCOLI

YIELDS 4 CUPS; SERVING SIZE: ½ CUP

4 cups rinsed and chopped broccoli florets

1 teaspoon olive oil

2 tablespoons lemon juice

1 tablespoon chopped walnuts

1 tablespoon raisins

1. Cook the broccoli until almost done by either boiling it in a pot of water or steaming in a Pyrex dish in ½" of water for about 2–3 minutes.

2. Coat a small or medium pan with the olive oil. Add the broccoli and lemon juice and sauté 5–7 minutes until lightly browned. Sprinkle with raisins and walnuts, heat for another minute, and then serve.

Nutritional Analysis (per serving): Calories: 35 | Protein: 1g | Carbohydrates: 3g | Fat: 1.5g | Saturated Fat: 0g | Cholesterol: 0mg | Sodium: 15mg | Fiber: 1g | PCF Ratio: 14-46-40 | Exchange Approx.: 1 Vegetable, ¼ Fat

BAKED CARROT FRIES

SERVES 8; SERVING SIZE: ⅛ RECIPE

6 cups baby carrots

2 tablespoons olive oil

Cooking spray

½ teaspoon salt

1. Preheat oven to 400°F. Add the carrots and the olive oil to a medium bowl and mix well.

2. Coat a baking pan with cooking spray and spread the carrots onto it. Sprinkle with salt and bake 15 minutes. Flip them over and bake another 15 minutes until lightly browned and tender when pierced with a fork.

Nutritional Analysis (per serving): Calories: 70 | Protein: 1g | Carbohydrates: 9g | Fat: 3.5g | Saturated Fat: 0g | Cholesterol: 0mg | Sodium: 190mg | Fiber: 2g | PCF Ratio: 6-50-44 | Exchange Approx.: 2 Vegetables, ½ Fat

MAPLE-GLAZED CARROTS WITH CRANBERRIES AND WALNUTS

SERVES 4; SERVING SIZE: ½ CUP

2 cups baby carrots

1 tablespoon olive oil

1 tablespoon dried cranberries

1 tablespoon chopped walnuts or pecans

2 tablespoons maple syrup

1. Cook the carrots until almost done by either boiling them in a pot of water or steaming them in a Pyrex dish in ½" of water for about 5–7 minutes.

2. Coat a small or medium pan with the olive oil and put on medium heat. Add the carrots and sauté for 2–4 minutes.

3. Sprinkle with cranberries and walnuts and heat for another minute. Turn off the heat, pour the maple syrup over, and toss to evenly coat the carrot mixture.

Nutritional Analysis (per serving): Calories: 130 | Protein: 1g | Carbohydrates: 15g | Fat: 8g | Saturated Fat: 1g | Cholesterol: 0mg | Sodium: 30mg | Fiber: 2g | PCF Ratio: 3-43-54 | Exchange Approx.: 1 Vegetable, ½ Other Carbohydrate, 1½ Fats

CAULIFLOWER WITH OLIVES AND PEPPERS

SERVES 4; SERVING SIZE: ¼ RECIPE

1 head of cauliflower, chopped into small florets (to yield about 4 cups)

2 teaspoons olive oil, divided

½ cup diced red bell pepper

2 tablespoons chopped kalamata olives

½ teaspoon garlic powder

½ teaspoon dried oregano

1. Cook the cauliflower until almost done. This can be done by either boiling it in a pot of water or steaming it in a Pyrex dish in ½" of water for about 3–5 minutes.

2. Add 1 teaspoon olive oil and the diced pepper to medium-sized pan and warm on high heat for about 3–5 minutes, stirring occasionally until slightly tender. Then add the cooked cauliflower, the remaining 1 teaspoon olive oil, the olives, the garlic powder, and the oregano and sauté until lightly browned and warmed though, about 3–5 minutes.

Nutritional Analysis (per serving): Calories: 60 | Protein: 1g | Carbohydrates: 7g | Fat: 3.5g | Saturated Fat: 0g | Cholesterol: 0mg | Sodium: 65mg | Fiber: 3g | PCF Ratio: 14-42-44 | Exchange Approx.: 1½ Vegetables, ½ Fat

HONEY-ROASTED CARROTS

YIELDS 3 CUPS; SERVING SIZE: ½ CUP

1 pound baby carrots

1 tablespoon honey

1 tablespoon olive oil

Cooking spray

1. Preheat oven to 375°F. Add the carrots to a medium bowl.

2. In a small bowl, whisk together the honey and olive oil. Pour the olive oil/honey mixture over the carrots and mix well to coat.

3. Spread the carrots on a baking sheet coated with cooking spray and roast for 15 minutes. Turn and toss the carrots and heat for another 5–7 minutes until lightly browned.

Nutritional Analysis (per serving): Calories: 70 | Protein: 1g | Carbohydrates: 11g | Fat: 2.5g | Saturated Fat: 0g | Cholesterol: 0mg | Sodium: 40mg | Fiber: 2g | PCF Ratio: 5-64-31 | Exchange Approx.: 1½ Vegetables, ½ Fat

CAULIFLOWER "RICE"

YIELDS ABOUT 4 CUPS; SERVING SIZE: 1 CUP

1 head of cauliflower

Ways to Use This Rice

Throw the raw granules into any of your favorite dishes that use rice, adding them during the last 3–4 minutes of cooking since they cook so fast. This "rice" can also be sprinkled raw on salads to add some crunch.

1. Rinse the head of cauliflower and cut into small to medium florets. (An average head of cauliflower will yield about 4 cups of florets, and 4 cups of florets will make approximately 4 cups of cauliflower rice.)

2. Add the florets to a food processor or chopper and pulse a few times until the cauliflower turns to small granules the size of rice/couscous. An alternative to using a food processor is preparing the granules by hand. Keep the cauliflower head whole and start shaving off the top using a serrated knife or grater with a plate/cutting board underneath to catch the granules. Then chop them a little more until desired consistency is reached.

3. Cooking the cauliflower takes little time. Put it in a microwave-safe dish, sprinkle a few drops of water on top, and heat for about a minute per cup of cauliflower. Pat any excess moisture off with a paper towel and serve. Another way to cook it is to add 1 teaspoon of olive oil to a small pan, put in the cauliflower, and sauté for 3–5 minutes until soft and slightly toasted/browned.

Nutritional Analysis (per serving): Calories: 25 | Protein: 2g | Carbohydrates: 5g | Fat: 0g | Saturated Fat: 0g | Cholesterol: 0mg | Sodium: 30mg | Fiber: 2g | PCF Ratio: 32-68-0 | Exchange Approx.: 1 Vegetable

CHAPTER 9

BEEF, PORK, LAMB, AND VENISON ENTRÉES

LEAN SLOPPY JOE FILLING

SERVES 4; SERVING SIZE: ¼ RECIPE

1 tablespoon olive oil

8 ounces lean ground beef

½ cup chopped white onion

½ cup chopped red bell pepper

½ cup shredded carrot

1¼ cups low-sodium tomato sauce

½ teaspoon chili powder

1 teaspoon paprika

½ teaspoon red pepper flakes

1. Coat a medium-sized pan with the olive oil, add the meat, and brown for about 5–7 minutes, stirring frequently. Remove meat from pan and set aside.

2. To the same pan, add the onions, bell peppers, and carrots and sauté on high heat until softened, about 6–7 minutes. Add the tomato sauce, browned meat, and spices; mix well and continue to cook, stirring occasionally until warmed through, about 5–8 minutes.

Nutritional Analysis (per serving): Calories: 150 | Protein: 13g | Carbohydrates: 12g | Fat: 6g | Saturated Fat: 1.5g | Cholesterol: 30mg | Sodium: 70mg | Fiber: 2g | PCF Ratio: 34-31-35 | Exchange Approx.: 2 Vegetables, 1½ Lean Meats, 1 Fat

SOUTHWEST BLACK BEAN BURGERS

SERVES 5; SERVING SIZE: 1 PATTY

1 cup cooked black beans

¼ cup chopped onion

1 teaspoon chili powder

1 teaspoon ground cumin

1 tablespoon minced fresh parsley

1 tablespoon minced fresh cilantro

½ teaspoon salt (optional)

¾ pound lean ground beef

1. Place beans, onion, chili powder, cumin, parsley, cilantro, and salt in food processor. Combine ingredients using pulse setting until beans are partially puréed and all ingredients are mixed. (If using canned beans, drain and rinse first.)

2. In a separate bowl, combine ground beef and bean mixture. Shape into five patties.

3. Meat mixture is quite soft after mixing and should be chilled or partially frozen prior to cooking. Grill or broil on oiled surface.

Nutritional Analysis (per serving): Calories: 230 | Protein: 20g | Carbohydrates: 10g | Fat: 12g | Saturated Fat: 4g | Cholesterol: 55mg | Sodium: 15.02mg | Fiber: 4g | PCF Ratio: 36-18-46 | Exchange Approx.: 2½ Lean Meats, ½ Starch, 1 Fat

SNAPPY STUFFED PEPPERS

SERVES 4; SERVING SIZE: 1 PEPPER

4 bell peppers

1 tablespoon olive oil

½ pound extra-lean ground beef

7 ounces crushed tomatoes

1 cup chopped mushrooms

¾ cup chopped white onion

1 teaspoon crushed garlic or 2 cloves chopped

1½ teaspoons paprika

1½ teaspoons ground cumin

½ cup corn (fresh, canned, or frozen thawed)

½ cup cooked brown rice

2 tablespoons chopped fresh cilantro

¼ teaspoon salt

½ cup shredded low-fat cheese

Changing Up the Beef

Not a ground beef fan? You can substitute lean ground turkey 1:1 instead.

1. Preheat oven to 350°F. Cut the tops of the peppers off, hollow out, remove seeds, and set aside. Cook the peppers until soft but still firm/maintaining their shape: Place them in a pot of boiling water or microwave them in a 4-quart Pyrex dish filled with ½" of water for about four minutes. Drain and set cooked peppers aside.

2. Coat a medium-sized pan with the olive oil, add the beef, and brown it for 5 minutes, stirring frequently. Add the crushed tomatoes, mushrooms, onion, garlic, paprika, and cumin; mix well and continue to cook, stirring occasionally for about 5–8 minutes.

3. Once the mixture is mostly cooked and the beef is well browned, mix in the corn, rice, cilantro, and salt and cook for another 1–2 minutes. Divide and add the mixture to the four cooked peppers. Cover the dish with the lid or aluminum foil and bake for 35 minutes. Uncover, sprinkle with cheese, and bake for another few minutes until slightly melted.

Nutritional Analysis (per serving): Calories: 260 | Protein: 19g | Carbohydrates: 26g | Fat: 10g | Saturated Fat: 3g | Cholesterol: 40mg | Sodium: 380mg | Fiber: 5g | PCF Ratio: 28-40-32 | Exchange Approx.: ¼ Starch, 3 Vegetables, 2 Lean Meats, 1 Fat

STOVETOP GRILLED BEEF LOIN

YIELDS 1 (5-OUNCE) LOIN; SERVING SIZE: 2½ OUNCES

1 lean beef tenderloin fillet, no more than 1" thick

½ teaspoon paprika

1½ teaspoons garlic powder

⅛ teaspoon cracked black pepper

¼ teaspoon onion powder

Pinch to ⅛ teaspoon ground cayenne pepper (according to taste)

⅛ teaspoon dried oregano

⅛ teaspoon dried thyme

½ teaspoon brown sugar

½ teaspoon olive oil

Weights and Measures: Before and After

Exchanges are based on cooking weights of meats; however, in the case of lean pork loin trimmed of all fat, very little weight is lost during the cooking process. Therefore, amounts given for raw pork loin in recipes equal cooked weights. If you find your cooking method causes more variation in weight, adjust accordingly.

1. Remove loin from refrigerator 30 minutes before preparing it to allow it to come to room temperature. Pat meat dry with paper towels.

2. Mix together all dry ingredients. Rub ¼ teaspoon of olive oil on each side of the fillet. (The olive oil is used in this recipe to help the "rub" adhere to the meat and to aid in the caramelization process.) Divide seasoning mixture; rub into each oiled side.

3. Heat a grill pan on high for 1–2 minutes until the pan is sizzling hot. Place beef fillet in pan, reduce heat to medium-high, and cook 3 minutes. Use tongs to turn fillet. (Be careful not to pierce meat.) Cook for another 2 minutes for medium or 3 minutes for well-done.

4. Remove from heat and let the meat rest in pan for at least 5 minutes, allowing juices to redistribute throughout meat and complete cooking process, which makes for a juicier fillet.

Nutritional Analysis (per serving): Calories: 105 | Protein: 15g | Carbohydrates: 1g | Fat: 4g | Saturated Fat: 1g | Cholesterol: 2mg | Sodium: 27mg | Fiber: 0g | PCF Ratio: 58-5-37 | Exchange Approx.: 2½ Lean Meats

THE ULTIMATE GRILLED CHEESEBURGER SANDWICH

SERVES 4; SERVING SIZE: ¼ SANDWICH

1 tablespoon olive oil

1 teaspoon butter

2 thick slices 7-Grain Bread (see recipe in Chapter 2)

1-ounce Cheddar cheese slice

½ pound (8 ounces) ground round

1 teaspoon Worcestershire sauce or to taste

Fresh minced garlic to taste

Balsamic vinegar to taste

Toppings of your choice such as stone-ground mustard, mayonnaise, etc.

The Olive Oil Factor

Once you've used an olive oil and butter mixture to butter the bread for a toasted or grilled sandwich, you'll never want to use just plain butter again! Olive oil helps make the bread crunchier and imparts a subtle taste difference to the sandwiches.

1. Preheat indoor grill. Combine olive oil and butter; use half to butter one side of each slice of bread. Place Cheddar cheese on unbuttered side of one slice of bread; top with other slice of bread, buttered-side up.

2. Combine ground round with Worcestershire sauce, garlic, and balsamic vinegar if using. Shape ground round into large, rectangular patty, a little larger than slice of bread. Grill patty and then cheese sandwich. (If you are using a large indoor grill, position hamburger at lower end, near area where fat drains; grill cheese sandwich at higher end.)

3. Once cheese sandwich is done, separate slices of bread, being careful not to burn yourself on cheese. Top one side with hamburger and add your choice of condiments and fixings.

Nutritional Analysis (per serving): Calories: 262 | Protein: 17g | Carbohydrates: 15g | Fat: 15g | Saturated Fat: 5g | Cholesterol: 60mg | Sodium: 252mg | Fiber: 1.22g | PCF Ratio: 26-24-50 | Exchange Approx.: 2 Lean Meats, 1 Fat, 1 Starch

HAM AND ARTICHOKE HEARTS SCALLOPED POTATOES

SERVES 4; SERVING SIZE: ¼ RECIPE

2 cups frozen artichoke hearts

Nonstick spray

1 cup chopped onion

4 small potatoes, thinly sliced

Sea salt and freshly ground black pepper to taste (optional)

1 tablespoon lemon juice

1 tablespoon dry white wine

1 cup Mock Cream (see recipe in Chapter 6)

½ cup nonfat cottage cheese

1 teaspoon dried parsley

1 teaspoon garlic powder

⅛ cup freshly grated Parmesan cheese

¼ pound (4 ounces) cubed lean ham

2 ounces grated Cheddar cheese (to yield ½ cup)

Simple Substitutions

Artichoke hearts can be expensive. You can substitute cabbage, broccoli, or cauliflower (or a mixture of all three) for the artichokes.

1. Preheat oven to 300°F.

2. Thaw artichoke hearts and pat dry with a paper towel. In deep casserole dish treated with nonstick spray, layer artichokes, onion, and potatoes; lightly sprinkle salt and pepper over top (if using).

3. In a food processor or blender, combine lemon juice, wine, Mock Cream, cottage cheese, parsley, garlic powder, and Parmesan cheese; process until smooth. Pour over layered vegetables; top with ham. Cover casserole dish (with a lid or foil); bake 35–40 minutes or until potatoes are cooked through.

4. Remove cover; top with Cheddar cheese. Return to oven another 10 minutes or until cheese is melted and bubbly. Let rest 10 minutes before cutting.

Nutritional Analysis (per serving, without salt): Calories: 269 | Protein: 21g | Carbohydrates: 31g | Fat: 8g | Saturated Fat: 4g | Cholesterol: 28mg | Sodium: 762mg | Fiber: 6g | PCF Ratio: 31-44-25 | Exchange Approx.: 1½ Lean Meats, ½ High-Fat Meat, 1½ Vegetables, 1 Starch

ITALIAN SAUSAGE

**YIELDS ABOUT 2 POUNDS (32 OUNCES);
SERVING SIZE: 2 OUNCES**

2 pounds (32 ounces) pork shoulder

1 teaspoon ground black pepper

1 teaspoon dried parsley

1 teaspoon Italian-style seasoning

1 teaspoon garlic powder

¾ teaspoon crushed anise seeds

⅛ teaspoon red pepper flakes

½ teaspoon paprika

½ teaspoon instant minced onion flakes

1 teaspoon kosher or sea salt (optional)

Simple (and Smart!) Substitutions

Game meats—buffalo, venison, elk, moose—are low in fat, as are ground chicken or turkey. Substitute one of these for pork in any of the sausage recipes in this chapter.

1. Remove all fat from meat; cut the meat into cubes. Put in food processor; grind to desired consistency.

2. Add remaining ingredients; mix until well blended. You can put sausage mixture in casings, but it works equally well broiled or grilled as patties.

Nutritional Analysis (per serving, without salt): Calories: 135 | Protein: 15g | Carbohydrates: 0g | Fat: 8g | Saturated Fat: 3g | Cholesterol: 45mg | Sodium: 27mg | Fiber: 0g | PCF Ratio: 47-0-53 | Exchange Approx.: 1 Medium-Fat Meat

ITALIAN SWEET FENNEL SAUSAGE

YIELDS ABOUT 2 POUNDS (32 OUNCES); SERVING SIZE: 2 OUNCES

1 tablespoon fennel seeds

¼ teaspoon ground cayenne pepper

2 pounds (32 ounces) pork butt

½ teaspoon black pepper

2½ teaspoons crushed garlic

1 tablespoon sugar

1 teaspoon kosher or sea salt (optional)

Better the Second Day

Ideally, sausage is made the night before and refrigerated to allow the flavors to merge. Leftover sausage can be frozen for up to 3 months.

1. Toast fennel seeds and cayenne pepper in nonstick skillet over medium heat, stirring constantly, until seeds just begin to darken, about 2 minutes. Set aside.

2. Remove all fat from meat; cut the meat into cubes. Put in food processor; grind to desired consistency. Add fennel and cayenne mixture plus remaining ingredients; mix until well blended. You can put sausage mixture in casings, but it works equally well broiled or grilled as patties.

Nutritional Analysis (per serving, without salt): Calories: 139 | Protein: 15g | Carbohydrates: 1g | Fat: 8g | Saturated Fat: 3g | Cholesterol: 45mg | Sodium: 27mg | Fiber: 0g | PCF Ratio: 46-3-51 | Exchange Approx.: 1 Medium-Fat Meat

MOCK CHORIZO 1

**YIELDS ABOUT 2 POUNDS (32 OUNCES);
SERVING SIZE: 2 OUNCES**

2 pounds (32 ounces) lean pork

4 tablespoons chili powder

¼ teaspoon ground cloves

2 tablespoons paprika

2½ teaspoons crushed fresh garlic

1 teaspoon crushed dried oregano

3½ tablespoons cider vinegar

1 teaspoon kosher or sea salt (optional)

Break from Tradition

Traditionally, chorizo is very high in fat.
The chorizo recipes in this chapter are
lower-fat alternatives. They make excellent
replacements for adding flavor to recipes
that call for bacon. In fact, 1 or 2 ounces
of chorizo can replace an entire pound of
bacon in cabbage, bean, or potato soup.

1. Remove all fat from meat; cut the meat into cubes. Put in food processor; grind to desired consistency. Add remaining ingredients; mix until well blended.

2. Tradition calls for aging this sausage in an airtight container in the refrigerator for 4 days before cooking. Leftover sausage can be stored in the freezer up to 3 months.

Nutritional Analysis (per serving, without salt): Calories: 137 | Protein: 15g | Carbohydrates: 1g | Fat: 8g | Saturated Fat: 3g | Cholesterol: 45mg | Sodium: 27mg | Fiber: 0g | PCF Ratio: 47-1-52 | Exchange Approx.: 1 Medium-Fat Meat

MOCK CHORIZO 2

**YIELDS ABOUT 1 POUND (16 OUNCES);
SERVING SIZE: 2 OUNCES**

1 pound (16 ounces) lean pork

2 tablespoons white wine vinegar

1 tablespoon dry sherry

2 teaspoons paprika

2 teaspoons chili powder

½ teaspoon dried oregano

¼ teaspoon ground cumin

½ teaspoon freshly ground black pepper

⅛ teaspoon ground cinnamon

⅛ teaspoon ground cloves

Pinch of ground coriander

Pinch of ground ginger

2 cloves garlic, crushed

Kosher or sea salt to taste (optional)

Tip

For chorizo stir-fry, consider decreasing the chili powder, adding some soy sauce or Bragg Liquid Aminos, and increasing the garlic and ginger.

1. Remove all fat from meat; cut the meat into cubes. Put in food processor; grind to desired consistency. Add remaining ingredients; mix until well blended.

2. Age sausage in an airtight container in the refrigerator for 4 days. Leftover sausage can be stored in the freezer up to 3 months.

Nutritional Analysis (per serving, without salt): Calories: 140 | Protein: 16g | Carbohydrates: 1g | Fat: 8g | Saturated Fat: 3g | Cholesterol: 45mg | Sodium: 27mg | Fiber: 0g | PCF Ratio: 46-2-52 | Exchange Approx.: 1 Medium-Fat Meat

KOUSA (SQUASH STUFFED WITH LAMB AND RICE)

SERVES 4; SERVING SIZE: 1 STUFFED SQUASH

3 cups chopped tomatoes

1 cup chopped onion

2 cups water

½ teaspoon salt

¼ teaspoon freshly ground pepper, divided

2 tablespoons minced fresh mint

4 small zucchini squash (7"–8" long)

¾ pound very lean ground lamb

½ cup rice

2 tablespoons pine nuts

½ teaspoon salt

⅛ teaspoon ground allspice

Summer Harvest

Kousa (stuffed squash) is a traditional Lebanese dish that uses a pale green summer squash very similar to zucchini. This squash is not always easy to find, but zucchini is very abundant and works quite well. If you have a large garden crop of zucchini, pick them small, hollow out the squash, blanch in boiling water for 2 minutes, then freeze. You'll have squash ready to stuff all year long.

1. Prepare tomato sauce first: Combine tomatoes, onion, water, salt, ⅛ teaspoon pepper, and fresh mint in a large pot. Bring to a boil; reduce heat and simmer 30 minutes.

2. Scrub squash and dry with paper towels. Remove stem ends of each squash and carefully core center, leaving about ¼" of shell.

3. Make stuffing: Thoroughly mix ground lamb, rice, pine nuts, salt, allspice, and remaining ⅛ teaspoon pepper.

4. Spoon stuffing into each squash, tapping bottom end of squash to get stuffing down. Fill each squash to top; stuffing should be loosely packed to allow rice to expand while cooking.

5. Place squash in tomato sauce, lying them on their sides. Bring sauce to a slow boil; cover and cook over low heat for 45–60 minutes or until squash is tender and rice has cooked. Serve squash with tomato sauce spooned over top.

Nutritional Analysis: Calories: 430 | Protein: 27g | Carbohydrates: 36g | Fat: 20g | Saturated Fat: 7g | Cholesterol: 82mg | Sodium: 692mg | Fiber: 5g | PCF Ratio: 25-33-42 | Exchange Approx.: 3 Lean Meats, 1 Starch, 3 Vegetables, 3 Fats

BAKED STUFFED KIBBEH

SERVES 8; SERVING SIZE: ⅛ RECIPE

Cooking spray

¾ cup fine-grind bulgur wheat

2 cups boiling water

1 pound lean ground lamb

1 cup grated onion, divided

1 teaspoon salt

¼ teaspoon pepper

Small bowl ice water

3 tablespoons butter, divided

¼ cup pine nuts

¼ teaspoon ground cinnamon

¼ teaspoon ground allspice

Making Lean Ground Lamb

Unless you have a butcher, very lean ground lamb is difficult to find. Make it yourself using chunks of meat trimmed from a leg of lamb. Be sure to remove all visible fat from the lamb and grind twice using a medium or fine grinder blade. Removing all visible fat prevents lamb from having a strong "mutton" taste.

1. Preheat oven to 350°F. Spray 9" × 9" baking dish with cooking spray.

2. Put bulgur wheat in small bowl. Cover with boiling water and allow wheat to absorb liquid, approximately 15–20 minutes.

3. Line colander with small piece of cheesecloth. Drop bulgur wheat into cloth; drain and squeeze as much liquid out of wheat as possible.

4. On large cutting board, combine lamb, ½ cup grated onions, wheat, salt, and pepper; mix with hands, kneading together all ingredients.

5. Divide meat mixture in half. Place half in bottom of baking dish by dipping hands into ice water to spread meat mixture smoothly over bottom of dish. Cover bottom of dish completely.

6. In a small pan, melt 1½ tablespoons of butter; sauté remaining ½ cup onions, pine nuts, cinnamon, and allspice until onions are soft.

7. Spread onion and pine nut mixture evenly over first layer of meat in baking dish. Take remaining half of meat mixture and spread smoothly on top, using procedure in step 5.

8. Score top in diamond shapes with a knife dipped in cold water. Melt remaining 1½ tablespoons of butter; drizzle over top of meat. Bake for approximately 40–45 minutes or until gold brown.

Nutritional Analysis (per serving): Calories: 226 | Protein: 18g | Carbohydrates: 13g | Fat: 12g | Saturated Fat: 4g | Cholesterol: 62mg | Sodium: 343mg | Fiber: 3g | PCF Ratio: 32-22-46 | Exchange Approx.: 1 Starch, 2 Lean Meats, 2 Fats

MAIN DISH PORK AND BEANS

SERVES 4; SERVING SIZE: ¼ RECIPE

Nonstick spray

1⅓ cups cooked pinto beans

2 tablespoons ketchup

¼ teaspoon Dijon mustard

¼ teaspoon dry mustard

1 teaspoon cider vinegar

4 tablespoons diced red onion

1 tablespoon 100% maple syrup

1 teaspoon brown sugar

¼ pound (4 ounces) slow-cooked shredded pork

⅛ cup (2 tablespoons) apple juice or cider

Preheat oven to 350°F. In casserole dish treated with nonstick spray, combine beans, ketchup, Dijon mustard, dry mustard, vinegar, onion, syrup, and brown sugar. Layer meat over top of bean mixture. Pour apple juice or cider over pork. Bake 20–30 minutes or until mixture is well heated and bubbling. Stir well before serving.

Nutritional Analysis (per serving): Calories: 153 | Protein: 11g | Carbohydrates: 24g | Fat: 2g | Saturated Fat: 1g | Cholesterol: 18mg | Sodium: 146mg | Fiber: 5g | PCF Ratio: 29-61-10 | Exchange Approx.: 2 Lean Meats, ½ Fruit/Misc. Carbohydrate

SLOW-COOKER PORK WITH PLUM SAUCE

SERVES 4; SERVING SIZE: ¼ RECIPE

Nonstick spray

½ pound (8 ounces) cooked shredded pork

1 clove garlic, crushed

½ teaspoon grated fresh ginger

⅛ cup apple juice

¼ teaspoon dry mustard

2 teaspoons Bragg Liquid Aminos or soy sauce

⅛ teaspoon dried thyme

⅛ cup plum jam

½ teaspoon cornstarch

1. In nonstick skillet treated with nonstick spray, stir-fry pork, garlic, and ginger for approximately 2 minutes.

2. In small bowl or measuring cup, combine remaining ingredients to make a slurry; pour over the heated pork, mixing well. Cook over low to medium heat until mixture thickens and juice is absorbed into pork, approximately 15 minutes.

Nutritional Analysis (per serving, with Bragg Liquid Aminos): Calories: 125 | Protein: 13g | Carbohydrates: 11g | Fat: 3g | Saturated Fat: 1g | Cholesterol: 36mg | Sodium: 148mg | Fiber: 0g | PCF Ratio: 42-37-21 | Exchange Approx.: 2 Lean Meats, ½ Fruit

SLOW-COOKER BEEF BRACIOLE

SERVES 4; SERVING SIZE: ¼ RECIPE

4 cups Quick Tomato Sauce (see recipe in Chapter 6)

1 tablespoon olive oil

¼ cup finely chopped onion

1 teaspoon finely chopped garlic

¼ cup finely chopped carrots

¼ cup finely chopped celery

2 slices whole-wheat bread, cubed

1 lightly beaten egg

1-pound beef round, cut into 4 thin slices

1. Add tomato sauce to slow cooker and maintain at medium heat.

2. Heat olive oil in large nonstick skillet; sauté onions, garlic, carrots, and celery until softened. Remove from heat.

3. Add cubed bread and egg to sautéed vegetables; mix well.

4. Pound each piece of beef on both sides to flatten and tenderize. Each slice of meat should be about ¼" thick. Place approximately ½ cup of bread and vegetable stuffing down center of each meat slice and press in place. Starting at one end, roll meat up like a jelly roll; secure with 6" wooden skewer.

5. Place meat rolls in tomato sauce. Set slow cooker on low to medium setting; cook for at least 4 hours. (On low setting, the meat rolls can be left in slow cooker for 6–8 hours.) Remove wooden skewers before serving.

Nutritional Analysis (per serving): Calories: 367 | Protein: 29g | Carbohydrates: 26g | Fat: 16g | Saturated Fat: 5g | Cholesterol: 69mg | Sodium: 162mg | Fiber: 5g | PCF Ratio: 32-29-39 | Exchange Approx.: 3½ Very Lean Meats, 2½ Fats, 3 Vegetables, 1 Starch

SOY AND GINGER FLANK STEAK

SERVES 4; SERVING SIZE: ¼ RECIPE

1-pound lean London broil

1 tablespoon minced fresh ginger

2 teaspoons minced fresh garlic

1 tablespoon reduced-sodium soy sauce

3 tablespoons dry red wine

¼ teaspoon pepper

½ tablespoon olive oil

Slicing Meats Against the Grain

Certain cuts of meat such as London broil (flank steak) and brisket have a distinct grain (or line) of fibers running through them. If you slice with the grain, meat will seem tough and difficult to chew. These cuts of meat should always be thinly sliced across (or against) the grain so fibers are cut through so meats remain tender and easy to chew.

1. Marinate meat at least 3–4 hours in advance: Place meat, ginger, garlic, soy sauce, red wine, pepper, and olive oil in shallow baking dish. Coat meat with marinade on both sides.

2. Cover and refrigerate meat in marinade, turning meat once or twice during marinating so all marinade soaks into both sides of meat.

3. Lightly oil barbecue grill and preheat. Place meat on grill. Grill, turning once, until done to your preference. Medium-rare will take approximately 12–15 minutes. Slice meat diagonally and against grain into thin slices.

Nutritional Analysis (per serving): Calories: 304 | Protein: 29g | Carbohydrates: 1g | Fat: 19g | Saturated Fat: 7g | Cholesterol: 95mg | Sodium: 213mg | Fiber: 0g | PCF Ratio: 40-2-58 | Exchange Approx.: 4 Lean Meats, 1½ Fats

PORK LO MEIN

SERVES 4; SERVING SIZE: ¼ RECIPE

1½ tablespoons reduced-sodium soy sauce

1 teaspoon grated fresh ginger

1 tablespoon rice vinegar

¼ teaspoon ground turmeric

¾-pound lean pork loin, cut into 1" cubes

½ tablespoon canola oil

½ cup sliced green onion

2 teaspoons minced garlic

2 cups shredded cabbage

1 cup (cut into 1" pieces) snap peas

¼ teaspoon crushed red pepper

2 cups cooked whole-grain spaghetti

1 teaspoon sesame oil

1 teaspoon sesame seeds

1. Combine soy sauce, ginger, rice vinegar, and turmeric in bowl. Mix in cubed pork; set aside.

2. In large skillet or wok, heat oil and sauté onion and garlic. Add meat; cook quickly until meat and onions are slightly browned.

3. Add in cabbage and snap peas; continue to stir-fry for another 3–4 minutes. Sprinkle in crushed red pepper.

4. When vegetables are crisp-tender, add cooked pasta, sesame oil, and sesame seeds. Toss lightly and serve.

Nutritional Analysis (per serving): Calories: 266 | Protein: 23g | Carbohydrates: 25g | Fat: 8g | Saturated Fat: 2g | Cholesterol: 50mg | Sodium: 386mg | Fiber: 5g | PCF Ratio: 35-38-27 | Exchange Approx.: 2½ Lean Meats, 1 Starch, 1 Vegetable

EASY OVEN BEEF BURGUNDY

SERVES 4; SERVING SIZE: ¼ RECIPE

1-pound beef round, cubed

2 tablespoons all-purpose flour

1 cup sliced carrots

1 cup chopped onions

1 cup sliced celery

1 clove garlic, finely chopped

¼ teaspoon pepper

¼ teaspoon ground marjoram

¼ teaspoon dried thyme

½ teaspoon salt

2 tablespoons balsamic vinegar

½ cup dry red wine

½ cup water

1 cup sliced fresh mushrooms

1. Preheat oven to 325°F.

2. Dredge meat cubes in flour; place in 3-quart covered baking dish or Dutch oven. Add carrots, onions, celery, garlic, pepper, marjoram, thyme, salt, and vinegar; combine.

3. Pour red wine and water over mixture. Cover and bake 1 hour.

4. Remove from oven; mix in mushrooms.

5. Return to oven for 1 hour or until beef cubes are tender.

Nutritional Analysis (per serving): Calories: 266 | Protein: 34g | Carbohydrates: 12g | Fat: 6g | Saturated Fat: 2g | Cholesterol: 82mg | Sodium: 388mg | Fiber: 2g | PCF Ratio: 56-20-23 | Exchange Approx.: 4 Lean Meats, 2 Vegetables, 1 Fat

PORK ROAST WITH CARAMELIZED ONIONS AND APPLES

SERVES 6; SERVING SIZE: ⅙ RECIPE

2-pound lean pork loin roast

Freshly ground pepper

½ tablespoon olive oil

½ tablespoon butter

2 cups chopped onion

1 tablespoon Marsala wine

⅓ cup low-sodium chicken broth

1 apple, peeled and chopped

1. Preheat oven to 375°F. Season pork loin with pepper. Heat olive oil in a large skillet; sear pork to brown all sides.

2. Transfer roast to 9" × 13" glass baking dish; place in oven for approximately 1 hour and 15 minutes.

3. While pork is roasting, prepare onions: In large nonstick skillet, melt butter and add onions. Sauté onions until soft; add wine, chicken broth, and apple. Continue cooking on low heat until onions are soft, brown in color, and have caramelized.

4. When roast has reached an internal temperature of 130°F, spoon onions over top; place a loose foil tent over roast and return to oven.

5. Remove roast from oven when an internal temperature of 145°F has been reached. (Temperature of roast will continue to rise as meat rests.) Keep roast loosely covered with foil and allow to stand for 10–15 minutes before slicing.

Nutritional Analysis (per serving): Calories: 373 | Protein: 31g | Carbohydrates: 8g | Fat: 23g | Saturated Fat: 9g | Cholesterol: 96mg | Sodium: 156mg | Fiber: 1g | PCF Ratio: 34-9-57 | Exchange Approx.: 1 Vegetable, 4 Lean Meats, 2 Fats

SWEET-AND-SOUR PORK SKILLET

SERVES 4; SERVING SIZE: ¼ RECIPE

12-ounce lean pork tenderloin, cut into 1" strips

1 tablespoon honey

2 tablespoons rice vinegar or white vinegar

2 teaspoons soy sauce

½ teaspoon grated fresh ginger

½ cup chopped onions

½ cup julienned carrots

2 cups cauliflower florets

¼ teaspoon Chinese five-spice powder

Aromatic Five-Spice Powder

Chinese five-spice powder is a blend of cinnamon, anise, fennel (or star anise), ginger, and clove. Five-spice powder is an essential base seasoning for many Chinese dishes. A little of this aromatic mix goes a long way, giving dishes a hint of sweet, savory, and sour.

1. In medium bowl, combine pork, honey, vinegar, soy sauce, and ginger. Coat pork strips with mixture; allow to marinate for at least 15 minutes.

2. Heat large nonstick skillet or wok. Add pork strips and onion; quickly stir-fry over high heat for 2–3 minutes. Reserve any leftover marinade to add with vegetables.

3. Add carrots, cauliflower, and marinade. Toss and continue to stir-fry, allowing marinade to coat all vegetables. Cook over high heat for an additional 3–4 minutes or until vegetables are crisp-tender.

4. Add five-spice powder and combine just before serving.

Nutritional Analysis (per serving): Calories: 198 | Protein: 26g | Carbohydrates: 12g | Fat: 5g | Saturated Fat: 2g | Cholesterol: 67mg | Sodium: 164mg | Fiber: 3g | PCF Ratio: 47-30-25 | Exchange Approx.: 3½ Very Lean Meats, 1½ Vegetables, ½ Other Carbohydrate, ½ Fat

FRUITED PORK LOIN ROAST CASSEROLE

SERVES 4; SERVING SIZE: ¼ RECIPE

Nonstick spray

4 small Yukon gold potatoes, peeled and sliced

2 (2-ounce) pieces trimmed boneless pork loin, pounded flat

1 apple, peeled, cored, and sliced

4 apricot halves

1 tablespoon chopped red onion or shallot

⅛ cup apple cider or apple juice

Olive oil, to taste (optional)

Grated Parmesan cheese, to taste (optional)

Salt and freshly ground pepper, to taste (optional)

Tip

To enhance the flavor of this dish, top with the optional ingredients when it's served. Just be sure to make the appropriate exchange approximation adjustments if you do.

1. Preheat oven to 350°F (325°F if using a glass casserole dish); treat casserole dish with nonstick spray.

2. Layer half the potato slices across bottom of dish; top with one piece of flattened pork loin. Arrange apple slices over top of loin; place apricot halves on top of apple. Sprinkle red onion over apricot and apples. Add second flattened pork loin; layer remaining potatoes atop loin. Drizzle apple cider over top of casserole.

3. Cover and bake for 45 minutes–1 hour or until potatoes are tender. Keep casserole covered and let sit for 10 minutes after removing from oven.

Nutritional Analysis (per serving, without salt): Calories: 170 | Protein: 7g | Carbohydrates: 27g | Fat: 4g | Saturated Fat: 1g | Cholesterol: 19mg | Sodium: 32mg | Fiber: 3g | PCF Ratio: 17-63-20 | Exchange Approx.: 1 Lean Meat, 1 Fruit, 1 Starch

WHITE WINE AND LEMON PORK ROAST

SERVES 4; SERVING SIZE: ¼ RECIPE

1 clove garlic, crushed

½ cup dry white wine

1 tablespoon lemon juice

1 teaspoon olive oil

1 tablespoon minced red onion or shallot

¼ teaspoon dried thyme

⅛ teaspoon ground black pepper

12-ounce pork loin roast

Nonstick spray

1. Make marinade by combining garlic, white wine, lemon juice, olive oil, red onion, thyme, and black pepper in heavy, freezer-style plastic bag. Add roast; marinate in refrigerator 1 hour or overnight, according to taste. (Note: Pork loin is already tender, so you're marinating the meat to impart the flavors only.)

2. Preheat oven to 350°F. Remove meat from marinade; put on nonstick spray–treated rack in roasting pan. Roast for 20–30 minutes or until meat thermometer reads 150°F–170°F, depending on how well done you prefer it.

Nutritional Analysis (per serving): Calories: 172 | Protein: 18g | Carbohydrates: 2g | Fat: 7g | Saturated Fat: 2g | Cholesterol: 50mg | Sodium: 47mg | Fiber: 0g | PCF Ratio: 53-5-42 | Exchange Approx.: 3 Lean Meats

PECAN-CRUSTED ROAST PORK LOIN

SERVES 4; SERVING SIZE: ¼ RECIPE

1 teaspoon olive oil

1 clove garlic, crushed

1 teaspoon brown sugar

Thyme, sage, and pepper to taste (optional)

12-ounce boneless pork loin roast

¼ cup chopped or ground pecans

1. Put olive oil, crushed garlic, brown sugar, and seasonings (if using) in a heavy, freezer-style plastic bag. Work bag until ingredients are mixed. Add roast; turn in bag to coat. Marinate in refrigerator for several hours or overnight.

2. Preheat oven to 400°F. Roll pork loin in chopped pecans; place in roasting pan. Make a tent of aluminum foil; arrange over pork loin, covering nuts completely so they won't char. Roast for 10 minutes, then lower heat to 350°F. Continue to roast for another 8–15 minutes or until meat thermometer reads 150°F–170°F, depending on how well done you prefer it.

Nutritional Analysis (per serving): Calories: 209 | Protein: 24g | Carbohydrates: 2g | Fat: 11g | Saturated Fat: 2g | Cholesterol: 67mg | Sodium: 47mg | Fiber: 1g | PCF Ratio: 47-4-49 | Exchange Approx.: 3½ Very Lean Meats, 2 Fats

BALSAMIC VENISON POT ROAST

SERVES 8; SERVING SIZE: 1/8 RECIPE

2½ tablespoons all-purpose flour

2 teaspoons paprika

2-pound venison roast

1½ tablespoons olive oil

14 ounces low-sodium beef broth

½ cup chopped onion

2 tablespoons dried onion flakes

⅓ cup balsamic vinegar

⅛ teaspoon Worcestershire sauce

1 teaspoon sugar

Recipe Adaptation

This recipe also works well cooked in a slow cooker for 6–8 hours until tender. Slow cookers with a ceramic interior maintain low temperatures better than those with a metal cooking surface.

1. Mix flour and paprika together; dredge venison in flour mixture until completely coated.

2. Heat oil in Dutch oven or deep skillet; brown roast on all sides.

3. Add beef broth, onion, onion flakes, balsamic vinegar, Worcestershire sauce, and sugar. Bring to a quick boil; reduce heat to low.

4. Cover and cook over low heat for 2–3 hours or until venison is tender and cuts easily. Serve with whole-grain noodles.

Nutritional Analysis (per serving): Calories: 188 | Protein: 28g | Carbohydrates: 6g | Fat: 6g | Saturated Fat: 2g | Cholesterol: 96mg | Sodium: 75mg | Fiber: 1g | PCF Ratio: 60-13-28 | Exchange Approx.: 4 Very Lean Meats, ½ Fat

VENISON PEPPER STEAK

SERVES 4; SERVING SIZE: ¼ RECIPE

2 tablespoons reduced-sodium soy sauce

1 clove garlic

1½ teaspoons grated fresh ginger

1-pound venison loin, cut across grain into ¼" strips

1 tablespoon canola oil

1 cup thinly sliced onion

1 cup (½" strips) green or red peppers

½ cup thinly sliced celery

1 tablespoon cornstarch

1 cup water

1½ cups chopped tomatoes

Whole-Grain Additions

Instead of serving white rice, substitute brown rice or quinoa mixed with sautéed vegetables with this dish.

1. Combine soy sauce, garlic, and ginger in bowl. Add sliced meat; mix well and set aside.

2. Heat canola oil in large wok or skillet. Add meat and cook for 2–3 minutes over high heat. Cover, reduce heat, and simmer for 15 minutes.

3. Add onions, peppers, and celery to meat; cover and cook on low heat for another 15 minutes or until sliced meat is tender.

4. Mix cornstarch with water; add to meat. Cook for 5 minutes or until sauce thickens slightly. Add tomatoes and heat through.

Nutritional Analysis (per serving): Calories: 237 | Protein: 26g | Carbohydrates: 12g | Fat: 9g | Saturated Fat: 3g | Cholesterol: 39mg | Sodium: 344mg | Fiber: 2g | PCF Ratio: 44-20-36 | Exchange Approx.: 3½ Very Lean Meats, 2 Vegetables, 1½ Fats

SLOW-COOKER VENISON AND VEGETABLE POT ROAST

SERVES 4; SERVING SIZE: ¼ RECIPE

1-pound venison roast

1 tablespoon all-purpose flour

1 tablespoon olive oil

1 tablespoon instant brown gravy mix

1 teaspoon Worcestershire sauce

1 cup chopped onions

½ pound potatoes, cut into 1" pieces

1 cup 1"-chopped carrots

1 cup chopped celery

½ cup crushed tomato

½ teaspoon dried thyme

Variation
You can also use ⅓ cup water and 2 tablespoons red wine for the liquid instead of crushed tomatoes.

1. Dredge roast in flour. Heat olive oil in large skillet; sear roast until browned on all sides. Put roast in slow cooker.

2. Sprinkle instant gravy mix and Worcestershire sauce over top of roast. Place onions, potatoes, carrots, and celery around roast; spoon crushed tomatoes evenly around vegetables. Sprinkle thyme over meat and vegetables.

3. Cook in slow cooker on low setting for 6–8 hours.

Nutritional Analysis (per serving): Calories: 309 | Protein: 27g | Carbohydrates: 28g | Fat: 10g | Saturated Fat: 3g | Cholesterol: 39mg | Sodium: 237mg | Fiber: 4g | PCF Ratio: 35-36-28 | Exchange Approx.: 3½ Very Lean Meats, 1 Starch, 3 Vegetables, 1½ Fats

SLOW-COOKED VENISON

YIELDS ABOUT 1 POUND; SERVING SIZE: 2 OUNCES

1-pound venison roast

1–2 tablespoons cider vinegar

1. Put venison in ceramic-lined slow cooker; add enough water to cover. Add vinegar; set on high. Once mixture begins to boil, reduce temperature to low. Allow meat to simmer for 8 or more hours.

2. Drain resulting broth from meat and discard. Remove any remaining fat from meat and discard. Weigh meat and separate into servings. Meat will keep for 1–2 days in refrigerator, or freeze portions for later use.

Nutritional Analysis (per serving): Calories: 90 | Protein: 18g | Carbohydrates: 0g | Fat: 2g | Saturated Fat: 1g | Cholesterol: 64mg | Sodium: 31mg | Fiber: 0g | PCF Ratio: 81-0-19 | Exchange Approx.: 2 Very Lean Meats

SLOW-COOKER VENISON BARBECUE

SERVES 12; SERVING SIZE: ¹/₁₂ RECIPE

1½ pounds (24 ounces) Slow-Cooked Venison (see recipe in this chapter)

1 cup water

½ cup dry white wine

½ cup Brooks Rich & Tangy Ketchup

1 tablespoon red wine vinegar

1 tablespoon stone-ground mustard

1 tablespoon dried onion flakes

⅛ cup (2 tablespoons) Homemade Worcestershire Sauce (see recipe in Chapter 6)

1 teaspoon dried minced garlic

1 teaspoon cracked black pepper

1 tablespoon brown sugar

Game Over
Instead of using the slow-cooker method to remove any gamy flavor from game meats, soak it in milk or tomato juice overnight. Drain the meat and discard the soaking liquid.

Add cooked venison to slow cooker. Mix remaining ingredients together; pour over venison. Add additional water if necessary to completely cover meat. Set slow cooker on high until mixture begins to boil. Reduce heat to low and simmer for 2 or more hours. Adjust seasonings if necessary.

Nutritional Analysis (per serving): Calories: 117 | Protein: 17g | Carbohydrates: 5g | Fat: 2g | Saturated Fat: 1g | Cholesterol: 63mg | Sodium: 185mg | Fiber: 0.04g | PCF Ratio: 65-20-16 | Exchange Approx.: 2 Very Lean Meats, 1 Free Condiment

VENISON WITH DRIED CRANBERRY VINEGAR SAUCE

SERVES 4; SERVING SIZE: ¼ RECIPE

⅛ cup (2 tablespoons) dried cranberries

1 tablespoon sugar

3 tablespoons water

⅛ cup (2 tablespoons) champagne vinegar
or white wine vinegar

2 teaspoons olive oil

1 tablespoon minced shallots or red onion

1 teaspoon minced garlic

⅛ cup (2 tablespoons) dry red wine

½ cup low-fat reduced-sodium chicken
broth

½ teaspoon cracked black pepper

½ pound (8 ounces) Slow-Cooked Venison
(see recipe in this chapter)

1 teaspoon cornstarch or potato flour
mixed with 1 tablespoon water

2 teaspoons butter

Operate Your Appliances Safely

When puréeing hot mixtures, leave the
vent uncovered on your food processor. If
using a blender, either remove the vent
cover from the lid or leave the lid ajar so
the steam can escape.

1. Add cranberries, sugar, water, and champagne vinegar to saucepan; bring to a boil. Reduce heat and simmer 5 minutes. Remove from heat and transfer to food processor or blender; process until cranberries are chopped (it isn't necessary to purée because you want some cranberry "chunks" to remain). Set aside.

2. Pour olive oil into a heated nonstick skillet. Add shallots and garlic; sauté for 30 seconds. Deglaze pan with red wine; cook, stirring occasionally, until wine is reduced by half. Add cranberry mixture and chicken broth; bring to a boil. Reduce heat to medium-low; season with pepper, add venison, and simmer for 3 minutes or until meat is heated through.

3. Thicken sauce using a slurry of 1 teaspoon cornstarch or potato flour and 1 tablespoon of water; simmer until sauce thickens. You'll need to cook the sauce a bit longer if you use cornstarch in order to remove the starchy taste. Remove from heat; add butter and whisk to incorporate into sauce.

Nutritional Analysis (per serving, without cornstarch or flour): Calories: 154 | Protein: 17g | Carbohydrates: 4g | Fat: 6g | Saturated Fat: 2g | Cholesterol: 69mg | Sodium: 77mg | Fiber: 0g | PCF Ratio: 49-12-38 | Exchange Approx.: 3 Very Lean Meats, 1 Fat

CORNED BEEF AND CABBAGE

SERVES 10; SERVING SIZE: 1/10 RECIPE

3 pounds corned beef brisket

3 medium carrots, peeled and cut into 3" pieces

3 medium onions, peeled and quartered

1 cup water

1/2 small head cabbage, cut into wedges

1. Place the beef, carrots, onions, and water in a slow cooker. Cover and cook on low for 8–10 hours.

2. Add the cabbage to the slow cooker; be sure to submerge the cabbage in liquid. Turn the heat up to high, cover, and cook for 2–3 hours.

Nutritional Analysis (per serving): Calories: 300 | Protein: 21g | Carbohydrates: 7g | Fat: 20g | Saturated Fat: 6g | Cholesterol: 75mg | Sodium: 129mg | Fiber: 2g | PCF Ratio: 28-10-62 | Exchange Approx.: 1 Vegetable, 3 Medium-Fat Meats, 1 Fat

STEAK AND MUSHROOM KABOBS

SERVES 3; SERVING SIZE: 1/3 RECIPE

3 tablespoons olive oil

1/4 cup balsamic vinegar

1 tablespoon Worcestershire sauce

1/2 teaspoon salt

2 cloves garlic, minced

Freshly ground black pepper to taste

1 pound sirloin steak, cut into 1½" cubes

1/2 pound large white mushrooms, washed and halved

1. Combine the oil, vinegar, Worcestershire sauce, salt, garlic, and pepper to make a marinade.

2. Place the steak and mushrooms in a shallow bowl with the marinade in the refrigerator for 1–2 hours.

3. Place the mushrooms and steak cubes on separate wooden or metal skewers. Grill at 350°F for about 4 minutes per side for medium-rare steak. You may need additional cooking time for the mushrooms.

Nutritional Analysis (per serving): Calories: 430 | Protein: 29g | Carbohydrates: 8g | Fat: 30g | Saturated Fat: 8g | Cholesterol: 90mg | Sodium: 540mg | Fiber: 0g | PCF Ratio: 27-7-66 | Exchange Approx.: 1 Vegetable, 4 Medium-Fat Meats, 3 Fats

POT ROAST WITH VEGETABLES AND GRAVY

SERVES 10; SERVING SIZE: 1/10 RECIPE

3-pound beef bottom-round roast, trimmed of fat

2 tablespoons canola oil

4 medium sweet onions, peeled and chopped

4 cloves garlic, chopped

4 medium carrots, peeled and chopped

4 celery stalks, chopped

8 small bluenose turnips, peeled and chopped

1" gingerroot, peeled and minced

1 (13-ounce) can beef broth

½ cup dry red wine

Salt and pepper to taste

1–2 tablespoons brown rice flour or almond flour

1. In a large pot, brown the beef in oil on medium-high heat and set aside. Add the onion, garlic, carrots, celery, turnips, and gingerroot to the pot and cook, stirring until softened, about 5–6 minutes. Return the beef to the pot and add the rest of the ingredients. Cover and cook over very low heat for 3 hours.

2. To serve, slice the beef across, not with, the grain. Serve surrounded by vegetables and place the gravy on the side or over the top.

Nutritional Analysis (per serving): Calories: 270 | Protein: 32g | Carbohydrates: 13g | Fat: 9g | Saturated Fat: 3g | Cholesterol: 85mg | Sodium: 300mg | Fiber: 3g | PCF Ratio: 50-20-30 | Exchange Approx.: ½ Starch, 1½ Vegetables, 4 Lean Meats, 1 Fat

GREEK MEATBALLS

SERVES 10; SERVING SIZE: ¹⁄₁₀ RECIPE

1 cup cooked buckwheat or quinoa

2 pounds lean ground beef

1 medium onion, peeled and minced

4 cloves garlic, minced

2 tablespoons Italian seasoning

1 bunch fresh mint leaves, chopped

2 teaspoons white vinegar

2 eggs, beaten

Salt and pepper to taste

½ cup olive oil

1. Preheat oven to 325°F. Mix the buckwheat, beef, onion, garlic, Italian seasoning, mint, vinegar, eggs, salt, and pepper in a bowl. Using your fingers, roll the mixture into meatballs.

2. Heat the oil in a medium frying pan over medium-high heat. Fry the meatballs in the oil in batches. Use a slotted spoon to move the balls in the oil to brown all sides.

3. Place the cooked meatballs on a paper towel to drain.

4. If the meatballs remain raw in the center, place them on a baking sheet and finish cooking them in the oven for 15–20 minutes.

Nutritional Analysis (per serving): Calories: 240 | Protein: 19g | Carbohydrates: 6g | Fat: 15g | Saturated Fat: 3g | Cholesterol: 50mg | Sodium: 65mg | Fiber: 1g | PCF Ratio: 32-10-58 | Exchange Approx.: ¼ Starch, ¼ Vegetable, 2 Lean Meats, 2¼ Fats

BOEUF BOURGUIGNON

SERVES 8; SERVING SIZE: 1/8 RECIPE

2 pounds stewing beef, cut into ½" cubes

Salt and pepper to taste

1 tablespoon olive oil

3 cloves garlic, minced

3 medium onions, peeled and quartered

2 cups red wine

¾ pound carrots, peeled and sliced

¾ pound white mushrooms, sliced

1 bunch chopped fresh rosemary

1 bunch chopped fresh thyme

2 cups water or as needed

1. Season the beef with the salt and pepper.

2. Add the olive oil to a large frying pan over medium heat. Place the beef in the pan and brown on the outside. Add the garlic and onions and cook until tender, about 3–5 minutes. Add the red wine, bring it to a boil, and then simmer.

3. Add the carrots, mushrooms, and herbs to the pan. Add 2 cups of water if you want a thinner stew and to keep the stew's sauce from cooking down. Cook for 3 hours, stirring occasionally.

Nutritional Analysis (per serving): Calories: 260 | Protein: 27g | Carbohydrates: 12g | Fat: 7g | Saturated Fat: 2g | Cholesterol: 70mg | Sodium: 100mg | Fiber: 2g | PCF Ratio: 52-18-30 | Exchange Approx.: 2 Vegetables, 3 Lean Meats, 1½ Fats

TOMATO-BRAISED PORK

SERVES 4; SERVING SIZE: ¼ RECIPE

1 (28-ounce) can crushed tomatoes

3 tablespoons tomato paste

1 cup loosely packed fresh basil

½ teaspoon freshly ground black pepper

½ teaspoon ground marjoram

1¼-pound boneless pork roast

1. Place the tomatoes, tomato paste, basil, pepper, and marjoram in a greased 4-quart slow cooker. Stir to create a uniform sauce. Add the pork.

2. Cook on low for 7–8 hours or until the pork easily falls apart when poked with a fork.

Nutritional Analysis (per serving): Calories: 226 | Protein: 34g | Carbohydrates: 10g | Fat: 5g | Saturated Fat: 2g | Cholesterol: 80mg | Sodium: 176mg | Fiber: 3g | PCF Ratio: 54-27-19 | Exchange Approx.: 2 Vegetables, 4 Lean Meats

GRASS-FED LAMB MEATBALLS

SERVES 6; SERVING SIZE: ⅙ RECIPE

¼ cup pine nuts

4 tablespoons olive oil, divided

1½ pounds ground grass-fed lamb

¼ cup minced garlic

2 tablespoons cumin

1. Over medium-high heat in a medium frying pan, sauté the pine nuts in 2 tablespoons of olive oil for 2 minutes until brown. Remove them from the pan and allow them to cool.

2. In a large bowl, combine the lamb, garlic, cumin, and pine nuts and form the mixture into meatballs.

3. Add the remaining olive oil to the pan and fry the meatballs until cooked through, about 5–10 minutes depending on size of meatballs.

Nutritional Analysis (per serving): Calories: 320 | Protein: 24g | Carbohydrates: 3g | Fat: 21g | Saturated Fat: 4.5g | Cholesterol: 75mg | Sodium: 75mg | Fiber: 1g | PCF Ratio: 32-64-4 | Exchange Approx.: 3½ Lean Meats, 3 Fats

GLAZED LEAN PORK SHOULDER

SERVES 8; SERVING SIZE: ⅛ RECIPE

3-pound bone-in pork shoulder, excess fat removed

3 apples, cored and thinly sliced

¼ cup apple cider

1 tablespoon brown sugar

1 teaspoon ground allspice

½ teaspoon ground cinnamon

¼ teaspoon ground nutmeg

Place the pork shoulder into a 4-quart slow cooker. Top with the remaining ingredients. Cook on low for 8 hours. Remove the lid and cook on high for 30 minutes or until the sauce thickens.

Nutritional Analysis (per serving): Calories: 218 | Protein: 31g | Carbohydrates: 10g | Fat: 5g | Saturated Fat: 1g | Cholesterol: 35mg | Sodium: 69mg | Fiber: 1g | PCF Ratio: 42-30-28 | Exchange Approx.: 1 Fruit, 3 Lean Meats

ROASTED PORK TENDERLOIN

SERVES 10; SERVING SIZE: ⅒ RECIPE

2½-pound pork loin

Juice of 1 large orange

3 tablespoons lime juice

2 tablespoons red wine

10 cloves garlic, minced

2 tablespoons dried rosemary

1 tablespoon ground black pepper

1. Combine all the ingredients in a shallow dish or large zip-top plastic bag. Refrigerate and marinate the pork for at least 2 hours.

2. Remove the pork from the marinade and bring it to room temperature. Preheat the oven to 350°F.

3. Place the pork in a roasting pan and cook for 20–25 minutes or until the internal temperature reaches 165°F. Allow the pork to rest for 5 minutes before carving.

Nutritional Analysis (per serving): Calories: 218 | Protein: 31g | Carbohydrates: 10g | Fat: 5g | Saturated Fat: 1g | Cholesterol: 35mg | Sodium: 69mg | Fiber: 1g | PCF Ratio: 42-30-28 | Exchange Approx.: 1 Fruit, 3 Lean Meats

MUSHROOM PORK MEDALLIONS

SERVES 2; SERVING SIZE: ½ RECIPE

1 tablespoon olive oil

1-pound pork tenderloin, sliced into ½"-thick medallions

1 small onion, peeled and sliced

¼ cup sliced fresh mushrooms

1 garlic clove, minced

2 teaspoons ground flaxseed

½ cup gluten-free beef broth

¼ teaspoon dried crushed rosemary

⅛ teaspoon ground black pepper

1. In a skillet, heat the olive oil over medium-high heat. Brown the pork in oil for 2 minutes on each side.

2. Remove the pork from the skillet and set it aside.

3. Add the onion, mushrooms, and garlic to the skillet and sauté for 1 minute.

4. Stir in the flaxseed until blended.

5. Gradually stir in the broth, rosemary, and pepper. Bring to a boil; cook and stir for 1 minute or until thickened.

6. Lay the pork medallions on top of the mixture. Reduce the heat, cover, and simmer for 15 minutes or until the meat juices run clear.

Nutritional Analysis (per serving): Calories: 380 | Protein: 51g | Carbohydrates: 7g | Fat: 17g | Saturated Fat: 4g | Cholesterol: 130mg | Sodium: 370mg | Fiber: 1g | PCF Ratio: 53-7-40 | Exchange Approx.: 6 Lean Meats, 2 Fats

PORK CHOPS WITH BALSAMIC GLAZE

SERVES 4; SERVING SIZE: 1 CHOP

4 (5-ounce) center-cut pork chops

1 teaspoon salt, divided

Freshly ground black pepper to taste

2 tablespoons olive oil

6 large shallots, peeled and quartered

½ cup balsamic vinegar

2 teaspoons agave nectar

1. Wash and pat dry the pork chops. Season them with ½ teaspoon salt and pepper.

2. Heat the oil in a large frying pan on medium-high heat. Add the pork and shallots to the pan and cook for 3 minutes. Flip the pork, stir the shallots, and cook an additional 3 minutes. Transfer the pork to a plate, cover it, and set it aside.

3. Add the vinegar, agave nectar, ½ teaspoon salt, and a pinch of pepper to the shallots in the pan. Cook until the liquid begins to thicken, about 1–2 minutes.

4. Turn the heat down to medium-low, return the pork to the pan, and coat the pork well with the sauce. Cook for 3–4 minutes; a thermometer inserted into pork should read 150°F.

5. Remove the pork from the pan, turn the heat up, and allow the remaining sauce to thicken. Pour the sauce over the pork chops before serving.

Nutritional Analysis (per serving): Calories: 288 | Protein: 30g | Carbohydrates: 10g | Fat: 12g | Saturated Fat: 2.5g | Cholesterol: 90mg | Sodium: 642mg | Fiber: 0g | PCF Ratio: 41-19-40 | Exchange Approx.: 1 Vegetable, 3 Lean Meats, 1 Fat

LAMB SHANKS WITH WHITE BEANS AND CARROTS

SERVES 4; SERVING SIZE: 1 LAMB SHANK

4 lamb shanks, well trimmed

Salt and pepper to taste

1 tablespoon olive oil

1 large yellow onion, peeled and chopped

4 garlic cloves, minced

1 medium carrot, peeled and cut into chunks

2 tablespoons tomato paste

1 cup dry red wine

1 cup gluten-free chicken broth

2 bay leaves

¼ cup chopped parsley

2 (13-ounce) cans white beans, drained and rinsed

Not Crazy about Lamb?

When people don't like lamb, it's usually the fat, not the lamb, they dislike. When you prepare roast lamb, stew, or shanks, be sure to remove all of the fat.

1. Sprinkle the lamb shanks with the salt and pepper. In a large frying pan over medium-high heat, add the olive oil, lamb, onion, garlic, and carrot and cook until the lamb is browned, about 5 minutes. Stir in the tomato paste, red wine, chicken broth, bay leaves, and parsley.

2. Cover the pot and simmer for 1 hour. Add the white beans and simmer for another 30 minutes. Remove the bay leaves before serving.

Nutritional Analysis (per serving): Calories: 417 | Protein: 31g | Carbohydrates: 44g | Fat: 12g | Saturated Fat: 3g | Cholesterol: 75mg | Sodium: 601mg | Fiber: 6g | PCF Ratio: 22-45-33 | Exchange Approx.: 2 Starches, 2 Vegetables, 3 Lean Meats, 1 Fat

LAMB AND ROOT VEGETABLE TAGINE

SERVES 6; SERVING SIZE: ⅙ RECIPE

2-pound leg of lamb, trimmed of fat and cut into bite-sized chunks

1 tablespoon olive oil

½ medium onion, peeled and chopped

1 clove garlic, minced

½ teaspoon ground black pepper

½ teaspoon salt

1 cup gluten-free chicken stock

½ pound (about 2 medium) sweet potatoes, peeled and cut into 1" chunks

⅓ cup dried apricots, cut in half

1 teaspoon ground coriander

1 teaspoon ground cumin

¼ teaspoon ground cinnamon

1. In a large skillet, brown the cubed lamb in the olive oil over medium-high heat, approximately 1–2 minutes per side. Add the lamb to a greased 4-quart slow cooker. Cook the onion and garlic in the same skillet over medium-high heat for 3–4 minutes until soft and then add them to the slow cooker.

2. Add the remaining ingredients to the slow cooker. Cook on high for 4 hours or on low for 8 hours.

Nutritional Analysis (per serving): Calories: 270 | Protein: 32g | Carbohydrates: 14g | Fat: 9g | Saturated Fat: 2.5g | Cholesterol: 100mg | Sodium: 480mg | Fiber: 2g | PCF Ratio: 50-20-30 | Exchange Approx.: ¼ Fruit, 4 Lean Meats, ½ Fat

CHAPTER 10

POULTRY

OVEN-FRIED CHICKEN THIGHS

SERVES 4; SERVING SIZE: 1 THIGH

4 chicken thighs, skin removed

1 tablespoon unbleached white all-purpose flour

1 large egg white

½ teaspoon sea salt

½ teaspoon olive oil (optional; see comparison analysis in sidebar for using olive oil)

1 tablespoon rice flour

1 tablespoon cornmeal

Nonstick cooking spray

If You Use Oil . . .

Comparison analysis (with olive oil): Calories: 78.53; Protein: 9.46g; Carbohydrates: 4.65g; Fat: 2.27g; Saturated Fat: 0.50g; Cholesterol: 34.03mg; Sodium: 331.03mg; Fiber: 0.06g; PCF Ratio: 49-24-27; Exchange Approx.: 2 Lean Meats.

1. Preheat oven to 350°F. Rinse and dry chicken thighs. Put white flour on plate. In small, shallow bowl, whip egg white with the sea salt. Add olive oil if using; mix well. Put rice flour and cornmeal on another plate; mix together. Place rack on baking sheet; spray both with nonstick cooking spray.

2. Roll each chicken thigh in white flour, dip it into egg mixture, and roll in rice flour mixture. Place thighs on rack so they aren't touching. Bake 35–45 minutes until meat juices run clear.

Nutritional Analysis (per serving, no oil): Calories: 74 | Protein: 9g | Carbohydrates: 5g | Fat: 2g | Saturated Fat: 1g | Cholesterol: 34mg | Sodium: 331mg | Fiber: 0g | PCF Ratio: 53-26-21 | Exchange Approx.: 2 Very Lean Meats

ANOTHER HEALTHY "FRIED" CHICKEN

SERVES 4; SERVING SIZE: ¼ RECIPE

Nonstick cooking spray

10 ounces raw boneless skinless chicken breasts (fat trimmed off)

½ cup nonfat plain yogurt

½ cup bread crumbs

1 teaspoon garlic powder

1 teaspoon paprika

¼ teaspoon dried thyme

Chicken Fat Facts

When faced with the decision of whether to have chicken with or without the skin, consider that ½ pound of skinless chicken breast has 9 grams of fat; ½ pound with the skin on has 38 grams!

1. Preheat oven to 350°F. Prepare baking pan with nonstick cooking spray. Cut each chicken breast into four equal pieces; marinate in yogurt for several minutes.

2. Mix together bread crumbs, garlic powder, paprika, and thyme; dredge chicken in crumb mixture. Arrange on prepared pan; bake 20 minutes. To give chicken a deep golden color, place pan under broiler last 5 minutes of cooking. Watch closely to ensure chicken "crust" doesn't burn.

Nutritional Analysis (per serving, without salt): Calories: 118 | Protein: 19g | Carbohydrates: 5g | Fat: 2g | Saturated Fat: 1g | Cholesterol: 44mg | Sodium: 91mg | Fiber: 0g | PCF Ratio: 66-18-16 | Exchange Approx.: 2 Very Lean Meats, ½ Starch

BUTTERMILK RANCH CHICKEN SALAD

SERVES 4; SERVING SIZE: ¼ RECIPE

1 tablespoon real mayonnaise

3 tablespoons nonfat plain yogurt

½ cup nonfat cottage cheese

½ teaspoon cider vinegar

1 teaspoon brown sugar

1 teaspoon Dijon mustard

½ cup buttermilk

2 tablespoons dried parsley

1 clove garlic, minced

2 tablespoons grated Parmesan cheese

¼ teaspoon sea salt (optional)

¼ teaspoon freshly ground pepper (optional)

1 cup chopped cooked chicken breast

½ cup sliced cucumber

½ cup chopped celery

½ cup sliced carrots

4 cups salad greens

½ cup red onion slices

Fresh parsley for garnish (optional)

Get More Mileage from Meals

Leftover chicken salad makes great sandwiches. Put it between two slices of bread with lots of lettuce for a quick lunch. The lettuce helps keep the bread from getting soggy if the sandwich is to-go.

1. In blender or food processor, combine mayonnaise, yogurt, cottage cheese, vinegar, brown sugar, mustard, buttermilk, parsley, garlic, cheese, salt, and pepper; process until smooth. Pour over the chicken, cucumber, celery, and carrots. Chill at least 2 hours.

2. To serve, arrange 1 cup of salad greens on each of four serving plates. Top each salad with an equal amount of chicken salad. Garnish with red onion slices and fresh parsley if desired.

Nutritional Analysis (per serving, without salt): Calories: 147 | Protein: 18g | Carbohydrates: 11g | Fat: 4g | Saturated Fat: 1g | Cholesterol: 33mg | Sodium: 184mg | Fiber: 2g | PCF Ratio: 49-29-22 | Exchange Approx.: 2 Very Lean Meats, ½ Vegetable, 1 Free Vegetable, ½ Skim Milk

PINEAPPLE-ORANGE GRILLED CHICKEN BREASTS

SERVES 4; SERVING SIZE: ¼ RECIPE

6 ounces pineapple juice

4 ounces orange juice

¼ cup cider vinegar

1 tablespoon chopped fresh tarragon

½ tablespoon fresh rosemary

1 pound boneless skinless chicken breast, cut into 4 pieces

1. Mix pineapple juice, orange juice, vinegar, tarragon, and rosemary in large shallow dish.

2. Add raw chicken breasts to marinade; cover and refrigerate 3–4 hours. Turn pieces of chicken to cover with marinade.

3. Heat grill to medium-high; place chicken on grill. Grill approximately 7–10 minutes on each side until chicken is cooked through.

Nutritional Analysis (per serving): Calories: 165 | Protein: 27g | Carbohydrates: 10g | Fat: 2g | Saturated Fat: 0g | Cholesterol: 58mg | Sodium: 75mg | Fiber: 0g | PCF Ratio: 67-25-9 | Exchange Approx.: 3½ Lean Meats, ½ Fruit

HERBED CHICKEN AND BROWN RICE DINNER

SERVES 4; SERVING SIZE: ¼ RECIPE

1 tablespoon canola oil

4 (4-ounce) boneless skinless chicken breast pieces

¾ teaspoon garlic powder, divided

¾ teaspoon dried rosemary, divided

1 (10½-ounce) can low-fat reduced-sodium chicken broth

⅓ cup water

2 cups uncooked instant brown rice

1. Heat oil in large nonstick skillet on medium-high heat. Add chicken; sprinkle with half the garlic powder and rosemary. Cover and cook 4 minutes on each side or until cooked through. Remove chicken from skillet and set aside.

2. Add broth and water to skillet; stir to deglaze pan and bring to a boil. Stir in rice and remaining garlic powder and rosemary. Top with chicken and cover; cook on low heat 5 minutes. Remove from heat and let stand covered 5 minutes.

Nutritional Analysis (per serving): Calories: 300 | Protein: 33g | Carbohydrates: 26g | Fat: 6g | Saturated Fat: 1g | Cholesterol: 75mg | Sodium: 112mg | Fiber: 0g | PCF Ratio: 45-36-19 | Exchange Approx.: 1½ Starches, 2 Very Lean Meats, 2 Lean Meats

WALNUT CHICKEN

SERVES 4; SERVING SIZE: ¼ RECIPE

¾ pound (12 ounces) boneless skinless chicken breast

1 teaspoon sherry

1 egg white

2 teaspoons peanut oil

2 drops toasted sesame oil (optional)

⅓ cup ground walnuts

Nonstick cooking spray

1. Preheat oven to 350°F. Cut chicken into bite-sized pieces; sprinkle with sherry and set aside.

2. In a small bowl, beat egg white and oils until frothy. Fold chicken pieces into egg mixture; roll individually in ground walnuts.

3. Arrange chicken pieces on baking sheet treated with nonstick cooking spray. Bake 10–15 minutes or until walnuts are lightly browned and chicken juices run clear. (Walnuts make the fat ratio of this dish high, so serve it with steamed vegetables and rice to bring the ratios into balance.)

Nutritional Analysis (per serving): Calories: 159 | Protein: 18g | Carbohydrates: 1g | Fat: 9g | Saturated Fat: 1g | Cholesterol: 44mg | Sodium: 51mg | Fiber: 1g | PCF Ratio: 47-3-51 | Exchange Approx.: 2 Very Lean Meats, 1½ Fats

CHICKEN AND MUSHROOM RICE CASSEROLE

SERVES 8; SERVING SIZE: ⅛ RECIPE

Nonstick cooking spray

1 recipe Condensed Cream of Chicken Soup (see recipe in Chapter 4)

1 cup diced chicken breast

1 large onion, chopped

½ cup chopped celery

1 cup uncooked rice (not instant rice)

Freshly ground black pepper to taste (optional)

1 teaspoon dried herbes de Provence (optional)

2 cups boiling water

2½ cups chopped broccoli florets

1 cup sliced fresh mushrooms

1. Preheat oven to 350°F. In 4-quart casserole dish (large enough to prevent boilovers in oven) treated with nonstick spray, combine condensed soup, chicken breast, onion, celery, rice, and seasonings; mix well. Pour boiling water over top; bake covered for 30 minutes.

2. Stir casserole; add broccoli and mushrooms. Replace cover; return to oven to bake additional 20–30 minutes or until celery is tender and rice has absorbed all liquid.

Nutritional Analysis (per serving): Calories: 165 | Protein: 9g | Carbohydrates: 30g | Fat: 1g | Saturated Fat: 0g | Cholesterol: 15mg | Sodium: 41mg | Fiber: 3g | PCF Ratio: 23-71-6 | Exchange Approx.: 1 Very Lean Meat, 1 Starch, 1 Vegetable

EASY CHICKEN PAPRIKASH

SERVES 4; SERVING SIZE: ¼ RECIPE

1 recipe Condensed Cream of Chicken Soup (see recipe in Chapter 4)

½ cup skim milk

2 teaspoons paprika

⅛ teaspoon ground cayenne pepper (optional)

¼ pound (4 ounces) chopped cooked boneless skinless chicken

1½ cups sliced steamed mushrooms

½ cup diced steamed onion

½ cup nonfat plain yogurt

4 cups cooked medium-sized egg noodles

For Best Results . . .

Homemade condensed soup recipes are used in the dishes in this book so that you know the accurate nutritional analysis information. In all cases, you can substitute commercial canned condensed soups; however, be sure to use the lower-fat and lower-sodium varieties.

1. In saucepan, combine soup, skim milk, paprika, and pepper (if using); whisk until well mixed. Bring to a boil over medium heat, stirring occasionally.

2. Reduce heat to low and stir in chicken, mushrooms, and onion; cook until chicken and vegetables are heated through, about 10 minutes. Stir in yogurt.

3. To serve, put 1 cup of warm, cooked noodles on each of four plates. Top each portion with an equal amount of chicken mixture. Garnish by sprinkling with additional paprika if desired.

Nutritional Analysis (per serving, using equal amounts of light and dark meat chicken): Calories: 376 | Protein: 22g | Carbohydrates: 58g | Fat: 6g | Saturated Fat: 2g | Cholesterol: 78mg | Sodium: 135mg | Fiber: 4g | PCF Ratio: 23-62-15 | Exchange Approx.: ½ Very Lean Meat, ½ Lean Meat, 2½ Starches, 1 Vegetable, 1 Skim Milk

CHICKEN AND BROCCOLI CASSEROLE

SERVES 4; SERVING SIZE: ¼ RECIPE

Nonstick cooking spray

2 cups broccoli florets

½ pound (8 ounces) chopped cooked chicken

½ cup skim milk

⅛ cup (2 tablespoons) real mayonnaise

¼ teaspoon curry powder

1 recipe Condensed Cream of Chicken Soup (see recipe in Chapter 4)

1 tablespoon lemon juice

½ cup (2 ounces) grated Cheddar cheese

½ cup bread crumbs

1 teaspoon melted butter

1 teaspoon olive oil

1. Preheat oven to 350°F. Treat 11" × 7" casserole dish with nonstick spray.

2. Steam broccoli until tender; drain.

3. Spread out chicken on bottom of dish; cover with steamed broccoli.

4. In medium bowl, combine milk, mayonnaise, curry powder, soup, and lemon juice; pour over broccoli.

5. In small bowl, mix together cheese, bread crumbs, butter, and oil; sprinkle over top of casserole. Bake 30 minutes.

Nutritional Analysis (per serving): Calories: 328 | Protein: 26g | Carbohydrates: 20g | Fat: 17g | Saturated Fat: 6g | Cholesterol: 67mg | Sodium: 254mg | Fiber: 3g | PCF Ratio: 31-24-45 | Exchange Approx.: 1 Very Lean Meat, 1 Lean Meat, ½ High-Fat Meat, 1 Fat, 1 Vegetable, 1 Skim Milk, ½ Starch

CHICKEN AND GREEN BEAN STOVETOP CASSEROLE

SERVES 4; SERVING SIZE: ¼ RECIPE

1 recipe Condensed Cream of Chicken Soup (see recipe in Chapter 4)

¼ cup skim milk

2 teaspoons Homemade Worcestershire Sauce (see recipe in Chapter 6)

1 teaspoon real mayonnaise

½ teaspoon onion powder

¼ teaspoon garlic powder

¼ teaspoon ground black pepper

1 (4-ounce) can sliced water chestnuts, drained

2½ cups frozen thawed green beans

1 cup sliced mushrooms, steamed

½ pound (8 ounces) cooked chopped chicken

1⅓ cups cooked brown long-grain rice

Veggie Filler

Steamed mushrooms are a low-calorie way to add flavor to a dish and "stretch" the meat. If you don't like mushrooms, you can substitute an equal amount of other low-calorie steamed vegetables like red and green peppers and not significantly affect the total calories in a recipe.

1. Combine soup, milk, Worcestershire, mayonnaise, onion powder, garlic powder, and pepper in a saucepan; bring to a boil.

2. Reduce heat; add water chestnuts, green beans, mushrooms, and chicken. Simmer until vegetables and chicken are heated through, about 10 minutes. Serve over rice.

Nutritional Analysis (per serving): Calories: 305 | Protein: 23g | Carbohydrates: 36g | Fat: 8g | Saturated Fat: 2g | Cholesterol: 48mg | Sodium: 101mg | Fiber: 6g | PCF Ratio: 30-46-24 | Exchange Approx.: 1 Very Lean Meat, 1 Lean Meat, 1 Vegetable, 1 Starch, 1 Skim Milk

CHICKEN PASTA WITH HERB SAUCE

SERVES 4; SERVING SIZE: ¼ RECIPE

1 recipe Condensed Cream of Chicken Soup (see recipe in Chapter 4)

¼ cup skim milk

½ teaspoon Homemade Worcestershire Sauce (see recipe in Chapter 6)

1 teaspoon real mayonnaise

¼ cup grated Parmesan cheese

¼ teaspoon chili powder

½ teaspoon garlic powder

¼ teaspoon dried rosemary

¼ teaspoon dried thyme

¼ teaspoon dried marjoram

1 cup sliced mushrooms, steamed

½ pound (8 ounces) chopped cooked chicken

4 cups cooked pasta

Freshly ground black pepper (optional)

1. Combine soup, milk, Worcestershire, mayonnaise, and cheese in saucepan; bring to a boil.

2. Reduce heat and add chili powder, garlic powder, rosemary, thyme, and marjoram; stir well. Add mushrooms and chicken; simmer for 10 minutes until heated through.

3. Serve over pasta and top with freshly ground pepper if desired.

Nutritional Analysis (per serving): Calories: 393 | Protein: 26g | Carbohydrates: 52g | Fat: 8g | Saturated Fat: 2g | Cholesterol: 48mg | Sodium: 71mg | Fiber: 4g | PCF Ratio: 27-53-20 | Exchange Approx.: 2 Lean Meats, 3 Starches, ½ Skim Milk

CHICKEN AND ASPARAGUS IN WHITE WINE SAUCE

SERVES 4; SERVING SIZE: ¼ RECIPE

½ tablespoon butter

1 tablespoon olive oil

1 teaspoon finely chopped garlic

½ cup finely chopped onion

4 boneless skinless chicken breast halves, pounded to ¼" thickness

10 ounces asparagus spears, cut diagonally in 2" pieces

½ pound mushrooms

¼ cup dry white wine

¼ cup water

1 tablespoon chopped fresh parsley

Salt and pepper to taste

1. Melt butter and olive oil in a large skillet over medium heat. Add chopped garlic and onions; sauté 1–2 minutes.

2. Add chicken; cook 5 minutes or until the chicken is brown on both sides. Remove chicken and set aside.

3. Add asparagus and mushrooms to skillet; cook 2–3 minutes.

4. Return chicken to skillet; add white wine and water. Bring to a quick boil; boil 2 minutes to reduce the liquid.

5. Reduce heat; cover and simmer 3 minutes or until chicken and vegetables are tender. Add chopped parsley, season with salt and pepper to taste, and serve.

Nutritional Analysis (per serving): Calories: 186 | Protein: 21g | Carbohydrates: 7g | Fat: 8g | Saturated Fat: 2g | Cholesterol: 51mg | Sodium: 57mg | Fiber: 2g | PCF Ratio: 46-16-38 | Exchange Approx.: 2½ Very Lean Meats, 1½ Vegetables, 1 Fat

CHICKEN KALAMATA

SERVES 4; SERVING SIZE: ¼ RECIPE

2 tablespoons olive oil

1 cup chopped onion

1 teaspoon minced garlic

1½ cups chopped green peppers

1 pound boneless skinless chicken breast, cut into 4 pieces

2 cups diced tomatoes

1 teaspoon dried oregano

½ cup pitted chopped kalamata olives

Are Olives Counted as a Fruit or Vegetable?

The short answer is: neither! Even though olives are a fruit that grows on trees, their flesh is filled with a significant amount of oil and therefore is counted as a fat. Nine black olives or ten green olives equal 1 Fat serving. The health benefits of olives (and olive oil) come from the monounsaturated fats they contain. Olives are usually cured in a brine, salt, or olive oil, so if you must watch your salt intake, be careful how many you eat.

1. Heat olive oil over medium heat in large skillet. Add onions, garlic, and peppers; sauté for about 5 minutes until onions are translucent.

2. Add chicken pieces; cook for about 5 minutes each side until lightly brown.

3. Add tomatoes and oregano. Reduce heat and simmer 20 minutes.

4. Add olives; simmer an additional 10 minutes before serving.

Nutritional Analysis (per serving): Calories: 311 | Protein: 31g | Carbohydrates: 25g | Fat: 11g | Saturated Fat: 2g | Cholesterol: 66mg | Sodium: 787mg | Fiber: 6g | PCF Ratio: 38-31-31 | Exchange Approx.: 4 Lean Meats, 2 Vegetables, 1 Starch, 2 Fats

CHICKEN BREASTS IN BALSAMIC VINEGAR SAUCE

SERVES 4; SERVING SIZE: ¼ RECIPE

1 pound boneless skinless chicken breasts, cut into 4 pieces

Pinch salt

¼ teaspoon pepper

1 tablespoon butter

1 tablespoon olive oil

¼ cup chopped red onion

2 teaspoons finely chopped garlic

3 tablespoons balsamic vinegar

1½ cups low-sodium chicken broth

1 teaspoon dried oregano

1. Sprinkle chicken with salt and pepper.

2. Heat butter and olive oil in large skillet over medium heat. Add chicken; cook until browned, about 5 minutes each side. Reduce heat and cook 12 minutes. Transfer to platter; cover and keep warm.

3. Add red onions and garlic to skillet; sauté over medium heat 3 minutes, scraping up browned bits. Add balsamic vinegar; bring to a boil. Boil 3 minutes or until reduced to a glaze, stirring constantly.

4. Add chicken broth; boil until reduced to about ¾ cup liquid. Remove sauce from heat; add oregano. Spoon sauce over chicken and serve immediately.

Nutritional Analysis (per serving): Calories: 200 | Protein: 28g | Carbohydrates: 2g | Fat: 8g | Saturated Fat: 3g | Cholesterol: 73mg | Sodium: 381mg | Fiber: 0g | PCF Ratio: 58-4-38 | Exchange Approx.: 4 Lean Meats, 1½ Fats

CHICKEN THIGHS CACCIATORE

SERVES 4; SERVING SIZE: 1 THIGH

2 teaspoons olive oil

½ cup chopped onion

2 cloves garlic, minced

4 chicken thighs, skin removed

½ cup dry red wine

1 (14-ounce) can unsalted diced tomatoes, undrained

1 teaspoon dried parsley

½ teaspoon dried oregano

¼ teaspoon pepper

⅛ teaspoon sugar

¼ cup grated Parmesan cheese

4 cups cooked spaghetti

2 teaspoons extra-virgin olive oil

For Cheese Lovers!

Indulge your love of extra cheese and still have a main dish that's under 400 calories. Prepare Chicken Thighs Cacciatore according to recipe instructions. Top each portion with 1 tablespoon freshly grated Parmesan cheese. With extra cheese, analysis is: Calories: 398; Protein: 21g; Carbohydrates: 48g; Fat: 11g; Saturated Fat: 3.6g; Cholesterol: 44mg; Sodium: 282mg; Fiber: 3.8g; PCF Ratio: 23-51-26; Exchange Approx.: 2 Lean Meats, 2½ Starches, 1 Fat, 1 Vegetable.

1. Heat deep, nonstick skillet over medium-high heat; add 2 teaspoons olive oil. Add onion; sauté until transparent. Add garlic and chicken thighs; sauté 3 minutes on each side or until lightly browned.

2. Remove thighs from pan; add wine, tomatoes and juices, parsley, oregano, pepper, and sugar. Stir well; bring to a boil. Add chicken back to pan; sprinkle Parmesan cheese over top. Cover, reduce heat, and simmer 10 minutes. Uncover and simmer 10 more minutes.

3. To serve, put 1 cup of cooked pasta on each of four plates. Top each serving with a chicken thigh; divide sauce between dishes. Drizzle ½ teaspoon extra-virgin olive oil over top of each dish and serve.

Nutritional Analysis (per serving): Calories: 370 | Protein: 19g | Carbohydrates: 48g | Fat: 9g | Saturated Fat: 2g | Cholesterol: 39mg | Sodium: 166mg | Fiber: 4g | PCF Ratio: 21-55-24 | Exchange Approx.: 1½ Lean Meats, 2½ Starches, 1 Fat, 1 Vegetable

CHICKEN WITH PORTOBELLO MUSHROOMS AND ROASTED GARLIC

SERVES 4; SERVING SIZE: 1 BREAST

1 tablespoon olive oil

4 boneless skinless chicken breasts

1 cup reduced-sodium chicken broth

1 bulb garlic, dry-roasted (see Garlic and Feta Cheese Dip in Chapter 3 for dry-roasting instruction) and mashed into paste

1 tablespoon butter

2 cups chopped portobello mushrooms

½ teaspoon dried thyme

2 tablespoons crumbled feta cheese

1. Heat olive oil in large nonstick skillet; brown chicken breasts on both sides over medium heat, about 5 minutes per side. Add chicken broth and roasted garlic paste to pan; cover and simmer on low 10 minutes.

2. Meanwhile, sauté mushrooms and thyme in butter in separate, smaller saucepan. Simmer 2 minutes.

3. Add the mushrooms and thyme mixture to the chicken and simmer for an additional 2 minutes.

4. When serving, top each chicken breast with 1½ teaspoons feta cheese and pour sauce over the top.

Nutritional Analysis (per serving): Calories: 335 | Protein: 26g | Carbohydrates: 39g | Fat: 10g | Saturated Fat: 4g | Cholesterol: 56mg | Sodium: 261mg | Fiber: 3g | PCF Ratio: 30-45-25 | Exchange Approx.: 2½ Lean Meats, ½ Fat, 1 Vegetable

CHIPOTLE CHICKEN WRAPS

SERVES 4; SERVING SIZE: 1 WRAP

12 ounces boneless skinless chicken breast, cut into ½" strips

1 tablespoon lime juice

1 tablespoon olive oil

1 teaspoon chipotle seasoning

⅛ teaspoon freshly ground pepper

4 whole-wheat tortillas

½ cup jarred salsa

1 cup chopped lettuce

What Is Chipotle?

A chipotle (chih-POTE-lay) is a dried, smoked jalapeño pepper used in Mexican or Tex-Mex dishes. You often see chipotle peppers canned in adobo sauce, but you can purchase dried chipotle peppers or a seasoning mix with chipotle peppers added. Mrs. Dash Southwest Chipotle Seasoning Blend is salt-free!

1. Place chicken, lime juice, olive oil, chipotle seasoning, and pepper in dish; mix well. Cover and allow chicken to marinate in refrigerator 1 hour.

2. Heat outdoor grill. Wrap tortillas in aluminum foil and place on top rack. Cook chicken strips 7–9 minutes until done, turning strips once during cooking.

3. When ready to make wraps, place chicken strips in center of each heated tortilla, add 2 tablespoons salsa to each, top with chopped lettuce, and wrap.

Nutritional Analysis (per serving): Calories: 284 | Protein: 24g | Carbohydrates: 28g | Fat: 8g | Saturated Fat: 2g | Cholesterol: 40mg | Sodium: 415mg | Fiber: 2g | PCF Ratio: 35-41-25 | Exchange Approx.: 2 Starches, ½ Vegetable, 3 Lean Meats

STOVETOP GRILLED TURKEY BREAST

SERVES 4; SERVING SIZE: ¼ RECIPE

1 teaspoon cider vinegar

1 teaspoon garlic powder

1 teaspoon Dijon mustard

1 teaspoon brown sugar

¼ teaspoon black pepper

2 teaspoons olive oil

4 (4-ounce) turkey breast cutlets

Tip

Cutlets prepared this way tend to cook faster than on an outdoor grill. If using an indoor grill that cooks both sides at once, allow 4–5 minutes total cooking time. You can also use a well-seasoned cast-iron skillet instead of a grill pan; however, you may need to introduce more oil to the pan to prevent the cutlets from sticking. Cooking time will be the same as with a grill pan. Be sure to adjust the Fat exchange if necessary.

1. In a medium bowl, combine vinegar, garlic powder, mustard, brown sugar, and black pepper; slowly whisk in olive oil to thoroughly combine and make a thin paste.

2. Rinse turkey cutlets and dry thoroughly on paper towels. If necessary to ensure a uniform thickness, put between sheets of plastic wrap and pound to flatten.

3. Pour paste into heavy-duty freezer-style resealable plastic bag. Add cutlets, moving around in mixture to coat all sides. Seal bag, carefully squeezing out as much air as possible. Refrigerate to allow turkey to marinate at least 1 hour or as long as overnight.

4. Place nonstick hard-anodized stovetop grill pan over high heat. When pan is heated thoroughly, add cutlets. Lower heat to medium-high; cook cutlets 3 minutes on one side. Use tongs to turn; cook another 3 minutes or until juices run clear.

Nutritional Analysis (per serving): Calories: 207 | Protein: 31g | Carbohydrates: 2g | Fat: 8g | Saturated Fat: 2g | Cholesterol: 85mg | Sodium: 68mg | Fiber: 0g | PCF Ratio: 62-3-35 | Exchange Approx.: 4 Very Lean Meats, ½ Fat

TURKEY MUSHROOM BURGERS

YIELDS 8 LARGE BURGERS; SERVING SIZE: 1 BURGER

1-pound turkey breast

1 pound fresh button mushrooms

1 tablespoon olive oil

1 teaspoon butter

1 clove garlic, minced

1 tablespoon chopped green onion

¼ teaspoon dried thyme

¼ teaspoon dried oregano

¼ teaspoon freshly ground black pepper

Ground cayenne pepper or red pepper flakes to taste (optional)

1. Cut turkey into even pieces about 1" square. Place cubes in freezer 10 minutes or long enough to allow turkey to become somewhat firm.

2. In a covered microwave-safe container, microwave mushrooms on high 3–4 minutes or until they begin to soften and sweat. Set aside to cool slightly.

3. Process turkey in food processor until ground, scraping down sides of bowl as necessary. Add oil, butter, garlic, onion, and mushrooms (and any resulting liquid from the mushrooms); process until mushrooms are ground, scraping down sides of bowl as necessary. Add remaining ingredients; pulse until mixed. Shape into eight equal-sized patties. Cooking times will vary according to method used and how thick burgers are.

Nutritional Analysis (per serving): Calories: 100 | Protein: 15g | Carbohydrates: 3g | Fat: 3g | Saturated Fat: 1g | Cholesterol: 34mg | Sodium: 36mg | Fiber: 1g | PCF Ratio: 60-10-30 | Exchange Approx.: 1 Lean Meat, 1 Vegetable, ½ Fat

TURKEY MARSALA WITH FRESH PEAS

SERVES 4; SERVING SIZE: ¼ RECIPE

¼ cup all-purpose flour

¼ teaspoon salt

¼ teaspoon pepper

½ teaspoon paprika

1 pound turkey breast cutlets, sliced ¼" thick

1 tablespoon olive oil

1 tablespoon butter

½ cup thinly sliced onion

½ cup Marsala wine

½ cup fresh or frozen peas

Quick Tip

It's easy to prepare quick and healthy meals if you keep skinless, boneless chicken or turkey in the freezer. If you use an indoor grill, you don't even need to thaw them first. You can prepare a quick sauce or glaze in the time it takes for the chicken or turkey to cook.

1. In a plastic zip-top bag, mix together flour, salt, pepper, and paprika. Place turkey cutlets in plastic bag; shake to coat cutlets with flour.

2. Heat olive and butter in large skillet; sauté onions for about 5 minutes until browned.

3. Add coated turkey cutlets; brown on both sides, approximately 7–8 minutes on each side.

4. Add Marsala to pan; stir well to combine. Bring to a boil; reduce heat. Turn cutlets to coat both sides.

5. Add peas; continue to cook, stirring, another 2–3 minutes. Serve.

Nutritional Analysis (per serving): Calories: 278 | Protein: 30g | Carbohydrates: 14g | Fat: 7g | Saturated Fat: 3g | Cholesterol: 78mg | Sodium: 208mg | Fiber: 2g | PCF Ratio: 50-24-27 | Exchange Approx.: 4 Very Lean Meats, ½ Starch, ½ Vegetable, 1 Fat

SPICY GRILLED TURKEY BURGERS

SERVES 4; SERVING SIZE: 1 PATTY

Nonstick cooking spray

1 pound ground turkey

¼ cup bread crumbs

1 tablespoon salt-free Cajun seasoning blend

1 egg

1 tablespoon finely chopped fresh cilantro

2 teaspoons minced jalapeño pepper

Proper Poultry and Meat Handling

Be sure to wash any utensil that comes in contact with raw poultry in hot, soapy water and rinse well. This includes washing any utensil each time it's used to baste grilling, roasting, or baking poultry.

1. Spray grill with nonstick cooking spray.

2. Combine remaining ingredients well; shape into four patties. Grill burgers approximately 6 minutes on each side or until cooked through.

Nutritional Analysis (per serving): Calories: 176 | Protein: 26g | Carbohydrates: 5g | Fat: 5g | Saturated Fat: 2g | Cholesterol: 125mg | Sodium: 155mg | Fiber: 0g | PCF Ratio: 63-12-25 | Exchange Approx.: 3½ Very Lean Meats, 1 Fat

TURKEY CHILI

SERVES 6; SERVING SIZE: ⅙ RECIPE

1 pound ground turkey

1 cup chopped onions

½ cup chopped green pepper

2 teaspoons finely chopped garlic

2 (28-ounce) cans crushed tomatoes

1 cup canned drained black beans

1 cup canned drained red kidney beans

3 tablespoons chili powder

1 tablespoon ground cumin

1 teaspoon crushed red pepper

Dash Tabasco

1. Brown ground turkey in large nonstick pot over medium-high heat.

2. Drain off any fat; add chopped onion, green pepper, and garlic. Continue cooking until onion is translucent, about 5 minutes.

3. Add remaining ingredients; bring to a slow boil.

4. Reduce heat, cover, and let simmer at least 2–3 hours before serving.

Nutritional Analysis (per serving): Calories: 281 | Protein: 26g | Carbohydrates: 38g | Fat: 4g | Saturated Fat: 1g | Cholesterol: 49mg | Sodium: 347mg | Fiber: 11g | PCF Ratio: 35-52-13 | Exchange Approx.: 2 Starches, 2 Vegetables, 3 Very Lean Meats, 1½ Fats

TURKEY KIELBASA WITH RED BEANS AND RICE

SERVES 5; SERVING SIZE: 1/5 RECIPE

2 cups canned, drained, and rinsed pinto beans

2 cups canned diced tomatoes

2 cups water, divided

1 cup diced onion

2 teaspoons Cajun seasoning blend

8 ounces turkey kielbasa sausage, cut into 1" pieces

1/2 cup brown rice

1. Combine pinto beans, canned tomatoes, 1/2 cup water, onion, Cajun seasoning, and kielbasa in slow cooker; set on low and cook 4–6 hours.

2. In separate saucepan, bring brown rice and 1 1/2 cups water to boil; reduce heat and simmer on low heat 35–40 minutes.

3. Serve beans and sausage over rice.

Nutritional Analysis (per serving): Calories: 297 | Protein: 15g | Carbohydrates: 41g | Fat: 9g | Saturated Fat: 3g | Cholesterol: 32mg | Sodium: 679mg | Fiber: 7g | PCF Ratio: 19-54-26 | Exchange Approx.: 2 Starches, 1 1/2 Vegetables, 1 Lean Meat, 1 Very Lean Meat, 3 Fats

CORNFLAKE CHICKEN

SERVES 4; SERVING SIZE: 1 CHICKEN BREAST

2 cups crushed cornflakes

Dashes of salt and pepper

¼ cup egg whites

2 tablespoons buttermilk or kefir

16 ounces (about 4 average-sized) raw chicken breasts

Cooking spray

1. Preheat oven to 425°F. Toss together the cornflakes, salt, and pepper in a small bowl, then spread them on a large plate.

2. Mix the egg whites and buttermilk/kefir in a shallow bowl.

3. Dip each chicken breast in the egg mixture to wet each side and then coat each side with cornflakes. Place the coated chicken breasts on a baking sheet coated with cooking spray and bake for 12–15 minutes. Flip them over and bake for another 12–15 minutes or until no longer pink in the center.

Nutritional Analysis (per serving): Calories: 230 | Protein: 36g | Carbohydrates: 12g | Fat: 3.5g | Saturated Fat: 1g | Cholesterol: 90mg | Sodium: 270mg | Fiber: 1g | PCF Ratio: 64-22-14 | Exchange Approx.: ¾ Starch, 4 Lean Meats

GRILLED CHICKEN AND VEGETABLE KABOBS

SERVES 6; SERVING SIZE: 1 KABOB

6 long skewers

1 tablespoon diced kalamata olives

2 tablespoons olive juice from the kalamata olives

1 tablespoon olive oil

¼ teaspoon dried oregano

¼ teaspoon garlic powder

1 tablespoon chopped fresh basil

⅛ teaspoon paprika

Salt and pepper (optional)

1 pound chicken breasts, cut into 1½" cubes

2 bell peppers, cut into 1½" squares

1 small white onion or ½ large, cut into 1½" squares

1. If using wooden skewers, soak them in water for 5–10 minutes to prevent them from burning on the grill.

2. In a small bowl, combine the olives, olive juice, olive oil, oregano, garlic powder, basil, and paprika and whisk together. Add it to a zip-top bag or sealable container with the chicken cubes and marinate in the fridge for about 1 hour.

3. Once the chicken has been marinated, preheat a grill on medium-high heat. Discard the marinade and assemble the skewers. Divide the chicken to make six skewers (about three cubes per skewer). Alternate the vegetables and chicken along the bamboo skewers. Add salt and pepper to taste (optional).

4. Grill the skewers over a medium-high flame for 15–20 minutes while turning every few minutes. The chicken should be fully cooked (no longer pink in the center) and vegetables should be slightly crisp but tender.

Nutritional Analysis (per serving): Calories: 120 | Protein: 16g | Carbohydrates: 3g | Fat: 3.5g | Saturated Fat: 1g | Cholesterol: 40mg | Sodium: 60mg | Fiber: 1g | PCF Ratio: 54-12-34 | Exchange Approx.: ½ Vegetable, 2 Lean Meats, ½ Fat

GREEK CHICKEN PIZZA

SERVES 1

1 whole-wheat pita

2 tablespoons low-sodium tomato sauce

1 tablespoon thinly sliced red or white onion

2 tablespoons finely chopped fresh basil

⅛ teaspoon dried oregano

2 tablespoons chopped olives

⅓ cup finely cubed cooked chicken

2 tablespoons low-fat feta cheese

Cooking spray

1. Preheat oven to 350°F. Spread the sauce on the pita and then add the onions, basil, oregano, olives, and chicken. Sprinkle the pita with the cheese.

2. Place the pita on a baking sheet coated with cooking spray and bake for about 15 minutes or until crust is lightly browned/crispy.

Nutritional Analysis (per serving): Calories: 320 | Protein: 25g | Carbohydrates: 40g | Fat: 8g | Saturated Fat: 2g | Cholesterol: 45mg | Sodium: 690mg | Fiber: 6g | PCF Ratio: 30-48-22 | Exchange Approx.: 2¼ Starches, ½ Medium-Fat Meat, 2 Lean Meats, ½ Fat

CHICKEN AND BRUSSELS SPROUT SKILLET

YIELDS 7 CUPS; SERVING SIZE: 1 CUP

1 teaspoon olive oil

2 cups sliced precooked chicken apple sausage

1 cup chopped white onion

4 cups halved Brussels sprouts

1 (8-ounce) package sliced button mushrooms

½ cup chicken or vegetable broth

2–3 tablespoons grainy Dijon mustard

1. Coat a large pan or pot with the olive oil and put in the sausage and onions. Sauté on medium-high heat until just starting to brown, about 5–7 minutes.

2. Cook the Brussels sprouts al dente by boiling them in a pot of water or steaming in a Pyrex dish in ½" of water on high heat for about 4 minutes.

3. Add the cooked Brussels sprouts, mushrooms, and broth to the pan/pot with the sausage and cover to simmer, stirring occasionally until the broth has evaporated and the whole mixture is brown and tender, about 5 minutes.

4. Uncover, stir in the mustard, and continue to cook for another 1–2 minutes until warmed through.

Nutritional Analysis (per serving): Calories: 130 | Protein: 10g | Carbohydrates: 17g | Fat: 4.5g | Saturated Fat: 1g | Cholesterol: 35mg | Sodium: 300mg | Fiber: 3g | PCF Ratio: 27-46-27 | Exchange Approx.: 2 Vegetables, ¼ Other Carbohydrate, 1 Lean Meat, ½ Fat

QUICK AND EASY CHICKEN ENCHILADAS

YIELDS 10 ENCHILADAS; SERVING SIZE: 1 ENCHILADA

1 teaspoon olive oil

¾ cup chopped white onion

1 cup chopped red bell peppers

2 cups cooked and shredded chicken

2–3 tablespoons chicken broth

¼ teaspoon garlic powder

2½ cups marinara sauce

1 cup enchilada sauce

10 corn tortillas

½ cup shredded reduced-fat Cheddar cheese

Sliced avocado (optional)

1. Preheat oven to 375°F. Coat a large pan or skillet with the olive oil and put in the onions and peppers. Sauté them on medium heat for about 3–5 minutes until lightly brown and softened. Add the chicken, broth, and garlic powder, then simmer for another 3–5 minutes until most of the liquid is evaporated. Remove from heat and set aside.

2. Mix the marinara and enchilada sauce in a medium bowl.

3. Assemble the enchiladas as follows: Spread a quarter of the sauce to thinly coat the bottom of a 9" × 12" pan. Microwave each tortilla for 10–20 seconds to soften. Place each heated tortilla on a clean surface or cutting board and spoon ⅓ cup of filling inside. Fold up the sides and then place in the pan with the folded side down. Repeat this step with each tortilla, placing them side by side, very close to each other, to make two rows of five.

4. Pour the rest of the sauce to evenly coat the enchiladas and bake for 20–25 minutes covered with aluminum foil. Remove from the oven, sprinkle the ½ cup cheese over them, and bake uncovered for another 5 minutes or until cheese is melted. Garnish with a few thin avocado slices if desired.

Nutritional Analysis (per serving): Calories: 170 | Protein: 12g | Carbohydrates: 19g | Fat: 4.5g | Saturated Fat: 1g | Cholesterol: 30mg | Sodium: 450mg | Fiber: 3g | PCF Ratio: 30-46-24 | Exchange Approx.: 1 Starch, ½ Vegetable, 1 Lean Meat, ½ Medium-Fat Meat

WALDORF CHICKEN LETTUCE CUPS

YIELDS 3½ CUPS; SERVING SIZE: ½ CUP

2 cups chopped cooked chicken

¾ cup chopped celery

½ cup sliced grapes

2 tablespoons chopped green onions

2 tablespoons chopped walnuts

½ cup nonfat Greek yogurt

¼ cup light mayonnaise

½ teaspoon rice vinegar

7 large iceberg or butter lettuce leaves, rinsed and patted dry

1. Put the chicken, celery, grapes, onions, and walnuts in a medium bowl.

2. In a smaller bowl, combine the yogurt, mayonnaise, and vinegar and pour over the chicken mixture. Mix well.

3. Add ½ cup of the chicken salad to each lettuce leaf and serve.

Nutritional Analysis (per serving): Calories: 120 | Protein: 14g | Carbohydrates: 4g | Fat: 5g | Saturated Fat: 1g | Cholesterol: 35mg | Sodium: 115mg | Fiber: 0g | PCF Ratio: 49-14-37 | Exchange Approx.: 1½ Lean Meats, 1 Fat

SLOW-COOKER BBQ CHICKEN

YIELDS 8 CUPS; SERVING SIZE: ½ CUP

3 pounds chicken breast

2 cups barbecue sauce

1 cup low-sodium chicken or vegetable broth

2 teaspoons brown sugar

Add all the ingredients to large slow cooker and cook on low for 4–4½ hours. Shred chicken with fork and then cook for another 30 minutes.

Nutritional Analysis (per serving): Calories: 150 | Protein: 18g | Carbohydrates: 14g | Fat: 2g | Saturated Fat: 0g | Cholesterol: 55mg | Sodium: 470mg | Fiber: 0g | PCF Ratio: 49-37-14 | Exchange Approx.: 1 Other Carbohydrate, 2 Lean Meats

BBQ CHICKEN SALAD WRAP

SERVES 6; SERVING SIZE: 1 WRAP

2 cups cooked chicken

¾ cup chopped celery

¼ cup corn

2 tablespoons pepitas

½ cup nonfat Greek yogurt

¼ cup light mayonnaise

3 tablespoons barbecue sauce

6 small whole-wheat tortillas

1. Put the chicken, celery, corn, and pepitas in a medium bowl.

2. In a smaller bowl, combine the yogurt, mayonnaise, and barbecue sauce and pour over the chicken mixture. Mix well.

3. Add ½ cup of the chicken salad per each tortilla and roll up for a total of six wraps.

Nutritional Analysis (per serving): Calories: 280 | Protein: 21g | Carbohydrates: 30g | Fat: 7g | Saturated Fat: 1.5g | Cholesterol: 40mg | Sodium: 510mg | Fiber: 3g | PCF Ratio: 31-45-24 | Exchange Approx.: 1½ Starches, ½ Other Carbohydrate, 2 Lean Meats, ½ Fat

SIMPLE GARLIC CHICKEN

SERVES 4; SERVING SIZE: 1 CHICKEN BREAST

1 pound (about 4 average-sized) boneless skinless chicken breasts

1 tablespoon olive oil

¼ teaspoon garlic powder

⅛ teaspoon salt

½ teaspoon pepper

1. Place the chicken breasts on a large plate. Put the olive oil in a small dish and use a brush to lightly coat both sides.

2. In a separate small dish, mix the garlic powder, salt, and pepper together. Sprinkle half the mixture over the chicken breasts on one side, flip, and coat the other side with the rest.

3. Preheat a large nonstick pan or barbecue grill on high heat and cook for 10–15 minutes on each side until no longer pink in the center.

Nutritional Analysis (per serving): Calories: 160 | Protein: 24g | Carbohydrates: 0g | Fat: 6g | Saturated Fat: 0g | Cholesterol: 95mg | Sodium: 200mg | Fiber: 0g | PCF Ratio: 66-0-34 | Exchange Approx.: 4 Lean Meats

CHICKEN CURRY

SERVES 4; SERVING SIZE: ¼ RECIPE

1 tablespoon plus 1 teaspoon olive oil, divided

1½ pounds chicken breast, cut into ¼" strips

¾ cup chopped white onion

2 cloves garlic, finely chopped

1 tablespoon plus ½ cup chicken or vegetable broth, divided

1½ cups light coconut milk

1½ tablespoons curry powder

How Do You Curry?

Serve a cup of this curry with ½ cup of brown rice or a serving of Whole-Wheat Dumplings (see recipe in Chapter 7). This will add 1½ to 2 Starch exchanges. For a lower-carb option, try wrapping the chicken in a large lettuce leaf.

1. Coat a large pan/skillet with 1 tablespoon olive oil. Turn on medium heat, add the chicken breast, and brown for a bit, about 3–5 minutes on each side; then remove from the pan and set aside.

2. Add 1 teaspoon of olive oil to the pan and put in the onions, garlic, and 1 tablespoon of broth and sauté on medium heat for 3–5 minutes until tender.

3. Return the chicken to the pan, add the coconut milk, curry powder, and remaining ½ cup of the broth. Cover and simmer for 15–20 minutes on low heat until chicken is tender.

Nutritional Analysis (per serving): Calories: 300 | Protein: 29g | Carbohydrates: 10g | Fat: 14g | Saturated Fat: 5g | Cholesterol: 95mg | Sodium: 135mg | Fiber: 1g | PCF Ratio: 47-13-40 | Exchange Approx.: 4 Lean Meats, 2½ Fats

PARMESAN-CRUSTED CHICKEN

SERVES 4; SERVING SIZE: 1 CHICKEN BREAST

2 whole-wheat English muffins

¼ cup grated Parmesan cheese

½ cup egg substitute or 2 egg whites

1 pound (about 4 average-sized) boneless skinless chicken breasts

Cooking spray

1. Preheat oven to 425°F.

2. Cut the English muffins into cubes and then grind in a blender or food processor on high for 10–15 seconds to produce coarse bread crumbs. Spread the bread crumbs on a large plate and mix with the Parmesan cheese.

3. Add the egg substitute/whites to a small plate or shallow bowl. Dip each chicken breast in the egg mixture to wet each side and then coat each side with bread crumbs.

4. Place the coated chicken breasts on a baking sheet coated with cooking spray and bake for 15 minutes. Flip them over and bake for another 15 minutes or until no longer pink in the center.

Nutritional Analysis (per serving): Calories: 230 | Protein: 30g | Carbohydrates: 15g | Fat: 6g | Saturated Fat: 2g | Cholesterol: 75mg | Sodium: 310mg | Fiber: 2g | PCF Ratio: 53-24-23 | Exchange Approx.: 1 Starch, 4 Lean Meats

SPICY BLACK BEAN AND TURKEY SAUSAGE SKILLET

YIELDS 7 CUPS; SERVING SIZE: ¾ CUP

1 teaspoon olive oil

1 pound spicy chicken sausage

1 white onion, chopped

2 red bell peppers, chopped

2 Anaheim chili peppers, finely chopped

1 (14-ounce) can lower-sodium black beans, rinsed well and patted dry

¼ cup low-sodium chicken or vegetable broth

Low-sodium Cajun seasoning (optional)

1. Add the olive oil to a large pan or pot and put in the sausage, onions, bell peppers, and chili peppers and sauté on medium-high heat until just starting to brown (about 7–10 minutes), stirring frequently.

2. Put in the black beans and broth, cover, and reduce heat to simmer, stirring occasionally, until the broth has mostly evaporated and the whole mixture is brown and tender (about 5–7 minutes). Sprinkle with additional seasoning if desired.

Nutritional Analysis (per serving): Calories: 150 | Protein: 12g | Carbohydrates: 15g | Fat: 5g | Saturated Fat: 1.5g | Cholesterol: 25mg | Sodium: 550mg | Fiber: 5g | PCF Ratio: 30-40-30 | Exchange Approx.: ½ Starch, 1 Vegetable, 1 Medium-Fat Meat

PORTOBELLO PIZZAS WITH BRUSSELS SPROUTS, TURKEY BACON, AND PARMESAN

YIELDS 4 PIZZAS; SERVING SIZE: 1 PIZZA

4 large portobello mushrooms (about 4"–5" in diameter)

Cooking spray

2 cups trimmed and quartered Brussels sprouts

1 tablespoon olive oil

½ cup diced white onion

½ cup chopped turkey bacon

¼ cup shredded Parmesan cheese

1. Preheat oven to 375°F. Rinse the mushrooms well, cut out the stems (without creating a hole in the bottom), pat dry, and place on a baking sheet coated with cooking spray, stem-side up. Bake for about 15 minutes.

2. While the mushrooms are baking, cook the Brussels sprouts until almost done by either boiling them in a pot of water or steaming them in the microwave in a Pyrex dish in ½" of water for about 3–5 minutes.

3. Add the oil, onions, and turkey bacon to a medium-sized pan and sauté on medium heat for about 3–5 minutes until lightly browned. Put in the cooked Brussels sprout quarters and continue to sauté until the Brussels sprouts are lightly browned and tender, about 3–5 minutes.

4. Remove the mushrooms from the oven and drain/blot any excess moisture. Top with the Brussels sprouts mixture, dividing it between the four mushrooms.

5. Place the filled mushrooms back in the oven and bake for 10–12 minutes. Remove from the oven, sprinkle each with 2 tablespoons cheese, and bake for another 2–3 minutes until cheese is slightly melted.

Nutritional Analysis (per serving): Calories: 150 | Protein: 11g | Carbohydrates: 10g | Fat: 9g | Saturated Fat: 3g | Cholesterol: 15mg | Sodium: 350mg | Fiber: 3g | PCF Ratio: 27-24-49 | Exchange Approx.: 2 Vegetables, 1 Lean Meat, ½ High-Fat Meat

FIESTA TURKEY BURGERS

SERVES 6; SERVING SIZE: 1 PATTY

1 pound extra-lean ground turkey

½ cup diced onion

1½ cups diced red bell pepper

½ cup egg whites

½ cup cooked black beans

½ cup cooked corn

2 tablespoons tomato sauce

1½ tablespoons taco seasoning

½ teaspoon ground cumin

¼ teaspoon chili powder

¼ teaspoon salt (if taco seasoning does not contain salt)

1. Mix all of the ingredients in a large bowl. Form six patties and place on a heated nonstick pan or grill.

2. Heat 7–10 minutes on each side on high heat or until no longer pink on the inside.

Nutritional Analysis (per serving): Calories: 140 | Protein: 23g | Carbohydrates: 10g | Fat: 1g | Saturated Fat: 0g | Cholesterol: 30mg | Sodium: 270mg | Fiber: 2g | PCF Ratio: 64-28-8 | Exchange Approx.: ½ Starch, ½ Vegetable, 2 Lean Meats

GARDEN TURKEY MEATLOAF

YIELDS 1 LOAF, 8 SLICES; SERVING SIZE: 1 SLICE

1 pound lean ground turkey

½ cup old-fashioned rolled oats

1 cup finely chopped veggies of your choice, such as onion, mushrooms, zucchini, carrots, peppers

½ cup tomato sauce

2 egg whites

1–2 teaspoons of two or more suggested seasonings: garlic powder, oregano, paprika, chili powder, Cajun seasoning, pepper

Cooking spray

1. Preheat oven to 350°F. In a large bowl, mix the turkey, oats, vegetables, tomato sauce, and egg whites. Add the desired seasonings and put into a large loaf pan coated with cooking spray.

2. Bake for 1 hour until no longer pink in the center and an instant-read thermometer registers 165°F.

Nutritional Analysis (per serving): Calories: 100 | Protein: 16g | Carbohydrates: 6g | Fat: 1g | Saturated Fat: 0g | Cholesterol: 30mg | Sodium: 120mg | Fiber: 1g | PCF Ratio: 64-28-8 | Exchange Approx.: ½ Vegetable, 2 Lean Meats

DIJON TURKEY CUTLETS

SERVES 6; SERVING SIZE: 1 CUTLET

1 tablespoon olive oil

1 pound (about 6 pieces) turkey breast cutlets

1 teaspoon crushed garlic or 2–3 cloves, diced

1 cup chopped white onion

3 cups sliced mushrooms

1 tablespoon plus ½ cup low-sodium chicken or vegetable broth

¼ cup grainy Dijon mustard

1 tablespoon white wine

1. Coat a large pan with the olive oil, add the turkey cutlets, and brown for about 3–5 minutes on each side. Remove from the pan and set aside.

2. Add the garlic, onions, mushrooms, and 1 tablespoon of broth to the pan and sauté for 5–7 minutes until tender.

3. Return the cutlets to the pan, add the remaining ½ cup of the broth, stir in Dijon mustard and wine, and simmer for 10–15 minutes on low heat until turkey is tender and no longer pink in the center.

Nutritional Analysis (per serving): Calories: 110 | Protein: 20g | Carbohydrates: 7g | Fat: 0.5g | Saturated Fat: 0g | Cholesterol: 30mg | Sodium: 320mg | Fiber: 1g | PCF Ratio: 71-24-5 | Exchange Approx.: 1 Vegetable, 2 Lean Meats

CHAPTER 11

FISH AND SEAFOOD ENTRÉES

ASIAN-STYLE FISH CAKES

SERVES 8; SERVING SIZE: 2 PATTIES

1-pound catfish fillet, cut into 1" pieces

2 green onions, minced

1 banana pepper, cored, seeded, and chopped

2 cloves garlic, minced

1 tablespoon grated or minced fresh ginger

1 tablespoon Bragg Liquid Aminos

1 tablespoon lemon juice

1 teaspoon grated lemon zest

Old Bay Seasoning (optional)

Nonstick cooking spray

Tip

For crunchy fish cakes, coat each side in rice flour and then lightly spritz the tops of the patties with olive or peanut oil before baking as directed.

1. Preheat oven to 375°F. Combine fish with green onions, banana pepper, garlic, ginger, Bragg Liquid Aminos, lemon juice, and lemon zest in food processor; process until chopped and mixed. (You do not want to purée this mixture; it should be a rough chop.) Add Old Bay Seasoning if using; stir to mix.

2. Form fish mixture into patties of about 2 tablespoons each; you should have sixteen patties total. Place patties on baking sheet treated with nonstick cooking spray; bake 12–15 minutes or until crisp. (Alternatively, you can fry these in a nonstick pan about 4 minutes on each side.)

Nutritional Analysis (per serving): Calories: 66 | Protein: 11g | Carbohydrates: 1g | Fat: 2g | Saturated Fat: 1g | Cholesterol: 41mg | Sodium: 112mg | Fiber: 0mg | PCF Ratio: 69-8-23 | Exchange Approx.: 1 Lean Meat, 1 Free Condiment

SLOW-ROASTED SALMON

SERVES 4; SERVING SIZE: 1 FILLET

2 teaspoons extra-virgin olive oil

4 (5-ounce) salmon fillets with skin, at room temperature

1 cup finely minced fresh chives

Sea or kosher salt and freshly ground white pepper to taste (optional)

Nonstick cooking spray

Sage sprigs for garnish

1. Preheat oven to 250°F. Rub ½ teaspoon of olive oil into flesh side of each salmon fillet. Completely cover fillets with chives; gently press into flesh. Season with salt and pepper if desired.

2. Place fillets skin-side down on nonstick oven-safe skillet or foil-lined cookie sheet treated with nonstick spray; roast 25 minutes. Garnish with sage sprigs.

Nutritional Analysis (per serving): Calories: 257 | Protein: 25g | Carbohydrates: 1g | Fat: 16g | Saturated Fat: 3g | Cholesterol: 710mg | Sodium: 69mg | Fiber: 1g | PCF Ratio: 41-1-59 | Exchange Approx.: 4 Lean Meats, ½ Fat

SALMON PATTIES

SERVES 5; SERVING SIZE: 1 PATTY

2 cups flaked cooked salmon (no salt added)

6 soda crackers, crushed

1 egg

½ cup skim milk

1 small onion, chopped

1 tablespoon chopped fresh parsley

1 tablespoon unbleached all-purpose flour

1 tablespoon olive oil

Ener-G Pure Rice Flour (optional)

1. Place flaked salmon in a bowl. Add crushed crackers, egg, milk, onion, parsley, and flour; mix well. Gently form five patties.

2. Heat oil in nonstick skillet over medium heat. (Optional: Lightly dust patties with some Ener-G Pure Rice Flour for crispier patties.) Fry on both sides until browned, about 5 minutes per side.

Nutritional Analysis (per serving): Calories: 168 | Protein: 17g | Carbohydrates: 3g | Fat: 9g | Saturated Fat: 2g | Cholesterol: 70mg | Sodium: 92mg | Fiber: 0g | PCF Ratio: 42-8-50 | Exchange Approx.: 2 Lean Meats, ½ Fat, ½ Starch

TRADITIONAL STOVETOP TUNA-NOODLE CASSEROLE

SERVES 4; SERVING SIZE: ¼ RECIPE

1⅓ cups egg noodles (yields 2 cups when cooked)

1 recipe Condensed Cream of Mushroom Soup (see recipe in Chapter 4)

1 teaspoon steamed chopped onion

1 tablespoon steamed chopped celery

½ cup skim milk

1 ounce shredded (to yield ¼ cup) American, Cheddar, or Colby cheese

1 cup frozen mixed peas and carrots

1 cup steamed sliced fresh mushrooms

1 can water-packed tuna, drained

Extra-Rich Stovetop Tuna-Noodle Casserole

Add 1 medium egg (beaten) and 1 table-spoon mayonnaise to give casserole taste of rich, homemade egg noodles while still maintaining good fat ratio. It's still less than 300 calories per serving, too! Nutritional Analysis: Calories: 275; Protein: 21g; Carbohydrates: 34g; Fat: 7g; Saturated Fat: 2g; Cholesterol: 94mg; Sodium: 281mg; Fiber: 4g; PCF Ratio: 30-48-21; Exchange Approx.: 1½ Breads, 1 Vegetable, 1 Meat, 1 Medium-Fat Meat.

1. Cook egg noodles according to package directions. Drain and return to pan.

2. Add all remaining ingredients to pan; stir to blend. Cook over medium heat, stirring occasionally until cheese is melted. (The nutritional analysis for this recipe assumes egg noodles were cooked without salt.)

Nutritional Analysis (per serving): Calories: 245 | Protein: 20g | Carbohydrates: 33g | Fat: 4g | Saturated Fat: 2g | Cholesterol: 46mg | Sodium: 241mg | Fiber: 4g | PCF Ratio: 32-53-15 | Exchange Approx.: 1½ Starches, 1 Vegetable, 1 Medium-Fat Meat

CRAB CAKES WITH SESAME CRUST

SERVES 5; SERVING SIZE: 2 CAKES

1 pound (16 ounces) lump crabmeat

1 egg

1 tablespoon minced fresh ginger

1 small scallion, finely chopped

1 tablespoon dry sherry

1 tablespoon freshly squeezed lemon juice

6 tablespoons real mayonnaise

Sea salt and freshly ground white pepper to taste (optional)

Old Bay Seasoning to taste (optional)

¼ cup lightly toasted sesame seeds

Nonstick cooking spray

1. Preheat oven to 375°F. In large bowl, mix together crab, egg, ginger, scallion, sherry, lemon juice, mayonnaise, and seasonings if using.

2. Form the mixture into ten equal cakes. Spread sesame seeds over sheet pan; dip both sides of cakes to coat them. Arrange cakes on baking sheet treated with nonstick spray. Typical baking time is 8–10 minutes, depending on thickness of cakes.

Nutritional Analysis (per serving, without salt and Old Bay):
Calories: 108 | Protein: 9g | Carbohydrates: 3g | Fat: 6g | Saturated Fat: 1g | Cholesterol: 45mg | Sodium: 171mg | Fiber: 1g | PCF Ratio: 34-11-55 | Exchange Approx.: 1 Very Lean Meat, 1½ Fats

CREAMY SHRIMP PIE WITH RICE CRUST

SERVES 4; SERVING SIZE: ¼ RECIPE

1⅓ cups cooked white rice

2 teaspoons dried parsley

2 tablespoons grated onion

1 teaspoon olive oil

1 tablespoon butter

1 clove garlic, crushed

1 pound shrimp, peeled and deveined

1 recipe Condensed Cream of Mushroom Soup (see recipe in Chapter 4)

1 teaspoon lemon juice

1 cup sliced steamed mushrooms

Fat-Free Flavor

To add the flavor of sautéed mushrooms or onions without the added fat of butter or oil, roast or grill them first. Simply spread them on a baking sheet treated with nonstick spray. Roasting for 5 minutes in a 350°F oven will be sufficient if the vegetables are sliced and will not add additional cooking time to the recipe.

1. Preheat oven to 350°F. Combine rice, parsley, and onion; mix well. Use olive oil to coat 10" pie plate; press rice mixture evenly around sides and bottom. This works best if the rice is moist; if necessary, add 1 teaspoon of water.

2. Melt butter in deep, nonstick skillet over medium heat; sauté garlic. Add shrimp; cook, stirring frequently, until pink, about 5 minutes.

3. Add soup and lemon juice to skillet; stir until smooth and thoroughly heated, about 5 minutes. (If the soup seems too thick, add some water 1 teaspoon at a time.) Stir mushrooms into soup mixture; pour over rice "crust." Bake 30 minutes or until lightly browned on top. Serve hot.

Nutritional Analysis (per serving): Calories: 273 | Protein: 26g | Carbohydrates: 27g | Fat: 6g | Saturated Fat: 2g | Cholesterol: 180mg | Sodium: 172mg | Fiber: 2g | PCF Ratio: 39-40-21 | Exchange Approx.: 2 Very Lean Meats, 2 Starches, 1 Fat

BARLEY-SPINACH-FISH BAKE

SERVES 4; SERVING SIZE: ¼ RECIPE

½ tablespoon olive oil

¼ cup chopped scallions

1 clove garlic, minced

¼ teaspoon dried rosemary

¼ teaspoon ground marjoram

¼ teaspoon salt

1 cup cooked pearl barley

5 ounces (½ box) frozen chopped spinach, thawed and drained

¼ cup chopped sun-dried tomatoes

4 (12") squares of aluminum foil

4 (4-ounce) fish fillets

3 tablespoons white wine

Salt and freshly ground pepper to taste

Cooking Barley

Pearl barley takes longer to cook than quick-cooking barley, so you will want to prepare it in advance. To prepare: bring ½ cup pearl barley and 1 cup water to a boil. Reduce heat, cover, and simmer for 35–45 minutes or until all water is absorbed. Pearl barley makes a good side dish on its own with the addition of spices or vegetables.

1. Preheat oven to 400°F (or outdoor grill can be used).

2. Heat oil in medium nonstick skillet; add scallions and sauté 2 minutes. Add garlic, rosemary, marjoram, and salt; continue to cook another 3 minutes until scallions are tender. Add cooked barley, spinach, and sun-dried tomatoes; mix well.

3. Place aluminum foil squares on work surface; place a fish fillet in center of each square. Divide barley mixture equally; place on top of each fillet. Sprinkle with white wine, salt, and pepper.

4. Fold aluminum foil loosely to enclose filling. Place packets on baking sheet (or directly on grill if using outdoor grill); bake 15 minutes or until fish is tender and flakes easily.

Nutritional Analysis (per serving): Calories: 239 | Protein: 26g | Carbohydrates: 15g | Fat: 8g | Saturated Fat: 1g | Cholesterol: 67mg | Sodium: 418mg | Fiber: 3g | PCF Ratio: 44-26-30 | Exchange Approx.: 3 Lean Meats, ½ Starch, 1 Vegetable, 1½ Fats

GRILLED SALMON WITH ROASTED PEPPERS

SERVES 4; SERVING SIZE: 1 STEAK

4 (4-ounce) salmon steaks

1 tablespoon reduced-sodium soy sauce

1 tablespoon brown sugar

1 tablespoon olive oil

2 large roasted red bell peppers, cut into strips

1 tablespoon balsamic vinegar

½ teaspoon dried thyme

¼ teaspoon freshly ground pepper

Wasabi Marinade

Wasabi, also known as Japanese horseradish, can be purchased in raw form or as a powder or paste. It adds a hot, pungent flavor to fish and works especially well with salmon. To make a marinade for salmon or other fish, mix 1 teaspoon wasabi powder (or paste) with 2 tablespoons low-sodium soy sauce, ½ teaspoon grated fresh ginger, and 1 teaspoon sesame oil. Coat fish with the marinade and grill.

1. Place salmon in shallow dish. Mix together soy sauce, brown sugar, and olive oil; pour over salmon and cover both sides with marinade. Set aside.

2. Sprinkle roasted pepper strips with balsamic vinegar, thyme, and pepper. Set aside.

3. Heat grill. Remove salmon from the marinade; grill over medium heat approximately 8 minutes on one side. Turn and grill on other side until salmon is cooked and tender, about 4–5 minutes longer. Remove from heat.

4. Top each salmon steak with marinated roasted red peppers.

Nutritional Analysis (per serving): Calories: 269 | Protein: 24g | Carbohydrates: 8g | Fat: 16g | Saturated Fat: 3g | Cholesterol: 67mg | Sodium: 321mg | Fiber: 1g | PCF Ratio: 36-11-53 | Exchange Approx.: 3½ Lean Meats, 1 Vegetable, 1 Fat

BAKED BREAD CRUMB–CRUSTED FISH WITH LEMON

SERVES 6; SERVING SIZE: ⅙ RECIPE

2 large lemons

¼ cup bread crumbs

Nonstick cooking spray

1½ pounds (24 ounces) halibut fillets

Sea or kosher salt and freshly ground white or black pepper to taste (optional)

Lemon Infusion

Mildly flavored fish such as catfish, cod, halibut, orange roughy, rockfish, and snapper benefit from the distinctive flavor of lemon. Adding slices of lemon to top of fish allows the flavor to infuse into fish.

1. Preheat oven to 375°F. Wash 1 lemon; cut into thin slices. Grate 1 tablespoon of zest from the second lemon, then juice it. Combine grated zest and bread crumbs in small bowl; stir to mix. Set aside.

2. Put lemon juice in shallow dish; arrange lemon slices in bottom of baking dish treated with nonstick spray. Dip fish pieces in lemon juice; set on lemon slices in baking dish.

3. Sprinkle bread crumb mixture evenly over fish pieces along with salt and pepper if using; bake until crumbs are lightly browned and fish is just opaque, 10–15 minutes. (Baking time will depend on thickness of fish.) Serve immediately using lemon slices as garnish.

Nutritional Analysis (per serving, without salt): Calories: 137 | Protein: 24g | Carbohydrates: 5g | Fat: 3g | Saturated Fat: 1g | Cholesterol: 36mg | Sodium: 73mg | Fiber: 2g | PCF Ratio: 68-14-18 | Exchange Approx.: 2 Very Lean Meats, ½ Starch, ½ Free Condiment

BAKED RED SNAPPER ALMANDINE

SERVES 4; SERVING SIZE: ¼ RECIPE

1 pound (16 ounces) red snapper fillets

Sea or kosher salt and freshly ground white
   or black pepper to taste (optional)

4 teaspoons all-purpose flour

2 teaspoons olive oil

2 tablespoons ground raw almonds

2 teaspoons unsalted butter

1 tablespoon lemon juice

1. Preheat oven to 375°F. Rinse red snapper fillets and dry between layers of paper towels. Season with salt and pepper if using; sprinkle with flour, front and back.

2. In an ovenproof nonstick skillet, sauté fillets in olive oil until nicely browned on both sides, about 5 minutes per side.

3. Combine ground almonds and butter in microwave-safe dish. Microwave on high 30 seconds or until butter is melted; stir to combine. Pour almond-butter mixture and lemon juice over fillets; bake 3–5 minutes or until almonds are nicely browned.

Nutritional Analysis (per serving, without salt): Calories: 178 | Protein: 24g | Carbohydrates: 3g | Fat: 7g | Saturated Fat: 2g | Cholesterol: 47mg | Sodium: 73mg | Fiber: 1g | PCF Ratio: 56-7-37 | Exchange Approx.: 3 Lean Meats

A-TASTE-OF-ITALY BAKED FISH

SERVES 4; SERVING SIZE: ¼ RECIPE

1 pound (16 ounces) cod fillets

Nonstick cooking spray

1 (14-ounce) can stewed tomatoes

¼ teaspoon dried minced onion

½ teaspoon dried minced garlic

¼ teaspoon dried basil

¼ teaspoon dried parsley

⅛ teaspoon dried oregano

⅛ teaspoon sugar

1 tablespoon grated Parmesan cheese

1. Preheat oven to 375°F. Rinse cod with cold water and pat dry with paper towels.

2. In 2–3-quart baking pan or casserole treated with nonstick cooking spray, combine remaining ingredients; mix.

3. Arrange fillets over mixture, folding thin tail ends under; spoon mixture over fillets. For fillets about 1" thick, bake uncovered 20–25 minutes or until fish is opaque and flaky.

Nutritional Analysis (per serving): Calories: 128 | Protein: 22g | Carbohydrates: 7g | Fat: 1g | Saturated Fat: 0g | Cholesterol: 50mg | Sodium: 312mg | Fiber: 1g | PCF Ratio: 68-23-9 | Exchange Approx.: 2½ Very Lean Meats, 1½ Vegetables

BAKED SNAPPER WITH ORANGE-RICE DRESSING

SERVES 4; SERVING SIZE: ¼ RECIPE

¼ cup chopped celery

½ cup chopped onion

½ cup orange juice

1 tablespoon lemon juice

1 teaspoon grated orange zest

1⅓ cups cooked rice

Water as needed to moisten rice

1 pound (16 ounces) red snapper fillets

Nonstick cooking spray

Sea or kosher salt and freshly ground white or black pepper to taste (optional)

2 teaspoons unsalted butter

2 tablespoons ground raw almonds

1. Preheat oven to 350°F.

2. In a microwave-safe bowl, mix celery and onion with juices and orange zest; microwave on high 2 minutes or until mixture comes to a boil. Add rice; stir to moisten, adding water 1 tablespoon at a time if necessary to thoroughly coat rice. Cover and let stand 5 minutes.

3. Rinse fillets and pat dry between paper towels. Prepare baking dish with nonstick spray. Spread rice mixture in dish; arrange fillets on top. Season fillets with salt and pepper if using.

4. Combine butter and almonds in a microwave-safe bowl; microwave on high 30 seconds or until butter is melted. Stir; spoon over top of fillets.

5. Cover and bake 10 minutes. Remove cover and bake another 5–10 minutes or until fish flakes easily when tested with a fork and almonds are lightly browned.

Nutritional Analysis (per serving, without salt): Calories: 257 | Protein: 26g | Carbohydrates: 25g | Fat: 5g | Saturated Fat: 2g | Cholesterol: 47mg | Sodium: 83mg | Fiber: 1g | PCF Ratio: 41-40-19 | Exchange Approx.: 2 Lean Meats, ½ Fruit, ½ Fat, 1 Starch

SHRIMP MICROWAVE CASSEROLE

SERVES 4; SERVING SIZE: ¼ RECIPE

1⅓ cups uncooked egg noodles (to yield four ½-cup servings)

1 cup chopped green onion

1 cup chopped green pepper

1 cup sliced mushrooms

1 recipe Condensed Cream of Celery Soup (see recipe in Chapter 4)

1 teaspoon Homemade Worcestershire Sauce (see recipe in Chapter 6)

4 drops Tabasco (optional)

¼ cup diced canned pimientos

½ cup pitted chopped olives

½ cup skimmed milk

½ pound (8 ounces) cooked, deveined, shelled shrimp

1. Cook egg noodles according to package directions; drain and keep warm.

2. Place green onion and green pepper in covered microwave-safe dish; microwave on high 1 minute. Add mushrooms; microwave another minute or until all vegetables are tender.

3. Add soup, Worcestershire sauce, Tabasco (if using), pimiento, olives, and milk; stir well. Microwave covered 1–2 minutes until mixture is hot and bubbly.

4. Add cooked shrimp and noodles; stir to mix. Microwave 30 seconds–1 minute or until mixture is hot.

Nutritional Analysis (per serving): Calories: 196 | Protein: 18g | Carbohydrates: 27g | Fat: 2g | Saturated Fat: 1g | Cholesterol: 131mg | Sodium: 290mg | Fiber: 2g | PCF Ratio: 35-56-9 | Exchange Approx.: 1 Starch, 1 Vegetable, 1 Medium-Fat Meat

CRUNCHY "FRIED" CATFISH FILLETS

SERVES 4; SERVING SIZE: ¼ RECIPE

Nonstick cooking spray

4 catfish fillets

1 egg white (from a large egg), room temperature

¼ cup bread crumbs

¼ cup enriched white cornmeal

1 teaspoon grated lemon zest

½ teaspoon crushed dried basil

¼ cup all-purpose flour

⅛ teaspoon kosher or sea salt (optional)

¼ teaspoon lemon pepper

Zesty Crunch

Grated lemon or lime zest is a great way to give added citrus flavor to a crunchy bread crumb topping for fish.

1. Preheat oven to 450°F; treat shallow baking pan with nonstick spray. Rinse catfish and dry between layers of paper towels.

2. In shallow dish, beat egg white until frothy. In another dish, combine bread crumbs, cornmeal, lemon zest, and basil. In third dish, combine flour, salt (if using), and lemon pepper.

3. Dip fish into flour mixture to coat one side of each fillet. Shake off any excess flour mixture, then dip flour-covered side of fillet into egg white. Next, coat covered side of fillet with bread crumb mixture.

4. Arrange prepared fillets side by side, coated-side up, on prepared baking pan. Tuck in any thin edges. Bake 6–12 minutes or until fish flakes easily with a fork.

Nutritional Analysis (per serving, without salt): Calories: 244 | Protein: 21g | Carbohydrates: 18g | Fat: 9g | Saturated Fat: 2g | Cholesterol: 53mg | Sodium: 248mg | Fiber: 1g | PCF Ratio: 35-30-35 | Exchange Approx.: 3 Lean Meats, 1 Starch

BAKED ORANGE ROUGHY WITH SPICY PLUM SAUCE

SERVES 4; SERVING SIZE: ¼ RECIPE

Nonstick cooking spray

1 pound (16 ounces) orange roughy fillets

1 teaspoon paprika

1 bay leaf

1 clove garlic, crushed

1 apple, peeled, cored, and cubed

1 teaspoon grated fresh ginger

1 small red or Spanish onion, chopped

1 teaspoon olive oil

¼ cup Plum Sauce (see recipe in Chapter 6)

¼ teaspoon Chinese five-spice powder

1 teaspoon frozen unsweetened apple juice concentrate

½ teaspoon Bragg Liquid Aminos

¼ teaspoon blackstrap molasses

1⅓ cups cooked brown rice

1. Preheat oven to 400°F. Treat baking dish with nonstick spray. Rinse orange roughy and pat dry between paper towels. Rub both sides of fish with paprika; set in prepared dish.

2. In covered microwave-safe bowl, mix bay leaf, garlic, apple, ginger, onion, and oil; microwave on high 3 minutes or until apple is tender and onion is transparent. Stir; discard bay leaf and top fillets with mixture. Bake uncovered 15–18 minutes or until fish is opaque.

3. While fish bakes, add Plum Sauce to microwave-safe bowl. Add five-spice powder, apple juice concentrate, Liquid Aminos, and molasses. Microwave on high 30 seconds; stir, add a little water if needed to thin mixture, and microwave another 15 seconds. Cover until ready to serve. If necessary, bring back to temperature by microwaving mixture another 15 seconds just prior to serving.

4. To serve, equally divide cooked rice among four serving plates. Top each with an equal amount of baked fish and Plum Sauce, drizzling sauce atop fish.

Nutritional Analysis (per serving): Calories: 221 | Protein: 19g | Carbohydrates: 31g | Fat: 3g | Saturated Fat: 1g | Cholesterol: 23mg | Sodium: 101mg | Fiber: 2g | PCF Ratio: 34-56-11 | Exchange Approx.: 2 Very Lean Meats, 1 Fruit, 1 Starch

JON'S FISH TACOS

SERVES 4; SERVING SIZE: 1 TACO

¼ cup light mayonnaise

½ cup plain nonfat yogurt

¼ cup chopped onion

2 tablespoons minced jalapeño pepper

2 teaspoons minced cilantro

2 cups shredded cabbage

¼ cup lime juice

1 clove garlic, minced

1 tablespoon canola oil

1 pound tilapia fillets

Aluminum foil

Nonstick cooking spray

4 (6" diameter) whole-wheat tortillas

1 cup chopped tomato

Freshly ground pepper (optional)

1. In medium bowl, whisk together mayonnaise, yogurt, onion, jalapeño, and cilantro. Stir in shredded cabbage; chill.

2. In separate bowl, combine lime juice, garlic, and canola oil to make a marinade for fish. Pour over fish; cover and refrigerate at least 1 hour.

3. Place fish on aluminum foil–lined grill (spray aluminum with cooking spray); cook 6–7 minutes on each side until fish is tender and beginning to flake.

4. While fish is cooking, loosely wrap whole-wheat tortillas in large piece of aluminum foil and place on grill to heat.

5. To assemble tacos, cut fish into strips; divide into four portions. Place strips in center of each heated tortilla. Top with coleslaw mixture and chopped tomatoes. Add pepper if desired.

Nutritional Analysis (per serving): Calories: 383 | Protein: 29g | Carbohydrates: 40g | Fat: 12g | Saturated Fat: 2g | Cholesterol: 60mg | Sodium: 400mg | Fiber: 4g | PCF Ratio: 30-42-28 | Exchange Approx.: 3½ Very Lean Meats, 2 Starches, 1 Vegetable, 1 Fat

SWEET ONION–BAKED YELLOWTAIL SNAPPER

SERVES 4; SERVING SIZE: ¼ RECIPE

2 cups sliced Vidalia onions

1 tablespoon balsamic vinegar

2 teaspoons brown sugar

4 teaspoons olive oil

1 pound (16 ounces) skinless yellowtail snapper fillets

Nonstick cooking spray

1 tablespoon Madeira Sauce (see recipe in Chapter 6)

1. In covered microwave-safe dish, microwave onion on high 5 minutes or until transparent. Carefully remove cover; stir in vinegar and brown sugar. Cover; allow to sit several minutes so onion absorbs flavors.

2. Heat a nonstick pan on medium-high heat; add olive oil. Transfer steamed onion mixture to pan; sauté until browned but not crisp. (Be careful, as onions will burn easily because of brown sugar; if onion browns too quickly, lower heat and add a few tablespoons of water.) Cook until all liquid has evaporated from pan, stirring often. Onions should have a shiny and dark caramelized color. (This can be prepared 2–3 days in advance; store tightly covered in refrigerator.)

3. Preheat oven to 375°F. Rinse snapper in cold water and dry between paper towels. Arrange on baking sheet treated with nonstick spray. Spoon caramelized onions over tops of fillets, pressing to form a light crust over top of fish. Bake 12–15 minutes or until fish flakes easily with a fork. Serve immediately with Madeira Sauce divided on four plates with fish placed on top.

Nutritional Analysis (per serving): Calories: 189 | Protein: 25g | Carbohydrates: 13g | Fat: 4g | Saturated Fat: 1g | Cholesterol: 42mg | Sodium: 77mg | Fiber: 1g | PCF Ratio: 53-28-19 | Exchange Approx.: 1 Lean Meat, 2 Very Lean Meats, 1 Vegetable, ½ Starch

STIR-FRIED GINGER SCALLOPS WITH VEGETABLES

SERVES 4; SERVING SIZE: ¼ RECIPE

1 pound (16 ounces) scallops

1 teaspoon peanut or sesame oil

1 tablespoon chopped fresh ginger

2 cloves garlic, minced

4 scallions, thinly sliced (optional)

1 teaspoon rice wine vinegar

2 teaspoons Bragg Liquid Aminos

½ cup low-fat, reduced-sodium chicken broth

2 cups broccoli florets

1 teaspoon cornstarch

¼ teaspoon toasted sesame oil

1. Rinse scallops and pat dry between layers of paper towels. If necessary, slice scallops so they're uniform size. Set aside.

2. Add peanut oil to heated nonstick deep skillet or wok; sauté ginger, garlic, and scallions if using 1–2 minutes, being careful ginger doesn't burn. Add vinegar, Liquid Aminos, and broth; bring to a boil. Remove from heat.

3. Place broccoli in large covered microwave-safe dish; pour chicken broth mixture over top. Microwave on high 3–5 minutes depending on preference. (Keep in mind that vegetables will continue to steam for a minute or so if cover remains on dish.)

4. Heat skillet or wok over medium-high temperature. Add scallops; sauté 1 minute on each side. (Do scallops in batches if necessary; be careful not to overcook.) Remove scallops from pan when done; set aside. Drain (but do not discard) liquid from broccoli; return liquid to bowl and transfer broccoli to heated skillet or wok. Stir-fry vegetables to bring up to serving temperature.

5. Meanwhile, in small cup or bowl, add enough water to cornstarch to make a slurry or roux. Whisk slurry into reserved broccoli liquid; microwave on high 1 minute. Add toasted sesame oil; whisk again. Pour thickened broth mixture over broccoli; toss to mix. Add scallops back to broccoli mixture; stir-fry over medium heat to return scallops to serving temperature. Serve over rice or pasta; adjust exchange approximations accordingly.

Nutritional Analysis (per serving): Calories: 145 | Protein: 22g | Carbohydrates: 8g | Fat: 3g | Saturated Fat: 1g | Cholesterol: 37mg | Sodium: 373mg | Fiber: 2g | PCF Ratio: 61-23-16 | Exchange Approx.: 3 Very Lean Meats, ½ Vegetable

SCALLOPS AND SHRIMP WITH WHITE BEAN SAUCE

SERVES 4; SERVING SIZE: ¼ RECIPE

½ cup finely chopped onion, steamed

2 cloves garlic, minced

2 teaspoons olive oil, divided

¼ cup dry white wine

¼ cup tightly packed fresh parsley leaves

¼ cup tightly packed fresh basil leaves

1⅓ cups canned, drained, and rinsed cannellini (white) beans

¼ cup low-fat reduced-sodium chicken broth

½ pound (8 ounces) shrimp, shelled and deveined

½ pound (8 ounces) scallops

1. In nonstick saucepan, sauté onion and garlic in 1 teaspoon of oil over moderately low heat for about 5 minutes until onion is soft.

2. Add wine; simmer until wine is reduced by half. Add parsley, basil, ⅓ cup of beans, and chicken broth; simmer, stirring constantly for 1 minute.

3. Transfer bean mixture to blender or food processor; purée. Pour purée back into saucepan; add remaining beans and simmer 2 minutes.

4. In nonstick skillet, heat remaining 1 teaspoon of oil over moderately high heat until it is hot but not smoking. Sauté shrimp 2 minutes on each side or until cooked through. Using slotted spoon, transfer shrimp to plate; cover to keep warm. Add scallops to skillet; sauté 1 minute on each side or until cooked through. To serve, divide bean sauce between four shallow bowls and arrange shellfish over top.

Nutritional Analysis (per serving): Calories: 231 | Protein: 27g | Carbohydrates: 18g | Fat: 4g | Saturated Fat: 1g | Cholesterol: 105mg | Sodium: 217mg | Fiber: 7g | PCF Ratio: 49-34-17 | Exchange Approx.: 3 Very Lean Meats, ½ Fat, 1 Starch, ½ Vegetable

SMOKED MUSSELS AND PASTA

SERVES 4; SERVING SIZE: ¼ RECIPE

1⅓ cups uncooked pasta (to yield 2 cups cooked pasta)

½ cup chopped leek

4 ounces smoked mussels, drained of all excess oil

⅛ teaspoon ground cayenne pepper

½ teaspoon dried oregano

¼ cup nonfat cottage cheese

⅛ cup nonfat plain yogurt

2 teaspoons grated Parmesan cheese

2 teaspoons extra-virgin olive oil

Cracked black pepper to taste

Savory Smoke

Smoked foods impart a strong, pleasant flavor to dishes, so you can use less to achieve a rich taste.

1. Cook pasta according to package directions; drain and set aside. In covered microwave-safe bowl, microwave leek on high 2–3 minutes or until limp and translucent. Add mussels and cayenne pepper; stir. Cover and microwave on high 30 seconds to heat mussels.

2. In blender, combine oregano, cottage cheese, yogurt, and Parmesan cheese; process until smooth. Combine cottage cheese and mussel mixtures; microwave on high until warm, about 30 seconds. Toss pasta with olive oil; stir in mussel mixture. Divide into four portions and serve immediately, topped with cracked pepper.

Nutritional Analysis (per serving): Calories: 206 | Protein: 10g | Carbohydrates: 22g | Fat: 8g | Saturated Fat: 2g | Cholesterol: 31mg | Sodium: 371mg | Fiber: 1g | PCF Ratio: 20-44-35 | Exchange Approx.: 1 Carbohydrate/Starch, 1 Lean Meat, ½ Fat, ½ Skim Milk

PASTA AND SMOKED TROUT WITH LEMON PESTO

SERVES 4; SERVING SIZE: ¼ RECIPE

2 cloves garlic

2 cups tightly packed fresh basil leaves

⅛ cup toasted pine nuts

2 teaspoons fresh lemon juice

2 teaspoons water

4 teaspoons extra-virgin olive oil

4 tablespoons grated Parmesan cheese, divided

1⅓ cups uncooked linguini or other pasta (to yield 2 cups cooked pasta)

2 ounces whole boneless smoked trout

Freshly ground black pepper to taste

1. Put garlic in food processor; pulse until finely chopped. Add basil, pine nuts, lemon juice, and water; process until just puréed. (Note: You can substitute fresh parsley for basil; supplement flavor by adding some dried basil, too, if you do.) Add olive oil and 3 tablespoons of Parmesan cheese; pulse until pesto is smooth, occasionally scraping down side of bowl if necessary. Set aside.

2. Cook pasta according to package directions. While it is cooking, flake trout. When pasta is cooked, pulse pesto to ensure it has remained blended; toss pesto and trout with pasta. Sprinkle remaining Parmesan and some pepper on top of each serving. (Although this recipe uses heart-healthy extra-virgin olive oil, it is a little higher in fat but still low in calories. Consult your dietitian if you have any question whether you should include this recipe in your meal plans.)

Nutritional Analysis (per serving): Calories: 209 | Protein: 10g | Carbohydrates: 23g | Fat: 8g | Saturated Fat: 1g | Cholesterol: 4mg | Sodium: 151mg | Fiber: 1g | PCF Ratio: 20-45-36 | Exchange Approx.: 1 Fat, 1½ Lean Meats, 1 Carbohydrate/Starch

GRILLED HADDOCK WITH PEACH-MANGO SALSA

SERVES 4; SERVING SIZE: ¼ RECIPE

2 tablespoons olive oil

2 tablespoons lime juice

¼ teaspoon salt

¼ teaspoon ground pepper

1 pound haddock, cut into 4 fillets

Nonstick cooking spray

2 cups Fresh Peach-Mango Salsa (see recipe in Chapter 6)

1. Mix olive oil, lime juice, salt, and pepper in a shallow dish; add haddock. Turn and coat fish with marinade.

2. Heat gas grill or broiler. Spray large piece of aluminum foil with nonstick cooking spray. Place fillets on foil; cook 7–8 minutes on each side or until fish is tender when pierced with a fork.

3. Top each piece of fish with ½ cup Fresh Peach-Mango Salsa.

Nutritional Analysis (per serving, including ½ cup Fresh Peach-Mango Salsa): Calories: 204 | Protein: 22g | Carbohydrates: 11g | Fat: 8g | Saturated Fat: 1g | Cholesterol: 65mg | Sodium: 467mg | Fiber: 2g | PCF Ratio: 43-22-35 | Exchange Approx.: 3 Very Lean Meats, 1 Fat, ½ Fruit

SESAME SHRIMP AND ASPARAGUS

SERVES 4; SERVING SIZE: ¼ RECIPE

2 teaspoons canola oil

2 cloves garlic, chopped

1 tablespoon grated fresh gingerroot

1 pound medium shrimp

2 tablespoons dry white wine

½ pound asparagus, cut diagonally into 1" pieces

2 cups cooked whole-grain pasta

½ teaspoon sesame seeds

¼ cup thinly sliced scallions

1 teaspoon sesame oil

1. Heat oil in wok or large nonstick skillet. Stir-fry garlic, gingerroot, and shrimp over high heat until shrimp begins to turn pink, about 2 minutes.

2. Add white wine and asparagus; stir-fry an additional 3–5 minutes.

3. Add pasta, sesame seeds, scallions, and sesame oil; toss lightly and serve.

Nutritional Analysis (per serving): Calories: 257 | Protein: 28g | Carbohydrates: 23g | Fat: 6g | Saturated Fat: 1g | Cholesterol: 172mg | Sodium: 173mg | Fiber: 3g | PCF Ratio: 44-35-21 | Exchange Approx.: 3 Very Lean Meats, ½ Vegetable, 1 Starch

SPICY "FRIED" FISH FILLET

SERVES 4; SERVING SIZE: ¼ RECIPE

⅓ cup cornmeal

½ teaspoon salt

1 teaspoon chipotle seasoning

1 egg

2 tablespoons 1% milk

16 ounces flounder, cut into 4 pieces

2 tablespoons olive oil

1. Combine cornmeal, salt, and chipotle seasoning in shallow dish.

2. Beat egg and milk together in shallow dish.

3. Dip fish in egg mixture; coat each fillet with cornmeal mixture.

4. Heat olive oil in nonstick skillet; brown fillets until golden and crispy, about 6–7 minutes each side.

Nutritional Analysis (per serving): Calories: 230 | Protein: 24g | Carbohydrates: 9g | Fat: 10g | Saturated Fat: 2g | Cholesterol: 116mg | Sodium: 412mg | Fiber: 1g | PCF Ratio: 44-17-39 | Exchange Approx.: 3 Very Lean Meats, 2 Fats, ½ Starch

GRILLED LEMON-AND-DILL SWORDFISH STEAKS

SERVES 4; SERVING SIZE: 1 STEAK

4 (4-ounce) swordfish steaks

1 tablespoon olive oil

1 lemon

4 dill sprigs

1. Lightly coat the swordfish steaks with olive oil.

2. Slice the lemon into rings and place them on top of the swordfish steaks.

3. Place a fresh dill sprig on each swordfish steak.

4. Grill over medium-high heat, about 10 minutes depending on the thickness of the steak.

Nutritional Analysis (per serving): Calories: 200 | Protein: 22g | Carbohydrates: 0g | Fat: 11g | Saturated Fat: 2.5g | Cholesterol: 75mg | Sodium: 90mg | Fiber: 0g | PCF Ratio: 48-0-52 | Exchange Approx.: 3 Lean Meats, 1 Fat

FRESH TOMATO AND CLAM SAUCE WITH WHOLE-GRAIN LINGUINI

SERVES 4; SERVING SIZE: ¼ RECIPE

3 dozen (36) littleneck clams

2 tablespoons olive oil

5 cloves garlic, chopped

½ cup chopped red bell pepper

4 cups peeled and chopped fresh tomatoes

3 tablespoons chopped fresh parsley

1 tablespoon chopped fresh basil

¼ teaspoon salt

¼ teaspoon red pepper flakes

½ teaspoon dried oregano

½ cup dry white wine

8 ounces whole-grain linguini

Tip

This recipe works well with canned clams if you are unable to get fresh. Canned clams are quite high in sodium, which will need to be taken into consideration. If using canned clams, you will need 1 (8-ounce) can of minced clams and 1 (10-ounce) can of whole clams. Reserve the clam juice and add to the sauce.

1. Before preparing this dish (preferably several hours or more), place clams in bowl of cold water with handful of cornmeal added; keep refrigerated. (This will help purge clams of any sand or other debris). When ready to cook, rinse and scrub clams.

2. Heat olive oil, garlic, and chopped red pepper in a deep skillet. Add tomatoes, parsley, basil, salt, red pepper flakes, and oregano; bring to quick boil, then reduce heat and simmer 15–20 minutes.

3. Stir in white wine; add clams on top of tomato sauce. Cover and steam until clams open.

4. Meanwhile, boil water and cook pasta to al dente.

5. Serve tomato sauce and clams over pasta.

Nutritional Analysis (per serving): Calories: 361 | Protein: 13g | Carbohydrates: 60g | Fat: 8g | Saturated Fat: 1g | Cholesterol: 7mg | Sodium: 356mg | Fiber: 8g | PCF Ratio: 14-66-20 | Exchange Approx.: 2½ Starches, 1½ Very Lean Meats, 3 Vegetables, 1½ Fats

SMOKED SHRIMP AND CHEESE QUESADILLAS

SERVES 4; SERVING SIZE: 1 QUESADILLA

4 (8") flour tortillas

4 teaspoons olive oil

2 ounces part-skim mozzarella or other mild cheese (such as fontina or baby Swiss)

1 jalapeño or banana pepper, finely chopped

2 cloves garlic, crushed

4 ounces smoked shrimp

1 cup thinly sliced red onion

½ cup roughly chopped fresh cilantro

Nonstick cooking spray

Cut Added Sodium

Reduce sodium content (salty flavor) from smoked seafood like mussels or shrimp by rinsing them in a little water.

1. Preheat oven to 375°F. Lightly brush one side of each tortilla with some olive oil. Mix cheese, pepper, and garlic with remaining olive oil; spread ¼ of cheese mixture in center of oiled half of each tortilla. Top with shrimp, red onion, and cilantro; fold tortilla in half to cover ingredients.

2. Place tortillas in baking pan treated with nonstick spray. Bake 3–5 minutes or until nicely browned and cheese is melted. Serve with your choice of tomato salsa.

Nutritional Analysis (per serving): Calories: 272 | Protein: 11g | Carbohydrates: 32g | Fat: 11g | Saturated Fat: 3g | Cholesterol: 39mg | Sodium: 428mg | Fiber: 3g | PCF Ratio: 17-46-37 | Exchange Approx.: 1 Carbohydrate/Starch, 1½ Lean Meats, 1 Fat, ½ Vegetable

CAJUN SALMON

SERVES 4; SERVING SIZE: ¼ RECIPE

Cooking spray

1 pound wild-caught salmon

2 teaspoons olive oil

¼ teaspoon cracked pepper

¼ teaspoon dried thyme

¼ teaspoon dried oregano

½ teaspoon onion powder

½ teaspoon garlic powder

1 teaspoon paprika

1 teaspoon Cajun seasoning

1. Coat the grill with cooking spray and preheat to high.

2. Rinse the salmon and slice off the skin. Pat dry and place on a plate. Spread each side with the olive oil using a basting brush or by hand.

3. Mix the pepper and all the spices in a small bowl. Sprinkle with half of the mixture to coat one side of the salmon, flip over, and coat the other side with the rest.

4. Place on the grill and heat on one side for 4–6 minutes, flip over, and heat for another 4–6 minutes or until the outside is slightly crispy. Cut into four equal-sized pieces and serve.

Nutritional Analysis (per serving): Calories: 190 | Protein: 23g | Carbohydrates: 1g | Fat: 10g | Saturated Fat: 1.5g | Cholesterol: 60mg | Sodium: 190mg | Fiber: 0g | PCF Ratio: 50-2-48 | Exchange Approx.: 4 Lean Meats

CHILI LIME SHRIMP SKEWERS

SERVES 4; SERVING SIZE: 1 SKEWER

¼ cup lime juice

4 teaspoons brown sugar

½ teaspoon chili powder

8 ounces (about 12–14) large shrimp, cleaned, peeled, and de-veined

4 skewers

1. Mix the lime juice, brown sugar, and chili powder in a small bowl.

2. Add the shrimp to a large zip-top bag or sealable container, pour in the lime juice marinade, and mix well to coat. Marinate in the refrigerator for 2–3 hours.

3. Preheat a barbecue grill on high heat. If using wooden skewers, soak them in water for 5–10 minutes to prevent them from burning on the grill.

4. Remove the shrimp from the container, discard the marinade, and add 3 or 4 pieces to each skewer. Grill a few minutes on each side until shrimp are slightly pink.

Nutritional Analysis (per serving): Calories: 60 | Protein: 8g | Carbohydrates: 6g | Fat: 0.5g | Saturated Fat: 0g | Cholesterol: 70mg | Sodium: 320mg | Fiber: 0g | PCF Ratio: 53-38-9 | Exchange Approx.: ¼ Other Carbohydrate, 1 Lean Meat

SHRIMP COCKTAIL

SERVES 4; SERVING SIZE: ¼ RECIPE

6 tablespoons grated horseradish root

1 tablespoon raw honey

1 (6-ounce) can organic no-salt-added tomato paste

Juice of 1 lemon

½ teaspoon red pepper flakes

1 pound cooked jumbo shrimp, peeled

Shrimp Facts

Shrimp is a great protein source. A single (4-ounce) serving of shrimp contains 24 grams of protein with less than 1 gram of fat. It contains a high level of selenium, vitamin D, and vitamin B_{12}. Selenium has been linked with cancer-fighting properties and is utilized in DNA repair.

In a small bowl, blend the horseradish, honey, tomato paste, lemon juice, and red pepper flakes. Serve immediately with the jumbo shrimp.

Nutritional Analysis (per serving): Calories: 152 | Protein: 19g | Carbohydrates: 16g | Fat: 2g | Saturated Fat: 0g | Cholesterol: 145mg | Sodium: 238mg | Fiber: 3g | PCF Ratio: 40-50-9 | Exchange Approx.: 3 Vegetables, 2 Lean Meats

GRILLED TROUT

SERVES 2; SERVING SIZE: 1 TROUT

2 whole trout, heads removed, cleaned, and butterflied

1 teaspoon ground black pepper

2 cloves garlic, minced

½ teaspoon chopped fresh rosemary

1 teaspoon chopped fresh parsley

6 sprigs fresh rosemary

1 lemon, halved; one half thinly sliced

Oily Fishes

There are many fishes that are good sources of beneficial fatty acids. These fish include trout, sardines, swordfish, whitebait, fresh tuna, anchovies, eel, kipper, mackerel, carp, bloater, smelt, and bluefish. The more varieties of fish that you try, the better fatty acid profile you will compile.

1. Place each trout on a square piece of aluminum foil.

2. Season both sides of trout with pepper, garlic, rosemary, and parsley.

3. Fold the fish closed and top with the rosemary sprigs and a few slices of lemon.

4. Squeeze the lemon half over each fish.

5. Wrap each fish securely inside the sheet of aluminum foil.

6. Grill the packets over medium-high heat for 7 minutes on each side or until the fish is flaky.

Nutritional Analysis (per serving): Calories: 176 | Protein: 25g | Carbohydrates: 0g | Fat: 8g | Saturated Fat: 1g | Cholesterol: 59mg | Sodium: 62mg | Fiber: 0g | PCF Ratio: 70-0-30 | Exchange Approx.: 3 Lean Meats, ½ Fat

SALMON IN PARCHMENT WITH BABY BRUSSELS SPROUTS

SERVES 2; SERVING SIZE: 1 FILLET

2 (4- to 5-ounce) salmon fillets or steaks

2 tablespoons frozen petite Brussels sprouts

2 cloves garlic, crushed

2 dashes lemon juice

1 tablespoon olive oil

1. Preheat the oven to 425°F.

2. Place each piece of salmon on a 12" circle of parchment paper.

3. Cover each salmon piece with a spoonful of Brussels sprouts, a clove of crushed garlic, a squeeze of lemon juice, and a drizzle of olive oil.

4. Fold the paper over into a packet and seal the edges by crimping and folding like a pastry. Place the packets on a baking sheet.

5. Bake for 15 minutes or until the fish flakes easily with a fork.

Nutritional Analysis (per serving): Calories: 330 | Protein: 29g | Carbohydrates: 2g | Fat: 22g | Saturated Fat: 5g | Cholesterol: 70mg | Sodium: 70mg | Fiber: 0g | PCF Ratio: 36-2-62 | Exchange Approx.: 4 Lean Meats, 3 Fats

SALMON SKEWERS

SERVES 4; SERVING SIZE: ¼ RECIPE

8 ounces salmon fillet, cut into 1"–2" cubes

1 medium red onion, peeled and cut into wedges

2 medium red bell peppers, seeded and cut into 2" squares

12 mushrooms

12 cherry tomatoes

Wild-Caught versus Farm-Raised Salmon

Salmon is one of the best sources of omega-3 fatty acids, but be sure to purchase wild-caught salmon. Farm-raised salmon are not exposed to the colder water; therefore, their fat reserves are not as robust as wild salmon's.

1. Preheat grill to 350°F.

2. Thread all the ingredients on metal skewers, alternating the vegetables and fish.

3. Grill over medium-high heat until vegetables are soft and the salmon is light pink, about 10 minutes depending on the thickness of the salmon fillet.

Nutritional Analysis (per serving): Calories: 107 | Protein: 15g | Carbohydrates: 6.5g | Fat: 3.5g | Saturated Fat: 0.5g | Cholesterol: 30mg | Sodium: 35mg | Fiber: 3g | PCF Ratio: 42-30-28 | Exchange Approx.: 2 Vegetables, 2 Lean Meats

CITRUS-BAKED SNAPPER

SERVES 6; SERVING SIZE: ⅙ RECIPE

1 (3-pound) whole red snapper, cleaned and scaled

3½ tablespoons grated fresh gingerroot

3 green onions, chopped

1 tomato, seeded and diced

¼ cup fresh-squeezed orange juice

¼ cup fresh-squeezed lime juice

¼ cup fresh-squeezed lemon juice

3 thin slices lime

3 thin slices lemon

Snapper and Omega-3

Snapper is not the fish that comes to mind when you're thinking about omega-3, but this cold-water fish does have some beneficial DHA fatty acid packed inside. Those with elevated blood triglycerides will benefit greatly from even small amounts of EPA and DHA, which are different types of very healthy omega-3 fatty acids.

1. Preheat the oven to 350°F.

2. Make three slashes across each side of the fish using a sharp knife. This will keep the fish from curling as it cooks.

3. Place the fish in a large, shallow baking dish or roasting pan.

4. Cover each side of the fish with the ginger, green onions, and tomatoes.

5. Combine the juices and drizzle them over the snapper.

6. Place the lime and lemon slices on top of the fish.

7. Cover the pan with aluminum foil and bake until the flesh is opaque and can be flaked with a fork, about 20 minutes.

Nutritional Analysis (per serving): Calories: 240 | Protein: 47g | Carbohydrates: 4g | Fat: 3g | Saturated Fat: 0.5g | Cholesterol: 85mg | Sodium: 150mg | Fiber: 0g | PCF Ratio: 82-6-12 | Exchange Approx.: 6 Lean Meats

MACKEREL WITH TOMATO AND CUCUMBER SALAD

SERVES 4; SERVING SIZE: ¼ RECIPE

15 ounces mackerel fillets, drained

1 clove garlic, crushed

1½ tablespoons flaxseed oil

1 tablespoon chopped fresh basil

½ teaspoon ground black pepper

10 cherry tomatoes, halved

½ cucumber, peeled and diced

1 small onion, peeled and chopped

2 cups mixed lettuce greens

1. Place the mackerel in a medium bowl with the garlic and flaxseed oil.

2. Add the basil and pepper to the mackerel mixture and place in a medium frying pan. Sauté over medium heat for 5–8 minutes each side or until brown.

3. Cut the cooked mackerel into bite-sized pieces and add to a large serving bowl.

4. Stir in the cherry tomatoes, cucumber, onion, and lettuce and serve.

Nutritional Analysis (per serving): Calories: 290 | Protein: 16g | Carbohydrates: 3.5g | Fat: 20g | Saturated Fat: 4g | Cholesterol: 75mg | Sodium: 115mg | Fiber: 2g | PCF Ratio: 30-8-62 | Exchange Approx.: 1 Vegetable, 3 Medium-Fat Meats, 1 Fat

HADDOCK FISH CAKES

SERVES 6; SERVING SIZE: 1 CAKE

1 pound haddock

2 medium leeks, trimmed and diced

1 medium red bell pepper, seeded and diced

2 egg whites

Freshly cracked black pepper to taste

1 tablespoon olive oil

1. Finely shred the raw fish with a fork. Combine all the ingredients except the oil in a medium bowl; mix well. Form the mixture into six small oval patties.

2. Heat the oil in a medium sauté pan over medium-high heat. Place the patties in the pan and loosely cover with the lid; sauté the fish cakes for 4–6 minutes on each side. Drain on a rack covered with paper towels; serve immediately.

Nutritional Analysis (per serving): Calories: 97 | Protein: 13g | Carbohydrates: 5g | Fat: 3g | Saturated Fat: 0g | Cholesterol: 45mg | Sodium: 67mg | Fiber: 1g | PCF Ratio: 59-16-25 | Exchange Approx.: ¼ Vegetable, 1½ Lean Meats, ½ Fat

LIME-POACHED FLOUNDER

SERVES 6; SERVING SIZE: ⅙ RECIPE

¾ cup sliced leek

¼ cup cilantro leaves (reserve stems)

1½ pounds flounder fillets

1¾ cups fish stock

2 tablespoons fresh lime juice

½ teaspoon grated lime zest

¼ teaspoon ground black pepper

1 cup shredded yellow onion

⅔ cup shredded carrot

⅔ cup shredded celery

2 tablespoons extra-virgin olive oil

Using Frozen Fish

Don't fret if you do not have fresh fish available. Using a quality fish frozen at sea is fine. In fact, sometimes the frozen fish is fresher than the fresh!

1. Place the leek slices and cilantro stems in a large skillet; lay the flounder on top.

2. Add the stock, lime juice, lime zest, and pepper. Turn on the heat and bring the mixture to a simmer, cover, and cook for 7–10 minutes until the flounder is thoroughly cooked. Remove from heat. Strain off and discard the liquid.

3. To serve, lay the shredded onions, carrots, and celery in separate strips on serving plates. Top with the flounder, drizzle with the extra-virgin olive oil, and sprinkle with the cilantro leaves.

Nutritional Analysis (per serving): Calories: 150 | Protein: 18g | Carbohydrates: 3.5g | Fat: 6g | Saturated Fat: 1.5g | Cholesterol: 40mg | Sodium: 218mg | Fiber: 1g | PCF Ratio: 43-13-44 | Exchange Approx.: 1 Vegetable, 2 Lean Meats, 1 Fat

FRESH TUNA WITH SWEET LEMON-LEEK SALSA

SERVES 6; SERVING SIZE: ⅙ RECIPE

Tuna

1½ pounds fresh tuna steaks (cut into 4-ounce portions)

¼–½ teaspoon extra-virgin olive oil

Freshly cracked black pepper to taste

Salsa

1 teaspoon extra-virgin olive oil

3 fresh leeks (light green and white parts only), thinly sliced

1 tablespoon fresh lemon juice

1 tablespoon honey

Tuna Packs a Punch

Tuna is truly a nutrient-dense food. This fish, rich in omega-3 fatty acids, has anti-inflammation written all over it with heaps of other valuable disease-fighting nutrients as well. Health authorities are urging consumers to eat fish two times per week to reap the significant health benefits.

1. Preheat the grill to medium-high.

2. Brush each portion of the tuna with the oil and drain on a rack. Season the tuna with the pepper and place on the grill; cook for 3 minutes. Shift the tuna steaks on the grill to form an *X* grill pattern on the fish; cook 3 more minutes.

3. Turn the steaks over and grill 3 more minutes; then change position again to create the grill pattern. Cook to desired doneness.

4. To make the salsa, heat the oil in a medium-sized sauté pan on medium heat; add the leeks. When the leeks are wilted, about 2–3 minutes, add the lemon juice and honey. Plate each tuna portion with a spoonful of salsa.

Nutritional Analysis (per serving): Calories: 171 | Protein: 21g | Carbohydrates: 9.5g | Fat: 5.5g | Saturated Fat: 0.5g | Cholesterol: 55mg | Sodium: 43mg | Fiber: 1g | PCF Ratio: 66-20-14 | Exchange Approx.: ¼ Other Carbohydrate, 3 Lean Meats

SALMON AND BROCCOLI STIR-FRY

SERVES 4; SERVING SIZE: ¼ RECIPE

½ pound broccoli florets

½ pound salmon fillet, skin removed

1 tablespoon canola oil

1 teaspoon sesame oil

1 teaspoon minced fresh gingerroot

2 slices pickled ginger, chopped

1 clove garlic, minced

1 teaspoon gluten-free hoisin sauce

1 cup brown rice (optional)

5 scallions, chopped

Food Safety

When preparing a dish that lists fish, seafood, or poultry as one of the ingredients, be sure to keep the fish, seafood, or poultry ice-cold during preparation to ensure food safety. If you will be doing a lot of handling of the ingredient or if the item will be standing on the counter for a long time, keep a bowl of ice nearby to place the ingredients in while you are tending to other steps of the recipe.

1. Blanch the broccoli in boiling water for 5 minutes; drain.

2. Toss the broccoli and salmon over medium-high heat in a large frying pan with the canola oil and sesame oil. Cook, stirring, for 3–4 minutes.

3. Add the gingerroot, pickled ginger, garlic, and hoisin sauce and serve over rice garnished with scallions.

Nutritional Analysis (per serving, including rice): Calories: 210 | Protein: 14g | Carbohydrates: 20g | Fat: 9g | Saturated Fat: 1g | Cholesterol: 30mg | Sodium: 95mg | Fiber: 3g | PCF Ratio: 26-38-36 | Exchange Approx.: 1 Vegetable, ¾ Starch, 2 Lean Meats, 1 Fat

PLANKED SALMON WITH DILL SAUCE

SERVES 10; SERVING SIZE: 1/10 RECIPE

1 cedar plank

Grapeseed oil as needed

1 large (3½-pound) salmon fillet, checked for bones

Juice of 1 lemon

8 juniper berries

Salt and pepper to taste

1 lemon, thinly sliced

1 cup mayonnaise

¼ cup chopped fresh dill weed

1 teaspoon horseradish

Fish Bones

The larger the fish, the more likely you will find bones in a fillet. Before cooking, hold a clean pair of pliers and run the finger of your other hand down the fillet, against the grain. Whenever you feel a bone, press down close to it. It will pop up, and you can then pull it out with the pliers.

1. Presoak the cedar plank in water for 2–6 hours before grilling. When thoroughly soaked, preheat the grill and then lightly oil the side of the cedar plank on which the salmon will lie. Set the salmon on the plank. Sprinkle with the lemon juice and press the juniper berries into the flesh at intervals. Add salt, pepper, and lemon slices.

2. Place the plank over indirect heat on a hot grill and close the lid. Roast for about 15–20 minutes or until the salmon begins to flake.

3. Mix the rest of the ingredients in a small bowl with more salt and pepper and serve with the fish.

Nutritional Analysis (per serving): Calories: 395 | Protein: 31g | Carbohydrates: 1g | Fat: 28g | Saturated Fat: 2.5g | Cholesterol: 95mg | Sodium: 432mg | Fiber: 0g | PCF Ratio: 33-1-66 | Exchange Approx.: 4½ Lean Meats, 3 Fats

GRILLED TUNA STEAK WITH VEGETABLES AND PINE NUTS

SERVES 2; SERVING SIZE: 1 STEAK

1 cup shredded napa cabbage

½ cup coarsely chopped pea pods

½ cup shredded carrots

3 tablespoons tomato sauce

¼ cup toasted pine nuts

2 (¼-pound) tuna steaks

1 teaspoon sesame oil

1 teaspoon lime juice

Salt and pepper to taste

1. Poach the vegetables in the tomato sauce for 8 minutes or until crisp-tender. Add the pine nuts and set aside.

2. Set grill on medium-high. Spread the tuna with sesame oil, lime juice, salt, and pepper. Grill for 4 minutes per side for medium.

3. Serve with tomato-poached vegetables.

Nutritional Analysis (per serving): Calories: 290 | Protein: 29g | Carbohydrates: 10g | Fat: 15g | Saturated Fat: 1.5g | Cholesterol: 55mg | Sodium: 190mg | Fiber: 3g | PCF Ratio: 40-13-47 | Exchange Approx.: 1 Vegetable, 4 Lean Meats, 1 Fat

GARLIC SHRIMP WITH BOK CHOY

SERVES 2; SERVING SIZE: ½ RECIPE

1 tablespoon sesame oil

3 cloves garlic, chopped

1 tablespoon grated fresh ginger

1 pound bok choy

1 cup broccoli florets

1 pound shrimp, peeled and deveined

¼ cup low-sodium soy sauce

1. Heat oil in a pan or wok over medium-high heat. Add garlic and ginger, stir, and cook for 30 seconds.

2. Turn heat up to high. Add bok choy and broccoli and stir-fry for 2–3 minutes. Add shrimp and continue stirring.

3. Add soy sauce and cook until shrimp are pink and completely done.

Nutritional Analysis (per serving): Calories: 290 | Protein: 37g | Carbohydrates: 14g | Fat: 9g | Saturated Fat: 1.5g | Cholesterol: 285mg | Sodium: 1000mg | Fiber: 4g | PCF Ratio: 51-19-30 | Exchange Approx.: 3 Vegetables, 3 Lean Proteins, 1 Fat

CORN-CRUSTED SALMON WITH PARSLEY AND RADISH TOPPING

SERVES 2; SERVING SIZE: 1 FILLET

4 radishes, thinly sliced

½ cup minced Italian flat-leaf parsley

4 tablespoons olive oil, divided

2 tablespoons red wine vinegar

½ teaspoon celery salt

2 (6-ounce) salmon fillets

1 tablespoon lemon juice

¼ cup cornmeal

¼ cup 2% milk

½ teaspoon dried dill

Red pepper flakes to taste

Nonstick spray

1. Mix the radishes, parsley, 1 tablespoon olive oil, vinegar, and celery salt. Set aside.

2. Make sure the salmon has no pin bones; sprinkle with lemon juice. Mix together the cornmeal, milk, dill, 3 tablespoons olive oil, and red pepper flakes. Spread on the salmon and rest it in the refrigerator for 30 minutes.

3. Preheat oven to 350°F. Prepare a baking dish or metal sheet with nonstick spray. Place salmon on the baking dish or sheet.

4. Bake the salmon for 20 minutes or until the topping is brown and the salmon flakes. Serve with radish-parsley topping.

Nutritional Analysis (per serving): Calories: 640 | Protein: 37g | Carbohydrates: 15g | Fat: 47g | Saturated Fat: 7g | Cholesterol: 95mg | Sodium: 360mg | Fiber: 2g | PCF Ratio: 23-10-67 | Exchange Approx.: 1 Starch, 5 Lean Meats, 7 Fats

CHAPTER 12

VEGETARIAN ENTRÉES

CORN CASSEROLE

SERVES 2; SERVING SIZE: ½ RECIPE

1 tablespoon finely chopped onion

1 tablespoon finely chopped green or red bell pepper

1 cup frozen or fresh corn kernels

⅛ teaspoon ground mace

Dash ground white or black pepper

¾ cup skim milk

¼ cup nonfat dry milk

1 egg

1 teaspoon butter

Spice Side Effects

Both ground mace and nutmeg can elevate blood pressure or cause an irregular heartbeat in some individuals. Check with your doctor or nutritionist before adding it to your diet.

1. Preheat oven to 325°F. In medium-sized bowl, combine onion, bell pepper, corn, mace, and pepper; toss to mix.

2. In blender, combine milk, dry milk, egg, and butter; process until mixed. Pour over corn mixture; toss to mix.

3. Pour entire mixture into glass casserole dish treated with nonstick spray. Bake 1 hour or until set.

Nutritional Analysis (per serving): Calories: 188 | Protein: 11g | Carbohydrates: 32g | Fat: 3g | Saturated Fat: 1g | Cholesterol: 10mg | Sodium: 133mg | Fiber: 2g | PCF Ratio: 23-65-13 | Exchange Approx.: 1½ Starches, 1 Skim Milk, ½ Fat

GNOCCHI

SERVES 8; SERVING SIZE: ⅛ RECIPE

1 cup boiled and mashed potatoes

2 cups all-purpose or semolina flour

1 egg

Old-Country Secrets

Italian cooks sometimes toss each helping of gnocchi in a teaspoon of melted butter and sugar, then sprinkle it with cinnamon to serve it as a dessert. This adds 1 Fat exchange and 1 Carbohydrate exchange to the recipe.

1. Combine potatoes, flour, and egg in large bowl; knead until dough forms a ball. Finished dough should be smooth, pliable, and slightly sticky.

2. Shape four equal portions of dough into long ropes, about ¾" in diameter. On floured surface, cut ropes into ½" pieces. Press thumb or forefinger into each piece to create an indentation. (Some gnocchi chefs also like to roll each piece with a fork to add a distinctive texture.)

3. Bring large pot of water to a boil. Drop in gnocchi, being careful amount you add doesn't stop water from boiling. Cook 3–5 minutes or until gnocchi rise to top. Remove from water with slotted spoon. Serve immediately, or if you make it in batches, put finished gnocchi on a platter to be set in a warm oven.

Nutritional Analysis (per serving): Calories: 139 | Protein: 4g | Carbohydrates: 28g | Fat: 1g | Saturated Fat: 0g | Cholesterol: 23mg | Sodium: 9mg | Fiber: 1g | PCF Ratio: 12-82-6 | Exchange Approx.: 1½ Starches

LAYERED VEGGIE CASSEROLE

SERVES 4; SERVING SIZE: ¼ RECIPE

Nonstick cooking spray

1 (10-ounce) package frozen mixed
  vegetables

½ cup diced onion

½ cup diced green pepper

1 cup unsalted tomato juice

⅛ teaspoon celery seed

⅛ teaspoon dried basil

⅛ teaspoon dried oregano

⅛ teaspoon dried parsley

¼ teaspoon garlic powder

3 tablespoons grated Parmesan cheese,
  divided

Season First

When readying vegetables for steaming,
add fresh or dried herbs, spices, sliced or
diced onions, minced garlic, grated ginger, or any other seasoning you'd normally
use. Seasonings will cook into vegetables
during steaming.

1. Preheat oven to 350°F. Using large casserole dish treated
   with nonstick spray, layer vegetables, onion, and pepper.
   Mix tomato juice, seasonings, and 2 tablespoons of
   Parmesan; pour over vegetables. Cover and bake 1 hour.

2. Uncover; sprinkle with remaining Parmesan. Continue to
   bake 10 minutes or until liquid thickens and mixture
   bubbles.

Nutritional Analysis (per serving): Calories: 84 | Protein:
5g | Carbohydrates: 16g | Fat: 1g | Saturated Fat:
1g | Cholesterol: 3mg | Sodium: 101mg | Fiber: 4g | PCF Ratio:
20-67-13 | Exchange Approx.: 1 Vegetable, 1 Starch

WINTER VEGETABLE CASSEROLE

SERVES 6; SERVING SIZE: ⅙ RECIPE

Cooking spray

1½ potatoes, peeled and thinly sliced

1½ sweet potatoes, peeled and thinly sliced

1 cup peeled and sliced parsnips

1 cup peeled and sliced turnips

3 tablespoons butter

3 tablespoons all-purpose flour

½ teaspoon salt

¼ teaspoon white pepper

1½ cups low-fat milk

½ cup chopped onions

1. Preheat oven to 350°F. Spray 2-quart casserole dish with cooking spray.

2. Combine potatoes, sweet potatoes, parsnips, and turnips.

3. In small saucepan, melt butter; add flour, salt, and pepper to make a roux.

4. Gradually stir in milk, cooking over low heat; stir well with wire whisk.

5. Bring milk to a boil, stirring constantly, until milk has thickened into a sauce, about 10 minutes. Remove from heat.

6. Arrange half of the sliced vegetables in casserole dish; top with half of the chopped onion and white sauce; repeat to make second layer. Cover and cook 45 minutes. Uncover and continue to cook until all vegetables are tender, about 60–70 minutes.

7. Let casserole stand 10 minutes before serving.

Nutritional Analysis (per serving): Calories: 218 | Protein: 5g | Carbohydrates: 36g | Fat: 7g | Saturated Fat: 1g | Cholesterol: 18mg | Sodium: 392mg | Fiber: 5g | PCF Ratio: 9-64-27 | Exchange Approx.: 1½ Starches, 1½ Vegetables, 1 Fat

CRUSTLESS ZUCCHINI AND ARTICHOKE QUICHE

SERVES 4; SERVING SIZE: ¼ RECIPE

Nonstick cooking spray

1 tablespoon olive oil

¼ cup chopped onions

¾ cup grated zucchini

1 cup canned artichoke hearts, cut into
    ½" pieces

1½ cups grated light Cheddar cheese

2 eggs

½ cup egg whites

½ cup fat-free cottage cheese

¼ teaspoon ground cayenne pepper

¼ teaspoon salt

⅛ teaspoon freshly ground pepper

1. Preheat oven to 375°F. Spray 9" pie plate with cooking spray.

2. In large nonstick skillet, heat olive oil; add onion and sauté until translucent.

3. Add zucchini and artichoke hearts; cook additional 3 minutes.

4. Sprinkle grated cheese in bottom of pie plate; add cooked vegetables on top of cheese.

5. In small bowl, whisk eggs, egg whites, cottage cheese, cayenne, salt, and pepper together; pour over vegetables.

6. Bake 35–40 minutes or until set and inserted toothpick comes out clean.

Nutritional Analysis (per serving): Calories: 224 | Protein: 24g | Carbohydrates: 9g | Fat: 10g | Saturated Fat: 4g | Cholesterol: 134mg | Sodium: 798mg | Fiber: 3g | PCF Ratio: 43-16-41 | Exchange Approx.: 1 Vegetable, 1½ Lean Meats, 1½ Fats

SPAGHETTI SQUASH AND VEGETABLE MIX

SERVES 6; SERVING SIZE: ⅙ RECIPE

2 pounds spaghetti squash, halved and seeded

Cooking spray

1 cup fresh or frozen peas

2 tablespoons butter

8 ounces cherry tomatoes, cut in half

1 ounce grated Romano cheese

¼ teaspoon freshly ground pepper

Pasta Alternative

Spaghetti squash is a wonderful alternative to pasta because it is packed with vitamins, minerals, and fiber. While it has a consistency similar to spaghetti, it is much lower in carbohydrates: 1 cup of cooked spaghetti squash has 15 grams of carbohydrates, while 1 cup of cooked spaghetti has approximately 45 grams!

1. Preheat oven to 400°F. Spray 9" × 13" baking dish with cooking spray; place squash halves face down. Bake for 45 minutes or until squash is soft-cooked.

2. When squash is cool enough to handle, use a fork to scoop out cooked squash from the outer shell. Scoop into a medium-sized microwaveable bowl.

3. In separate small saucepan, lightly steam peas 2–3 minutes. Add to squash along with butter; mix well.

4. Place covered bowl in microwave; cook on high 2–3 minutes.

5. Add cherry tomato halves and top with Romano cheese and pepper before serving.

Nutritional Analysis (per serving): Calories: 127 | Protein: 4g | Carbohydrates: 16g | Fat: 6g | Saturated Fat: 3g | Cholesterol: 5mg | Sodium: 169mg | Fiber: 2g | PCF Ratio: 12-47-41 | Exchange Approx.: 1 Starch, 1 Fat

GREENS IN GARLIC WITH PASTA

SERVES 4; SERVING SIZE: ¼ RECIPE

2 teaspoons olive oil

4 cloves garlic, crushed

6 cups tightly packed loose-leaf greens
(baby mustard, turnip, chard)

2 cups cooked pasta

2 teaspoons extra-virgin olive oil

¼ cup freshly grated Parmesan cheese

Salt and freshly ground black pepper to
taste (optional)

Sweet or Salty?

In most cases, when you add a pinch (less
than ⅛ teaspoon) of sugar to a recipe, you
can reduce the amount of salt without
noticing a difference. Sugar acts as a flavor enhancer and magnifies the effect of
the salt.

1. Place sauté pan over medium heat. When hot, add
   2 teaspoons of olive oil and garlic. Cook while stirring
   frequently until golden brown, 3–5 minutes, being careful
   not to burn garlic, as that makes it bitter.

2. Add greens; sauté until coated in garlic oil. Remove from
   heat.

3. In large serving bowl, add pasta, cooked greens, 2 teaspoons
   of extra-virgin olive oil, and Parmesan cheese; toss to mix.
   Serve immediately and season as desired.

Nutritional Analysis (per serving, without salt): Calories:
176 | Protein: 8g | Carbohydrates: 26g | Fat: 5g | Saturated Fat:
1g | Cholesterol: 0mg | Sodium: 17mg | Fiber: 3g | PCF Ratio:
17-58-25 | Exchange Approx.: 1 Free Vegetable, 1 Fat, 1 Starch,
½ Lean Meat

VEGETABLE FRITTATA

SERVES 4; SERVING SIZE: ¼ RECIPE

1½ tablespoons olive oil

4 ounces chopped red pepper

3 large eggs

4 ounces egg substitute (or egg whites)

4 ounces asparagus, cut diagonally into 1" pieces

¾ cup cooked and cubed potatoes

⅓ cup crumbled feta cheese

1 teaspoon dried oregano

1. Preheat oven to 350°F. Using ovenproof nonstick skillet, heat olive oil over medium heat. Add red peppers; cook until softened.

2. In medium bowl, beat together eggs and egg substitute. Add asparagus, potatoes, feta, and oregano.

3. Pour eggs into skillet; gently stir until eggs on bottom of pan begin to set. Gently pull cooked eggs from side of skillet, allowing liquid uncooked egg on top to come in contact with heated skillet. Repeat, working all around skillet until most of eggs on top have begun to set.

4. Transfer skillet to oven; bake until top is set and dry to the touch, about 3–5 minutes. Loosen frittata around edges of skillet and invert onto serving plate.

Nutritional Analysis (per serving): Calories: 171 | Protein: 12g | Carbohydrates: 11g | Fat: 9g | Saturated Fat: 4g | Cholesterol: 195mg | Sodium: 252mg | Fiber: 2g | PCF Ratio: 28-24-48 | Exchange Approx.: 1 Vegetable, 1 Lean Meat, 2½ Fats

EGGPLANT GRILLED CHEESE

SERVES 4; SERVING SIZE: 1 "SANDWICH"

1 large eggplant, sliced into eight ¼"–½"- thick rounds

2 tablespoons olive oil, divided

4 (1-ounce) slices of cheese (Gouda, white Cheddar, or mozzarella)

Delicious Additions

Optional add-ins to this recipe include chopped olives, sliced tomatoes, fresh basil, a dollop of tomato sauce, or chopped fresh tomatoes. Simply place them on top of the cheese before it is covered by the top eggplant round.

1. Place the eggplant slices on a plate. Add 1 tablespoon of olive oil to a small dish and brush the slices lightly with the oil on each side.

2. Coat a large pan with the remaining 1 tablespoon of olive oil and put on medium-high heat. Add the slices, cover, and heat for 4–5 minutes until lightly browned; flip over and heat for another 4–5 minutes. Remove four of the rounds and set aside.

3. Put one slice of cheese on each of the four rounds in the pan. Then top them with the other four rounds, cover, and heat for about 1–2 minutes until the cheese is melted.

Nutritional Analysis (per serving): Calories: 160 | Protein: 7g | Carbohydrates: 9g | Fat: 9.5g | Saturated Fat: 3.5g | Cholesterol: 15mg | Sodium: 190mg | Fiber: 4g | PCF Ratio: 20-25-55 | Exchange Approx.: 1½ Vegetables, 1 Medium-Fat Meat, 1 Fat

CHOCK-FULL O' VEGGIES CHILI

YIELDS 12 CUPS; SERVING SIZE: 1 CUP

1 (28-ounce) can crushed tomatoes

2 (15-ounce) cans black beans, drained and rinsed

1 (15-ounce) can kidney beans, drained and rinsed

3½ cups sliced cremini mushrooms

2½ cups shredded carrots

2 cups cubed yellow squash

2 cups chopped onion

1 cup chopped red pepper

1 cup chopped yellow pepper

1 cup chopped orange pepper

1 cup finely diced Anaheim chili peppers

3 tablespoons chili powder

1 tablespoon paprika

1 teaspoon crushed garlic

Topping It Off

Make this delicious chili even better by topping it with a dollop of nonfat sour cream/yogurt and sprinkling it with shredded low-fat Cheddar cheese and chopped chives.

1. Add the canned tomatoes, beans, mushrooms, carrots, squash, onion, red pepper, yellow pepper, and orange pepper to a large pot. Place on high heat for 15 minutes uncovered, stirring occasionally.

2. Add the chili peppers, chili powder, paprika, and garlic and continue to cook on medium-high heat uncovered for another 15 minutes, stirring occasionally. Then reduce to low heat, cover, and simmer, stirring occasionally, until vegetables are tender, another 25–30 minutes.

Nutritional Analysis (per serving): Calories: 150 | Protein: 7g | Carbohydrates: 30g | Fat: 0.5g | Saturated Fat: 0g | Cholesterol: 0mg | Sodium: 160mg | Fiber: 8g | PCF Ratio: 19-78-3 | Exchange Approx.: 1 Starch, 2 Vegetables, ½ Lean Meat

EASY MEDITERRANEAN TOSTADA

SERVES 1

1 whole-wheat pita

2 heaping tablespoons hummus

2 tablespoons chopped tomato

2 tablespoons chopped cucumber

1 tablespoon sliced olives

2 tablespoons crumbled reduced-fat feta cheese

1 teaspoon chopped fresh basil

Toast the pita. Spread with hummus and then layer on the tomato, cucumber, olives, and cheese. Sprinkle with basil and serve.

Nutritional Analysis (per serving): Calories: 300 | Protein: 11g | Carbohydrates: 43g | Fat: 12g | Saturated Fat: 2g | Cholesterol: 5mg | Sodium: 720mg | Fiber: 3g | PCF Ratio: 16-58-26 | Exchange Approx.: 2 Starches, 1 Vegetable, 1 Medium-Fat Meat, ½ Fat

ZUCCHINI SPAGHETTI PRIMAVERA

YIELDS 4 CUPS; SERVING SIZE: 1 CUP

1 tablespoon olive oil

3 cups sliced mushrooms

2 cups chopped red bell pepper

½ cup chopped white onion

4 cups raw Zucchini "Noodles" (see recipe in Chapter 8)

1 cup marinara sauce

¼ teaspoon garlic powder

Chopped fresh basil (optional)

Grated Parmesan cheese (optional)

1. Coat a large pan with the olive oil; add the mushrooms, peppers, and onions and sauté on medium heat for 8–10 minutes until lightly browned and softened.

2. Add the zucchini noodles, marinara sauce, and garlic powder and mix well. Continue to heat for about 5–7 minutes covered, stirring occasionally, until softened and cooked through. Top with basil and Parmesan cheese if desired.

Nutritional Analysis (per serving): Calories: 90 | Protein: 3g | Carbohydrates: 13g | Fat: 3g | Saturated Fat: 0g | Cholesterol: 0mg | Sodium: 300mg | Fiber: 4g | PCF Ratio: 15-57-30 | Exchange Approx.: 2 Vegetables, 1 Fat

EASY SPAGHETTI SQUASH MAC 'N CHEESE FOR ONE

SERVES 1

1 cup cooked spaghetti squash (see Maple Spaghetti Squash with Walnuts and Goat Cheese recipe in Chapter 8 for instructions on cooking spaghetti squash)

1 teaspoon butter or margarine

¼ cup shredded reduced-fat Cheddar cheese

1. Put the spaghetti squash in a small dish, add the margarine/butter, and microwave on high for 30 seconds. Remove and stir well to evenly coat.

2. Sprinkle in the cheese and mix well. Return to microwave and heat for another 30 seconds or until cheese is melted

Nutritional Analysis (per serving): Calories: 160 | Protein: 8g | Carbohydrates: 11g | Fat: 10g | Saturated Fat: 4.5g | Cholesterol: 20mg | Sodium: 290mg | Fiber: 2g | PCF Ratio: 19-27-54 | Exchange Approx.: ½ Starch, 1 Medium-Fat Meat, 1 Fat

PORTOBELLO MUSHROOM FAJITAS

SERVES 6; SERVING SIZE: 1 FAJITA

1 tablespoon olive oil

1 green bell pepper, seeded and sliced lengthwise

1 red bell pepper, seeded and sliced lengthwise

½ medium onion, peeled and sliced lengthwise

2 large or 4 or 5 small portobello mushroom caps, stems removed, sliced into ¼"-thick strips

1 teaspoon taco seasoning

6 small corn or flour tortillas

1. Add the olive oil, peppers, and onions to a large skillet or pan and sauté on medium-high heat for 3–5 minutes.

2. Put in the mushrooms and taco seasoning and continue to sauté until the veggies are browned and tender, about 5–7 minutes. Divide and spoon the mixture onto the tortillas and serve.

Nutritional Analysis (per serving): Calories: 100 | Protein: 2g | Carbohydrates: 16g | Fat: 3g | Saturated Fat: 0g | Cholesterol: 0mg | Sodium: 40mg | Fiber: 2g | PCF Ratio: 9-63-28 | Exchange Approx.: ¾ Starch, 1 Vegetable, ½ Fat

LENTIL TACO FILLING

YIELDS 6 CUPS; SERVING SIZE: 1 CUP

1 teaspoon olive oil

2 cups diced red bell pepper

1½ cups finely chopped white onion

4 cups chopped button mushrooms

3 cups cooked or canned rinsed lentils

3 teaspoons taco seasoning

⅛ teaspoon garlic powder

Serving Suggestions

Enjoy this filling in corn tortillas, lettuce wraps, or even over salad. Top with avocado, low-fat cheese, salsa, and nonfat Greek yogurt.

1. Coat a large pan with the olive oil, add the bell pepper and onion to it, and brown for about 5–7 minutes, stirring frequently.

2. Add in the chopped mushrooms, cover, and cook for another few minutes, stirring occasionally. Put in the lentils, taco seasoning, and garlic powder and stir well. Heat uncovered for 3–5 minutes until warmed through.

Nutritional Analysis (per serving): Calories: 170 | Protein: 11g | Carbohydrates: 29g | Fat: 2g | Saturated Fat: 0g | Cholesterol: 0mg | Sodium: 80mg | Fiber: 10g | PCF Ratio: 25-68-7 | Exchange Approx.: 1 Starch, 2 Vegetables, ½ Fat

INDIAN CHILI

YIELDS 5 CUPS; SERVING SIZE: 1 CUP

1 teaspoon olive oil

1 teaspoon finely chopped garlic

2 cups chopped carrot

2 cups peeled ¼"-cubed eggplant

1 cup chopped white onion

¾ cup tomato sauce

¼ cup low-sodium chicken or vegetable broth

1½ cups cooked or canned rinsed lentils

1½ cups canned rinsed kidney beans

1 teaspoon ground cumin

¾ teaspoon curry powder

¼ teaspoon ground cinnamon

1. Add the olive oil, garlic, carrots, eggplant, and onion to a large pot and sauté on medium heat for 5 minutes, stirring often.

2. Put in the tomato sauce, broth, lentils, kidney beans, and spices and heat 7–12 minutes until the beans are very soft and the vegetables are tender.

Nutritional Analysis (per serving): Calories: 230 | Protein: 13g | Carbohydrates: 40g | Fat: 2g | Saturated Fat: 0g | Cholesterol: 0mg | Sodium: 240mg | Fiber: 15g | PCF Ratio: 21-71-8 | Exchange Approx.: 2 Starches, 2 Vegetables, 1 Lean Meat

MEDITERRANEAN-STYLE SAUCE FOR PASTA OR RICE

YIELDS 8 CUPS; SERVING SIZE: 1 CUP

1 teaspoon olive oil

1 large eggplant, cut into ½" cubes

2 cloves garlic, finely chopped, or
    2 teaspoons crushed/jarred

1 cup chopped white onion

1 cup chopped red bell pepper

1 (15-ounce) can diced tomatoes

1 (15-ounce) can tomato sauce

1 (8-ounce) package sliced white or cremini
    mushrooms

¼ cup chopped green olives

¼ cup capers

2 teaspoons dried oregano

2 tablespoons red wine (optional)

Chopped fresh basil and grated Parmesan
    cheese (optional)

Making This Sauce Into a Meal

Serve this sauce over ⅔ cup brown rice or
whole-wheat pasta, which will add
30 grams of carbohydrates and 2 starch
servings. Or go for a low-carbohydrate
option and serve this over 2 cups Zucchini
"Noodles" (see recipe in Chapter 8) for
only 8 additional carbohydrates and
2 vegetable servings.

1. Coat a large pan or skillet with the olive oil and add the
   eggplant, garlic, onion, and peppers and sauté on medium
   heat for about 3–5 minutes until soft and starting to brown.

2. Put in the tomatoes, tomato sauce, mushrooms, olives,
   capers, oregano, and wine if using and simmer for
   12–17 minutes until all the veggies are very soft and tender.
   Garnish with basil and Parmesan cheese if desired.

Nutritional Analysis (per serving): Calories: 80 | Protein:
3g | Carbohydrates: 15g | Fat: 1.5g | Saturated Fat:
0g | Cholesterol: 0mg | Sodium: 440mg | Fiber: 4g | PCF Ratio:
14-68-18 | Exchange Approx.: 2½ Vegetables, ½ Fat

MEXICAN PIZZA

SERVES 4; SERVING SIZE: 1 PIZZA

2 teaspoons olive oil

4 corn tortillas

Cooking spray

¼ cup enchilada sauce

¼ cup finely diced white onion

½ cup diced bell peppers

½ cup finely chopped mushroom

½ cup canned rinsed black beans

¼ cup shredded Cheddar cheese

4 teaspoons chopped fresh cilantro

4 tablespoons chopped avocado

1. Preheat oven to 425°F. Put the olive oil in a small dish and lightly brush both sides of each tortilla and place them on a baking sheet coated with cooking spray.

2. Spread 1 tablespoon of enchilada sauce over each tortilla; top with the onion, peppers, mushrooms, and black beans.

3. Bake in the oven for 10 minutes or until the edges of the tortilla are crispy. Remove from oven, sprinkle 1 tablespoon of cheese over each tortilla, return to oven, and bake for another 2 minutes or until cheese is melted. Garnish each with 1 teaspoon cilantro and 1 tablespoon avocado and serve.

Nutritional Analysis (per serving): Calories: 160 | Protein: 5g | Carbohydrates: 20g | Fat: 6g | Saturated Fat: 1.5g | Cholesterol: 5mg | Sodium: 230mg | Fiber: 4g | PCF Ratio: 13-60-27 | Exchange Approx.: 1 Starch, 1 Vegetable, ¼ Medium-Fat Meat, 1 Fat

SAUTÉED SPAGHETTI SQUASH WITH SPINACH AND MUSHROOMS

YIELDS 4 HEAPING CUPS; SERVING SIZE: 1 HEAPING CUP

1 tablespoon olive oil

4 cloves garlic, finely chopped

4 heaping cups fresh baby spinach

2 (8-ounce) packages sliced mushrooms

4 cups cooked spaghetti squash (see Maple Spaghetti Squash with Walnuts and Goat Cheese recipe in Chapter 8 for instructions on cooking spaghetti squash)

Grated Parmesan cheese (optional)

1. Coat a large pan with ½ tablespoon of the oil, put in the garlic, and sauté on medium heat for a few minutes until lightly browned.

2. Add the remaining ½ tablespoon of olive oil, the spinach, and the mushrooms and continue to sauté for a few more minutes, stirring frequently.

3. Stir in the cooked spaghetti squash and heat through for about 3–5 minutes. Serve with Parmesan cheese as a garnish if desired.

Nutritional Analysis (per serving): Calories: 120 | Protein: 5g | Carbohydrates: 19g | Fat: 4g | Saturated Fat: 0.5g | Cholesterol: 0mg | Sodium: 85mg | Fiber: 4g | PCF Ratio: 14-58-28 | Exchange Approx.: ½ Starch, 1½ Vegetables, 1 Fat

GRILLED VEGGIE WRAPS

SERVES 2; SERVING SIZE: 1 WRAP

1 red bell pepper, cut lengthwise into 4–6 large strips

6 asparagus spears

1 cup broccoli florets

2 tablespoons light cream cheese

2 whole-wheat tortillas

1–2 tablespoons chopped red onion

8 olives, sliced

¼ cup chopped fresh basil

½ cup shredded carrot

Garlic powder (optional)

Grated Parmesan cheese (optional)

1. Grill the peppers, asparagus, and broccoli on a barbecue or a grill pan on high heat for about 3–5 minutes each side until just slightly soft. Set aside to cool.

2. Spread 1 tablespoon of cream cheese on each tortilla to thinly coat.

3. Add the onions, olives, basil, carrots, and the cooked broccoli, asparagus, and red bell pepper, layering them in the middle. Sprinkle with garlic powder and/or Parmesan cheese to taste if desired, roll up, and serve.

Nutritional Analysis (per serving): Calories: 240 | Protein: 9g | Carbohydrates: 35g | Fat: 7g | Saturated Fat: 2.5g | Cholesterol: 10mg | Sodium: 340mg | Fiber: 8g | PCF Ratio: 15-57-28 | Exchange Approx.: 1½ Starches, 2 Vegetables, 1½ Fats

BAKED EGGPLANT PARMESAN

SERVES 8; SERVING SIZE: 1 EGGPLANT ROUND

2 whole-wheat English muffins

4 tablespoons grated Parmesan cheese

4 egg whites or ½ cup liquid egg whites

1 large eggplant, sliced into eight ½ –1"-thick rounds

Cooking spray

2 cups marinara sauce

2 tablespoons chopped fresh basil

½ cup shredded low-fat mozzarella cheese

1. Preheat oven to 425°F.

2. Cut the English muffins into cubes and then grind in a blender or food processor on high for 10–15 seconds to produce coarse bread crumbs. Spread the bread crumbs on a large plate and mix with the Parmesan cheese.

3. Pour the egg whites into a shallow bowl. Dip each eggplant round in the egg mixture to wet each side and then coat each side with the bread crumbs/cheese mixture.

4. Place the coated rounds on a baking sheet coated with cooking spray and bake for 10 minutes. Flip them over and bake for another 10 minutes.

5. While the eggplant is baking, pour 1 cup of marinara sauce to coat the bottom of a 9" × 12" baking dish.

6. Once done, place the baked eggplant rounds to line the dish and then top with the other 1 cup sauce. Bake covered with aluminum foil for 15 minutes. Uncover, sprinkle with the basil and mozzarella cheese, and bake uncovered for another 5 minutes or until cheese is melted.

Nutritional Analysis (per serving): Calories: 140 | Protein: 7g | Carbohydrates: 16g | Fat: 5g | Saturated Fat: 2g | Cholesterol: 10mg | Sodium: 450mg | Fiber: 4g | PCF Ratio: 20-46-34 | Exchange Approx.: ¾ Starch, 1 Vegetable, ¼ Medium-Fat Meat, ½ Fat

VEGGIE FRIED RICE

YIELDS 4 CUPS; SERVING SIZE: ½ CUP

2 cups cooked brown rice

1 tablespoon sesame oil

½ cup diced green onion

1 cup diced celery

1 cup chopped carrots

½ cup corn or peas (fresh or frozen thawed)

1 cup chopped broccoli

2 tablespoons low-sodium soy sauce

¼ cup chopped fresh basil

2 tablespoons chopped peanuts or cashews

1. Coat a large skillet or wok with the sesame oil and add all the vegetables. Sauté them on medium heat, stirring constantly. Cook for about 7–10 minutes or until they are slightly tender and then remove from heat.

2. Add cooked rice into the pan with the veggies. Return to medium heat; add the soy sauce, basil, and chopped nuts; stir well. Heat until warm, about 2–3 minutes.

Nutritional Analysis (per serving): Calories: 110 | Protein: 3g | Carbohydrates: 19g | Fat: 3.5g | Saturated Fat: 0g | Cholesterol: 0mg | Sodium: 170mg | Fiber: 2g | PCF Ratio: 9-66-25 | Exchange Approx.: 1 Starch, ½ Vegetable, ½ Fat

200-CALORIE GRILLED CHEESE

SERVES 1

1 teaspoon light butter or margarine

2 slices light/reduced-calorie whole-wheat bread

1 slice reduced-fat Cheddar cheese

1. Spread ½ teaspoon of the margarine/butter on one side of each bread slice. Place the bread slices buttered-side down and put the cheese in between them.

2. Put the sandwich in a small pan on medium heat and warm for 1–2 minutes each side until golden brown and the cheese is melted.

Nutritional Analysis (per serving): Calories: 180 | Protein: 10g | Carbohydrates: 21g | Fat: 9g | Saturated Fat: 4g | Cholesterol: 15mg | Sodium: 490mg | Fiber: 6g | PCF Ratio: 19-41-40 | Exchange Approx.: 1¼ Starches, 1 Medium-Fat Meat, ½ Fat

LOW-CARB VEGGIE LASAGNA

SERVES 9; SERVING SIZE: ⅑ RECIPE

1 large eggplant

2 red bell peppers

2 large carrots

3 medium zucchini

¾ cup chopped fresh basil

1 (15-ounce) container low-fat ricotta cheese

Salt and pepper (optional)

Cooking spray

2 cups marinara sauce

1 cup sliced button mushrooms

2 cups shredded low-fat mozzarella cheese

1. Preheat oven to 375°F. Wash and cut the eggplant, peppers, carrots, and zucchini lengthwise into ⅛"–¼" slices. Grill them in batches on the barbecue or a large nonstick pan on high heat for about 5–7 minutes each side until just slightly soft. Place aside to cool.

2. In a small bowl, combine the chopped basil and ricotta, adding salt and pepper to taste if desired.

3. To assemble, coat a 9" × 13" baking pan with cooking spray and layer with eggplant to cover the bottom. Spread the ricotta/basil mixture over the eggplant and then layer zucchini and peppers on top. Pour on the marinara to evenly coat, top with carrots and mushrooms, and then bake for 30 minutes. Sprinkle the mozzarella cheese on top and bake another 5–7 minutes until cheese is melted.

Nutritional Analysis (per serving): Calories: 180 | Protein: 16g | Carbohydrates: 18g | Fat: 7g | Saturated Fat: 4g | Cholesterol: 30mg | Sodium: 550mg | Fiber: 4g | PCF Ratio: 32-36-32 | Exchange Approx.: 2½ Vegetables, 1 Lean Meat, 1 Medium-Fat Meat

GRILLED PORTOBELLO MUSHROOM BURGERS WITH CARAMELIZED BALSAMIC ONIONS

SERVES 2; SERVING SIZE: 1 "BURGER"

2 large (about 4"–5" in diameter) portobello mushrooms

2 tablespoons balsamic vinegar

½ teaspoon brown sugar

1 teaspoon olive oil

1 cup sliced red onion

2 slices reduced-fat cheese

2 whole-wheat buns

1. Rinse the mushrooms well, dry, and cook them on the barbecue or a nonstick pan on high heat, about 7–10 minutes stem-side up first. Pat dry any moisture that has collected, flip over, and heat another 7–10 minutes.

2. While the mushrooms are cooking, mix the balsamic vinegar and brown sugar in a small bowl and set aside. Then add the olive oil and onions to a separate small pan and sauté on medium heat until the onions are lightly browned, about 5–7 minutes. Reduce heat to low and add the balsamic-brown sugar mixture and sauté until it is fully absorbed, about 1–2 minutes.

3. Once the mushrooms are nearly done, add a slice of cheese on top for the last minute of cooking and heat until lightly melted. Place each cooked mushroom on a bun, top with the onions, and serve.

Nutritional Analysis (per serving): Calories: 260 | Protein: 10g | Carbohydrates: 33g | Fat: 10g | Saturated Fat: 3.5g | Cholesterol: 15mg | Sodium: 400mg | Fiber: 4g | PCF Ratio: 27-24-49 | Exchange Approx.: 2 Starches, 1 Vegetable, 1 Medium-Fat Meat

SESAME NOODLE STIR-FRY

YIELDS 6 CUPS; SERVING SIZE: 1 CUP

4 ounces dry soba noodles or whole-wheat spaghetti

1 tablespoon plus 1 teaspoon sesame oil, divided

1 cup diced onion

1 cup diced celery

2 cups chopped mushrooms

1 cup chopped yellow, orange, or red bell peppers

1 cup ½"-cubed eggplant

1 cup snap peas or pea pods

½ teaspoon crushed garlic or a few cloves diced

¼ cup chopped nuts such as peanuts or cashews

½ cup chopped fresh basil

Low-sodium soy sauce and red pepper flakes (optional)

Stir-Fry Swaps

If you don't care for one or more of the above vegetables, you can substitute a cup of another chopped vegetable of your choice such as broccoli, carrots, and water chestnut, as long as there are 6 cups of raw veggies total.

1. Cook noodles according to package directions.

2. While the noodles are cooking, put all the veggies in a large skillet coated with 1 tablespoon sesame oil and sauté on medium heat, stirring constantly.

3. Add the crushed garlic after about 5 minutes as the veggies begin to soften and continue to stir. Warm for another 5 minutes or until they are slightly tender.

4. Once the noodles are done, drain them in a strainer and add them into the pan with the veggies. Add 1 teaspoon of sesame oil, the chopped nuts, and the basil and stir well to coat and warm for another 2–3 minutes.

5. Serve with low-sodium soy sauce and red pepper flakes if desired.

Nutritional Analysis (per serving): Calories: 140 | Protein: 6g | Carbohydrates: 22g | Fat: 4g | Saturated Fat: 0.5g | Cholesterol: 0mg | Sodium: 60mg | Fiber: 5g | PCF Ratio: 16-60-24 | Exchange Approx.: 1 Starch, 1½ Vegetables, ½ Fat

HONEY MUSTARD BAKED TOFU

YIELDS 2 CUPS; SERVING SIZE: ½ CUP

12 ounces extra-firm tofu

Cooking spray

1 tablespoon olive oil

2 tablespoons honey mustard

½ teaspoon honey

1. Remove the tofu from the package, rinse, and pat dry. Place it on a plate in between two paper towels. Top with another plate with a heavy object (such as a can) on top of that. Let it sit for 20–30 minutes to press out excess water. Then cut it into ½" cubes.

2. Preheat oven to 350°F and coat a baking sheet with cooking spray.

3. Add the olive oil, mustard, and honey to a medium-sized bowl and whisk together.

4. Put the tofu in the bowl and gently stir with a spatula to coat the cubes with the sauce. Transfer to prepared baking sheet.

5. Bake for 40 minutes, flipping the cubes over halfway through the baking.

Nutritional Analysis (per serving): Calories: 120 | Protein: 8g | Carbohydrates: 4g | Fat: 7g | Saturated Fat: 1g | Cholesterol: 0mg | Sodium: 50mg | Fiber: 1g | PCF Ratio: 27-15-58 | Exchange Approx.: ¼ Other Carbohydrate, 1 Medium-Fat Meat, ½ Fat

SIMPLE SAUTÉED TOFU

12 ounces extra-firm tofu

1 tablespoon cornstarch

1 tablespoon canola oil

Tofu: A Blank, Not a Bland, Slate

This tofu comes out nice and firm with a slightly crispy texture. The cornstarch and oil help keep it from sticking to the pan. Plain tofu absorbs flavor well, so liven it up with low-sodium soy sauce, BBQ sauce, or your favorite salad dressing, or try it with the Peanut Sauce (see recipe in Chapter 6).

1. Remove the tofu from the package, rinse, and pat dry. Place it on a plate in between two paper towels. Top with another plate with a heavy object (such as a can) on top of that. Let it sit for 20–30 minutes to press out excess water. Then cut the tofu into ½" cubes. Add the cornstarch to a medium bowl; add the tofu cubes and toss to coat.

2. Coat a large pan with the canola oil and warm on medium-high heat.

3. Add the tofu and sauté for 7–10 minutes, flipping it every 1–2 minutes until all cubes are slightly crispy and browned.

Nutritional Analysis (per serving): Calories: 110 | Protein: 8g | Carbohydrates: 4g | Fat: 7g | Saturated Fat: 1g | Cholesterol: 0mg | Sodium: 20mg | Fiber: 1g | PCF Ratio: 28-13-59 | Exchange Approx.: ¼ Other Carbohydrate, 1 Medium-Fat Meat, ½ Fat

CHAPTER 13

DESSERTS AND BEVERAGES

INDIVIDUAL SPONGE CAKES

**YIELDS 12 CUPCAKES; SERVING SIZE:
1 CUPCAKE**

1 cup flour

½ teaspoon salt

1 teaspoon baking powder

3 eggs

¾ cup granulated sugar

1 tablespoon lemon juice

½ teaspoon lemon zest (optional)

6 tablespoons hot milk

Nonstick spray

Snack Cakes

Use a pastry bag to pump nonfat whipped topping or low-sugar jelly (or a mixture of the two) into the center of the Individual Sponge Cakes, and you have a healthier homemade snack-cake alternative.

1. Preheat oven to 350°F. Mix together flour, salt, and baking powder. In food processor or mixing bowl, beat eggs until fluffy and lemon colored. Add sugar, lemon juice, and lemon zest if using. Add flour mixture; process only enough to blend. Add milk; process until blended.

2. Pour into a twelve-section muffin pan treated with nonstick spray. (Also works well as twenty-four mini muffins.) If lining muffin pan, use foil liners. Bake for 15 minutes or until toothpick inserted in center of cupcake comes out clean. Cakes will be golden brown and firm to the touch. Move cupcakes to a rack to cool.

Nutritional Analysis (per serving): Calories: 108 | Protein: 3g | Carbohydrates: 21g | Fat: 2g | Saturated Fat: 1g | Cholesterol: 62mg | Sodium: 163mg | Fiber: 1g | PCF Ratio: 12-74-14 | Exchange Approx.: 1½ Starches

GLAZED CARROT CAKE

SERVES 9; SERVING SIZE: 1/9 RECIPE

1½ cups unbleached all-purpose flour

1 teaspoon baking powder

1 teaspoon baking soda

1½ teaspoons ground cinnamon

¼ teaspoon ground cloves

¼ teaspoon ground allspice

⅛ teaspoon ground nutmeg

1 tablespoon sugar

⅛ cup (2 tablespoons) frozen unsweetened apple juice concentrate

2 eggs

¼ cup water

2 tablespoons ground flaxseed

1 teaspoon vanilla extract

3 tablespoons nonfat plain yogurt

1 cup canned unsweetened crushed pineapple, ¼ cup of liquid retained

1 cup finely shredded carrots

¼ cup seedless raisins

Nonstick spray

Glaze

⅛ cup (2 tablespoons) frozen unsweetened apple juice concentrate

1 tablespoon water

1. Preheat oven to 350°F. Sift together dry ingredients and spices.

2. Using food processor or mixer, blend sugar, apple juice concentrate, and eggs until well mixed. Stir water and flaxseed together in small microwave-safe bowl; microwave on high for 30 seconds, then stir. (Mixture should be consistency of egg whites; if it isn't, microwave in 15-second increments until it is.) Gradually beat into egg mixture, along with vanilla, yogurt, and ¼ cup pineapple liquid.

3. Stir in dry ingredients. Fold in pineapple (drained of any remaining juice), carrots, and raisins.

4. Treat 8" baking pan with nonstick spray. Spoon mixture into pan; bake for 20–25 minutes. Allow cake to cool slightly while you prepare glaze.

5. Mix apple juice concentrate and water until concentrate is melted. (You can microwave the mixture for 15–20 seconds if necessary.) Spread evenly over cake.

Nutritional Analysis (per serving): Calories: 149 | Protein: 5g | Carbohydrates: 28g | Fat: 2g | Saturated Fat: 1g | Cholesterol: 42mg | Sodium: 220mg | Fiber: 2g | PCF Ratio: 13-74-13 | Exchange Approx.: 1 Starch, ½ Vegetable, 1 Fruit

LINZERTORTE MUFFINS

YIELDS 12 MUFFINS; SERVING SIZE: 1 MUFFIN

Nonstick spray

¼ cup ground blanched hazelnuts (filberts)

2 cups unbleached all-purpose flour

2 teaspoons baking powder

½ teaspoon salt

1 teaspoon ground cinnamon

⅛ teaspoon ground allspice

⅛ teaspoon ground ginger

⅛ cup granulated sugar

¼ cup firmly packed brown sugar

½ cup applesauce

1 egg

1 teaspoon grated lemon zest

½ teaspoon vanilla extract

1 cup skim milk

12 teaspoons seedless black raspberry jam

1. Preheat oven to 400°F. Spray muffin pan with nonstick spray or use lining cups with cupcake papers.

2. Add all dry ingredients, including spices, to food processor; pulse until everything is well mixed. Add remaining ingredients except for jam; process to mix. (If you're using a mixer, cream egg, applesauce, and sugars. Mix in milk and vanilla, then add dry ingredients and lemon zest. Fold in nuts.)

3. Spoon a tablespoonful of batter into each of the twelve muffin sections. Top batter with a teaspoonful of seedless black raspberry jam per muffin, being careful no jam touches sides of muffin pan. Evenly divide remaining muffin batter between the muffins, using it to top jam. Gently spread batter to cover jam. Bake 15–20 minutes or until lightly browned.

Nutritional Analysis (per serving): Calories: 147 | Protein: 4g | Carbohydrates: 30g | Fat: 2g | Saturated Fat: 1g | Cholesterol: 16mg | Sodium: 294mg | Fiber: 1g | PCF Ratio: 10-80-10 | Exchange Approx.: 1 Starch, 1 Fruit

MOCK WHIPPED CREAM

YIELDS 3½ CUPS; SERVING SIZE: 2 TABLESPOONS

1 envelope Knox Unflavored Gelatine

¼ cup cold water

½ cup hot water

2 tablespoons almond oil

3 tablespoons powdered sugar

1 teaspoon vanilla extract

1 cup ice water

1¼ cups nonfat milk powder

Know Your Ingredients

Although any unflavored gelatine will work, the nutritional analyses for all recipes are based on the Knox brand.

1. Allow gelatine to soften in cold water; pour into blender. Add hot water; blend for 2 minutes until gelatine is dissolved.

2. While continuing to blend mixture, gradually add almond oil, powdered sugar, and vanilla. Chill in freezer for 15 minutes or until mixture is cool but hasn't begun to set.

3. Using hand mixer or whisk, add ice water and nonfat milk powder to a chilled bowl; beat until peaks start to form. Add gelatine mixture to whipped milk; continue to whip for 10 minutes until stiffer peaks begin to form. This whipped topping will keep several days in refrigerator. Whip again to introduce more air into topping before serving.

Nutritional Analysis (per serving): Calories: 24 | Protein: 1g | Carbohydrates: 2g | Fat: 1g | Saturated Fat: 0g | Cholesterol: 1mg | Sodium: 17mg | Fiber: 0g | PCF Ratio: 21-41-38 | Exchange Approx.: ½ Fat

DATE-NUT ROLL

SERVES 12; SERVING SIZE: 1 SLICE

12 graham crackers

¼ cup finely chopped walnuts

12 dates, chopped

¼ cup Mock Whipped Cream (see recipe in this chapter)

1. Place graham crackers in plastic bag; use rolling pin to crush or process into crumbs in food processor. Mix crumbs with chopped walnuts and dates. Gently fold in Mock Whipped Cream.

2. Turn mixture out onto a piece of aluminum foil (if you plan to freeze it) or onto plastic wrap (if you'll only be chilling it until you're ready to serve it). Shape into a log; wrap securely in foil or plastic wrap. Chill for at least 4 hours before serving. Cut into twelve slices.

Nutritional Analysis (per serving): Calories: 103 | Protein: 2g | Carbohydrates: 18g | Fat: 3g | Saturated Fat: 1g | Cholesterol: 0mg | Sodium: 95mg | Fiber: 1g | PCF Ratio: 7-66-27 | Exchange Approx.: 1 Fat, ½ Starch, ½ Fruit

CHOCOLATE CHEESECAKE MOUSSE

SERVES 4; SERVING SIZE: ¼ RECIPE

1 tablespoon semisweet chocolate chips

¾ cup Mock Whipped Cream (see recipe in this chapter), divided

1 ounce cream cheese

1½ teaspoons cocoa

1 teaspoon vanilla extract

1. Put chocolate chips and 1 tablespoon of Mock Whipped Cream in microwave-safe bowl; microwave on high for 15 seconds.

2. Add cream cheese; microwave on high for another 15 seconds. Whip mixture until well blended and chocolate chips are melted.

3. Stir in cocoa and vanilla; fold in remaining Mock Whipped Cream. Chill until ready to serve.

Nutritional Analysis (per serving): Calories: 83 | Protein: 3g | Carbohydrates: 7g | Fat: 5g | Saturated Fat: 2g | Cholesterol: 9mg | Sodium: 47mg | Fiber: 0g | PCF Ratio: 13-32-55 | Exchange Approx.: ½ Skim Milk, 1 Fat

NONFAT WHIPPED MILK BASE

YIELDS ABOUT 3 CUPS

¼ cup nonfat milk powder

⅛ cup powdered sugar

1 cup chilled skim milk, divided

1½ envelopes Knox Unflavored Gelatine

Whipping Methods

Because you don't need to whip the Nonfat Whipped Milk Base into stiff peaks, you can use a blender or food processor; however, you won't be whipping as much air into the mixture if you do, so the serving sizes will be a bit smaller.

1. In chilled bowl, combine milk powder and sugar; mix until well blended. Pour ¼ cup milk and gelatine into blender; let sit for 1–2 minutes for gelatine to soften.

2. In microwave-safe container, heat remaining milk on high until it almost reaches boiling point, 30–45 seconds. Add milk to blender with gelatine; blend 2 minutes or until gelatine is completely dissolved. Chill for 15 minutes or until mixture is cool but gelatine hasn't yet begun to set.

3. Using hand mixer or whisk, beat until doubled in size. (It won't form stiff peaks like whipped cream; however, you'll notice it will get creamier in color.) Chill until ready to use in desserts. If necessary, whip again immediately prior to folding in other ingredients.

Nutritional Analysis (per recipe): Calories: 290 | Carbohydrates: 42g | Protein: 28g | Fat: 1g | Saturated Fat: 0g | Cholesterol: 11mg | Sodium: 310mg | Fiber: 0g | PCF Ratio: 39-59-2 | Exchange Approx.: 2 Skim Milks, 1 Carbohydrate

WHIPPED LEMON CHEESECAKE MOUSSE

SERVES 10; SERVING SIZE: ½ CUP

4 ounces room temperature cream cheese

1 tablespoon lemon juice

1 teaspoon lemon zest

¼ cup powdered sugar

1 recipe Nonfat Whipped Milk Base (see recipe in this chapter)

In small bowl, combine cream cheese, lemon juice, lemon zest, and sugar; using fork or whisk, beat until well blended. Fold mixture into Nonfat Whipped Milk Base. Chill for at least 1 hour before serving.

Nutritional Analysis (per serving): Calories: 81 | Protein: 4g | Carbohydrates: 8g | Fat: 4g | Saturated Fat: 3g | Cholesterol: 14mg | Sodium: 65mg | Fiber: 0g | PCF Ratio: 18-38-44 | Exchange Approx.: 1 Skim Milk

CHOCOLATE ALMOND SAUCE

YIELDS 10 SERVINGS; SERVING SIZE: 2 TABLESPOONS

½ cup cocoa powder

5 or 6 packets Splenda or other artificial sweetener

1 cup (8 ounces) evaporated skim milk

1 teaspoon almond extract

Something Sweet!

Try this rich sauce over ½ cup of ice cream or a small slice of plain cake. It can be used warm or cold. Mix into 8 ounces skim milk and heat in microwave for hot cocoa. Store sauce in a jar in refrigerator up to 2 weeks.

1. Combine the cocoa and Splenda in small saucepan. Add 1–2 tablespoons evaporated milk and almond extract; stir to make a paste.

2. Add remaining evaporated milk; mix well using whisk. Cook over low heat, stirring constantly until mixture begins to bubble.

3. Reduce heat and continue cooking for 10 minutes or until sauce has thickened to consistency of honey.

Nutritional Analysis (per serving): Calories: 36 | Protein: 3g | Carbohydrates: 5g | Fat: 0g | Saturated Fat: 0g | Cholesterol: 1mg | Sodium: 26mg | Fiber: 1g | PCF Ratio: 28-61-11 | Exchange Approx.: ½ Other Carbohydrate

PEACH BREAD PUDDING

SERVES 9; SERVING SIZE: ½ CUP

Nonstick cooking spray

2 cups 1% milk

2 tablespoons butter

2 eggs

⅓ cup egg whites

1 teaspoon vanilla extract

2 teaspoons ground cinnamon

⅓ cup Splenda Brown Sugar Blend

6 slices whole-wheat bread, cubed

2 cups sliced peaches

1. Preheat oven to 350°F. Spray 9" × 9" baking dish with nonstick cooking spray.

2. Heat milk in small saucepan; melt butter in milk. Cool.

3. In medium bowl, beat eggs, egg whites, vanilla, cinnamon, and Splenda.

4. Combine milk and egg mixtures.

5. Place cubed bread in baking dish. Place sliced peaches on top of bread cubes. Pour egg mixture over bread and peaches. Bake for 40–45 minutes.

Nutritional Analysis (per serving): Calories: 164 | Protein: 7g | Carbohydrates: 23g | Fat: 5g | Saturated Fat: 3g | Cholesterol: 63mg | Sodium: 175mg | Fiber: 2g | PCF Ratio: 16-55-29 | Exchange Approx.: 1 Starch, ½ Fruit, 1 Fat

WHIPPED MOCHA MOUSSE

SERVES 10; SERVING SIZE: ½ CUP

¼ cup cold water

1 envelope Knox Unflavored Gelatine

¾ cup hot water

2 teaspoons instant espresso powder

½ cup sugar

¼ cup unsweetened cocoa

1½ teaspoons vanilla extract

1 recipe Nonfat Whipped Milk Base (see recipe in this chapter)

Ground cinnamon (optional)

1. Pour cold water into blender and sprinkle gelatine over it; let stand for 1 minute.

2. Add hot water and instant espresso powder; blend at low speed until gelatine is completely dissolved. Add sugar, cocoa, vanilla, and cinnamon if using; process at high speed until blended. Allow mixture to cool to at least room temperature before folding into Nonfat Whipped Milk Base. Chill until ready to serve.

Nutritional Analysis (per serving): Calories: 82 | Protein: 4g | Carbohydrates: 16g | Fat: 1g | Saturated Fat: 0g | Cholesterol: 1mg | Sodium: 37mg | Fiber: 1g | PCF Ratio: 19-77-3 | Exchange Approx.: 1 Skim Milk

KEY LIME PIE

SERVES 10; SERVING SIZE: 1 SLICE

1 cup graham cracker crumbs

1 tablespoon plus ½ cup Splenda Granulated, divided

2 tablespoons melted butter

½ teaspoon lime zest

6 ounces low-fat (Neufchâtel) cream cheese

1 package instant sugar-free vanilla pudding mix

½ cup 1% milk

1 cup lime juice (from 5 or 6 limes), divided

1 tablespoon Knox Unflavored Gelatine

Mock Whipped Cream (optional; see recipe in this chapter)

1. Preheat oven to 350°F.

2. Prepare graham cracker crust: Combine graham crumbs and 1 tablespoon Splenda. Add melted butter; mix well. Press crumbs into 9" pie plate with help of flat surface such as bottom of glass. Bake for 10 minutes; remove from oven and cool.

3. In mixer or food processor, combine lime zest and ½ cup Splenda. Add cream cheese; process for 30 seconds. Add pudding mix and milk; blend well.

4. Pour ¼ cup lime juice into small measuring cup or bowl; heat in microwave for 1 minute. Add gelatine to heated juice; dissolve completely.

5. Mix dissolved gelatine in rest of lime juice. Turn on mixer or food processor with filling mixture; pour lime juice into mixture slowly. Process until all ingredients are well combined.

6. Pour filling into pie shell; refrigerate for 3–4 hours before serving. If desired, top with Mock Whipped Cream.

Nutritional Analysis (per serving): Calories: 203 | Protein: 4g | Carbohydrates: 29g | Fat: 8g | Saturated Fat: 4g | Cholesterol: 20mg | Sodium: 331mg | Fiber: 1g | PCF Ratio: 8-57-35 | Exchange Approx.: 1½ Starches, 1½ Fats

FALL FRUIT WITH YOGURT SAUCE

SERVES 8; SERVING SIZE: ½ CUP

2 cups cubed apples

1½ cups halved red seedless grapes

1½ cups cubed pears

2 teaspoons lemon juice, divided

8 ounces light vanilla yogurt

1 tablespoon honey

¼ cup chopped walnuts

1. Combine apples, grapes, and pears in medium bowl. Drizzle 1 teaspoon lemon juice over fruit to prevent turning brown.

2. In small bowl, combine yogurt, 1 teaspoon lemon juice, and honey.

3. Portion ½ cup fruit per serving. Spoon yogurt dressing over fruit and top with chopped walnuts.

Nutritional Analysis (per serving): Calories: 126 | Protein: 3g | Carbohydrates: 26g | Fat: 3g | Saturated Fat: 1g | Cholesterol: 2mg | Sodium: 48mg | Fiber: 3g | PCF Ratio: 10-72-19 | Exchange Approx.: 1 Fruit, ½ Milk

FRUIT COMPOTE

SERVES 4; SERVING SIZE: ½ CUP

2 cups chopped apples

2 tablespoons dried cranberries

6 dried apricots, diced

¼ teaspoon ground cinnamon

2 tablespoons water

1 tablespoon brandy (optional; if not used, add additional 3 tablespoons water)

1 tablespoon finely chopped walnuts

1. Combine apples, cranberries, apricots, cinnamon, water, and brandy in small saucepan.

2. Cook over medium heat until apples are softened, about 10 minutes. Remove from heat and cover 5 minutes. Stir in walnuts before serving.

Nutritional Analysis (per serving): Calories: 117 | Protein: 1g | Carbohydrates: 24g | Fat: 2g | Saturated Fat: 1g | Cholesterol: 3mg | Sodium: 29mg | Fiber: 3g | PCF Ratio: 3-80-17 | Exchange Approx.: 1½ Fruits, ½ Fat

FAUX CHOCOLATE BAVARIAN CREAM

SERVES 4; SERVING SIZE: ½ CUP

1 envelope Knox Unflavored Gelatine

⅛ cup cold water

1½ cups plus 2 tablespoons skim milk, divided

¼ cup nonfat milk powder

2 tablespoons unsweetened cocoa

4 teaspoons sugar

⅛ cup hot water

Tip

This cream is best served right away, but if you have to wait, give it a quick blend just before using to mix in any ingredients that may have separated.

1. Soak gelatine in cold water for at least 3 minutes; heat 1½ cups skim milk in saucepan over medium heat just until bubbles begin to form around edges. Turn heat as low as it will go; add milk powder, cocoa, and sugar; stir until they dissolve. Add hot water to gelatine; stir until gelatine dissolves. Add gelatine to milk mixture; stir well. Refrigerate until set, at least 3 hours.

2. Once gelatine has set completely, put in blender with remaining 2 tablespoons of skim milk. Blend until mixture has pudding-like consistency. If necessary, add more milk.

Nutritional Analysis (per serving): Calories: 79 | Protein: 7g | Carbohydrates: 13g | Fat: 1g | Saturated Fat: 0g | Cholesterol: 3mg | Sodium: 79mg | Fiber: 1g | PCF Ratio: 33-61-6 | Exchange Approx.: 1 Skim Milk

STRAWBERRY RICOTTA PIE

SERVES 8; SERVING SIZE: 1 SLICE

2 cups part-skim ricotta cheese

1 cup graham cracker crumbs

1 tablespoon plus ¼ cup plus
   2 tablespoons Splenda Granulated,
   divided

2 tablespoons melted butter

2 eggs, separated

1 teaspoon lemon extract

2 tablespoons honey

¼ cup egg whites

¼ teaspoon cream of tartar

2 cups sliced strawberries

1 tablespoon cornstarch

1 tablespoon lemon juice

1 teaspoon balsamic vinegar

1. Place ricotta cheese in fine mesh strainer lined with coffee filter; allow excess water to drain from cheese for 2–3 hours.

2. Preheat oven to 350°F.

3. Prepare graham cracker crust: Combine graham crumbs and 1 tablespoon Splenda. Add melted butter; mix well. Press crumbs into 9" pie plate with help of flat surface such as bottom of glass. Bake for 10 minutes; remove from oven and cool.

4. Prepare pie filling: In medium bowl, mix ricotta cheese, egg yolks, lemon extract, honey, and ¼ cup Splenda.

5. In mixer bowl, beat egg whites (2 separated plus ¼ cup additional egg whites) with cream of tartar until soft peaks begin to form. Gently fold egg whites into ricotta mixture. Turn out into pie shell; bake for 45 minutes or until mixture is set and top is golden brown. Remove to wire rack and cool completely.

6. Prepare glaze: In medium saucepan, combine strawberries, cornstarch, and remaining 2 tablespoons Splenda until dry ingredients have coated strawberries. Add lemon juice and balsamic vinegar; cook over medium heat, stirring constantly. Cook mixture for 5–7 minutes or until cornstarch liquid is clear and gently bubbling. Cool.

7. Spread cooled strawberry glaze on top of cooled pie. Chill until ready to serve.

Nutritional Analysis (per serving): Calories: 238 | Protein: 10g | Carbohydrates: 27g | Fat: 10g | Saturated Fat: 5g | Cholesterol: 86mg | Sodium: 183mg | Fiber: 1g | PCF Ratio: 18-45-37 | Exchange Approx.: 1 Starch, 1 Lean Meat, 2 Fats

SUMMER FRUIT COBBLER

SERVES 8; SERVING SIZE: ½ CUP

Nonstick cooking spray

1½ cups raspberries

1½ cups peeled and sliced peaches

1 cup sliced strawberries

¼ cup plus 1 tablespoon sugar, divided

1 tablespoon Splenda Granulated

2 tablespoons plus ¾ cup whole-wheat pastry flour, divided

1 teaspoon ground cinnamon

1½ teaspoons baking powder

½ teaspoon salt

2½ tablespoons canola oil

2 tablespoons milk

2 tablespoons egg whites

Fun Fruits

Any combination of fresh fruit will work well with this recipe. You will need a total of 4 cups of fruit. Fruit suggestions include blueberries, blackberries, peaches, mangoes, or plums. Keep in mind that the nutritional analysis will vary somewhat with different fruit combinations.

1. Preheat oven to 350°F. Spray 9" × 9" square baking pan with nonstick cooking spray. Put fruit in bottom of baking dish.

2. In small bowl, mix ¼ cup sugar, Splenda, 2 tablespoons flour, and cinnamon; sprinkle evenly over fruit.

3. In small bowl, sift together ¾ cup flour, 1 tablespoon sugar, baking powder, and salt. Add oil, milk, and egg whites; stir quickly until just mixed.

4. Drop dough by spoonfuls over fruit. If desired, loosely spread dough over fruit. Bake for 25–30 minutes until dough is golden brown.

Nutritional Analysis (per serving): Calories: 152 | Protein: 3g | Carbohydrates: 26g | Fat: 5g | Saturated Fat: 0g | Cholesterol: 0mg | Sodium: 248mg | Fiber: 4g | PCF Ratio: 8-65-27 | Exchange Approx.: ½ Starch, ½ Fruit, 1 Fat

BUBBLY BERRY BLAST

SERVES 6; SERVING SIZE: ½ CUP

2 envelopes Knox Unflavored Gelatine

½ cup frozen unsweetened apple juice concentrate

3 cups (24 ounces) unsweetened sparkling water

1 cup sliced strawberries

1 cup blueberries

1. Mix gelatine and apple juice in small saucepan; stir and let stand for 1 minute. Place mixture over low heat; stir until completely dissolved, about 3 minutes. Cool slightly. (Alternatively, blend gelatine and apple juice in small microwave-safe bowl, let stand 1 minute, then microwave on high for 45 seconds; stir until gelatine is completely dissolved.)

2. Stir in sparkling water. Refrigerate until mixture begins to gel or is consistency of unbeaten egg whites when stirred.

3. Fold fruit into partially thickened gelatine mixture. Pour into 6-cup mold. Refrigerate for 4 hours or until firm.

Nutritional Analysis (per serving): Calories: 61 | Protein: 2g | Carbohydrates: 13g | Fat: 0g | Saturated Fat: 0g | Cholesterol: 0mg | Sodium: 11mg | Fiber: 1g | PCF Ratio: 15-81-4 | Exchange Approx.: 1 Fruit

BAKED PEAR CRISP

SERVES 4; SERVING SIZE: ½ CUP

Nonstick cooking spray

2 pears

2 tablespoons frozen unsweetened pineapple juice concentrate

1 teaspoon vanilla extract

1 teaspoon rum

1 tablespoon butter

⅛ cup Ener-G Pure Rice Flour

⅓ cup firmly packed brown sugar

½ cup oat bran flakes

1. Preheat oven to 375°F. Treat 9" × 13" baking dish or large flat casserole dish with nonstick cooking spray. Core and cut up pears; place in baking dish. (Except for any bruised spots, it's okay to leave skins on.)

2. In glass measuring cup, microwave frozen juice concentrate for 1 minute. Stir in vanilla and rum; pour over pears.

3. Using same measuring cup, microwave butter 30–40 seconds until melted; set aside.

4. Toss remaining ingredients in bowl, being careful not to crush cereal. Spread uniformly over pears; dribble melted butter over top. Bake for 35 minutes or until mixture is bubbling and top is just beginning to brown. Serve hot or cold.

Nutritional Analysis (per serving): Calories: 200 | Protein: 2g | Carbohydrates: 42g | Fat: 4g | Saturated Fat: 2g | Cholesterol: 8mg | Sodium: 53mg | Fiber: 3g | PCF Ratio: 3-82-15 | Exchange Approx.: 1 Fruit, 1 Fat, 1 Starch

BAKED PUMPKIN CUSTARD

SERVES 6; SERVING SIZE: ½ CUP

2 cups solid pack or mashed cooked pumpkin

¼ cup sugar

⅓ cup Splenda Granulated

2 teaspoons ground cinnamon

½ teaspoon ground ginger

⅛ teaspoon ground cloves

2 eggs, slightly beaten

¼ cup egg whites

12 ounces evaporated skim milk

Pumpkin Pie

If using this recipe for pumpkin pie, pour filling into prepared pie shell and bake in a 350°F oven for 40–45 minutes or until filling is set. The nutritional analysis per serving is: Calories: 244; Protein: 8g; Carbohydrates: 33g; Fat: 9g; Saturated fat: 3g; Cholesterol: 63mg; Sodium: 206mg; PCF Ratio: 13-33-54; Exchange Approx.: 1 Starch, 1 Milk, 1 Vegetable, 3 Fats.

1. Preheat oven to 350°F.

2. Mix together pumpkin, sugar, Splenda, cinnamon, ginger, and cloves. Add eggs, egg whites, and evaporated milk; whisk until well blended.

3. Pour into six custard cups or 1½-quart casserole dish. Set cups or casserole in large baking pan; put pan on rack in oven and pour hot water into pan to within ½" of top of custard.

4. Bake in custard cups for 40–45 minutes, 1½-quart casserole for 60–70 minutes, until knife inserted in center comes out clean. Remove immediately from hot water. Serve warm or chilled.

Nutritional Analysis (per serving): Calories: 130 | Protein: 7g | Carbohydrates: 23g | Fat: 2g | Saturated Fat: 1g | Cholesterol: 63mg | Sodium: 89mg | Fiber: 2g | PCF Ratio: 20-68-12 | Exchange Approx.: 1 Milk, 1 Vegetable, ½ Fat

STRAWBERRY RHUBARB COBBLER

SERVES 9; SERVING SIZE: ½ CUP

Nonstick cooking spray

4 cups chopped rhubarb

2 cups thickly sliced strawberries

¼ teaspoon lemon zest

⅓ cup sugar

¼ cup Splenda Granulated

2 tablespoons cornstarch

2 tablespoons water

¾ cup whole-wheat pastry flour

1 tablespoon sugar

¼ teaspoon ground ginger

1½ teaspoons baking powder

½ teaspoon salt

2½ tablespoons canola oil

2 tablespoons milk

2 tablespoons egg whites

1. Preheat oven to 375°F. Spray 8" × 8" baking dish with nonstick cooking spray.

2. In mixing bowl, combine rhubarb, strawberries, lemon zest, sugar, and Splenda. Dissolve cornstarch in water. Pour over fruit; stir to coat. Place in prepared baking dish; set aside.

3. In small bowl, sift together flour, sugar, ginger, baking powder, and salt. Add oil, milk, and egg whites; stir quickly until just mixed.

4. Drop dough by spoonfuls over fruit. If desired, loosely spread dough over fruit. Bake for 25–30 minutes until dough is golden brown.

Nutritional Analysis (per serving): Calories: 138 | Protein: 3g | Carbohydrates: 27g | Fat: 3g | Saturated Fat: 0g | Cholesterol: 7mg | Sodium: 223mg | Fiber: 3g | PCF Ratio: 7-76-17 | Exchange Approx.: ½ Starch, ½ Fruit, ½ Fat

ALMOND BISCOTTI

YIELDS 42 COOKIES; SERVING SIZE: 1 COOKIE

1 cup sugar

½ cup unsalted butter

1 tablespoon grated orange zest

2 eggs

3½ cups all-purpose flour

1 teaspoon baking powder

½ teaspoon sea salt

⅓ cup ground almonds

1. Preheat oven to 350°F.

2. Beat sugar, butter, orange zest, and eggs in small bowl.

3. Mix together flour, baking powder, and salt in large bowl; stir in egg mixture and almonds.

4. Divide dough in half; shape each half into 10" × 3" rectangle. Place on ungreased baking sheet and bake about 20 minutes or until inserted toothpick comes out clean.

5. Cool on baking sheet for 15 minutes. Cut into ½" slices; place cut-side down on baking sheet. Bake for another 15 minutes or until crisp and light brown. Cool on a wire rack.

Nutritional Analysis (per serving): Calories: 86 | Protein: 2g | Carbohydrates: 13g | Fat: 3g | Saturated Fat: 1g | Cholesterol: 9mg | Sodium: 65mg | Fiber: 0g | PCF Ratio: 8-60-32 | Exchange Approx.: ½ Fat, ½ Starch

CRANBERRY PECAN BISCOTTI

YIELDS 30 BISCOTTI; SERVING SIZE: 1 BISCOTTI

4 tablespoons sweet butter, softened

½ cup sugar

½ cup Splenda Granulated

2 eggs

½ cup egg whites

1 teaspoon vanilla extract

1 teaspoon lemon zest

2½ cups all-purpose flour

⅛ teaspoon salt

½ teaspoon baking powder

½ cup chopped pecans

½ cup dried cranberries

1. Preheat oven to 350°F. In medium bowl, beat butter, sugar, Splenda, eggs, egg whites, vanilla, and lemon zest until smooth.

2. In separate bowl, sift flour, salt, and baking powder. Add dry ingredients to liquid ingredients; mix well. Add pecans and cranberries. Chill dough for 1–2 hours, which makes it easier to handle.

3. Divide dough in half; shape each half into slightly flattened 3" × 9" loaf. Place loaves on greased cookie sheet; bake for 25 minutes.

4. Remove from oven; when cooled enough to handle, cut into ½" slices. Lay out slices on cookie sheet and return to oven for 20 minutes until toasted on bottom.

5. Remove from oven; turn over and bake for 15 minutes until other side is toasted as well. Remove from oven and cool on wire rack.

Nutritional Analysis (per serving): Calories: 98 | Protein: 3g | Carbohydrates: 15g | Fat: 3g | Saturated Fat: 1g | Cholesterol: 20mg | Sodium: 39mg | Fiber: 2g | PCF Ratio: 10-59-3 | Exchange Approx.: 1 Starch, ½ Fat

STRAWBERRY-BANANA SHERBET

SERVES 4; SERVING SIZE: ½ CUP

1⅓ cups strawberry halves

2 tablespoons sugar

1 ripe (but not overly ripe) banana, peeled and mashed

1 tablespoon frozen orange juice concentrate

2 tablespoons water

1 tablespoon lemon juice

1 cup 1% milk

2 tablespoons nonfat milk powder

1. Sprinkle sugar over strawberries. Mash strawberries with fork; allow 5 minutes or so for sugar to dissolve and draw juice out of strawberries.

2. Combine all ingredients in blender or food processor; process to desired consistency. (Some people prefer chunks of fruit; others like a smoother sherbet.)

3. Pour mixture into ice-cream maker; freeze according to manufacturer's directions or pour into ice-cube trays or covered container and freeze overnight.

Nutritional Analysis (per serving): Calories: 98 | Protein: 4g | Carbohydrates: 22g | Fat: 1g | Saturated Fat: 0g | Cholesterol: 0mg | Sodium: 45mg | Fiber: 2g | PCF Ratio: 13-83-4 | Exchange Approx.: ½ Skim Milk, ½ Fruit, ½ Carbohydrate

BANANAS FOSTER

SERVES 4; SERVING SIZE: 3 OUNCES

4 bananas, peeled and sliced

¼ cup apple juice concentrate

Grated zest of 1 orange

¼ cup fresh orange juice

1 tablespoon ground cinnamon

12 ounces nonfat frozen vanilla yogurt

Know Your Ingredients

Overripe bananas are higher in sugar and can adversely affect blood glucose levels. Freeze bananas in skins until ready to use. Doing so makes them perfect additions for fruit smoothies or fruit cups. Remove from freezer and run a little water over peel to remove any frost. Peel using a paring knife and slice according to recipe directions. Frozen bananas can be added directly to smoothies and other recipes.

1. Combine all ingredients except yogurt in nonstick skillet. Bring to a boil; cook until bananas are tender.

2. Put 3 ounces frozen yogurt in each dessert bowl or stemmed glass; spoon heated banana sauce over top.

Nutritional Analysis (per serving): Calories: 220 | Protein: 2g | Carbohydrates: 51g | Fat: 1g | Saturated Fat: 0g | Cholesterol: 0mg | Sodium: 43mg | Fiber: 4g | PCF Ratio: 4-92-4 | Exchange Approx.: 2½ Fruits, 1 Skim Milk

RASPBERRY TRIFLE

SERVES 4; SERVING SIZE: ¼ RECIPE

4 Individual Sponge Cakes (see recipe in this chapter)

1 (1.3-ounce) package vanilla sugar-free instant pudding mix

2 cups 1% milk, for pudding

1 teaspoon almond extract

2 packets Splenda

1½ cups fresh raspberries

1. Slice each sponge cake into four small slices.

2. Follow package directions for pudding mix. Add almond extract to pudding while mixing.

3. Add Splenda to fresh raspberries; mix gently until Splenda has dissolved.

4. Assemble trifle: Arrange half the cake slices in circle in bottom of small glass bowl or dish. (You can also use individual glass goblets and follow same procedure.) Place half of raspberries over top of cakes. Spread half of pudding over fruit, leaving ½" border all around. Repeat layer of cake, raspberries, and pudding. Wrap bowl in plastic wrap; refrigerate for at least 6 hours.

Nutritional Analysis (per serving): Calories: 211 | Protein: 7g | Carbohydrates: 34g | Fat: 5g | Saturated Fat: 1g | Cholesterol: 62mg | Sodium: 464mg | Fiber: 4g | PCF Ratio: 15-64-21 | Exchange Approx.: ½ Milk, ½ Starch, ½ Fruit, 1 Fat

APPLE COOKIES WITH A KICK

**YIELDS 24 COOKIES; SERVING SIZE:
1 COOKIE**

1 tablespoon ground flaxseed

¼ cup water

¼ cup firmly packed brown sugar

⅛ cup granulated sugar

¾ cup cooked drained pinto beans

⅓ cup unsweetened applesauce

2 teaspoons baking powder

⅛ teaspoon sea salt

1 teaspoon ground cinnamon

½ teaspoon ground nutmeg

¼ teaspoon ground cloves

¼ teaspoon ground allspice

1 cup VitaSpelt White Spelt Flour

1 medium-sized Golden Delicious apple

1 cup dried unroasted, unsalted sunflower seeds

Nonstick cooking spray

Creative Substitutions

Adding nuts and, of all things, beans to dessert recipes increases the amount of protein and fiber. Just because it's dessert doesn't mean it has to be all empty calories.

1. Preheat oven to 350°F.

2. Put flaxseed and water in microwave-safe container; microwave on high for 15 seconds or until mixture thickens and has consistency of egg whites. Add flaxseed mixture, sugars, beans, and applesauce to mixing bowl; mix well.

3. Sift dry ingredients together; fold into bean mixture. (Do not overmix; this will cause muffins to become tough.)

4. Peel, core, and chop apple; fold into batter with sunflower seeds.

5. Drop by teaspoonful onto baking sheet treated with nonstick spray; bake for 12–18 minutes.

Nutritional Analysis (per serving): Calories: 64 | Protein: 2g | Carbohydrates: 12g | Fat: 1g | Saturated Fat: 0g | Cholesterol: 0mg | Sodium: 67mg | Fiber: 1g | PCF Ratio: 12-71-17 | Exchange Approx.: 1 Fruit

PINEAPPLE UPSIDE-DOWN CAKE

SERVES 8; SERVING SIZE: 1 SLICE

Nonstick cooking spray

1 tablespoon brown sugar

1 (8¼-ounce) can unsweetened crushed pineapple in juice (drained, juice reserved)

1 envelope Knox Unflavored Gelatine

2 eggs

1 egg white

¾ cup granulated sugar

1 teaspoon vanilla

¾ cup all-purpose flour

1 teaspoon baking powder

¼ teaspoon salt

1. Preheat oven to 375°F. Line 9" × 1½" round baking pan with waxed paper and spray with nonstick cooking spray. Sprinkle brown sugar on waxed paper. Spread crushed pineapple evenly in bottom of pan; sprinkle gelatine over top.

2. In large bowl, beat eggs and egg white until very thick. Gradually beat in granulated sugar. Add enough water to reserved pineapple juice to measure ⅓ cup; beat into egg mixture along with vanilla.

3. In separate bowl, mix flour, baking powder, and salt; gradually add to egg mixture, beating until batter is smooth. Pour into pan. Bake about 25–30 minutes or until inserted toothpick comes out clean. Immediately loosen cake from edge of pan with knife; invert pan on plate. Carefully remove waxed paper; slice into eight pieces.

Nutritional Analysis (per serving): Calories: 138 | Protein: 3g | Carbohydrates: 32g | Fat: 0g | Saturated Fat: 0g | Cholesterol: 0g | Sodium: 83g | Fiber: 1mg | PCF Ratio: 7-92-1 | Exchange Approx.: 1 Starch, 1 Fruit

WHOLE-GRAIN MAPLE-WALNUT BREAD PUDDING

SERVES 8; SERVING SIZE: 1 WEDGE

1 cup skim milk

⅜ cup dry nonfat milk powder

2 teaspoons unsalted butter

2 eggs

1 teaspoon vanilla extract

3 tablespoons maple syrup

1 tablespoon brown sugar

Pinch of sea salt (optional)

4 ounces (4 thick slices with crusts removed) 7-Grain Bread (see recipe in Chapter 2)

¼ cup chopped walnuts

1. Preheat oven to 350°F.

2. Put milk, milk powder, butter, eggs, vanilla, syrup, brown sugar, and salt if using in food processor or blender; process until mixed.

3. Tear crustless bread into pieces; place in mixing bowl. Pour blended milk mixture over bread and add chopped walnuts; toss to mix.

4. Pour mixture into nonstick cake pan. Bake for 20 minutes or until egg is set. Cut into eight pie-shaped wedges. Serve warm or chilled.

Nutritional Analysis (per serving): Calories: 140 | Protein: 6g | Carbohydrates: 18g | Fat: 5g | Saturated Fat: 1g | Cholesterol: 55mg | Sodium: 103mg | Fiber: 1g | PCF Ratio: 16-51-33 | Exchange Approx.: 1 Starch, 1 Fat, ½ Misc. Carbohydrate

CHOCOLATE CANDY SUBSTITUTE

YIELDS 15–20 PIECES; SERVING SIZE: 1 PIECE

1 tablespoon cocoa

1 tablespoon sugar

¾ cup fresh pineapple chunks

1–3 teaspoons nonfat dry milk (optional)

Tip

The exchange approximations given for this recipe are for the entire amount; however, it's intended to be used as a way to curb a candy craving. (You grab a frozen chunk from the freezer and eat it like candy.) Discuss this recipe with your dietitian to see how you can fit it into your meal plan.

1. In small bowl, mix cocoa and sugar.

2. Place waxed paper on baking sheet. Dip each piece of pineapple in cocoa-sugar mixture. (The choice whether to coat only one side of the pineapple or all sides depends on whether you prefer a dark, bittersweet chocolate taste or a milder one.) Add dry milk powder to mixture if you prefer milk chocolate. Place each piece of pineapple on waxed paper–covered baking sheet. Place baking sheet in freezer for several hours.

3. Once pineapple is frozen, layer "candies" on waxed paper in airtight freezer container. Place a piece of aluminum foil over top layer before putting on lid to prevent freezer burn.

Nutritional Analysis (per serving): Calories: 11 | Protein: 0g | Carbohydrates: 2g | Fat: 0g | Saturated Fat: 0g | Cholesterol: 0mg | Sodium: 0mg | Fiber: 0g | PCF Ratio: 0-100-0 | Exchange Approx. (for entire recipe, without dry milk): 1 Fruit, 1 Carbohydrate/Sugar, 1 Free Drink

HONEY RAISIN BARS

YIELDS 18 BARS; SERVING SIZE: 1 BAR

½ cup unbleached all-purpose flour

¼ teaspoon baking soda

⅛ teaspoon sea salt

¼ teaspoon ground cinnamon

¾ cup quick-cooking oats

1 egg white, slightly beaten

2½ tablespoons sunflower oil

¼ cup honey

¼ cup skim milk

½ teaspoon vanilla extract

½ cup golden raisins

Nonstick cooking spray

Tip

If you like chewier cookies or need to cut the fat in your diet, you can substitute applesauce, plums, prunes, or mashed banana for the sunflower oil.

1. Preheat oven to 350°F.

2. Sift flour, soda, salt, and cinnamon together into bowl; stir in oatmeal.

3. In another bowl, mix egg white, oil, honey, milk, vanilla, and raisins; add to dry ingredients.

4. Drop by teaspoonful onto cookie sheets treated with nonstick spray; bake for 12–15 minutes. (Longer baking time will result in crispier cookies.) Cool on baking rack.

5. For cookie bars, spread mixture in an even layer on piece of parchment paper placed on cookie sheet; bake for 15–18 minutes. Cool slightly, then use sharp knife or pizza cutter to slice into eighteen equal pieces (six down, three across).

Nutritional Analysis (per serving): Calories: 71 | Protein: 1g | Carbohydrates: 12g | Fat: 2g | Saturated Fat: 0g | Cholesterol: 0mg | Sodium: 39mg | Fiber: 1g | PCF Ratio: 7-66-26 | Exchange Approx.: ½ Starch, ½ Misc. Carbohydrate

NO-BAKE CHOCOLATE–PEANUT BUTTER–OATMEAL COOKIES

SERVES 12; SERVING SIZE: 1 COOKIE

2 tablespoons butter

¼ cup cocoa

½ cup granulated sugar

¼ cup Mock Cream (see recipe in Chapter 6)

Dash of sea salt

1 teaspoon vanilla

1 tablespoon peanut butter

1½ cups oats

1. Add butter to deep, microwave-safe bowl; microwave on high for 20–30 seconds or until butter is melted.

2. Add cocoa; stir to blend. Stir in sugar, Mock Cream, and salt; microwave on high for 70 seconds to bring to full boil. (Should you need to microwave batter more, do so in 10-second increments. You want a full boil, but because it will continue to cook for a while once it's removed from microwave, heating too long can cause mixture to scorch.)

3. Add vanilla and peanut butter; stir until mixed. Fold in oats. Drop by tablespoonful on waxed paper and allow to cool.

Nutritional Analysis (per serving, with granulated sugar): Calories: 87 | Protein: 2g | Carbohydrates: 13g | Fat: 3g | Saturated Fat: 2g | Cholesterol: 5mg | Sodium: 26mg | Fiber: 1g | PCF Ratio: 7-61-32 | Exchange Approx.: ½ Fat, 1 Starch

SPARKLING FRUITED ICED TEA

SERVES 4; SERVING SIZE: ¼ RECIPE

3 cups decaffeinated tea

1 cup unsweetened orange juice

4 teaspoons fresh lemon juice

1 (12-ounce) can carbonated ginger ale

Seltzer water, club soda, or other unsweetened carbonated water

1. In pitcher, mix together tea, orange juice, and lemon juice. In tall iced-tea glasses (16- to 20-ounce size), place 4 or 5 ice cubes.

2. Pour tea and juice mixture over ice; evenly divide ginger ale between glasses.

3. Add carbonated water to finish filling glasses; stir to mix. Serve.

Nutritional Analysis (per serving): Calories: 62 | Protein: 0g | Carbohydrates: 16g | Fat: 0g | Saturated Fat: 0g | Cholesterol: 0mg | Sodium: 12mg | Fiber: 0g | PCF Ratio: 3-97-1 | Exchange Approx.: 1 Fruit

GINGER LIME ICED TEA

SERVES 6; SERVING SIZE: ⅙ RECIPE

6 cups boiling water

4 green tea bags

2 tablespoons honey

1 tablespoon lime juice

1 tablespoon coarsely chopped crystallized ginger

1. In ceramic or glass container, pour boiling water over tea bags, honey, lime juice, and ginger; cover and allow to steep for 5 minutes. Stir until honey is dissolved.

2. Remove teabags and ginger. Chill in refrigerator and serve over ice. (May also be served hot.)

Nutritional Analysis (per serving): Calories: 23 | Protein: 0g | Carbohydrates: 6g | Fat: 0g | Saturated Fat: 0g | Cholesterol: 0mg | Sodium: 0mg | Fiber: 0g | PCF Ratio: 1-99-0 | Exchange Approx.: ½ Misc. Carbohydrate

HOT SPICED TEA

SERVES 4; SERVING SIZE: ¼ RECIPE

2 tea bags

14 whole cloves

1 cinnamon stick

1 strip (about 3") fresh orange peel

2 cups boiling water

¼ cup orange juice

1½ tablespoons lemon juice

1. Put tea bags, spices, and orange peel in ceramic or glass container; pour boiling water over. Cover and allow to steep for 5 minutes.

2. Strain; stir in orange and lemon juices. Reheat if necessary. You can also chill it and serve over ice for a refreshing iced tea.

Nutritional Analysis (per serving): Calories: 8 | Protein: 0g | Carbohydrates: 2g | Fat: 0g | Saturated Fat: 0g | Cholesterol: 0mg | Sodium: 3mg | Fiber: 0g | PCF Ratio: 5-93-2 | Exchange Approx.: ½ Free

ICED AND SPICED CHAI-STYLE TEA

SERVES 4; SERVING SIZE: ¼ RECIPE

2 cups skim milk

¼ cup honey (optional)

½ teaspoon ground cinnamon

¼ teaspoon ground ginger

⅛ teaspoon ground allspice

4 tea bags

2 cups chilled unflavored, unsweetened carbonated water

Tip

This tea is also terrific when served warm in mugs; just replace the carbonated water with warm water.

1. In medium saucepan, bring milk just to boil. Stir in remaining ingredients except for carbonated water. Reduce heat to low and simmer uncovered for 3 minutes.

2. Remove tea bags and strain; chill. Serve over ice, adding an equal amount of carbonated water to each serving.

Nutritional Analysis (per serving): Calories: 108 | Protein: 4g | Carbohydrates: 23g | Fat: 1g | Saturated Fat: 0g | Cholesterol: 0mg | Sodium: 65mg | Fiber: 0g | PCF Ratio: 14-82-4 | Exchange Approx.: 1 Misc. Carbohydrate, ½ Skim Milk

SPICED CHAI-STYLE CREAMER MIX

YIELDS 15 TEASPOONS; SERVING SIZE: 1 TABLESPOON

½ cup nonfat dry milk

1½ teaspoons ground cinnamon

¼ teaspoon ground nutmeg

¼ teaspoon ground cloves

½ teaspoon ground ginger

¼ teaspoon ground allspice

¼ cup sugar

Combine all ingredients in lidded jar; shake to mix. Store in a cool, dry place. Because this recipe uses noninstant nonfat milk, it must be stirred into hot liquid. For iced tea, you can mix in "creamer" using a blender.

Nutritional Analysis (per serving): Calories: 86 | Protein: 4g | Carbohydrates: 17g | Fat: 0g | Saturated Fat: 0g | Cholesterol: 0mg | Sodium: 65mg | Fiber: 0g | PCF Ratio: 20-78-2 | Exchange Approx.: 1 Misc. Carbohydrate

TANGY LIMEADE

6 fresh limes

½ cup granulated sugar

2½ cups water

½ teaspoon salt (optional)

12 ice cubes or 1½ cups cold water

Carbonated Limeade

To make a concentrate that can be stored in refrigerator for up to 3 days, reduce the boiling water to 1 cup. In a glass, combine 3 tablespoons of the concentrate with enough seltzer water or club soda to fill an 8- to 12-ounce glass. Remember that more carbonated water will produce a weaker-tasting beverage. Exchange approximations: 1 Misc. Carbohydrate, ½ Fruit.

1. Roll limes on cutting board using hard pressure to loosen flesh and release juices. Cut limes in half and juice them, minus any seeds and pith. Place rinds in noncorrosive metal or glass container; cover with sugar and set aside.

2. Bring water to boil, pour over rinds and sugar mixture and add lime juice. Allow to steep for 5–10 minutes, depending on your taste. (Two minutes is sufficient for an intense lime flavor; 10 minutes will have a hint of bitterness. If you prefer a sweeter limeade, omit rinds and steep mixture with juice and pulp.)

3. If you're using optional salt, add it now and stir thoroughly. Strain warm liquid. Add ice cubes; stir until ice is melted. Serve over additional ice cubes.

Nutritional Analysis (per serving, without salt): Calories: 65 | Protein: 0g | Carbohydrates: 18g | Fat: 0g | Saturated Fat: 0g | Cholesterol: 0mg | Sodium: 1mg | Fiber: 1.41g | PCF Ratio: 2-97-1 | Exchange Approx.: 1 Misc. Carbohydrate

ORANGE-PINEAPPLE FROTH

SERVES 1

1 tablespoon frozen orange juice
concentrate

1 tablespoon frozen pineapple juice
concentrate

1 cup skim milk

½ cup chilled water

½ teaspoon vanilla extract

Combine all ingredients in blender; process until mixed.
Serve in chilled glass.

Nutritional Analysis (per serving): Calories: 153 | Protein:
9g | Carbohydrates: 27g | Fat: 1g | Saturated Fat:
0g | Cholesterol: 5mg | Sodium: 129mg | Fiber: 0g | PCF Ratio:
24-73-3 | Exchange Approx.: 2 Fruits, 1 Skim Milk

PINEAPPLE-BANANA BLAST

SERVES 1

¼ frozen banana, peeled and sliced

1 tablespoon frozen pineapple juice
concentrate

3 tablespoons water

½ cup buttermilk

Combine all ingredients in blender; process until mixed.
Serve in chilled glass.

Nutritional Analysis (per serving): Calories: 109 | Protein:
5g | Carbohydrates: 21g | Fat: 1g | Saturated Fat:
1g | Cholesterol: 4mg | Sodium: 129mg | Fiber: 1g | PCF Ratio:
16-74-10 | Exchange Approx.: 1 Fruit, ½ Skim Milk

MINTED RASPBERRY LEMONADE

SERVES 8; SERVING SIZE: ⅛ RECIPE

½ cup raspberries

1½ cups lemon juice

8 packets sweetener or to taste

6 cups water

1 tablespoon finely chopped fresh mint or
1 teaspoon dried mint

Bubbly Touch-of-Fruit Taste Drink

Another soft drink option is to pour 1 cup of chilled, unsweetened club soda or seltzer over fresh or frozen fruit. The fruit imparts subtle flavor and sweetness to the beverage, and when the drink is gone, you can eat the fruit for dessert. Nutritional analysis depends on the chosen fruit, but for any choice, exchange approx.: ½ Fruit.

1. Mash raspberries; press through fine mesh sieve to remove seeds.

2. Add raspberries, lemon juice, sweetener, water, and mint to 2-quart pitcher; stir. Serve chilled over ice.

Nutritional Analysis (per serving): Calories: 19 | Protein: 0g | Carbohydrates: 6g | Fat: 0g | Saturated Fat: 0g | Cholesterol: 0mg | Sodium: 4mg | Fiber: 1g | PCF Ratio: 5-93-2 | Exchange Approx.: ½ Fruit

KIWI-LIME COOLER

SERVES 2; SERVING SIZE: ½ RECIPE

1 cup ice cubes

1 tablespoon lime juice

1 cup light vanilla yogurt

2 ripe kiwi, peeled and sliced

1 or 2 packets artificial sweetener or to taste

The Chinese Gooseberry

Kiwi is also known as Chinese gooseberry. Kiwi is a very nutrient-dense food rich in vitamin C, fiber, and potassium. This versatile little fruit can be used in beverages, salads, and salsas, or as a beautiful edible garnish. Native to China, kiwi is now grown in many parts of the world and is easy to find in grocery stores and produce markets.

Combine all ingredients in blender; process until mixed. Serve in chilled glass.

Nutritional Analysis (per serving): Calories: 135 | Protein: 8g | Carbohydrates: 26g | Fat: 1g | Saturated Fat: 0g | Cholesterol: 2mg | Sodium: 97mg | Fiber: 3g | PCF Ratio: 23-73-5 | Exchange Approx.: 1 Skim Milk, 1 Fruit

STRAWBERRY COOLER

SERVES 1

½ cup frozen strawberries

¼ cup apple juice

Sparkling water

In a large tumbler, add ½ cup frozen strawberries. Pour ¼ cup apple juice over strawberries; finish filling glass with sparkling water. Stir and serve with an iced-tea spoon.

Nutritional Analysis (per serving): Calories: 52 | Protein: 1g | Carbohydrates: 13g | Fat: 0g | Saturated Fat: 0g | Cholesterol: 0mg | Sodium: 3mg | Fiber: 2g | PCF Ratio: 4-91-6 | Exchange Approx.: 1 Fruit

NECTARINE COCKTAIL

SERVES 4; SERVING SIZE: ¼ RECIPE

2 cups buttermilk

2 large chilled nectarines, peeled and cut into pieces

⅛ cup brown sugar

Combine buttermilk, nectarines, and brown sugar in blender; process until nectarines are puréed. Serve in chilled glass.

Nutritional Analysis (per serving): Calories: 109 | Protein: 5g | Carbohydrates: 21g | Fat: 1g | Saturated Fat: 1g | Cholesterol: 4mg | Sodium: 131mg | Fiber: 1g | PCF Ratio: 17-72-11 | Exchange Approx.: 1 Fruit, ½ Skim Milk

STRAWBERRY ALMOND TARTS

**YIELDS 16 MINI TARTS; SERVING SIZE:
1 TART**

½ cup creamy almond butter

¼ cup plus 1 tablespoon honey, divided

¾ cup old-fashioned rolled oats

2 tablespoons oat flour or all-purpose flour

Cooking spray and mini muffin liners

¾ cup sliced fresh strawberries

⅓ cup light cream cheese

1 tablespoon lemon juice

Serving Tip
These tarts will get very soft if left out for more than 10–15 minutes, so they are best served while they are frozen or only slightly thawed.

1. To make the crust, mix the almond butter, ¼ cup honey, oats, and flour in a medium-sized bowl. Add sixteen mini muffin liners to a mini muffin tin and spray them lightly with cooking spray. Roll the dough out into an 8" × 8" square and cut into sixteen equal-sized pieces. Roll each square up into a ball; add to the muffin tin. Press a hole in the middle and then press the dough against the edges of the tin to form the shape of the crust for sixteen tarts.

2. To make the filling, add the strawberries, cream cheese, 1 tablespoon honey, and the lemon juice to a medium-sized bowl and whip with an electric mixer until blended together and the strawberries are mostly puréed to a uniform mixture. (There will be small bits of berries here and there.)

3. Spoon the filling into the tin with the crusts, dividing it evenly amongst the tarts. Freeze for about 3–4 hours until the centers are very firm. Serve frozen.

Nutritional Analysis (per serving): Calories: 100 | Protein: 3g | Carbohydrates: 10g | Fat: 6g | Saturated Fat: 1g | Cholesterol: 5mg | Sodium: 60mg | Fiber: 1g | PCF Ratio: 14-38-48 | Exchange Approx.: ¼ Starch, ½ Other Carbohydrate, 1 Fat

RASPBERRY BANANA ALMOND BARS

YIELDS 16 BARS; SERVING SIZE: 1 BAR

Cooking spray

½ heaping cup creamy or crunchy unsalted almond butter

½ cup pure maple syrup

1 packed cup mashed overripe banana

½ cup egg whites

1 tablespoon vanilla extract

½ teaspoon baking powder

1¾ cups old-fashioned rolled oats

¾ cup chopped fresh raspberries

Storage and Serving Tip

These bars are very moist, almost cake-like, and can be a bit crumbly. They are best stored in an airtight container in the fridge to keep longer. Pop them in the microwave for 10 seconds to warm them up for a nice treat.

1. Preheat oven to 350°F. Coat a 9" × 9" pan with cooking spray.

2. Add the almond butter, maple syrup, banana, egg whites, vanilla, and baking powder to a medium bowl and blend using an electric mixer.

3. Stir in the oats and the raspberries by hand and add the batter to the pan.

4. Bake for 35–40 minutes until the top is set and lightly browned on the edges. Cut into squares and serve.

Nutritional Analysis (per serving): Calories: 130 | Protein: 4g | Carbohydrates: 18g | Fat: 5g | Saturated Fat: 0g | Cholesterol: 0mg | Sodium: 30mg | Fiber: 2g | PCF Ratio: 12-54-32 | Exchange Approx.: ¾ Starch, ¼ Fruit, ½ High-Fat Meat

BANANA CAKE

SERVES 12; SERVING SIZE: 1 SQUARE

Cooking spray

1¼ cups oat flour

1½ teaspoons baking soda

½ teaspoon baking powder

1 egg

½ cup packed brown sugar

¼ cup margarine, softened

¼ cup light pancake syrup

½ cup nonfat Greek yogurt

1 cup smashed ripe banana

½ teaspoon vanilla extract

1. Preheat oven to 350°F. Coat a 9" × 9" pan with cooking spray.

2. Mix the flour, baking soda, and baking powder in a small bowl.

3. In a larger bowl, beat the egg, brown sugar, margarine, syrup, Greek yogurt, banana, and vanilla.

4. Slowly add the flour mixture to the larger bowl with the egg/sugar mixture and stir until a soft, thick batter is formed.

5. Pour the batter into the pan and bake for 25 minutes or until a toothpick placed in the center comes out mostly clean and the top is set and lightly brown. Cut the cake into twelve squares and serve.

Nutritional Analysis (per serving): Calories: 140 | Protein: 2g | Carbohydrates: 21g | Fat: 5g | Saturated Fat: 1g | Cholesterol: 15mg | Sodium: 240mg | Fiber: 1g | PCF Ratio: 6-62-32 | Exchange Approx.: ¼ Starch, ¾ Other Carbohydrate, ¼ Fruit, 1 Fat

CORNFLAKE ENERGY BITES

YIELDS 16 BITES; SERVING SIZE: 1 BITE

½ cup creamy or crunchy peanut butter

¼ cup pure maple syrup or honey

1 teaspoon vanilla extract

¼ cup dried cranberries

1½ cups crushed cornflakes

Wax or parchment paper or cooking spray

1. In a medium bowl, combine the peanut butter, maple syrup or honey, and vanilla and mix well. Stir in the cranberries and cornflakes and continue to mix until well incorporated.

2. Form into balls and place on wax/parchment paper or a container lightly coated with cooking spray and refrigerate for at least 1 hour. Store in the fridge in an airtight container.

Nutritional Analysis (per serving): Calories: 80 | Protein: 2g | Carbohydrates: 8g | Fat: 4g | Saturated Fat: 0.5g | Cholesterol: 0mg | Sodium: 50mg | Fiber: 1g | PCF Ratio: 10-42-48 | Exchange Approx.: ½ Starch, 1 Fat

RASPBERRY YOGURT POPS

YIELDS 6 POPSICLES; SERVING SIZE: 1 POPSICLE

2 (8-ounce) containers nonfat raspberry yogurt

½ heaping cup washed and halved fresh raspberries

1 teaspoon vanilla extract

6 (6-ounce) popsicle holders with sticks

Mix the yogurt, raspberries, and vanilla in a small bowl. Carefully spoon all of the mixture into the popsicle holders, add sticks, and freeze for 2–4 hours until set.

Nutritional Analysis (per serving): Calories: 50 | Protein: 3g | Carbohydrates: 10g | Fat: 0g | Saturated Fat: 0g | Cholesterol: 0mg | Sodium: 40mg | Fiber: 0g | PCF Ratio: 21-76-3 | Exchange Approx.: ⅔ Skim Milk

SIMPLE SUNFLOWER BARS

YIELDS 16 SQUARES; SERVING SIZE: 1 SQUARE

½ cup creamy sunflower butter

¼ cup pure maple syrup

¼ teaspoon vanilla extract

1 cup old-fashioned rolled oats

¼ cup sunflower seeds

Wax or parchment paper

1. In a medium-sized bowl, combine the sunflower butter, maple syrup, and vanilla and mix well. Stir in the oats and sunflower seeds and mix some more.

2. To press mixture into an 8" × 8" pan, line the pan with a large rectangular piece of parchment paper, place the mixture on one side, and then fold the paper over to press down (this works nicely since the dough is sticky).

3. Chill in the refrigerator for 1 hour or more, cut into sixteen squares, and serve. Store squares in the refrigerator in an airtight container.

Nutritional Analysis (per serving): Calories: 90 | Protein: 3g | Carbohydrates: 8g | Fat: 5g | Saturated Fat: 0.5g | Cholesterol: 0mg | Sodium: 40mg | Fiber: 2g | PCF Ratio: 10-36-54 | Exchange Approx.: ¼ Starch, ¼ Other Carbohydrate, 1 Fat

ALMOND CRANBERRY WHITE CHOCOLATE OAT BARS

YIELDS 16 SQUARES; SERVING SIZE: 1 SQUARE

½ cup creamy or crunchy unsalted almond butter

½ cup light pancake syrup

½ teaspoon vanilla

1 cup old-fashioned rolled oats

2 tablespoons white chocolate chips

2 tablespoons dried cranberries

2 tablespoons shredded unsweetened coconut

Wax or parchment paper

1. In a medium-sized bowl, combine the almond butter, syrup, and vanilla and mix well. Stir in the oats, white chocolate chips, cranberries, and coconut and mix some more.

2. To press mixture into an 8" × 8" pan, line the pan with a large rectangular piece of parchment paper, place the mixture on one side, and then fold the paper over to press down (this works nicely since the dough is sticky). Chill in the refrigerator for 1 hour or more, cut into squares, and serve. Store in the refrigerator.

Nutritional Analysis (per serving): Calories: 80 | Protein: 2g | Carbohydrates: 7g | Fat: 5g | Saturated Fat: 1g | Cholesterol: 0mg | Sodium: 15mg | Fiber: 1g | PCF Ratio: 12-31-57 | Exchange Approx.: ¼ Starch, ¼ Other Carbohydrate, 1 Fat

PUMPKIN SPICE CAKE

SERVES 12; SERVING SIZE: 1 SQUARE

Cooking spray

1¼ cups oat flour

1½ teaspoons baking soda

½ teaspoon baking powder

1 teaspoon pumpkin pie spice

½ teaspoon ground cinnamon

1 egg

1 cup packed brown sugar

¼ cup margarine, softened

¼ cup light pancake syrup

½ cup nonfat Greek yogurt

1 cup canned or fresh cooked pumpkin purée (not pumpkin pie filling)

1. Preheat oven to 350°F. Coat a 9" × 9" pan with cooking spray.

2. Mix the flour, baking soda, baking powder, pie spice, and cinnamon in a small bowl. In a larger bowl, beat together the egg, brown sugar, margarine, syrup, Greek yogurt, and pumpkin.

3. Slowly add the flour mixture to the larger bowl with the egg/sugar mixture and stir until a soft, thick batter is formed.

4. Pour the batter into the pan and bake for 30–35 minutes or until a toothpick placed in the center comes out mostly clean and the top is set and lightly brown. Cut the cake into twelve squares and serve.

Nutritional Analysis (per serving): Calories: 160 | Protein: 2g | Carbohydrates: 27g | Fat: 5g | Saturated Fat: 1g | Cholesterol: 15mg | Sodium: 250mg | Fiber: 2g | PCF Ratio: 5-67-28 | Exchange Approx.: ½ Starch, 1 Other Carbohydrate, 1 Fat

PEANUT BUTTER RICE KRISPIES TREATS

YIELDS 16 BARS; SERVING SIZE: 1 BAR

1 cup creamy or crunchy peanut butter

½ cup pure maple syrup or honey

1 teaspoon vanilla extract

2½ cups Rice Krispies

¼ cup chocolate chips

Wax or parchment paper

1. In a medium bowl, combine the peanut butter, syrup or honey, and vanilla and mix well. Stir in the Rice Krispies and chocolate chips and continue to mix until well incorporated.

2. To press mixture into an 8" × 8" pan, line the pan with a large rectangular piece of parchment paper, place the mixture on one side, and then fold the paper over to press down (this works nicely since the dough is sticky). Refrigerate for at least 1 hour, cut into squares, and serve. Store in the refrigerator in an airtight container.

Nutritional Analysis (per serving): Calories: 160 | Protein: 5g | Carbohydrates: 16g | Fat: 9g | Saturated Fat: 1.5g | Cholesterol: 10mg | Sodium: 90mg | Fiber: 2g | PCF Ratio: 11-39-50 | Exchange Approx.: ¼ Starch, ½ Other Carbohydrate, ½ High-Fat Meat, 1 Fat

CARROT CAKE MACAROONS

YIELDS 30 COOKIES; SERVING SIZE: 1 COOKIE

Cooking spray

4 tablespoons white whole-wheat flour

¼ teaspoon ground nutmeg

¼ teaspoon ground cinnamon

⅛ teaspoon ground ginger (optional)

2 cups unsweetened, finely shredded coconut

½ cup liquid egg whites

½ cup honey

2 tablespoons chopped pecans

2 tablespoons raisins

A Few Helpful Tips

Oat flour and all-purpose flour also work well in this recipe. Using a small scooper to portion out the cookie dough helps them keep a nice round shape.

1. Preheat oven to 350°F. Coat two or three baking sheets with cooking spray.

2. Combine the flour, spices, and coconut in a small bowl. In a larger bowl, beat together the egg whites and honey.

3. Slowly add the flour/coconut mixture to the larger bowl with the egg whites and honey and stir until thoroughly mixed. Fold in the pecans and raisins.

4. Drop in small spoonfuls onto the greased cookie sheets to make thirty cookies and bake 11–15 minutes until tops are firm and bottoms are very lightly browned.

Nutritional Analysis (per serving): Calories: 70 | Protein: 1g | Carbohydrates: 7g | Fat: 4.5g | Saturated Fat: 3.5g | Cholesterol: 0mg | Sodium: 0mg | Fiber: 1g | PCF Ratio: 3-41-56 | Exchange Approx.: ½ Other Carbohydrate, 1 Fat

WHITE CHOCOLATE WALNUT COOKIES

YIELDS 24 COOKIES; SERVING SIZE: 1 COOKIE

Cooking spray

1¼ cups oat flour

½ cup old-fashioned rolled oats

½ teaspoon baking powder

1 egg

½ cup margarine, slightly softened

¾ cup brown sugar

½ cup white chocolate chips

¼ cup finely chopped walnuts

1. Preheat oven to 350°F and coat two baking sheets with cooking spray.

2. Mix flour, oats, and baking powder in a small to medium bowl. In a larger bowl, beat together the egg, margarine, and brown sugar.

3. Slowly add the flour mixture to the larger bowl with the egg/sugar mixture and stir until a soft, thick dough is formed. Fold in the white chocolate chips and walnuts. Refrigerate the dough overnight or at least a few hours for best results.

4. Drop the cookie dough in rounded spoonfuls onto the baking sheets to make twenty-four cookies. Bake for 10–15 minutes or until lightly browned around the edges.

Nutritional Analysis (per serving): Calories: 110 | Protein: 1g | Carbohydrates: 13g | Fat: 6g | Saturated Fat: 1.5g | Cholesterol: 10mg | Sodium: 55mg | Fiber: 1g | PCF Ratio: 4-47-49 | Exchange Approx.: ¼ Starch, ½ Other Carbohydrate, 1 Fat

LIGHT CREAM CHEESE FROSTING

YIELDS 12 TABLESPOONS; SERVING SIZE: 1 TABLESPOON

1 (8-ounce) tub light cream cheese

2 tablespoons powdered sugar

Put both ingredients in a medium bowl and mix well by hand or with an electric mixer. Store unused portions in an airtight container in the refrigerator for up to 1 week.

Nutritional Analysis (per serving): Calories: 45 | Protein: 1g | Carbohydrates: 2g | Fat: 3g | Saturated Fat: 2g | Cholesterol: 10mg | Sodium: 81mg | Fiber: 0g | PCF Ratio: 22-22-56 | Exchange Approx.: ¼ Other Carbohydrate, ½ Fat

MAPLE GLAZE

YIELDS ¼ CUP; SERVING SIZE: 1 TEASPOON

½ cup powdered sugar

2 teaspoons water

½ teaspoon maple flavoring/extract

Great Ways to Glaze
This glaze is delicious served over Autumn Apple Cake and Fall Pumpkin Cookies (see recipes in this chapter).

Whisk all of the ingredients together in a small bowl until a smooth glaze is formed.

Nutritional Analysis (per serving): Calories: 20 | Protein: 0g | Carbohydrates: 5g | Fat: 0g | Saturated Fat: 0g | Cholesterol: 0mg | Sodium: 80mg | Fiber: 0g | PCF Ratio: 0-100-0 | Exchange Approx.: ¼ Other Carbohydrate

AUTUMN APPLE CAKE

SERVES 12; SERVING SIZE: 1 SQUARE

Cooking spray

1¼ cups whole-wheat pastry flour

1½ teaspoons baking soda

1 teaspoon ground cinnamon

1 egg

½ cup packed brown sugar

¼ cup margarine, softened

¼ cup light pancake syrup

½ cup nonfat Greek yogurt

3 cups chopped apples

1. Preheat oven to 350°F. Coat a 9" × 9" pan with cooking spray.

2. Mix the flour, baking soda, and cinnamon in a small bowl. In a larger bowl, beat together the egg, brown sugar, margarine, syrup, and Greek yogurt.

3. Slowly add the flour mixture to the larger bowl with the egg/sugar mixture and stir until a soft, thick batter is formed. Fold in the chopped apples.

4. Pour the batter into the pan and bake for 35 minutes or until a toothpick placed in the center comes out mostly clean and the top is set and lightly brown. Cut the cake into twelve squares and serve.

Nutritional Analysis (per serving): Calories: 140 | Protein: 3g | Carbohydrates: 23g | Fat: 4g | Saturated Fat: 1g | Cholesterol: 15mg | Sodium: 233mg | Fiber: 2g | PCF Ratio: 9-66-25 | Exchange Approx.: ¼ Starch, 1 Other Carbohydrate, 1 Fat

FALL PUMPKIN COOKIES

YIELDS 24 COOKIES; SERVING SIZE: 1 COOKIE

Cooking spray

1 cup whole-wheat pastry flour

1¼ cups old-fashioned rolled oats

1 teaspoon baking soda

1½ teaspoons pumpkin pie spice or ground cinnamon

1 cup brown sugar

1 egg

¼ cup margarine, softened

¾ cup fresh cooked or canned pumpkin (not pumpkin pie filling)

½ cup raisins

1. Preheat oven to 350°F. Coat two baking sheets with cooking spray.

2. Mix the flour, oats, baking soda, and pumpkin pie spice in a small to medium bowl. In a larger bowl, mix the brown sugar, egg, margarine, and pumpkin.

3. Slowly add the flour mixture to the larger bowl with the egg/sugar mixture and stir until a soft, thick dough is formed. Fold in the raisins. Refrigerate the dough overnight or at least a few hours for best results.

4. Drop the cookie dough in rounded spoonfuls onto the baking sheets to make twenty-four cookies. Bake for 14–17 minutes or until lightly browned.

Nutritional Analysis (per serving): Calories: 90 | Protein: 1g | Carbohydrates: 17g | Fat: 2.5g | Saturated Fat: 0.5g | Cholesterol: 10mg | Sodium: 75mg | Fiber: 1g | PCF Ratio: 6-70-24 | Exchange Approx.: ½ Starch, ½ Other Carbohydrate, ¼ Fat

CHEWY OAT RAISIN COOKIES

YIELDS 24 COOKIES; SERVING SIZE: 1 COOKIE

Cooking spray

1 cup whole-wheat pastry flour

1½ cups old-fashioned rolled oats

1 teaspoon baking soda

1 teaspoon ground cinnamon

¾ cup brown sugar

1 egg

¼ cup margarine, softened

½ cup applesauce

1 teaspoon vanilla extract

¾ cup raisins

1. Preheat oven to 350°F and coat two baking sheets with cooking spray.

2. Mix flour, oats, baking soda, and cinnamon in a small to medium bowl. In a larger bowl, mix the brown sugar, egg, margarine, applesauce, and vanilla.

3. Slowly add the flour mixture to the larger bowl with the egg/sugar mixture and stir until a soft, thick dough is formed. Stir in the raisins and drop the cookie dough in rounded spoonfuls onto the baking sheets to make twenty-four cookies. Bake for 15 minutes or until lightly browned.

Nutritional Analysis (per serving): Calories: 80 | Protein: 1g | Carbohydrates: 15g | Fat: 2.5g | Saturated Fat: 0.5g | Cholesterol: 10mg | Sodium: 75mg | Fiber: 1g | PCF Ratio: 4-48-48 | Exchange Approx.: ¼ Starch, ¼ Fruit, ½ Other Carbohydrate

BAKED APPLES

YIELDS 4 LARGE BAKED APPLES; SERVING SIZE: ½ APPLE

4 large apples

1 tablespoon brown sugar

1 teaspoon ground cinnamon

2 tablespoons light pancake syrup

1 tablespoon plus ⅔ cup water, divided

2 tablespoons chopped pecans or walnuts

2 tablespoons dried cranberries or raisins

1 teaspoon light margarine

1. Preheat the oven to 350°F. Core through the middle of the apples, stopping short of going through the bottom (leaving about ½"). Place them in a shallow 2-quart baking dish.

2. In a small bowl, mix the brown sugar and cinnamon together, whisk in the syrup and the 1 tablespoon water, and stir in the nuts and dried fruit. Spoon the mixture into the apples.

3. Divide the teaspoon of margarine between the apples, putting a dollop on each.

4. Add the ⅔ cup water to the bottom of the dish and cover with a lid or aluminum foil. Bake for about 40 minutes or until apples are soft when pierced with a fork or toothpick.

Nutritional Analysis (per serving): Calories: 90 | Protein: 1g | Carbohydrates: 21g | Fat: 2g | Saturated Fat: 0g | Cholesterol: 0mg | Sodium: 15mg | Fiber: 3g | PCF Ratio: 2-79-19 | Exchange Approx.: 1 Fruit, ¼ Other Carbohydrate, ¼ Fat

RESOURCES

AS YOU LEARN MORE ABOUT DIABETES, YOU may have more questions or want to find additional information. The following resources provide a wealth of information regarding diabetes in general, as well as diets, forums, and frequently asked questions.

RECOMMENDED WEBSITES

Ask the Dietitian

www.dietitian.com
Joanne Larsen, MS, RD, LD, maintains this site. Post specific diet-related questions or read the answers to questions from other visitors.

American Diabetes Association

www.diabetes.org
This site, maintained by the recognized authority on diabetes, is dedicated to poviding up-to-date information regarding medications and diabetes research findings.

Academy of Nutrition and Dietetics

www.eatright.org
The Academy of Nutrition and Dietetics is the world's largest organization of food and nutrition professionals. This site provides nutrition information and resources on a variety of topics and includes a tool to find a dietitian in your area.

dLife

www.dLife.com
An interactive diabetes website that includes diabetes information, tips for healthy eating, a recipe bank, and a diabetic community.

National Institute of Diabetes and Digestive and Kidney Disease

www.niddk.nih.gov
Site for general diabetes information, where brochures and articles can be downloaded.

The U.S. National Library of Medicine and National Institutes of Health

www.nlm.nih.gov/medlineplus/diabetes.html
This site has research, references, an interactive tutorial, consumer materials, and guidebooks to download or order online.

Cornerstones4Care

www.conerstones4care.com
An interactive website with information and a personalized action plan for managing diabetes.

ONLINE SOURCES FOR INGREDIENTS AND EQUIPMENT

The quality of the foods you prepare is based on the quality of the ingredients you use; that's elementary. The equipment you use can make a difference, too. Even if you don't have a gourmet grocery or cooking supply store nearby, you don't have to forego using out-of-the-ordinary ingredients or products you've been wanting to try. Chances are you can order them online through one of these sites:

CHEFS Catalog

www.chefscatalog.com

McCormick

www.mccormick.com

Bob's Red Mill

www.bobsredmill.com

King Arthur Flour

www.kingarthurflour.com

Cabot

www.cabotcheese.coop

Ancient Harvest

www.ancientharvest.com

Mrs. Dash

www.mrsdash.com

MexGrocer.com

www.mexgrocer.com

Barilla

www.barillaus.com

Whole Foods Market

www.wholefoodsmarket.com

Trader Joe's

www.traderjoes.com

LocalHarvest

www.localharvest.org
Use this website to find farmers' markets, family farms, and other sources of sustainably grown food in your area where you can buy produce, grass-fed meats, and many other locally grown foods.

EXCHANGE LIST

BECAUSE FOOD EXCHANGE LISTS CAN BE AN important part of arriving at an individualized meal plan, this appendix covers many of the common foods found on such lists. Please remember that the information contained in this book is not intended as medical advice. Consult your dietitian with any questions or details regarding the diet he or she has designed specifically for you. The information presented here is intended as a general guide only.

KEY
† = 3 grams or more of fiber per serving
‡ = High in sodium; if more than 1 serving is eaten, these foods have 400mg or more of sodium.
1 Carbohydrate Exchange List choice = 15g carbohydrates
1 Protein Exchange List choice = 7g protein
1 Milk Exchange List choice = 12g carbohydrates and 8g protein
1 Fat Exchange List choice = 5g fat

STARCHES AND BREAD

These are the foods found on the bottom tier of the food pyramid. Each exchange in this category contains about 15 grams of carbohydrates, 3 grams of protein, and a trace of fat, for a total of 80 calories. Serving sizes may vary. A general rule is that ½ cup of cooked cereal, grain, or pasta equals 1 exchange, and 1 ounce of a bread product is 1 serving. Those foods within this category that contain 3 grams or more of fiber are identified using a † symbol.

Plain roll, small	1 (1 ounce)
Raisin, unfrosted	1 slice
Rye†, pumpernickel	1 slice (1 ounce)
Tortilla, 6" across	1
White (including French, Italian)	1 slice (1 ounce)
Whole wheat	1 slice

CEREALS AND PASTA	
food	amount
Bran cereals†, concentrated	
Fiber One	⅔ cup
Kellogg's All-Bran	⅓ cup
Kellogg's All-Bran Complete Wheat Flakes	1 cup
Kellogg's Bran Buds	⅓ cup
Post 100% Bran	⅔ cup
Bran cereals†, flaked	
Bulgur, cooked	½ cup
Cereals, most ready to eat	
Unsweetened, plain	¾ cup
Cheerios†	1 cup
Cooked cereals	½ cup
Corn Flakes	¾ cup
Frosted Flakes	¼ cup
Grape Nuts	3 tablespoons
Grits, cooked	½ cup
Kix	1 cup
Life	½ cup
Puffed cereal, rice or wheat	1½ cups

CEREALS AND PASTA	
food	amount
Rice Krispies	⅔ cup
Shredded Wheat, biscuit	1 cup
Shredded Wheat, spoon size	½ cup
Shredded Wheat Wheat'n Bran†	½ cup
Special K	1 cup
Total	¾ cup
Wheat Chex†	½ cup
Wheaties†	⅔ cup

GRAINS	
food	amount
Barley, cooked	⅓ cup
Buckwheat, cooked	½ cup
Bulgur, cooked	⅓ cup
Cornmeal, dry	2½ tablespoons
Cornstarch	2 tablespoons
Couscous, cooked	⅓ cup
Flour	3 tablespoons
Kasha, cooked	⅓ cup
Millet, dry	3 tablespoons
Oat bran, cooked	¼ cup
Pasta, cooked	⅓ cup
Quinoa, cooked	⅓ cup
Rice, white or brown, cooked	⅓ cup
Rice, wild, cooked	½ cup
Wheat berries, cooked	⅔ cup
Wheat germ†	¼ cup (1 carb and 1 low-fat protein)

CRACKERS AND SNACKS	
food	amount
Animal crackers	8
Cheese Nips, reduced fat	22
Club Crackers Reduced Fat	6
Finn Crisp	4
Graham crackers, (2½" square)	3
Matzoh	1 (¾ ounce)
Matzoh with bran	1 (¾ ounce)
Manischewitz Whole Wheat Matzos	7

CRACKERS AND SNACKS

food	amount
Melba toast, rectangles	5
Melba toast, rounds	10
Orville Redenbacher's SmartPop! popcorn	3 cups
Popcorn, air popped, no fat added	3 cups
Pretzels‡	¾ ounce
Rye crisp, 2" × 3½"	4
Saltine-type crackers‡	6
Town House Reduced Fat‡	8
Triscuit Reduced Fat‡	8
Wasa Hearty Crispbread	2
Wasa Lite Rye Crispbread	2

DRIED BEANS, LENTILS, AND PEAS

Note: All portions given are for cooked amounts.

food	amount
Baked beans†	⅓ cup
Beans†, white	½ cup
Chickpeas/garbanzo beans†	½ cup
Kidney beans†	½ cup
Lentils†	½ cup
Lima beans†	⅔ cup
Navy beans†	½ cup
Peas†, black-eyed	½ cup
Peas†, split	½ cup
Pinto beans†	½ cup

STARCHY VEGETABLES

food	amount
Corn†	½ cup
Corn on the cob†, 6" long	1
Lima beans†	½ cup
Mixed vegetables, with corn or peas	⅔ cup
Peas†, green (canned or frozen)	½ cup
Plantain†	½ cup
Potato, baked or boiled	1 small (3 ounce)
Potato, mashed	½ cup
Pumpkin	1 cup
Squash, winter (acorn, butternut)	1 cup

STARCHY VEGETABLES

food	amount
Yam, sweet potato	½ cup

STARCHES AND BREADS PREPARED WITH FAT

These count as 1 starch/bread plus 1 fat choice.

food	amount
Biscuit, 2½" across	1
Chow mein noodles	½ cup
Cornbread, 2" cube	1 (2 ounce)
Crackers	
Arrowroot	4
Butter cracker‡, round	7
Butter cracker‡, rectangle	6
Cheese Nips‡	20
Cheez-It‡	27
Club Crackers‡	6
Combos‡	1 ounce
Lorna Doone	3
Oyster‡	20
Peanut butter crackers‡	3
Pepperidge Farm Bordeaux cookies	3
Pepperidge Farm Goldfish‡	36
Popcorn, microwave, light	4 cups
Ritz Crackers‡	7
Sociables‡	9
Stella D'oro Sesame Breadsticks	2
Teddy Grahams	15
Triscuit‡	5
Town House‡	6
Vanilla wafers	6
Wasa Fiber Crispbread	4
Wasa Sesame Crispbread	2
Wheat Thins Reduced Fat‡	13
French fries (2"–3" long)	10 (1½ ounces)
Muffin, plain, small	1
Pancake, 4" across	2
Stuffing, bread (prepared)	¼ cup
Taco shell, 6" across	2
Waffle, 4" square	1

VEGETABLES

Vegetables fall within the second tier of the food pyramid. Each vegetable serving is calculated to contain 5 grams of carbohydrates, 2 grams of protein, between 2 and 3 grams of fiber, and 25 calories. Vegetables are a good source of vitamins and minerals. Fresh or frozen vegetables are preferred because of their higher vitamin and mineral content; however, canned vegetables are also acceptable, with the preference being for low-sodium or salt-free varieties. As a general rule, 1 Vegetable exchange is usually equal to ½ cup cooked, 1 cup raw, or ½ cup juice.

Not all vegetables are found on the Vegetable Exchange List. Starchy vegetables such as corn, peas, and potatoes are part of the Starches and Bread Exchange List. Vegetables with fewer than 10 calories per serving are found on the Free Food Exchange List.

VEGETABLE EXCHANGE LIST

Cooked or steamed serving.

food	amount
Artichoke	½ medium
Asparagus	1 cup
Bamboo shoots	1 cup
Bean sprouts	½ cup
Beet greens	½ cup
Beets	½ cup
Broccoli	½ cup
Brussels sprouts	½ cup
Cabbage	1 cup
Carrots	½ cup
Cauliflower	½ cup
Celery	1 cup
Collard greens	1 cup
Eggplant	½ cup
Fennel leaf	1 cup
Green beans	1 cup
Green pepper	1 cup
Kale	½ cup

VEGETABLE EXCHANGE LIST

Cooked or steamed serving.

food	amount
Kohlrabi	½ cup
Leeks	½ cup
Mushrooms, fresh	1 cup
Mustard greens	1 cup
Okra	½ cup
Onions	½ cup
Pea pods	½ cup
Radishes	1 cup
Red pepper	1 cup
Rutabaga	½ cup
Sauerkraut‡	½ cup
Spaghetti sauce, jar	¼ cup
Spaghetti squash	½ cup
Spinach	½ cup
Summer squash	1 cup
Tomato	1 medium
Tomato, canned‡	½ cup
Tomato, paste‡	1½ tablespoons
Tomato sauce, canned‡	⅓ cup
Tomato/vegetable juice‡	½ cup
Turnip greens	1 cup
Turnips	½ cup
Water chestnuts	6 whole or ½ cup
Wax beans	½ cup
Zucchini	1 cup

FRUITS

One Fruit exchange has about 15 grams of carbohydrates, which totals 60 calories. The serving sizes for fruits vary considerably, so consult the list. Also, note that portion amounts are given for fruit that is dried, fresh, frozen, or canned packed in its own juice with no sugar added.

FRESH, FROZEN, AND UNSWEETENED CANNED FRUIT	
food	amount
Apple, raw, 2" across	1
Apple, dried	4 rings
Applesauce, unsweetened	½ cup
Apricots, canned	4 halves or ½ cup
Apricots, dried	8 halves
Apricots, fresh, medium	4
Banana, 9" long	½
Banana flakes or chips	3 tablespoons
Blackberries, raw	¾ cup
Blueberries†, raw	¾ cup
Boysenberries	1 cup
Canned fruit, unless otherwise stated	½ cup
Cantaloupe, 5" across	⅓
Cantaloupe, cubes	1 cup
Casaba, 7" across	⅙ melon
Casaba, cubed	1⅓ cups
Cherries, large, raw	12 whole
Cherries, canned	½ cup
Cherries, dried (no sugar added)	2 tablespoons
Cranberries, dried (no sugar added)	2 tablespoons
Currants	2 tablespoons
Dates	3
Fig, dried	1
Figs, fresh, 2" across	2
Fruit cocktail, canned	½ cup
Grapefruit, medium	½
Grapefruit, sections	¾ cup
Grapes, small	15
Guavas, small	1½
Honeydew melon, medium	⅛
Honeydew melon, cubes	1 cup
Kiwi, large	1
Kumquats, medium	5
Loquats, fresh	12
Lychees, dried or fresh	10
Mandarin oranges	¾ cup
Mango, small	½
Nectarine, 2½" across	1

FRESH, FROZEN, AND UNSWEETENED CANNED FRUIT	
food	amount
Orange, 3" across	1
Papaya, fresh, 3½" across	½
Papaya, fresh, cubed	1 cup
Peach, 2¾" across	1 peach or ¾ cup
Peaches, canned	2 halves or 1 cup
Peach, fresh, 2½" across	1
Pear, small	1
Pears, canned	2 halves or ½ cup
Persimmon, medium, native	2
Pineapple, raw	¾ cup
Pineapple, canned	⅓ cup
Plantain, cooked	⅓ cup
Plum, raw, 2" across	2
Pomegranate†	½
Prunes, dried, medium	3
Raisins	2 tablespoons
Raspberries†, raw	1 cup
Strawberries†, raw, whole	1¼ cups
Tangerine, 2½" across	2
Watermelon, cubes	1¼ cups

DRIED FRUIT†	
food	amount
†Apples	4 rings
†Apricots	8 halves
Dates, medium	2½
†Figs	1½
†Prunes, medium	3
Raisins	2 tablespoons

FRUIT JUICE	
food	amount
Apple cider	½ cup
Apple juice, unsweetened	½ cup
Cranapple juice, unsweetened	⅜ cup
Cranberry juice cocktail	⅓ cup
Cranberry juice, low-calorie	1⅛ cups
Cranberry juice, unsweetened	½ cup

FRUIT JUICE

food	amount
Grapefruit juice	½ cup
Grape juice	⅓ cup
Orange juice	½ cup
Pineapple juice	½ cup
Prune juice	⅓ cup

MILK

Milk servings are usually marked at 1 cup or 8 ounces. Like meats, the Milk Exchange Lists are divided into categories depending on the fat content of the choices. Each Milk exchange has about 12 grams of carbohydrates and 8 grams of protein; however, the calories in each exchange will vary according to the fat content.

SKIM OR VERY LOW-FAT MILK

food	amount
½% milk	1 cup
1% milk	1 cup
Buttermilk, low-fat or 1%	1 cup
Nonfat milk, dry	⅓ cup
Skim milk	1 cup
Skim milk, evaporated	½ cup
Yogurt, plain, nonfat	8 ounces

LOW-FAT MILK

food	amount
2% milk	1 cup
Yogurt, plain, low-fat with added nonfat milk solids	8 ounces

WHOLE MILK

The whole-milk group has much more fat per serving than the skim and low-fat groups. Whole milk has more than 3¼ percent butterfat, so you should limit your choices from this group as much as possible.

food	amount
Whole milk	1 cup
Whole milk, evaporated	½ cup
Yogurt, plain, whole milk	8 ounces

MEATS

Each serving of meat or meat substitute has about 7 grams of protein. As shown in the tables below, the Meats Exchange Lists are divided depending on the fat content of the meat or meat substitute choice. (See Chapter 9 for suggestions on the healthiest ways to prepare meats.)

Make your selections from the lean and medium-fat meat, poultry, and fish choices in your meal plan as much as possible. This helps you keep the fat intake in your diet low, which may help decrease your risk for heart disease. Remember that the meats in the high-fat group have more saturated fat, cholesterol, and calories, so you should consult with your dietitian about whether or not your diet should include any meats from that group. When they are permitted, most dietitians recommend limiting your choices from the high-fat group to a maximum of three times per week.

Meats and meat substitutes that have 400 milligrams or more of sodium per exchange are indicated with the ‡ symbol.

Meats Exchange List portions are generally 1 ounce of cooked meat (using the 4 ounces of raw meat results in 3 ounces of cooked meat standard). Beef, pork, fish, poultry, cheese, eggs, and, when they're used as meat substitutes, dried beans, legumes, and some nuts fall within the Meats Exchange List categories. Because the calorie counts vary so widely (as do the cholesterol and saturated fat content), your dietitian will advise from which lists you are to choose your selections.

exchange	carbohydrate	protein (g)	fat(g)	calories
Very Lean Meats	0	7	0–1	35
Lean Meats	0	7	3	55
Medium-Fat Meats	0	7	5	75
High-Fat Meats	0	7	8	100

VERY LEAN MEATS (AND MEAT SUBSTITUTES)

Meats in this category are usually the reduced-fat varieties, like Healthy Choice, and contain 4 percent or fewer calories from fat, which unless otherwise noted are at 1 ounce per food exchange list portion. Name-brand foods come and go, with new ones introduced regularly that phase out others. Check product labels or with your dietitian to ascertain which products currently fall within this category.

One choice provides about 35–45 calories, 7 grams of protein, no carbohydrates, and 0–2 grams of fat.

food	amount
Buffalo	1 ounce
Chicken, white meat, skinless	1 ounce
Cornish hen, white meat, skinless	1 ounce
Cottage cheese, fat-free or 1%	¼ cup
Ricotta, 100 percent fat-free‡	1 ounce
Egg substitute, plain (if less than 40 calories per serving)	¼ cup
Fish and seafood, fresh or frozen, cooked: clams, cod, crab, flounder, haddock, halibut, imitation crabmeat, lobster, scallops, shrimp, trout, tuna (in water)	2 ounces
Ostrich	1 ounce
Turkey, ground, 93–99 percent fat-free	1 ounce
Turkey, white meat, skinless	1 ounce
Turkey sausage, 97 percent fat-free‡	1 ounce
Venison	1 ounce

LEAN MEATS (AND MEAT SUBSTITUTES)

One choice provides about 55 calories, 7 grams of protein, no carbohydrates, and 3 grams of fat.

food	amount
95 percent fat-free luncheon meat	1 ounce
Beef, of lean beef such as:	
Chipped beef‡ (USDA Good or Choice grade)	1 ounce
Flank steak (USDA Good or Choice grade)	1 ounce
Round steak (USDA Good or Choice grade)	1 ounce
Sirloin steak (USDA Good or Choice grade)	1 ounce
Tenderloin (USDA Good or Choice grade)	1 ounce
Clams, fresh or canned in water‡	2 ounces
Cottage cheese, any variety	¼ cup
Crab	2 ounces

LEAN MEATS (AND MEAT SUBSTITUTES)

One choice provides about 55 calories, 7 grams of protein, no carbohydrates, and 3 grams of fat.

food	amount
Diet cheese‡ (with fewer than 55 calories per ounce)	1 ounce
Duck, without skin	1 ounce
Egg substitutes (with fewer than 55 calories per ¼ cup)	¼ cup
Egg whites	3
Fish, all fresh and frozen catfish, salmon, and other fattier fish	1 ounce
Goose, without skin	1 ounce
Grated Parmesan	2 tablespoons
Herring, uncreamed or smoked	1 ounce
Lobster	2 ounces
Oysters, medium	6
Pheasant, without skin	1 ounce
Boiled ham‡	1 ounce
Canadian bacon‡	1 ounce
Canned ham‡	1 ounce
Cured ham‡	1 ounce
Fresh ham	1 ounce
Tenderloin	1 ounce
Chicken, dark meat, without skin	1 ounce
Cornish game hen, dark meat, without skin	1 ounce
Turkey, dark meat, without skin	1 ounce
Rabbit	1 ounce
Sardines, canned, medium	2
Scallops	2 ounces
Shrimp	2 ounces
Squirrel	1 ounce
Tofu	3 ounces
Veal, all cuts are lean except for veal cutlets (ground or cubed)	1 ounce
Venison	1 ounce

MEDIUM-FAT MEATS (AND MEAT SUBSTITUTES)

One choice provides about 75 calories, 7 grams of protein, no carbohydrates, and 5 grams of fat.

food	amount
86 percent fat-free luncheon meat‡	1 ounce
Chuck roast	1 ounce
Cubed steak	1 ounce
Ground beef	1 ounce
Meat loaf	1 ounce
Porterhouse steak	1 ounce
Rib roast	1 ounce
Rump roast	1 ounce
T-bone steak	1 ounce
Diet cheeses‡ (with 56–80 calories per ounce)	1 ounce
Mozzarella (skim or part-skim milk)	1 ounce
Ricotta (skim or part-skim milk)	¼ cup
Egg (high in cholesterol, so limit to 3 per week)	1
Egg substitutes (with 56–80 calories per ¼ cup)	¼ cup
Heart (high in cholesterol)	1 ounce
Kidney (high in cholesterol)	1 ounce
Lamb chops	1 ounce
Lamb leg	1 ounce
Lamb roast	1 ounce
Liver (high in cholesterol)	1 ounce
Parmesan cheese‡	3 tablespoons
Pork chops	1 ounce
Pork loin roast	1 ounce
Boston butt	1 ounce
Pork cutlets	1 ounce
Chicken (with skin)	1 ounce
Duck, domestic, well drained of fat	1 ounce
Goose, domestic, well drained of fat	1 ounce
Ground turkey	1 ounce
Romano cheese	3 tablespoons
Sweetbreads (high in cholesterol)	1 ounce
Tofu (2½" × 2¾" × 1")	4 ounce
Tuna‡, canned in oil, drained	¼ cup
Salmon‡, canned	¼ cup
Veal cutlet, ground or cubed, unbreaded	1 ounce

HIGH-FAT MEATS (AND MEAT SUBSTITUTES)

Remember, these items are high in saturated fat, cholesterol, and calories, and should be eaten only three or fewer times per week. One choice provides about 100 calories, 7 grams of protein, no carbohydrates, and 8 grams of fat. One exchange choice is equal to any one of the following items:

food	amount
Most USDA Prime cuts of beef	1 ounce
Beef‡, corned	1 ounce
Ribs, beef	1 ounce
Bologna‡	1 ounce
Cheese, all regular cheese‡:	
American	1 ounce
Blue	1 ounce
Cheddar	1 ounce
Monterey Jack	1 ounce
Swiss	1 ounce
Fish, fried	1 ounce
Hotdog‡:	
Chicken, 10/pound	1 frank
Turkey, 10/pound	1 frank
Lamb, ground	1 ounce
Peanut butter (contains unsaturated fat)	1 tablespoon
Pimiento loaf‡	1 ounce
Pork chop	1 ounce
Pork, ground	1 ounce
Spareribs	1 ounce
Steak	1 ounce
Salami‡	1 ounce
Sausage‡:	
Bratwurst‡	1 ounce
Italian	1 ounce
Knockwurst, smoked	1 ounce
Polish	1 ounce
Pork sausage‡ (patty or link)	1 ounce
Counts as 1 High-Fat Meat plus 1 Fat exchange:	
Hotdog‡—beef, pork, or combination, 400mg or more of sodium per exchange, 10/pound	1 frank

FATS

Each Fat Exchange List serving will contain about 5 grams of fat and 45 calories. Fats are found in margarine, butter, oils, nuts, meat fat, and dairy products. Saturated fat amounts and sodium contents can vary considerably, depending on the choice. Most dietitians recommend polyunsaturated or monounsaturated fats whenever possible.

UNSATURATED FATS	
food	amount
Almonds, dry-roasted	6
Avocado, medium	⅛
Cashews, dry-roasted	1 tablespoon or 6
Cooking oil (corn, cottonseed, safflower, soybean, sunflower, olive, peanut)	1 teaspoon
Hazelnuts (filberts)	5
Macadamia nuts	3
Margarine	1 teaspoon
Margarine, diet‡	1 tablespoon
Mayonnaise	1 teaspoon
Mayonnaise, reduced-calorie‡	1 tablespoon
Olives, black, large‡	9
Olives, green, large‡	10
Other nuts	1 tablespoon
Peanuts, large	10
Peanuts, small	20
Pecan halves	4
Pine nuts	1 tablespoon
Pistachio	12
Pumpkin seeds	2 teaspoons
Salad dressing, all varieties, regular	1 tablespoon
Salad dressing, mayonnaise-type, reduced-calorie	1 tablespoon
Salad dressing, mayonnaise-type, regular	2 teaspoons
Salad dressing, reduced-calorie‡ (2 tablespoons of low-calorie dressing is a Free Food exchange)	2 tablespoons
Sesame seeds	1 tablespoon
Sunflower seeds, without shells	1 tablespoon
Tahini	2 teaspoons
Walnut halves	4

SATURATED FATS	
food	amount
Bacon‡	1 slice
Butter	1 teaspoon
Butter, whipped	2 teaspoons
Chitterlings	½ ounce
Coconut, shredded	2 tablespoons
Coffee whitener, liquid	2 tablespoons
Coffee whitener, powder	4 tablespoons
Cream, heavy	1 tablespoon
Cream, light, coffee, table	2 tablespoons
Cream, sour	2 tablespoons
Cream, whipping	1 tablespoon
Cream cheese	1 tablespoon
Salt pork‡	¼ ounce

FREE FOODS

A free food is any food or drink that contains fewer than 20 calories per serving. Unless a serving size is specified, you can eat as much as you want of these foods. You are limited to eating two or three servings per day of those foods with a specific serving size.

FREE DRINKS	
food	amount
Bouillon or canned broth without fat‡	
Bouillon, low sodium	
Broth, low sodium	
Carbonated drinks, sugar-free	
Carbonated water	
Club soda	
Cocoa powder, unsweetened	1 tablespoon
Coffee	
Drink mixes, sugar-free	
Tea	
Tonic water, sugar-free	

FREE FRUITS AND VEGETABLES

food	amount
Cranberries, unsweetened	½ cup
Rhubarb, unsweetened	½ cup
Vegetables, raw	1 cup
Alfalfa sprouts	
Cabbage	
Celery	
Chinese cabbage†	
Cucumber	
Endive	
Escarole	
Green onion	
Hot peppers	
Lettuce	
Mushrooms	
Parsley	
Pickles, unsweetened‡	
Pimento	
Radishes	
Romaine	
Salad greens	
Spinach	
Watercress	
Zucchini†	

FREE SWEETS

food	amount
Candy, hard, sugar-free	
Gelatin, sugar-free	
Gum, sugar-free	
Jam/jelly, low sugar	2 teaspoons
Jam/jelly, sugar-free	2 teaspoons
Pancake syrup, sugar-free	1–2 tablespoons
Sugar substitutes (saccharin, aspartame, Splenda)	
Whipped topping	2 tablespoons

FREE CONDIMENTS

food	amount
Horseradish	
Ketchup	1 tablespoon
Mustard	
Nonstick pan spray	
Pickles, dill, unsweetened‡	
Salad dressing, low calorie	2 tablespoons
Taco sauce	1 tablespoon
Vinegar	

FREE SEASONINGS

Seasonings can be very helpful in making foods taste better, but be careful how much sodium you use. Read labels to help you choose seasonings that do not contain sodium or salt.

food	amount
Basil	
Celery seeds	
Chili powder	
Chives	
Cinnamon	
Curry	
Dill	
Garlic	
Garlic powder	
Herbs	
Hot pepper sauce	
Lemon	
Lemon juice	
Lemon pepper	
Lime	
Lime juice	
Mint	
Onion powder	
Oregano	
Paprika	
Pepper	
Pimiento	
Soy sauce, low sodium ("lite")	
Soy sauce‡	

FREE SEASONINGS

Seasonings can be very helpful in making foods taste better, but be careful how much sodium you use. Read labels to help you choose seasonings that do not contain sodium or salt.

food	amount
Spices	
Wine, used in cooking	¼ cup
Worcestershire sauce‡	

FREE FLAVORING EXTRACTS

Almond	
Butter	
Lemon	
Peppermint	
Vanilla	
Walnut	

MEAT-SUBSTITUTE PROTEIN FOODS

Note: Foods on this list equal 1 Protein Food Exchange List serving (0g carb, 7g protein, 0–5g fat).

food	amount
Egg substitute	¼ cup
Soy cheese	1 ounce
Tofu, firm	½ cup (4 ounces)

BEANS USED AS A MEAT SUBSTITUTE

food	amount	exchanges
Dried beans†	1 cup, cooked	1 Lean Meat, 2 Starches
Dried lentils†	1 cup, cooked	1 Lean Meat, 2 Starches
Dried peas†	1 cup, cooked	1 Lean Meat, 2 Starches

NUTS AND SEEDS USED AS MEAT SUBSTITUTES

Note: Foods on this list equal 1 Protein and 2 or 3 Fat Exchange List servings (0g carb, 7g protein, 10–15g fat). Consult product label to determine fat content for your choice.

food	amount
Almonds	¼ cup
Pecans	¼ cup
Peanuts	¼ cup
Pine nuts	2 tablespoons

NUTS AND SEEDS USED AS MEAT SUBSTITUTES

Note: Foods on this list equal 1 Protein and 2 or 3 Fat Exchange List servings (0g carb, 7g protein, 10–15g fat). Consult product label to determine fat content for your choice.

food	amount
Pistachios	¼ cup (1 ounce)
Pumpkin seeds	¼ cup
Sesame seeds	¼ cup
Squash seeds	¼ cup
Sunflower seeds	¼ cup
Walnut halves	16–20

COMBINATION FOODS

Food is often mixed together in various combinations that do not fit into only one exchange list. Each of the recipes in this book gives the exchange list exchanges for that dish. The following is a list of average exchange list values for some typical combination foods. Ask your dietitian for information about these or any other combination of foods you'd like to eat.

FAT FOODS USED AS A MEAT SUBSTITUTE

Note: Foods on this list equal 1 Fat Exchange List serving (0g carb, 5g fat).

food	amount	exchanges
Almond butter	1 tablespoon	2 Fats
Cashew butter	1 tablespoon	2 Fats
Flaxseed oil	1 teaspoon	1 Fat
Peanut oil	1 teaspoon	1 Fat
Sesame butter	1 tablespoon	2 Fats

FOODS FOR SPECIAL TREATS

These foods, despite their sugar or fat content, are intended to be added to your meal plan in moderate amounts, as long as your dietitian agrees and if, despite consuming them, you can still maintain blood-glucose control. Your dietitian can also advise how often you can eat these foods. Because these special treats are concentrated sources of carbohydrates, the portion sizes are very small.

COMBO FOODS

food	amount	exchanges
Bean soup†‡	1 cup (8 ounces)	1 Lean Meat, 1 Starch, 1 Vegetable
Casserole	1 cup (8 ounces)	2 Medium-Fat Meats
Homemade casserole	1 cup (8 ounces)	2 Starches, 1 Fat
Cheese pizza‡, thin crust	¼ of 15-ounce pizza	1 Medium-Fat Meat
Cheese pizza‡	10" pizza	2 Starches, 1 Fat
Chili with beans, commercial†‡	1 cup (8 ounces)	2 Medium-Fat Meats, 2 Starches, 2 Fats
Chow mein†‡ (without noodles or rice)	2 cups (16 ounces)	2 Lean Meats, 1 Starch, 2 Vegetables
Chunky soup, all varieties‡	10¾-ounce can	1 Medium-Fat Meat, 1 Starch, 1 Vegetable
Cream soup‡ (made with water)	1 cup (8 ounces)	1 Starch, 1 Fat
Macaroni and cheese‡	1 cup (8 ounces)	1 Medium-Fat Meat, 2 Starches, 2 Fats
Spaghetti and meatballs, canned‡	1 cup (8 ounces)	1 Medium-Fat Meat, 1 Fat, 2 Starches
Sugar-free pudding (made with skim milk)	½ cup	1 Starch
Vegetable soup‡	1 cup (8 ounces)	1 Starch

FOODS FOR SPECIAL TREATS

food	amount	exchanges
Angel-food cake	1/12 cake	2 Starches
Cake, no icing	1/12 cake (3" square)	2 Starches, 2 Fats
Cookies	2 small (1¾" across)	2 Starches, 1 Fat
Frozen fruit yogurt	⅓ cup	1 Starch
Gingersnaps	3	1 Starch
Granola	¼ cup	1 Starch, 1 Fat
Granola bars	1 small	1 Starch, 1 Fat
Ice cream, any flavor	½ cup	1 Starch, 2 Fats
Ice milk, any flavor	½ cup	1 Starch, 1 Fat
Sherbet, any flavor	¼ cup	1 Starch
Snack chips‡, all varieties	1 ounce	1 Starch, 2 Fats
Vanilla wafers	6 small	1 Starch, 2 Fats

MISCELLANEOUS FOODS

food	amount	food group	carbo-hydrate grams	calo-ries
Jam, regular	1 tablespoon	1 Carbohydrate	13g	80
Jelly, regular	1 tablespoon	1 Carbohydrate	13g	80
Honey, regular	1 tablespoon	1 Carbohydrate	13g	80
Sugar	1 tablespoon	1 Carbohydrate	12g	46
Syrup, light	2 tablespoons	1 Carbohydrate	13g	80
Syrup, regular	2 tablespoons	1 Carbohydrate	27g	160
Yogurt, regular, with fruit	1 cup	1 Carbohydrate	45g	240

OTHER SPECIAL FOODS

food	amount	exchanges
Brewer's yeast	3 tablespoons	1 Bread
Carob flour	⅛ cup	1 Bread

OTHER SPECIAL FOODS		
food	amount	exchanges
Kefir	1 cup	1 milk, 1 Fat
Miso	3 tablespoons	1 Bread, ½ Lean Meat
Sea vegetables, cooked	½ cup	1 Vegetable
Soy flour	¼ cup	1 Lean Meat, ½ Bread
Soy grits, raw	⅛ cup	1 Lean Meat
Soymilk	1 cup	1 Milk, 1 Fat
Tahini	1 teaspoon	1 Fat
Tempeh	4 ounces	1 Bread, 2 Protein
Wheat germ	1 tablespoon	½ Bread

starch group	uncooked	cooked
Cream of wheat	2 level tablespoons	½ cup
Dried beans	3 tablespoons	⅓ cup
Dried peas	3 tablespoons	⅓ cup
Grits	3 level tablespoons	½ cup
Lentils	2 tablespoons	⅓ cup
Macaroni	¼ cup	½ cup
Noodles	⅓ cup	½ cup
Oatmeal	3 level tablespoons	½ cup
Rice	2 level tablespoons	⅓ cup
Spaghetti	¼ cup	½ cup
meat group	uncooked	cooked
Chicken	1 small drumstick	1 ounce
Chicken	½ chicken breast	3 ounces
Hamburger	4 ounces	3 ounces

MEASURING FOODS

Portion control is an important part of implementing a diet based on the food exchange lists. This helps ensure you eat the right serving sizes of food. Liquids and some solid foods (such as tuna, cottage cheese, and canned fruits) can be measured using a measuring cup. Measuring spoons are useful to guarantee correct amounts for foods used in smaller portions, like oil, salad dressing, and peanut butter. A scale can be very useful for measuring almost anything, especially meat, poultry, and fish.

Similar in manner to how professional chefs cook, you will eventually learn how to estimate food amounts. Until then, it can be useful to remember that 1 cup is about equal in size to an average woman's closed fist. A thumb is about the size of 1 tablespoon or a 1-ounce portion of cheese. The tip of the thumb equals about 1 teaspoon, a useful gauge when trying to determine how much butter to add to your bread or dressing to add to a salad when you're dining out and don't have measuring spoons available.

Many raw foods will weigh less after they are cooked. This is especially true for most meats. On the other hand, starches often swell during cooking, so a small amount of uncooked starch results in a much larger amount of cooked food. Some examples:

INDEX